CROSSING THE RUBICON

CROSSING
THE RUBICON

CAESAR'S
DECISION
AND THE FATE
OF ROME

LUCA FEZZI

TRANSLATED FROM THE ITALIAN BY RICHARD DIXON

YALE UNIVERSITY PRESS
NEW HAVEN AND LONDON

For information about this and other Yale University Press publications, please contact:
U.S. Office: sales.press@yale.edu   yalebooks.com
Europe Office: sales@yaleup.co.uk   yalebooks.co.uk

Set in Adobe Garamond Pro by IDSUK (DataConnection) Ltd
Printed in Great Britain by TJ International Ltd, Padstow, Cornwall

Library of Congress Control Number: 2019947812

ISBN 978-0-300-24145-7

A catalogue record for this book is available from the British Library.

10 9 8 7 6 5 4 3 2 1

CONTENTS

MAPS

A NOTE ON THE TEXT

The chronological references relating to the events and to the early sources are all to be understood as BC, unless otherwise indicated. The dates are those of the republican calendar prior to Caesar's reform in 46 BC (and which made it necessary, among other things, to recover more than two months in order to bring the official year in line with the astronomical year).[1] The 11 and 12 January 49 (official calendar), the two possible dates when Caesar crossed the Rubicon, might correspond, in the astronomical calendar, to 24 and 25 November 50 (Groebe) or to 16 and 17 December 50 (Le Verrier).[2]

TRANSLATOR'S NOTE

The translations of all quotations throughout this book are my own. Where possible, I have consulted the translations referred to in the Bibliography and Further Notes below, in particular the translations of Cicero's letters published by Cambridge University Press, but have also used the invaluable Perseus Digital Library and other online resources. My special thanks to Giuliana Paganucci for her advice on the interpretation of particular words and phrases, and to Peter Greene for his comments and suggestions for improvements to the translation.

A NOTE ON SOURCES

In retelling the events of 49 BC, I draw extensively on Cicero's letters. Marcus Tullius Cicero (106–43) was an orator, politician and tireless letter-writer – and an important contemporary voice. His letters, much more authentic inasmuch as they were not meant for publication, reveal their author to be 'the personality of the ancient world whom we know best in the hidden corners of his mind'.[1] The letters also offer a lively glimpse of Rome's 'short century', or its age of 'revolution', populated by the restless and extraordinary 'last generation' of the *res publica*. Among his correspondents were Caesar and Pompey.

The material is vast and hitherto undervalued. The letters, often referred to as 'hysterical', have only fuelled depictions of Cicero as incapable of political judgement and struck by 'chronic blindness'.

As historians, we are fortunate to possess such a rich testimony for this crucial period – rich, although unreliable in its objectivity since Cicero vacillated in his views as a result of partial or false news that he received about the war. Nonetheless, not all of Caesar's adversaries could boast equal lucidity, coherence, nor indeed heroism. The correspondence is therefore valuable, particularly those letters addressed in the early months of 49 to Titus Pomponius Atticus (110–32) who was not only a friend but also his brother-in-law (Titus's sister Pomponia had married Cicero's brother Quintus). It is also valuable as long as we keep in mind that it is the product of a man from the 'ruling class' – a 'class' which had in Pompey an uncertain leader and strategist. The correspondence therefore reflects the elite's anxieties at that time.

Atticus himself, a cultured intellectual and very well-informed businessman, was a point of reference for many people during those days of turmoil. To friends leaving to join Pompey 'he gave what was necessary from his own pocket and in this way did not offend the feelings of Pompey' (whose wife Cornelia was related to Atticus' maternal uncle); Caesar appreciated his neutrality, so much as to prize him.[2] This at least is what we read in the single idealized biography of this figure, written with much encouragement from him, and circulated while he was still alive (and supplemented after his death with a few closing chapters). Cicero also remained in contact with both contenders, as is recalled with hagiographical excess in the biography dedicated to him by Plutarch of Chaeronea (c.AD 45–c.125).[3] 'He would have preferred to follow the chariot of triumphant Caesar' so long as the two contenders came to an agreement; he gave advice to the former, pleading several times with the latter, trying to 'mollify and pacify both of them'. When the situation deteriorated and Pompey left Rome, Cicero did not flee but 'seemed to be trying to attach himself to Caesar'. Tormented by doubts, he did not know which side to take. The jurist Gaius Trebatius Testa wrote to him 'that, in Caesar's view, he ought to have joined his side'; but if he felt unable 'by reason of advanced age, he would be better off going to Greece and living there in peace, far away from both'. Cicero, amazed that Caesar hadn't written to him personally, 'replied angrily that he would do nothing that was unworthy of his past political record. The episode in question can be read in his letters.'

In the chaotic tragedy of the *res publica*, Cicero's correspondence seems in our view, as it did to Plutarch, to be a mine of information: on the lack of preparation in Pompey's camp, on the difficulties in communication, on the opportunistic behaviour of the ruling class, on the fate of the ancient city-state which had now become a megalopolis and which Cicero feared could be prey to anarchy and starvation. Neither of these last two events, like many of his other predictions, actually took place. The correspondence offers many possible ideas for an alternative history, if matters had ended otherwise. In August of 50, his friend Marcus Caelius Rufus (82–48) wrote: 'great and amusing is the entertainment that Fortune is preparing for you'.[4] Caesar himself, on 16 April 49, advised him to 'follow Fortune (now everything turns in our favour and against our opponents)'.[5] In August 46 Cicero was again confiding to a friend who was still peacefully in Greece: 'matters have gone like this, partly by chance, partly through our own fault'.[6]

Map 1 The Roman world and the Civil War of 49–45

xiv

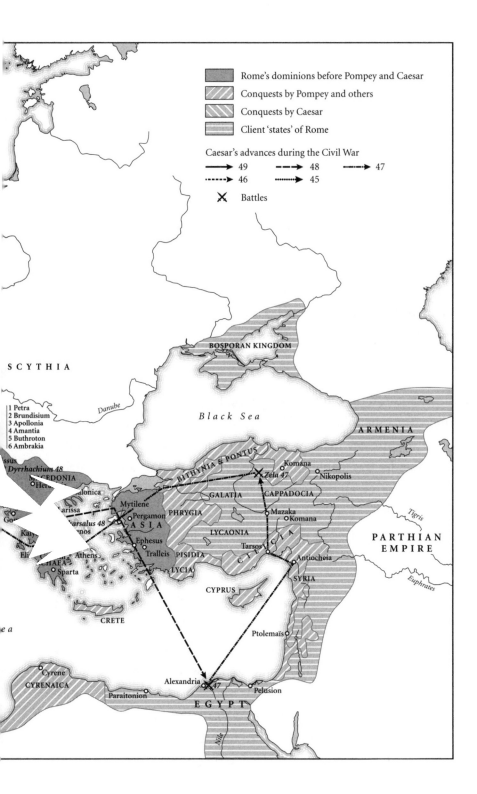

Rome's dominions before Pompey and Caesar

Conquests by Pompey and others

Conquests by Caesar

Client 'states' of Rome

Caesar's advances during the Civil War

→ 49   ---→ 48   —·—→ 47

·-·-→ 46   ·····→ 45

✗   Battles

SCYTHIA

1 Petra
2 Brundisium
3 Apollonia
4 Amantia
5 Buthroton
6 Ambrakia

Danube

Black Sea

BOSPORAN KINGDOM

ARMENIA

Komana

Zela 47   Nikopolis

BITHYNIA & PONTUS

Dyrrhachium 48

MACEDONIA

Her...

...alonica

...arissa

Pharsalus 48

...enos

Mytilene

Pergamon

ASIA

GALATIA   CAPPADOCIA

PHRYGIA

Ephesus   LYCAONIA   Mazaka

Tralleis   PISIDIA   Komana

Athens   Tarsos   CILICIA

ACHAEA   LYCIA   Antiocheia

Sparta

Tigris

PARTHIAN
EMPIRE

SYRIA

CYPRUS

Euphrates

CRETE

Ptolemaïs

e a

Cyrene

CYRENAICA   Alexandria   47   Pelusion

Paraitonion

EGYPT

Nile

XV

PROLOGUE

What he did after he left Ravenna
and leapt the Rubicon, was such a flight,
as neither tongue nor pen could follow.

Dante, Paradise, 6,61–3

In 49 BC, a crowd of soldiers was waiting for its commander to arrive. For some time, the soldiers had been gathered along the northern bank of one of the streams that crossed their route towards nearby Rimini. The commander was making his way to them under the cover of night, but had got lost several times. Forced to abandon his mules and wagon, he sought the help of a local guide who led him on foot along narrow paths. Finally, he arrived in the early morning of 11 or 12 January and stood before his troops. He hesitated.

Gaius Julius Caesar, patrician, *pontifex maximus* and proconsul, knew that when he led his men across the small stream ahead – the Rubicon – he would trigger a war he could not be sure of winning. The Rubicon was the border between the south-eastern corner of Cisalpine Gaul and *terra Italia*. Cisalpine Gaul was a province, a territory subject to Rome and governed at that time by Caesar; *terra Italia* was the peninsular area of Italy, whose inhabitants some forty years before had received Roman citizenship. By crossing the Rubicon, Caesar's men would be defying a twofold prohibition and an ultimatum recently issued by

Rome. The twofold prohibition forbade the leading of armies outside a commander's own province – particularly in *terra Italia* – without the authorization of the Senate (the assembly of ex-magistrates that regulated Roman foreign policy). The ultimatum, which was issued soon after the declaration of a state of emergency, instructed Caesar to disband his troops.

Caesar knew that crossing the Rubicon was the point of no return. But he had a strategic objective to achieve. His aim was to occupy Ariminum (present-day Rimini), an ancient *colonia* built as a garrison against Gallic invaders and the first *municipium* – urban centre of Roman citizens – to be reached on entering *terra Italia* from the *via Popilia*. This was the first step in his plan to attain candidacy for the consulship, chief magistracy of Rome – a city-state born on the seven hills that now ruled over a Mediterranean empire.

Suddenly, an enormous, superhuman figure appeared, sat down and began playing a reed pipe. Then the figure stood up, snatched a bugle from the nearest soldier and, loudly blowing the battle signal, crossed to the other bank. Caesar, feeling reassured, spoke (perhaps in Greek) the few words that would soon become famous: 'let the die be thrown'. This was subsequently popularized, in modern times, as 'the die is cast'. Following the apparition, he finally led his men south. This, at least, is the most credible of many versions of that fateful episode.

By that symbolic crossing of the border at the head of a legion (or half a legion), Caesar knew he was risking a new war of frightening proportions, one which would drive Romans not against barbarians but against other Romans. Crossing the Rubicon would cause a *bellum civile*, the worst of the internecine struggles that wracked ancient city-states. In Rome, founded upon a fratricide, a new conflict between the city's armies would bring back the grim period initiated in 88 by the consul Lucius Cornelius Sulla. But the chain of events leading to war was not set in motion by Caesar alone, and equally if not more decisive were the actions of his former ally, Gnaeus Pompeius Magnus (Pompey the Great). As

Rome's highly skilled proconsul, Pompey had been entrusted with a task of utmost importance – that of defending the *res publica*. When faced with the threat Caesar posed, Pompey's actions were unprecedented, beginning with the disastrous order to abandon Rome.

The clash between these two titans of ancient history, and the civil war that erupted in that fateful year of 49, would eventually result in the end of the Roman Republic, and lead to the beginning of a new chapter in world history. This book aims to tell that story.

PART I
BACKGROUND

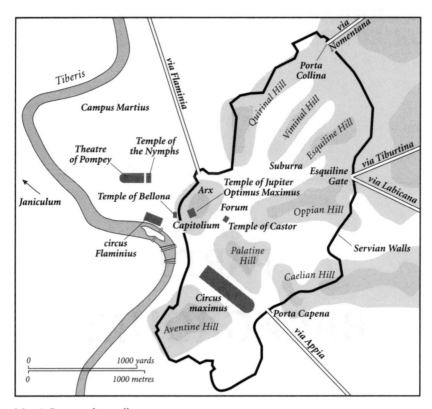

Map 2 Rome and its walls

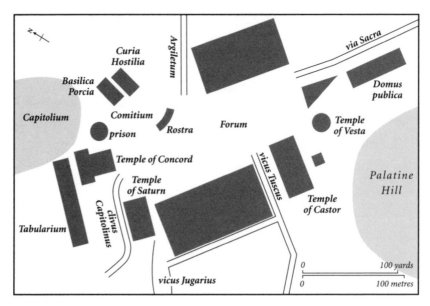

Map 3 Forum, Comitium and Curia

1

THE STAGE AND ITS MAIN CHARACTERS

This is Rome, a city established by the gathering of nations, a
city full of trickery, fraud, vices of every kind, in which you have
to tolerate the insolence, rancour, scorn, hatred and irritation
of many.

Cicero, *Handbook on Electioneering*, 54

THE (TOO) BIG HEART OF THE *RES PUBLICA*

*In that fateful year 49, the strategies of the 'attacker' and of the 'defenders'
would originate, in part, from the conflicting interpretations of a more or
less abstract entity called the* res publica. *The city of Rome, now the stage
for world ambitions, continued to be its heart . . . ever larger and more
troubled.*

In the hectic years between 54 and 51, Cicero celebrated the perfect
construction of the *res publica*, the result of generations of experience.
In his imaginary political dialogue set in 129, Publius Cornelius Scipio
Aemilianus, the destroyer of Carthage, observed: 'the *res publica* is [. . .]
that which belongs to the people. But the people does not mean every
multitude of men assembled together in any manner whatsoever, but
rather an organized society whose foundation is the observance of justice
and the sharing of interests.'[1] The ultimate aim, the eternal government
of an extraordinary city.

Far from the sea and from its dangers – whether from pirates or the corruption of customs – Rome could make the most of its advantages, thanks to the Tiber: Romulus seemed to have foreseen its destiny as 'a seat and centre of an immense empire'.[2] It was also well protected.

> Through the wisdom of Romulus and the kings who came after him, a continuous wall enclosed the city all round, bounded by rough and craggy hills; the only entrance, which opened between the Esquiline and the Quirinal hills, was obstructed by an enormous barrier, and on blocks of stone cut almost vertically and on crags so inaccessible stood the citadel, safe and intact even at the time of the terrible invasions by the Gauls. The place chosen by him was also plentiful in springs and healthy, even if the region was pestilent: the hills around are indeed ventilated and have shaded valleys.[3]

According to tradition, the wall around the city was built by the penultimate king, Servius Tullius. Immediately behind it was the *pomerium*, the ancient ditch traced out by a plough, which marked the boundary of the sacred space originally identified by Romulus and then expanded over time. Inside, among other things, it was forbidden to carry weapons: likewise, any commander who went inside lost his *imperium*, his full military power. Remus's fatal mistake, according to the most accredited version of the legend, had been to leap, in scorn, across the first walls built by his brother. Over five centuries, urban expansion had naturally spread the city far beyond the 'Servian' wall: by the middle of the first century BC, the population of the city, now master of the Mediterranean, had perhaps reached 500,000. Many were recent immigrants, including Cicero, born in 106 at Arpinum (present-day Arpino, in southern Latium) – where Gaius Marius had been born – from a family of knights (*equites*). This is how he describes the relationship between his birthplace and Rome:

this, in truth, is the home my brother and I share. Here we were born of ancient stock; here are our *penates*,[4] here are our family and many memories of our forebears. [. . .] In this place I too was born, while my grandfather was still living and the house was still small [. . .] in the same way we must call home just as much the place where we are born as where we dwell. [. . .] I will never disown Arpinum as my home, even though much greater is that other home, from which every man, whatever might be his *municipium* of origin, receives the right of citizenship and which he thinks of as his only home.[5]

This is another idealized vision, this time in his *Laws*, a political dialogue begun in 52 but, according to some, left incomplete since everything was now changing. It is a vision, nevertheless, that is consistent with the positions he adopted on that fateful 17 January 49. While Pompey urged his senators to follow him, because 'the *res publica* is not bound by walls', Cicero observed that the *res publica* was 'in the temples and in the hearths'.[6] Caesar, however, seemed to have a quite different idea: 'the *res publica* is nothing, merely a word without form or substance'.[7]

In reality, for every citizen – who was originally a citizen-soldier – the *res publica* meant much, if not everything. Every male adult could elect magistrates – administrators, generally annually – and could express his views, today we would say by 'referendum', on laws. Voting took place only in Rome, in a single place, in the open air, which ended up creating an aberration in favour of citizens living in Rome. Indeed, after the devastating Social War, fought by the *res publica* against the rebel allies (90–88), Roman citizenship was recognized for more or less all free inhabitants of *terra Italia*. This brought a momentous change, as emerges from the increase in the number of male adult citizens: from 394,000 in 114 to 910,000 in 69, the year of the last census of the republican period.

In a world that had no parliamentary representation and, of course, no international bodies, those citizens who could be present in Rome at the moment of the vote had the feeling that their own views counted. With certain distinctions, of course. The vote of the wealthier families carried greater weight, either they lived in the city or could afford to travel in to vote.

Economic privilege was systemically entrenched in the Centuriate Assembly, which had most prestige, where the wealthier were divided at that time into 89 *centuriae*, out of a total of just over 190. Therefore, not 'one man one vote' but 'one *centuria* one vote'. The decision of the first 89 represented the view of the wealthier families, in other words the 'first class' and the *equites*, 'knights'. The disparity was very clear: in just one of the remaining *centuriae* 'there were almost more registered citizens than in the whole "first class"'.[8] The voting and proclamation of results were 'progressive', in descending order among the 'classes', until the absolute majority of *centuriae* was reached.

Those who still had to vote were further swayed by the casting of lots among the 'first class' in a *centuria praerogativa*, which was required to express itself openly and first. The assembly met in the Campus Martius, outside the *pomerium*, a legacy from when it represented the city's army: those who could afford the cost of complete armour and fought in the front line were guaranteed more weight when it came to decision-making. This however was a hangover from the past since, by the end of the second century, voluntary enlistment had become particularly popular among men of more humble and rural background, as tends to happen in many other times and places. And in 218 a vast gulf had been created between 'first class' and 'knights'. A tribunician law had in fact limited freedom of trade by senators and their sons. They would – unless they used a 'nominee' – therefore become involved in land investment in *terra Italia*. The 'knights', who would soon represent a social class rather than being part of the army itself (which was gradually replaced by non-Roman auxiliaries), could occupy themselves full-time with trade and finance in Italy, but above all in the Roman provinces – those regions outside Italy that were subject to Rome.

The Tribal Assembly, on the other hand, decided on the principle of 'one tribe one vote'. The division of citizens into thirty-five *tribus* was along territorial lines, something like a modern-day 'electoral college'. Yet here too it ended up favouring those who could afford the cost of travel or who lived in Rome but came from – and, more importantly, had property in – *terra Italia*. This enabled them to register with one of the thirty-one rural tribes, those most coveted. In the four urban tribes, with large numbers of poor residents and *liberti* (slaves freed by their masters), the individual vote carried much less weight. Things were balanced out by poor recent immigrants who had not yet been subject to the census (completed for the last time in 69): they kept their tribe of origin even if they weren't owners of land in *terra Italia*. The *concilium plebis* must have been organized in a similar way to the Tribal Assembly. Summoned by ten tribunes – magistrates who had to live in the city – it voted for the *plebiscita*, which now decided the majority of legislative measures. The only important difference compared to the Tribal Assembly was the exclusion of patricians, the ancient aristocracy of blood that had now dwindled to a mere handful, and included Caesar's own family.

Decisive then was the amorphous group of the urban populace that grew from year to year thanks to a particular privilege: the *frumentationes*. Beginning from a *plebiscitum* proposed by Gaius Sempronius Gracchus (123), the adult male citizen resident in Rome was guaranteed the regular right – apart from just one interruption between 82 and 73 – to obtain a monthly quantity of grain (5 *modii*, equivalent to a little under 44 litres)[9] at a fixed price. This price would often change, as would the criteria for deciding who was eligible – a number that gradually rose.

The provision of grain was a major logistical problem. Transport by land, at prohibitive costs, had to be limited as much as possible. The only viable route, for a commodity that was essential but bulky and relatively cheap, was by sea. The cargoes of ships docking at Puteoli (present-day Pozzuoli) or Ostia were therefore moved onto smaller boats which were then rowed or towed up the Tiber as far as Rome, the principal consumer. The 'imperialistic' power therefore preferred to exploit productive Tyrrhenian areas accessible to the sea, such as the provinces of Sicily, Sardinia and Africa. In 58, what was by now the free distribution of grain led to a sharp increase in the migration of Roman citizens into the city and the freeing of slaves. For many masters, transforming slaves into *liberti* – who then, as citizens, were entitled to public grain – was a way of saving on their upkeep while, at the same time, continuing to enjoy the services guaranteed by *clientela*, the institutionalized relationship between a *patronus* and someone of humbler origins.

In an environment that had no structures for mediating consensus (no party system), even that ancient constraint contributed towards mobilizing the electors, especially the urban populace. There was no set quorum, so the actual turnout could be around 5–6 per cent of those entitled to vote (i.e. of all adult male Roman citizens who were living in *terra Italia*). A minority that was resolute and organized, for whatever reason, could therefore easily win the day. Another relevant factor, electoral corruption (*ambitus*), erupted when voting became secret (at the end of the second century), so that control of society was taken over by economic factors such as bribery. In short, there was nothing 'more fickle than the populace, more enigmatic than the will of men, more deceptive than the general conduct of assemblies'.[10] Less scrupulous politicians illegally embroiled slaves and other non-citizens through the *collegia*, the ancient trade or religious associations that included a wide and varied section of society and which, due to being spread throughout the city, made it easier to win and manage popular approval. Lastly, the absence of a 'police force' allowed situations to degenerate into violence.

Ideas naturally had their own importance. But what moved the mass? In the *Defence of Sestius*, a speech that Cicero gave during a trial in 56, he states that 'on three occasions can the will of the Roman people be substantially displayed in political terms: in the *contiones*, in assemblies, and at games and gladiatorial spectacles'.[11] The former were assemblies officially organized by a magistrate entirely for purposes of information:

8

the populace had no right to vote in them but could nevertheless take part (how, and within what limits, is a matter of much debate).

There were, however, methods of control. These included the veto *(intercessio)*, a right typically held by tribunes, who could exercise it in relation to laws proposed by higher magistrates and, generally speaking, against decisions of senators. It was also often used against colleagues: 'what college indeed is so ill-composed as not to have at least one reasonable person among its 10 members?'[12] An alternative system was the *obnuntiatio*, the communication of unfavourable celestial signs – including thunder, lightning and flights of birds – in accordance with the complex rules of an ancient 'science' of Etruscan origin. When it came to very popular proposals, this system was more prudent than the veto: 'often indeed the immortal gods restrained with augurs the unjust impulse of the people'.[13] Moreover, during the whole time that the *spectio* – the observation of such signs – was declared, the assemblies could make no decision.

Very few citizens, of course, could have access to the *cursus honorum*, the course of honours, which was the highest ambition for every Roman. *Ambitio*, moreover, indicated literally the action of a person who 'goes around asking', an activity typical of candidates at any time (while *ambitus* was none other than the corrupt side of the same action). Even the city layout adapted itself to this. On the northern slopes of the Palatine Hill, families of the ruling class built their houses, symbols of power and ideal places to observe the movements of opponents and to receive *clientes* who accompanied politicians in the spectacle of their daily wanderings in the Forum below.

The *cursus honorum* was an ever-narrowing pyramid whose steps were formed by the various magistracies. At the higher levels, in order: quaestorship, tribunate (from which patricians were excluded), aedileship, praetorship, consulship, in rare cases the office of censor (generally elected every five years) and very rarely dictatorship (created only in moments of crisis). The key to access was not just family prestige – *nobilitas*, 'renown', determined by positions of high office held by ancestors, as opposed to *novitas* – but also money. Offices, in fact, were not remunerated and electoral campaigns, self-financed and ever more costly, often ended in debt. Generally speaking, to cover costs it was necessary to reach the end of a term of office. Only then were consuls and praetors, on becoming proconsuls and propraetors, awarded the government of a province, and therefore the possibility of exploitation. Lower magistrates – quaestors, aediles and tribunes – had to climb further in order to reach the next step. The whole 'course' from quaestor to consul, if all went well, took twelve years, considering not only the minimum ages of entry to each magistracy but also the obligatory gaps between each of them. More ambitious politicians, however, could rely on one ally: on the general enthusiasm for an 'imperialistic' policy. This, among other things, had already, in 167, released all the people of Rome from property taxes . . . at the expense, of course, of those who lived in the provinces. It was indeed the wealth of those subjects – officially confiscated each year as war reparations – that provided citizens with important 'social safety nets'. These were principally: grain at a fixed price for residents in Rome, public works and an ever more professional army that offered opportunities for those who had no property. For 'knights', the equestrian class, who at the highest levels included bankers and *publicani* – the inexorable and all-powerful tax collectors – the advantages were even more apparent. Nor were those advantages any less for the great landowners of *terra Italia*, subsidized by ever cheaper and more plentiful slave labour from overseas victories. The politicians, of course, didn't hold back. Many of them, thanks to the mechanisms triggered by 'imperialism', became rich as landowners, a very few as victorious generals, and a fair number as governors.

In particular, thanks to foreign conquests, magistrates with *imperium* increased their prestige out of all proportion, establishing also a privileged relationship with soldiers. These, now more loyal to their general and to their comrades than to the *res publica*, could be just as useful in peacetime, exerting pressure on citizens or simply turning out en masse to vote. The cost of such great advantages fell on the general public: the largest items of public expenditure included pay for the legions and parcels of land for retired veterans.

The political elite was split, however, into two factions, created in the latter half of the second century and destined to clash right up to the last years of the *res publica*. On the one side were the 'Populares', who 'wanted, in their words and deeds, to please the mass of the people',[14] and, on the other, the 'Optimates', the self-styled 'best', whom we might describe as 'conservatives'.

A frequently used concept – and for that reason ambiguous, as in every age – was 'freedom', personified in *Libertas*. In a society already fundamentally divided between free men and slaves, freedom was invoked by the Optimates to defend the rules of a *res publica* which was to all intents and purposes oligarchic, and by the Populares to protect the citizen. They were two often conflicting interpretations but both ascribable to what came to be described in the nineteenth century as 'liberty of the ancients', inseparable from involvement in the political life of an all-absorbing city-state, which suppressed the 'private sphere' in terms that could not be applied to 'moderns'. We may note however that, at the time of Cicero, figures like Atticus – and all knights in general – could happily keep a low profile.

Among the more markedly 'popular' assertions of *libertas* was *provocatio*, which gave the possibility for every citizen condemned to death to appeal to the final judgement of the people. It was an ancient right, which had been reasserted in 123 by the tribune Gaius Gracchus, who remembered the killing of his brother Tiberius and the judicial persecution of his supporters a decade earlier. A frequent alternative for anyone facing capital punishment was voluntary exile (prohibited only for the most heinous crimes); for a politician, banishment from the city was much the same as death.

In a world where separation of powers was unknown, justice itself was a natural terrain for conflict between Optimates and Populares. It has been observed that 'the "show-trial" is an invention of the Romans'.[15] During those years, judicial proceedings were generally conducted on large open-air tribunes, platforms in the central area of the Forum. Every court of judgment, each specializing in a single type of crime, had its own tribune, with positions for the president, jury, witnesses and orators. Surrounding it, at ground level, was an often sizeable crowd of onlookers or, often, 'supporters' who, at times, were violent. The trial of a politician, in any event, was always a political trial.

A third powerful force, alongside the people and the magistrates, was the Senate, a permanent assembly that automatically included anyone who had been a magistrate. This therefore brought together those who, at least once in their life, had enjoyed the favour of the electorate and had gained experience in public affairs. The office of senator was for life, open to review only by the censors (generally elected every five years to keep order among every class of citizen), following criteria of morality and wealth. The Senate held overall authority on questions of religion and foreign policy, where stability – helped by a low turnover among its members – was more necessary. Each year it also appointed the governors of provinces.

The Senate was a consultative body assembled at the request of a magistrate in office (generally a consul), who, acting as president, chose the place, date and agenda. The place was an inaugurated site: *in primis* the ancient Curia Hostilia which, according to tradition, dated back to the third king, or a *templum*, either inside the *pomerium* or outside (but within a radius of a mile,[16] to allow tribunes to exercise their veto). The possibility of meeting was extensive; only after 61 could they not take place on days set aside for popular assemblies. Prior notice could also be very short, if an emergency arose. The whole procedure for consultation had to take place between sunrise and sunset and – apart from the preliminaries – on the initiative of the president. The senators at that point were consulted in decreasing order of seniority: each was required to express a view. As there was no time limit for each intervention, a long speech could bring proceedings to a standstill.

Otherwise, they proceeded to vote – where serving magistrates did not take part and which was generally open to the tribunician veto. Voting took place *per discessionem*, in other words by moving to two different sectors of the meeting place. The opinion expressed in this way, called the *senatus consultum*, was recorded by the president. The doors stayed open throughout the whole session; a crowd that gathered outside would be kept informed by word of mouth, and this sometimes made it necessary for the assembly to be protected by guards.

The Senate, in line with Roman tradition, used to maintain its composition. But during the time of Sulla it underwent a major change. The dictator doubled the number of its members to 600, favouring the entry of his own supporters while at the same time removing his opponents, even through physical elimination. This had an important consequence that was exactly the opposite of what Sulla had anticipated. After the re-emergence of pro-Populares tendencies, the assembly's loss of authority became a permanent problem.

In 56, during his *Defence of Sestius*, Cicero spoke of the Senate as the 'highest perennial moderator of the *res publica*'.[17] In the *Laws*, while his friend Atticus noted that such order 'would tire not just the censors, but all the judges too', Cicero reminded him: 'may the order of the Senate be unblemished and an example to others'.[18] And again:

> nor must a speech ever be too long, except when the Senate fails in its duty – as often happens in the case of intrigues – and it is useless to let a day be lost without the intervention of a magistrate, or when the importance of the argument requires eloquence on the part of the orator to persuade and clarify: and our Cato is remarkable in both of these instances. [. . .] It is necessary for the senator to be well informed about the conditions of the *res publica*, the power of the army, the state of the treasury, what are the foreign alliances, friends, taxable populations, laws, conditions and treaties, and he must also know about the formulas used by our forebears in issuing decrees.[19]

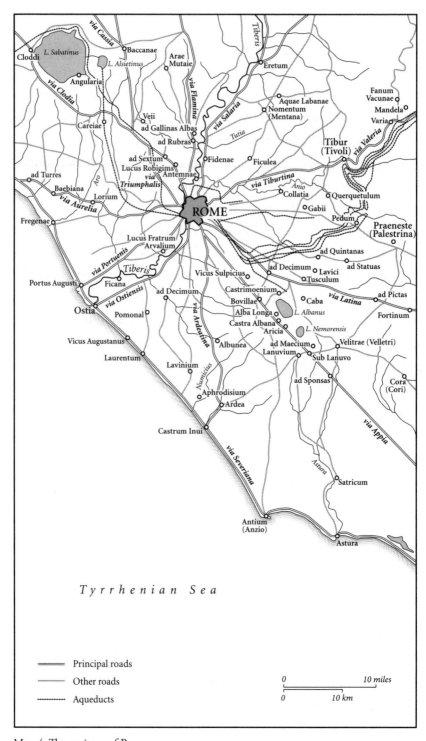

Map 4 The environs of Rome

The crisis would have particularly dramatic consequences in relation to the institution of the *senatus consultum ultimum*. This was a controversial resolution which, from the latter half of the second century, was adopted in cases where the *res publica* and the city of Rome were in danger. 'THE CONSULS SHALL TAKE STEPS TO ENSURE THAT THE *RES PUBLICA* SUFFERS NO HARM'; the underlying problem, however, was the generic nature of the formula and of the powers granted: 'to raise troops, to conduct war, to require the obedience in every respect of allies and citizens, therefore to have maximum judicial and military authority at home and in the field'.[20] At that point, any magistrate who acted on the basis of that authority – but without absolute *imperium*, both military and civil, guaranteed by the ancient institution of dictatorship – would be exposed to the risk of later repercussions, particularly if he had curtailed the right of *provocatio*.

In any event, the defence of the city of Rome still remained an absolute priority.

ROME: A CITY EVER PROTECTED

Prior to the unprecedented order given by Pompey on that fateful 17 January 49, the city of Rome had always been defended, from both outside and inside attacks: indeed raids and 'marches on Rome' have a very long history.

Back in the legendary times of Romulus, it is recorded that after the abduction of the Sabine women, the men of King Titus Tatius managed to corrupt the young Tarpeia with gold and occupy the Arx (the northern summit of the Capitolium). But the Romans, it is said, guided by Romulus and protected by Jupiter Stator, held out on the Palatine Hill, prompting a bitter conflict in the valley between the two hills . . . until the Sabine women themselves, by intervening, secured peace and the joint reign of the two monarchs.

There were many subsequent expeditions towards Rome. These were particularly frequent in its earliest times, when the city had limited territory and enemies all around.

But the *res publica* came about due to another legendary though peaceful incursion, dating back to 509. When the noble Lucretia was raped by the son of King Lucius Tarquinius 'the Proud' and committed suicide, Lucius Junius Brutus arrived in Rome at the head of a volunteer army recruited from nearby Collatia (in the area of present-day Castel dell'Osa). The city made no attempt to defend itself on that occasion, but only because the action wasn't seen as hostile: public opinion sided instead against the tyrant. Nor was any defence required when Tarquinius returned in due course from Ardea: quite simply 'the gates were shut in his face and he was informed of his banishment'.[21] Soon after, the situation deteriorated. Tarquinius called for assistance from Lars Porsenna, king of the Etruscan city of Clusium (present-day Chiusi). According to the more 'pro-Roman' version (stating an effective resistance against the etruscan occupation), everyone moved from the country districts into the city, encircled by defences. The enemies succeeded in capturing the Janiculum on the other side of the River Tiber, but the heroic Horatius Cocles stopped them by valiantly defending the bridge, the *pons Sublicius*, until his comrades had managed to demolish it. Porsenna's siege, which followed, conducted also from the river, came to nothing. During the same siege, Gaius Mucius Scaevola, having failed to murder the Etruscan king, managed to persuade the latter to negotiate through his show of determination in thrusting his right arm – the one that had failed to kill him – into the flames of a fire.

The *res publica* remained at the centre of the ambitions of the city's neighbours; to defend it, from 501 onward, dictators were also appointed. On successive occasions hostile armies came as far as the city walls, sometimes encouraged by in-fighting between patricians and plebeians. The latter, through concessions or other means, always ended up defending it. This dark and frantic period saw an occupation of the Capitolium and its citadel by exiles and slaves led by the Sabine Appius Herdonius (460); it saw the banishment of many senators through the high-handedness of the *decemviri* – the plenipotentiary commission appointed to draft the Law of the XII Tables – as well as two peaceful 'marches' of soldiers towards the Aventine Hill, who in both cases were allowed to enter (450). But the city, when faced with serious danger, was always defended.

The events of 390 were terrible: the trauma caused would be exorcized – and only partially – more than three centuries later, thanks to Caesar's conquest of Gaul. A Celtic army led by Brennus brought the city to its knees, despite heroic resistance. The 'pro-Roman' version of what happened – which differs from many other accounts (not ruling out a total and long celtic occupation) – is the one passed down by the historian Titus Livius, better known as Livy (59 BC–AD 17). Living during the time of the principate of Augustus – who good-naturedly called him 'Pompeianus' for his marked 'republican' sensibility[22] – Livy states that he was unable to rely on documents, 'most of which were lost' in the Gallic conflagration.[23] In our view, this offers all the more reason why his 'exemplary' reconstruction of what took place must also have been inspired to some extent by the 'marches' on Rome that were more recent in time, and not least by the unprecedented flight decreed on that fateful 17 January 49.

According to Livy, the *casus belli* of 390 was a gross diplomatic error. Three young Roman patricians who went to the Etruscan city of Clusium to act as mediators, took up arms against the Celts. The Celts demanded satisfaction; the Senate refused and the populace even elected the three perpetrators of the insult as military tribunes (the magistrates who at that time replaced the consuls). During that period there was no dictator: 'at such a point destiny blinds men's minds'.[24]

The Roman army was led by incompetent commanders, with little concern for new levies and scornful of the widespread fear about those people who had come from the far reaches of the Ocean. They ordered the camp to be set up in an unsuitable place, unprotected by a trench, nor did they worry about taking the *auspicia* (to test the favour of the divinity) or performing sacrifices. At the River Allia (11 miles north from Rome), the army was routed (on 18 July). Many took refuge in the recently captured Etruscan city of Veii (present-day Veio); those who returned to Rome forgot to shut the city gates. When they heard 'the savage cries and dissonant songs of the barbarians that roamed in swarms around the walls',[25] panic took over. The young men of military age and the able-bodied senators retreated, with their wives, children, weapons and provisions, to the Arx and the Capitolium, to defend 'from that stronghold the gods, men, and the name of Rome'.[26] The plebeians, now short of grain, fled beyond the Janiculum, scattering in the fields or making for nearby towns. The vestals – patrician priestesses who from childhood had taken a vow of chastity for thirty years, and to keep the city's holy flame alight in the Temple of Vesta – buried certain sacred objects and carried others into the Etruscan town of Caere (present-day Cerveteri). A plebeian carried them on his wagon, having got his wife and children to dismount. The more illustrious old men remained in their homes, ready for death, wearing their official robes.

The Celts, having entered the Colline Gate incredulous and afraid, set about sacking the city. Those on the citadel held out, watching the ruin of the city below. An initial attack was held back; it marked the beginning of the siege, which in reality placed the attackers under great hardship: all the grain from the nearby fields had just been taken to Veii. A band of Gauls also attacked Ardea, where the former dictator and patrician Marcus Furius Camillus was living in exile. He urged his new fellow citizens to make a sortie, slaughtering enemy soldiers. Men then began to converge on Veii, and it was decided to call back Camillus, who had captured the city some time before. A messenger was sent to the Capitolium, 'such was the respect for the law and the distinction of authority even in that desperate moment',[27] to seek the resolution of the Popular Assembly to recall him from exile and for the Senate to name him dictator. This is what happened. Camillus, taken to Veii, could then lead the counter-attack. Meanwhile, hunger raged among both besiegers and besieged, and Brennus, rigging the scales that weighed the 1,000 pounds of gold agreed as a ransom,[28] exclaimed the cruel words 'Woe to the conquered!' Eventually, the dictator, urging his men to 'win their country back with iron', gained the upper hand, annihilating the enemies and winning the title of 'second Romulus', father of his country.[29]

The 'pro-Roman' version records that the resistance of the Arx and the Capitolium was also helped by the alarm raised by the sacred geese of Juno, which, together with Jupiter and Minerva, protected the Capitolium and the city. This is the version that finally prevailed, demonstrated also by the honours reserved for the descendants of those heroic birds. Fed by the censors, every year they were 'honoured with a splendid procession, during which a goose was carried on a litter';[30] but dogs, having failed to keep guard, 'paid with crucifixion, hung alive by their shoulders on a gibbet of elder wood'.[31]

Returning to Livy's account, Camillus persuaded his fellow citizens to rebuild Rome after its recapture rather than moving to Veii, as some people, particularly the plebeians, were suggesting. The temples were purified and covenants created with the people of Caere, who had given hospitality to the holy objects and the priestesses, thereby ensuring that 'worship of the gods'[32] had not been interrupted. The Capitoline Games were established, since Jupiter Optimus Maximus had defended 'his own abode and the citadel of the Roman people'.[33] The gold collected for the ransom was declared sacred and placed under the throne of Jupiter; the matrons, by virtue of their offerings, were granted the honour of having eulogies pronounced at their funerals. Since the tribunes continued to urge people to abandon Rome, Camillus, together with the senators, climbed onto the *rostra*, the platform of the orators in front of the Comitium. Expressing his own bitterness, he recalled how he had been banished, asked why having taken Rome it should then be abandoned, and recalled misfortunes and the need to continue worshipping the gods. These acts, he observed, were performed not just on specific days but in specific places: there were rituals to be performed on the Capitolium; there was the fire of Vesta, whose priestesses could live in no other place. The *flamen* (priest) of Jupiter was also forbidden to spend more than one night outside the *pomerium*. Finally, Camillus spoke words that recall Cicero's *De re publica*:

[D]uring my absence, each time my home city came to mind, my thought ran to all of these places, to the hills, to the fields, to the Tiber, to this region so familiar to my eyes, to this sky beneath which I was born and grew up. [. . .] Not without cause did the gods and men choose this place for the foundation of our city, its healthier hills, a convenient river for the transport of agricultural goods from inland and for receiving provisions that arrive by sea, a place close to the sea as our needs require but not exposed, through excessive proximity, to the threats of foreign fleets, situated at the centre of Italy, particularly suitable for the expansion of the city. The greatness of the city so recently built is the very proof of it. [. . .] Here is the Capitolium, where once, when a human skull (*caput*) had been found, it was prophesied that this would be the capital (*caput*) and the place that ruled the world.[34]

His speech was followed by a voice, heard by senators gathered in the Curia Hostilia. A centurion in the Forum ordered a patrol of guards to plant the ensign, saying: 'here we will stay most excellently';[35] *hic manebimus optime*, a motto that would serve well in the nineteenth century for Quintino Sella and Rome as capital of Italy, and later for Gabriele D'Annunzio and his occupation of Fiume.

The Romans followed the advice and the prophecy. Ten years later, the appointment of a dictator was enough to persuade attackers from Praeneste (present-day Palestrina) to withdraw from the walls of Rome; further attempts by neighbouring populations – as well as the Celts – came to nothing. The city of Rome for some time found peace.

The problem re-emerged dramatically in 280 when Pyrrhus, king of Epirus, defeated a Roman army in battle and drove his troops as far as Anagnia (present-day Anagni) or, according to another version, to Praeneste. They were pushed back by diplomacy: Etruria had unexpectedly made peace, and the Roman army that found itself there could return to the city; at the same time, Pyrrhus had failed in his attempts to corrupt the senators and ambassadors who had been sent to him. An even more difficult moment followed. In 211, having wreaked panic and destruction throughout Italy, Hannibal, still undefeated, set up camp just 3 miles from the city. The Roman army was employed at that time in the siege of Capua (present-day Santa Maria Capua Vetere), but Rome had to be defended at all costs. According to the historian Polybius of Megalopolis (c.200–c.120) the situation was resolved by chance: the consuls were carrying out new levies and had recruited a legion which was at the city that same day. The soldiers were lined up at that very moment outside the walls, stopping the enemy in its tracks.

Livy doesn't record this fortunate coincidence but states, on the contrary, that it was proposed that all troops spread throughout *terra Italia* be recalled. This proved unnecessary, however: 15,000 men arrived from Capua, led by the proconsul Quintus Fulvius Flaccus. Livy states that he was given the title of consul, which was necessary to govern inside the *pomerium*. Hannibal was persuaded to hold back by divine omens and by the confidence of his enemies, who had not even lowered land values.[36] Plutarch tells how five years earlier, after the defeat at Cannae (between present-day Barletta and Canosa di Puglia) – when friends had already advised Hannibal to march on Rome – the ex-dictator Quintus Fabius Maximus 'the Delayer' had posted 'sentries at the gates ordering them to prevent the crowd from going out and abandoning the city'.[37] The fear of the Carthaginians, during those terrible years, was equal to that more ancient fear of the Celts.

In 91, according to an otherwise unconfirmed account, the Marsian general Quintus Poppaedius Silo is said to have attempted to march on Rome with 10,000 men with weapons hidden under their tunics. In league with the plebeian tribunes in Rome, their purpose was to force the Senate to make them citizens. Silo was stopped along the way by a certain Gaius Domitius (perhaps Gnaeus Domitius Ahenobarbus, censor in 92 and father of Lucius, the anti-Caesarian consul of 54), who, thanks to his 'moderate and calm discourse', persuaded him to see reason.[38]

Sometimes it was the citizens themselves who attacked the city, but even then it was always defended. The first of these attacks came from the banished patrician Gnaeus Marcius Coriolanus who, in 488, transformed internal strife into 'an armed conflict'.[39] Having captured a series of districts, starting with Circei (present-day San Felice Circeo), he arrived within 5 miles of Rome, at the head of an army of Volsci. The consuls prepared to defend the city, according to the historian Dionysius of Halicarnassus (c.60 BC–c.AD 7), enlisting as many men as possible, organizing night watchmen and collecting a 'substantial amount of money, grain, weapons'.[40] The population, without even receiving orders, took their own initiatives: there were those who climbed onto the city walls, who flocked to the gates, who armed their slaves and made their stand on the roofs of the houses, and who 'took up position on the citadel of the Capitolium and in other fortified areas of the city'.[41] An embassy was sent without success. To the contrary, Coriolanus, after capturing other nearby cities, brought a much stronger army even closer to the city, which meanwhile strengthened its defences. Conflict was avoided only thanks to the intervention of the rebel's wife and his mother. She, according to Livy, asked her son: 'did not this thought come to you, when Rome was in sight: "Within those walls are my house and my household gods, my mother, my wife, my children"?'[42] Nevertheless, according to Livy, it was the population of Rome, with little appetite for war, who immediately pressed for a diplomatic solution.

A group of rebel soldiers – less than a thousand – also took the initiative in 342. In the middle of a military rebellion at Capua, having left Anxur (present-day Terracina), they forced the patrician Titus Quinctius, a soldier and politician who had retired from public life to the district of Tusculum (near present-day Grottaferrata), to become their leader. And so they arrived, through their own initiative more than the wishes of their commander, 'advancing in hostility as far as the eighth milestone of what is today the *via Appia*'; they would have immediately marched on the city 'had they not heard that an army was coming to oppose them under Marcus Valerius Corvus, who had been appointed dictator, with Lucius Aemilius Mamercus as master of the cavalry'.[43] The sight of the banners and the memory of their home city stopped them: 'they were not yet so hardy in shedding the blood of fellow citizens, nor did they know wars other than external ones'.[44] Corvus persuaded them by remembering the wars they had fought together, the peaceful secessions of the plebeians, the women who had stopped Coriolanus and his army, not of Romans, but of Volscians. At Quinctius' pleading, the soldiers surrendered to the dictator, who did not take vengeance on them.

Two centuries later, however, political strife began to degenerate into violence. The first act was the assassination of Tiberius Gracchus (in 133) on the personal initiative of the *pontifex maximus* Publius Cornelius Scipio Nasica Serapio (consul in 138), who wanted to stop his re-election as tribune, which he regarded as illegal; the consul Publius Mucius Scaevola, though asked, hadn't dared to intervene. Led by Serapio, the senators and a throng of citizens then attacked the tribune and his supporters, who had occupied the area of the Capitolium waiting for the vote of the *concilium plebis* that had been assembled there; they pursued them and hurled many from the rock. Along with Tiberius – it seems – 300 of his followers died, all attacked with cudgels and stones (in the *pomerium* it was forbidden to carry arms). The fate of his brother Gaius (tribune in 123 and 122) was different, also from a legal point of view. A 'final' decree of the Senate, in 121, directed the consul Lucius Opimius and his men to drive Gaius and his followers from the Aventine Hill, which they had occupied. Gaius, now on the run, had himself killed by a slave. The repressions that followed are said to have resulted in 3,000 dead.

With a city now divided between Populares and Optimates, the factions began warring between themselves. Rome was under attack 'as though it were an enemy city, and for those present there were ruthless massacres, for others sentences of death, banishment and confiscation, for some terrible tortures'.[45] This was a radical change: the emergence of the *bellum civile*, fighting between citizen armies . . . but even then the city always found its 'defenders'.

The dark age began with Sulla. In 88, while consul, he led six legions from Campania, declaring that he wanted to protect the *res publica*. The situation was very tense: at a certain point, due to in-fighting, political activities were suspended. It was Marius – a former Popularis consul and, above all, a Roman hero – who sparked disorder. Twenty years before, he and his army had resolved the embarrassing stalemate in the African conflict against King Jugurtha of Numidia. Soon after, in Narbonese and Cisalpine Gaul, he had annihilated the Teutons and Cimbri, Germanic populations that were threatening to invade Italy. In that grim year 88, however, with the aid of a tribune, Marius had removed Sulla from his prestigious command over the war against Mithridates VI, king of Pontus. The consul, now followed by soldiers – but not by 'officials', apart from a quaestor – and supported by his colleague, consul Quintus Pompeius Rufus, marched on Rome. In reality, he did so with much hesitation, reaffirming his reasons several times to justify his actions. He managed to reach the Esquiline Hill with two legions, but the inhabitants 'sought to drive him back by throwing missiles from above, until he threatened to burn down the houses'.[46] The two factions then clashed in the Forum: 'and so there was a true battle between enemies, the first of its kind in Rome . . . with bugles and standards in keeping with the rules of war'.[47] Sulla was then joined by reinforcements, while his enemies, in vain, sought help from their fellow citizens and promised slaves their freedom. Sulla's victory was followed not by looting but by many of the losers being executed, some as they tried to escape. At the end of the day, the whole action bore some vestiges of legality: from a certain point of view the two consuls, by joint agreement, had quelled a domestic revolt.

The following year, in 87, however, something entirely new occurred: the city was struck down by famine. The 'attacker' this time was the Popularis Lucius Cornelius Cinna, former consul, whom the Senate had dismissed for fomenting serious disorder. Having gathered an army from the towns and villages of Latium and Campania, he marched against Rome but found it fortified with ditches and protected by war machines. The Senate also called for the help of Gnaeus Pompeius Strabo, father of Pompey, who had a loyal army which had been strengthened by a recent victory against rebel Italian allies.

But Cinna's army was joined by other forces, led by Quintus Sertorius – hero of the Cimbrian War – and by Marius himself. The Populares laid siege to Rome from the coast, sacked Ostia, and sent troops north to Marius' allies in Ariminum to block the arrival of reinforcements from Gaul. Thanks to the betrayal of a tribune, Marius made a first entry into Rome but was driven back by consular forces. He then blocked supplies from the south by sea, and from the north by river, and attacked the surrounding towns, where provisions were stored. Cinna meanwhile persuaded slaves to desert by promising freedom, and the Senate, fearing serious consequences from the populace 'if the shortage of wheat worsened',[48] reached a hard-fought agreement. Marius and Cinna could then enter the city but, despite their promises, they gave the go-ahead for looting and revenge. Many heads went to decorate the *rostra*, while corpses were left prey to dogs and birds. Sulla was deposed and declared a public enemy; his house was destroyed, along with those of anyone who aspired to the *regnum*, the ancient monarchic power.

Revenge led to two other 'marches' on Rome, both in 82. Sulla, after re-conquering *terra Italia* at the head of an army already victorious over Mithridates, and protagonist of the ruthless siege of Athens, could, for the first time, enter a Rome that had lost many of its protectors and was ready to open its gates to him. Its inhabitants, 'in the grip of starvation', were 'accustomed always to tolerating, in place of immediate sufferings, those who were worse'.[49] Having driven out their adversaries – who couldn't have expected such popular support – Sulla moved first on Clusium, then on Praeneste, where one of the two consuls, the young son of Marius, had taken refuge: he would soon commit suicide (his colleague, Gnaeus Papirius Carbo, had meanwhile escaped to Africa).

At that point, Rome faced an even greater risk. Now 'with neither defenders nor food supplies',[50] it faced an army of Samnites, led by Pontius Telesinus and Marian leaders. The arrival of historic enemies, who had been ruthlessly defeated during the Social War and were now thirsting for revenge was, for the *res publica*, a threat worse than 'Hannibal camped less than three miles away'; Telesinus went about telling his men 'the last day is at hand for the Romans, and he shouted out loud that the city had to be overthrown and destroyed', adding that 'the wolves that ravaged Italian liberty would always exist unless the forest which is their customary shelter is cut down'.[51] Chaos then broke loose, 'with women crying and people running in every direction'.[52] Sulla managed to intercept the attackers, who had already surrounded the city and were camped at the Colline Gate.

The battle was bloody and chaotic. The wing led by Marcus Licinius Crassus quickly drove away the attackers; the other wing led by Sulla, pinned against the walls, managed to win only at dawn. Some 50,000 men were left dead on the field, but the number of victims soon increased even further. The Samnite prisoners were put to death at the *villa publica*: the senators assembled nearby at the Temple of Bellona – the Roman goddess of war – could hear their screams. Then came the proscriptions: an indeterminate number of Romans (estimates vary between 1,660 and 9,000) fell under the blows of 'head hunters' in search of revenge or the possessions of those they killed, who were often 'guilty' just for being wealthy.

In 77, Rome was once again in peril after an attack upon the laws imposed by Sulla. The dictator had resigned from office in 79 and died of natural causes the following year. The Popularis consul Marcus Aemilius Lepidus had already proposed the repeal of various reforms. Having gone to Etruria to put down a revolt, he had been called back in vain by the Senate to preside over the elections for the following year. In 77, he and his army marched on Rome to find it protected – following a *senatus consultum ultimum* – by a line of defences that extended from the Milvian Bridge to the Janiculum. Not far from the Campus Martius he was driven back and defeated by his Optimate colleague, consul Quintus Lutatius Catulus, before escaping from the Italian peninsula.

Before moving on towards the events of that fateful year 49, we must finally record the last serious attempt at resistance in the republican period, against another 'march' on Rome, that of Octavian, the future Augustus. Even though both consuls had died in the final stage of the War of Mutina (present-day Modena) in April 43, the Senate had refused to grant the supreme political office to the propraetor, Caesar's adopted son, who was not yet 20 years old. In response, he had crossed the Rubicon 'from Cisalpine Gaul to Italy, exactly the same that his father had crossed bringing the start of the civil war',[53] at the head of eight legions. Following a *senatus consultum ultimum*, citizens of military age would be called to arms; two legions and 1,100 horsemen would arrive from Africa, meeting up with the legion already there. The contingents, on the orders of the city praetors, would guard the Janiculum, where the public treasury had been taken, and the bridge over the river; at the port, others held at the ready 'boats, ships, money, in case they were defeated and had to escape by sea'; by doing this 'valiantly with much speed they hoped to frighten Octavian'.[54] They were not to succeed: on reaching the gates of Rome, Octavian calmed the turbulent crowd and occupied the far edge of the Quirinal Hill unopposed. The citizens greeted him with joy, heartened by the discipline shown by his troops. The rebel would finally cross the *pomerium*, amid widespread rejoicing, soon to obtain the consulship.

POMPEY: TRAINING AND DOMINANCE OF A 'TEENAGE BUTCHER'

In that fateful year 49, Caesar's main opponent would be Gnaeus Pompeius 'Magnus'. From a very young age he had managed to bring himself to the city's attention thanks to military victories that were so great as to put his innate aversion to politics into second place.

Pompey (106–48), the main figure over the whole twenty-year period after Sulla, was born some six years before Caesar. Plutarch's biography recalls, not without exaggeration, that 'no Roman enjoyed greater good-will on the part of his countrymen'.[55] He lists his qualities: simplicity, loyalty, affability and generosity. There was general admiration for his abilities to command, and from it he derived an objective power from military *clientelae*. His alleged, though dubious, physical resemblance to Alexander the Great did the rest. Unlike everyone else – including the patrician Caesar – his advance through his career was so rapid that it might be thought not to have happened at all: he became consul not only before he was legally old enough, but also without ever previously having being an elected magistrate.

The way was opened by war, and indicated by the example of Strabo, his father. This tough landowner from Picenum had distinguished himself in the devastating conflict between Rome and its former Italian allies. He besieged and stormed Asculum (present-day Ascoli Piceno), where hostilities against Rome had begun, an enterprise that guaranteed him – the first of his family – the office of consul and a triumph.

A triumph was the procession of the victorious general, preceded by captured treasures and prisoners, and followed by generals and soldiers, along a route from the Campus Martius to the Forum, reaching its climax on the Capitolium. There, a sacrifice was performed to Jupiter Optimus Maximus, while the prisoners, kept alive so that the Romans could 'enjoy a magnificent spectacle and the fruit of the victory', were taken to the prison and put to death.[56] Strabo paraded with his son, a 17-year-old soldier, behind him. In keeping with Roman policy, which was to quell rebellion by offering citizenship to those who surrendered, he offered Latin citizenship (precursor to Roman citizenship) to Transpadanians, those who lived in that part of Cisalpine Gaul north of the River Po, where he could build new *clientelae*.

Thanks to his father, this youth must immediately have understood the importance of a loyal army. At the end of his mandate as consul,

Strabo refused to hand over command, hoping perhaps to renew his appointment; his men went as far as assassinating his legitimate successor. There were no reprisals: he was soon required to defend Rome from the 'march' of Marius and Cinna. Strabo died in the process, from unknown causes. The inhabitants of Rome, in any event, must have disliked him: during his funeral 'they dragged his body from the funeral chariot and insulted it'.[57] His young son, forced to defend himself from the Populares, went home to Picenum. Just a few years later he came back on the scene, joining Sulla, who had landed at Brundisium (present-day Brindisi) and was marching to power. Having recruited three legions of 'hungry sons of a poor and populous region',[58] from 'his' Picenum, Pompey could therefore distinguish himself in various battles.

He also learned about the importance of the fleet and of food supplies. Now 24, but already a key figure in Sulla's army, he obtained from the dictator – now his father-in-law – a command to drive Marius' forces from the *provinciae frumentariae*: from Sicily (where his father, in 104, had been quaestor), Sardinia and Africa. He commanded 6 legions, 120 warships and 800 transport ships, and quickly resolved the situation: Sicily, 'surrounded by perils on every side, was liberated not with the terror of war but with the promptness of his decisions'.[59] While untainted by the proscriptions that were causing bloodshed throughout the peninsula, he managed all the same to earn the nickname 'teenage butcher'.[60] He put to death Gnaeus Papirius Carbo, three times consul, who was captured in hiding on the island of Pantelleria. Yet he showed moderation towards followers of Marius and to Sicilians, thus enlarging his own *clientela*. Having landed in Africa, in just forty days he defeated and put to death Marius' commander Gnaeus Domitius Ahenobarbus (perhaps a brother of Lucius Domitius Ahenobarbus, consul in 54), captured Prince Hiarbas, invaded Numidia, and brought about a settlement in relations between sovereigns. He also found time to go lion and elephant hunting, because 'in Africa not even the wild beasts must be ignorant of Roman strength and courage'.[61]

His father's example remained. Despite clear orders from Rome, his troops, having proclaimed him *imperator* (victorious general), didn't want to be separated from him. After various attempts – though we do not know how sincere – to make them change their minds, Pompey returned, followed by his whole army. Sulla unenthusiastically greeted him as 'Great' but this wasn't enough for him: soon after, he obtained the triumph (the first ever granted to a non-senator).

Sulla stood down as dictator, dying a natural death a year later. Pompey accompanied his body, at the head of many veterans who had come in from the countryside, braving the hostility of the consul Lepidus. It was Lepidus, by rebelling against the Senate, who gave him cause to defend the *res publica*. In 77, Pompey had a command in the north of the peninsula and in Cisalpine Gaul. Having built an army with *clientelae* from Picenum and Gaul, he managed to block movement in and out of *terra Italia*, occupying Mutina as well and putting to death the legate Marcus Junius Brutus (tribune in 83). Lepidus was forced back to just outside the *pomerium*, at the Campus Martius, by Catulus. Now on the run, according to one version Lepidus was intercepted and defeated by Pompey close to Cosa (near present-day Ansedonia in southern Tuscany). It is certain that he managed to embark with many soldiers for Sardinia, from where he hoped to stop supplies to Rome or continue on to Spain. Instead he died there, hunted down by the governor of the island.

Once again, despite an express order, Pompey failed to discharge his troops but kept them not far from Rome. The dangerous stalemate was resolved by the emergency created in Spain, which Sertorius had reduced to a Marian stronghold, and by the reluctance of the consuls to make a move. The Senate sent Pompey, who thus gained the experience of a long-drawn-out war on land fought alongside the proconsul – and *pontifex maximus* – Quintus Caecilius Metellus Pius. While Sertorius received help from Mithridates, and perhaps from pirates, the Senate sent further reinforcements only in 75. The turning point, however, came in 73 or 72, when Sertorius was betrayed and killed, and replaced by another rebel, who was soon defeated. Pompey left a monument in the Pyrenees to record his exploits, on which he claimed victory over 876 cities from the Alps to Spain.

His return offered him another opportunity. After years of hardship, marred by famine and political struggles to repeal Sulla's 'constitutional' system, something happened between 73 and 71 that was even more disturbing. This was the last, most serious, and most famous rebellion of slaves, the ubiquitous 'machines' that turned the wheels of the Roman economy. It was led by Spartacus of Thrace. The original band of gladiators on the run from Capua was soon transformed into an army of tens of thousands of men that persistently routed the regular armies. Marcus Licinius Crassus, as propraetor, was given command of operations against that belligerent but elusive enemy.

The son of Publius Licinius Crassus Dives (consul in 97 and censor in 89), he had been forced to escape after Marius' victory of 87, following which his father and brother had been killed. He had then returned at Sulla's side, taking a leading role in the battle at the Colline Gate. His love of wealth wasn't his only defect but, 'having become the most powerful, it made the others fade'.[62] He had made himself rich through Sulla's proscriptions, before then thinking up, among other things, an activity that says much about the housing situation in Rome. Having acquired slaves, architects and builders, he began buying up burnt-out houses and those nearby that had now lost their value, soon becoming the owner of the 'major part of Rome'.[63]

He went about quelling the revolt with a firm hand and with no expense spared. Pompey – a man he had never liked – hurried back: the Popular Assembly had probably directed him to intervene. Crassus, on seeing that the time for glory was running out, hastened to defeat the rebels in Calabria and to crucify 6,000 prisoners along the *via Appia*, from Rome to Capua. Pompey, in turn, intercepted and surrounded 5,000 survivors escaping north, killing them there and then: in that way he could write to the Senate that he had eliminated the roots of the revolt.

Both generals arrived in Rome with their troops. Pompey waited until he could formally celebrate the triumph, which was delayed because Metellus Pius was still in Spain. The less popular Crassus asked him to form an electoral alliance with a joint objective: the office of consul. The Senate then offered Pompey exemption in relation to previous offices . . . not because of any irregularity, but because he hadn't held any. We don't know whether other candidates had the courage to put themselves forward. What is certain is that the two men, with armed forces at the gates of Rome, ought not to have done it. They did so all the same, and Pompey obtained the larger number of votes. During his first *contio*, he promised to restore the powers of the people's tribunes, thereby repudiating his own Sullan origins. Having celebrated the triumph at the end of the year, on Metellus Pius's return, he disbanded his troops. Crassus followed his example, and at some point – we don't know when – the two were reconciled, to the joy of the people.

Pompey, at that point, was suddenly caught up in the world of Roman politics at the highest level, and discovered he didn't like it. Now required to preside over a Senate in which he had never taken part – and where Crassus was much more popular – he asked his erudite friend Marcus Terentius Varro to prepare a manual for him. He frequently disagreed with his colleague, but that year marked a decisive blow for what remained of Sulla's 'constitutional' system. In particular, restoring the power of the tribunes would have many repercussions.

CAESAR: A PATRICIAN IN POMPEY'S SHADOW

In that fateful year 49, Caesar would act, once more, as though he were 'predestined'. Such a conviction intensified just as Pompey was asserting his own dominance.

Caesar was born a patrician. On the side of his father, who had the same name, he belonged to the *gens Julia*, which boasted kinship with the goddess Venus through Julus, son of Aeneas and founder of Alba Longa, birthplace of Romulus and Remus. His father's sister had married the Popularis Gaius Marius. On his mother's side he came from the *Aurelii Cottae*, a family of ancient plebeian origin that had produced various consuls.

Caesar was not yet 20 when the death of his uncle Marius brought a change of fortune, bringing Sulla's dictatorship with it. The reign of terror forced him to leave everything, to hide, to go into exile. Unlike young Pompey, he couldn't rely on an Italic 'feudal domain' ready to welcome him. His many contacts enabled him nonetheless to distinguish himself in military and diplomatic campaigns. These took place in Asia and Cilicia (both in Anatolia), particularly difficult fronts because of King Mithridates and piracy. And so he was awarded the civic crown, the chaplet of oak leaves – sacred to Jupiter – given to those who had saved a comrade in war. Returning to Rome after the death of Sulla, he had refused, despite Lepidus' offers, to play any part in the revolt. Instead he became involved in Populares struggles: the reintegration of the sons of exiles and judicial proceedings against Sullans who had committed abuses. Back in the east, with a small militia he kept control of the cities of Caria, in south-western Turkey: he eventually returned to Rome, where he became *pontifex* in place of his dead uncle Gaius Aurelius Cotta (Popularis consul in 75 and proconsul in Cisalpine Gaul). Then, in 70, he supported an amnesty for supporters of Sertorius and that same year was elected quaestor.

Having quickly established himself as one of the finest orators of his age, Caesar was brave or reckless enough, in a funeral speech for the widow of Marius, to declare:

My aunt Julia, on her mother's side, was descended from the Kings; on her father's side she was related to the immortal gods. Indeed the *Marcii Reges*, to whose family her mother belonged, are descended from Ancus Marcius, but the Julii descend from Venus, and my family is a branch of those people. Flowing into our stock, therefore, is the sacred character of kings, who have supreme power among men, and the sanctity of gods, on whom kings themselves depend.[64]

He therefore took full advantage of one of the key moments in Roman public life when generations could be brought together. In funeral ceremonies dedicated to illustrious men – and matrons – a close relative, speaking from the *rostra*, would list the merits and deeds of the deceased and their ancestors.

For these occasions, players would wear wax masks showing the faces of the most famous forebears that were kept on display in the family home, giving the idea of the continuity of the family and its glory. In the front row, Caesar paraded the masks of Marius and his son, the consul who had committed suicide at Praeneste during Sulla's siege. The inevitable protests of the Optimates were silenced by popular enthusiasm.

Caesar then left for Hispania Ulterior (one of the two Roman provinces in Spain, precisely the farther one). During his first important office, as quaestor for the dependencies of the governor of that province, he managed to win the affection of its Roman subjects. But he returned in haste, driven by the desire to rival the glory of Alexander the Great, or rather by a dream: that he had 'raped his own mother', which could be interpreted as a sign of power over the whole earth, mother of mankind.[65] This would be followed by the attempt, described only by his biographer Gaius Suetonius Tranquillus (AD 70–126), to make converts in the Latin *coloniae* (settlements with Latin right) who were clamouring to obtain Roman citizenship.

In 67, Caesar's consistent and 'popular' path merged with the much more sinuous path followed by Pompey. The ex-quaestor supported the ex-consul in a political challenge that had unexpected consequences.

Rome and its empire was threatened by pirates, hunters of bounty and of humans to sell on the flourishing slave market. With them,

Sertorius and Spartacus, like Mithridates before them, had concluded – or at least attempted to conclude – unscrupulous agreements. Rome, in turn, had until that time raised fleets supplied mostly by allied cities, without venturing beyond 'makeshift politics'.[66]

Cicero, in 66, would point out to fellow senators that the *res publica* had been unsuccessful in defending the provinces, in guaranteeing tax revenues and protecting its allies. For years the sea had been impenetrable; foreign ambassadors were taken prisoner on their way to Rome and Roman ambassadors held to ransom; magistrates and strategic ports had fallen into enemy hands: 'Caieta (present-day Gaeta), a famous harbour and full of ships, was plundered by pirates under the eyes of the praetor'; then 'at Misenum (present-day Miseno) they kidnapped the daughter of that same man who had previously waged war against them'; another disaster at Ostia, 'foul and shameful for the *res publica* to think that almost under our eyes raiders capture and sink a fleet commanded by a consul of the Roman people'.[67]

The problem was even more awkward: in Rome 'goods were not arriving and the importation of grain had completely stopped'[68] or, at least, its inhabitants were 'hard pressed by the lack of supplies and by the fear of a great famine'.[69] This extraordinary threat had to be eliminated, without delay. Besides, 'the pirate does not count as an enemy of war, but he is a common enemy of all, and with him we cannot share faith or allegiance'.[70]

Just as exceptional was the solution: a special appointment, not by the Senate but by the plebeian assembly. In January 67, the tribune Aulus Gabinius, also from Picenum, publicized the proposal without naming Pompey. The people approved, the Senate much less: everyone understood whom he was seeking to involve. It was the offer of a three-year command in the Mediterranean and the Black Sea to within 50 miles of the coast, with authority equal to that of the governors of the individual provinces, the power to appoint legates and also large loans and enormous land and sea forces. Caesar alone supported the proposal. Years earlier he had been captured by pirates while sailing to Rhodes and released only after payment of a ransom. Now, moreover, he was looking for popular approval. In the Senate, Gabinius risked being killed; the crowd, on hearing of this, drove out members of the assembly and besieged the consul Gaius Calpurnius Piso, who was only saved from being lynched by Gabinius. Two tribunes tried in vain to use their veto; one was dismissed from office by popular vote, the other greeted 'with a cry so loud and threatening, that a crow flying over the crowd was stunned and fell to the ground as though struck by lightning'.[71] The observations addressed to the people by the illustrious Catulus (consul in 78), who criticized – perhaps with some justification – the excessive powers granted by the proposal, were in vain. Pompey spent the day of the vote in the countryside, returned to Rome, and patriotically accepted. Perhaps he obtained further concessions. The price of foodstuffs fell immediately and the people, delighted, 'thought that Pompey's name alone had already resolved the war'.[72] Speculation must have been very great.

Pompey showed perfect efficiency, thanks perhaps to lengthy, secret preparations. In spring, even before the season favourable for navigation, Rome assembled the largest combined force ever, 'limited' however to 270 vessels. The Mediterranean was divided into twelve zones, plus that of the Black Sea. Each official, with boats, legionaries and horsemen, had to control their own zone, also from land. For pirates it was the beginning of the end.

Pompey, who had well understood the importance of the *provinciae frumentariae* since the time of Sulla, pacified first Sicily, then Africa and finally Sardinia. He then moved on to Spain and Gaul, liberating the western Mediterranean in just six weeks. Having sent ships to wait for him at Brundisium, he landed in Etruria and moved towards Rome, where the consul Piso sought to oppose him, in particular by preventing conscription in Cisalpine and Narbonese Gaul (the provinces assigned to him). But everyone crowded into the streets, prompted 'by the unexpected rapidity of the change that had filled the marketplace with provisions'.[73] The results were extraordinary even in the more difficult eastern sector, haunted by many gangs of pirates. The enemies surrendered en masse; those who didn't were driven towards Cilicia, where there was a final showdown in the bay of Coracesium (the present-day Turkish seaport of Alanya). Pompey is said to have taken more than 20,000 prisoners; to many he guaranteed land and adequate living conditions. It was perhaps a temporary success, but its impact was enormous.

In Rome, meanwhile, there were other tensions regarding a recent law on *ambitus*, consular elections, and an unsuccessful proposal by the tribune Gaius Manilius to distribute *liberti* among all tribes. The last of these would have altered the electoral body, to the undoubted advantage of the proponent. The Senate rejected it, and the populace – jealous of their own privileges – were 'highly indignant'.[74] To regain popularity, Manilius made a further proposal, once again in 66.

It was supported again by Caesar, who found himself this time in larger company. It involved the command against Mithridates, who had earlier been defeated by Sulla and, more recently, by the Optimate and proconsul Lucius Licinius Lucullus. But Lucullus was opposed by the knights (for having reduced taxation on the provinces) and by the Populares (who wouldn't forgive his past support for Sulla). A mutiny of soldiers at Nisibis (the present-day eastern Turkish city of Nusaybin), stirred up by his young brother-in-law Publius Claudius Pulcher probably at the instigation of Pompey, had triggered a series of military disasters, plunging the finances of Rome into a dire situation.

Manilius proposed that Pompey should assume supreme command of the armies that were already in the region, with power to appoint legates and negotiate settlements. Also in favour was the praetor Cicero, who delivered his oration *In Defence of the Manilian Law*, the 'manifesto' of Roman 'imperialism', in front of the people. Opposition from the Optimates was pointless. Catulus, unheeded, 'began shouting from the tribune, urging the senators to seek out, like their forebears, a mountain and sheer rock to find shelter and preserve freedom'[75] – a reference to the Gallic sack of Rome.

Pompey received news of his appointment while he was still in Cilicia. Predictably, he accepted with reluctance, though well aware that this would allow him to emulate Alexander the Great. Having abandoned negotiations in order to launch hostilities, he set up a naval blockade along the whole coast of Asia Minor, from Phoenicia to the Bosporus, calling on the support of every ally: he would leave Mithridates with 'an enemy stronger than him, hunger'.[76] The logistical involvement was enormous, and long sieges were made possible by advanced engineering works. Mithridates, once surrounded and finally betrayed by his son Pharnaces, committed suicide. Between the summer and autumn of 63, on the proposal of Cicero, the consul at that time, the Senate voted a *supplicatio* of unprecedented length: ten whole days. It was a solemn ceremony of thanksgiving during which the temples were opened and statues of the gods put on public display for the people to honour them with offerings and prayers.

Pompey had defeated Rome's deadliest enemy since the times of Hannibal and had overcome its worst threat since the wars against the Cimbri and Teutons, expanding its influence as far as Syria and Judaea. His greatest glory – he would later declare to the people – was 'to have received Asia as a frontier province and to have restored it to his country as an internal province'.[77] Having organized conquests and created a permanent fleet in the eastern Mediterranean, he sent another dispatch. Towards the end of March 62, the Senate voted a new *supplicatio*, of another twelve days. In December the victor landed at Brundisium, expecting a third, well-deserved triumph. It was feared, however, that he might 'march' on Rome 'to establish absolute power', so much so that Crassus left secretly with his children and possessions, 'either because he was truly afraid, or more likely, that he wanted to give credibility to such calumny'.[78]

But Pompey discharged his troops. At this news, an unimaginable number of jubilant people accompanied him to Rome.

2

PLOTS AND SCANDALS

Having discovered the plot, the people who, at first, too much desirous of a change of government, were inclined to war, changed their mind and began to denounce the plans of Catiline, extolling Cicero; they were gripped by an extraordinary joy, as if they had been snatched from slavery; indeed they expected the other events of the civil war would bring more spoils than harm, whereas the burning of the city was an enormous cruelty and particularly disastrous for them, since the plebeians' only wealth was their everyday things and the clothes they wore.

Sallust, *Conspiracy of Catiline*, 48,1–2

AMONG THE SCUM OF ROMULUS

In that fateful year 49, the two main actors would be joined by others. These would include Cicero and Cato who, in 63, unlike Caesar, took the view that the defence of Rome and the res publica *ought to take priority over the fundamental rights of individual citizens.*

While Pompey was still conquering the east, discontent was brewing in Rome. His rival Crassus, to oppose him, began lending money to more ambitious politicians, including Caesar . . . as would later be immortalized, among others, by Bertolt Brecht.[1] The two may have been involved in attempting a series of political actions of varying success.

First, there seems to have been a tentative but aborted conspiracy aimed at eliminating the two Optimate consuls of 65, who had taken the place of the real winners, two Populares forced to retire because of a conviction for *ambitus*. The plan, hatched by the Populares, also envisaged a massacre of senators, the armed occupation of the Capitolium, the appointment of Crassus as dictator, and of Caesar as master of the cavalry. None of this happened because, according to one version, Caesar had failed to give the agreed signal. There were no legal repercussions – a further reason for thinking that the story was later exaggerated.

There then followed the questions of the annexation of Egypt – which had been left to the Roman people by the dubious will of Ptolemy XI – and of Roman citizenship for inhabitants of Transpadane Gaul. Crassus, as censor, pushed both projects ahead, but was opposed by his colleague Catulus. In the same year 65, Caesar, as aedile, organized lavish public entertainments, animal hunts, and games in memory of his father: these involved 320 pairs of gladiators, a number bordering on the illegal, equipped with silver weapons and armour. All of this sidelined his Optimate colleague Marcus Calpurnius Bibulus, his enemy during their joint consulate in 59 as well as in that fateful year 49. One night, Caesar, perhaps out of resentment for not having obtained a mission in Egypt that had been opposed by the Optimates, restored Marius' trophies of his victories over Jugurtha, over the Cimbri and over the Teutons, which Sulla had had removed. The Marians went up to the Capitolium to celebrate, and Catulus accused Caesar of trying to undermine the institutions.

Caesar then presided over a tribunal that convicted a murderer hired by Sulla but acquitted another defendant who, during the same period, at the head of a gang of Celt warriors, had wreaked carnage among his fellow citizens, staining his own hands with blood. The killing of proscribed men had, however, been legalized by the dictator. Caesar was able to acquit, it seems, thanks to the request for too harsh a sentence. The defendant was Lucius Sergius Catilina, better known as Catiline.

Shortly before the trial, having previously been prevented through various accusations from standing for office, Catiline had appeared at the consular elections in summer 64. He had promised the distribution of public lands and remission of debts, angering a large portion of the ruling class. Despite the support of Caesar and Crassus, he had been defeated.

Cicero received the most votes. His main asset was his fame as an orator. He had quickly risen to the higher magistracies: quaestorship (in 75), aedileship (in 69) and praetorship (in 65). Extraneous to the *nobilitas*, he was supported by knights and new Italic citizens but yet was not disliked by the Optimates. Besides, the ruling class had their own fears: the Senate, as a precaution, had even ordered the dissolution of *collegia*.

Such fears were not unfounded. The year 63 began, it seems, with disturbing celestial signs. Politically, it started with a proposal by the tribune Publius Servilius Rullus, supported perhaps by Crassus and Caesar, to distribute public lands in *terra Italia* and in the provinces. Cicero, the new consul, in his appeal to the people and to the Senate, was sending out a clear message. It was better to remain in Rome, being kept at the expense of the *res publica*, than to go working on remote and pestilential plots of land. The alienation of the fertile countryside of Campania – whose rent was collected by *publicani* – would have deprived Rome of a granary but even more of a tax resource. He managed to get the proposal withdrawn. The result, no doubt, was welcomed by the large tenants – not infrequently illegal occupiers – of public lands, and often owners of the villas scattered along the coast of Campania, the most fashionable part of *terra Italia*. In reality, not all of those who benefited from monthly distributions – who by 73 already numbered between 40,000 and 80,000 – must have had an interest in agricultural life. Thirty years before, the city populace, who were careful to guard their privileges, had opposed an allocation of land proposed by the tribune Lucius Ap(p)uleius Saturninus 'since the law gave advantage to the Italic people'.[2] But now they seemed indifferent. Cicero also defeated a tribunician request to cut debts and an attempt to re-establish the rights of the sons of proscripts: both proposals, he argued, could upset a fragile equilibrium (which Cicero had sought to shore up by foregoing the governorship of the province of Macedonia in favour of his colleague Gaius Antonius Hybrida, and then also of Cisalpine Gaul).

Preparations for rebellion, fomented by Catiline, were centred on Faesulae (present-day Fiesole), in Etruria, earlier the breeding ground for Lepidus' revolt. The old Sullan centurion Gaius Manlius took military command. Other active centres were Capua, whose mass of slaves had responded to Spartacus' appeal, and Transpadane Gaul, which was still awaiting citizenship. In Rome, the plan attracted the violent underclass, debtors, ambitious young *nobiles* and, not least, senators. But it seems that broad sections of the urban plebs were also sympathetic to Catiline's plans: 'the cesspit of the city, the numerous and deadly throng of your companions'.[3] It must have been more than a few people: Catiline told the Senate that 'the *res publica* has two bodies, one weak with a fragile head, the other strong but with no head; this second, if it behaves well towards me, will never lack a head so long as I live'.[4]

Cicero was waging, above all, a 'war of information': adducing various pieces of evidence, the consul managed to convince the Senate of the guilt of a *nobilis* and a patrician who, moreover, was supported by Caesar and Crassus.

Before that, an old controversy had resurfaced relating to the defence of Rome itself. Gaius Rabirius, an elderly senator with little influence, was accused by the tribune Titus Labienus (a loyal supporter of Caesar up to that fateful year 49) of involvement in the death of Saturninus and his followers thirty-seven years earlier, when he was still a knight. Saturninus, an ally of the then consul Marius and newly confirmed as tribune for the third time, had arranged for the favoured candidate for the consular elections to be beaten to death. The Senate had therefore instructed the consuls – and accordingly Marius – to take hold of the situation. The rebels had barricaded themselves on the Capitolium, but their water supply had been cut. Marius had then imprisoned them in the Curia Hostilia so that he could act legally and avoid his responsibilities in relation to the *senatus consultum ultimum*. But others, 'reckoning that this was an excuse, had opened up the roof and attacked the Apuleians, killing them'.[5] It was said that Rabirius had then carried the head of Saturninus 'in jest, around various feasts'.[6]

The terms of the accusation are not clear, nor the dynamics of the whole trial, which took place in two stages. In the first stage it is thought that Labienus had brought the charge before the *praetor urbanus* and that Caesar and his kinsman Lucius Julius Caesar (consul in 64) were involved in their capacity as *duumviri*, magistrates appointed since ancient times to punish *perduellio*, high treason (a charge long superseded by *maiestas*, the *lèse-majesté* versus the Roman people). In other words, an archaic procedure was revived which, in theory, carried a sentence of crucifixion, the punishment for slaves. Cicero – or the populace itself – at some point in the proceedings, we don't know when or why, prevented the worst from happening. Labienus then repeated the charge on the basis of his own authority as tribune. In defence of Rabirius, Cicero spoke before the Centuriate Assembly, sustaining the lawfulness of the *senatus consultum ultimum*. He also guaranteed, with a remarkable prescience of what would soon happen, that, in similar circumstances, he would have reacted like Rabirius. The assembly was dissolved before it could reach its verdict.

Caesar recovered from the setback thanks to two important electoral victories. The first guaranteed him the position of *pontifex maximus*, an office for life as supreme custodian of a tradition that united religion and politics. The post had become vacant with the death of Metellus Pius (who, as proconsul in Spain, had fought with Pompey in the war against Sertorius). The rival Catulus offered Caesar money to persuade him to withdraw. Instead, he ran up incredible debts and won. Having previously lived in the popular district of the Suburra, he now moved into the *domus publica*, residence of the *pontifex maximus*, on the *via Sacra*. There is no exact information about his second victory: the office of praetor. All eyes were fixed on the consular elections.

Catiline stood again as candidate, putting forward the same programme. Cicero, whose life – so his informers told him – was at risk, delayed the calling of the Centuriate Assembly over which he was to preside. Then, on the day of the vote, he arrived with a bodyguard of knights and a cuirass well visible beneath his toga. Catiline left defeated.

At that very moment, Marcus Porcius Cato (96–46), grandson of the homonymous, famous 'Censor' and himself a man of legendary charisma, risked spoiling everything. He was incorruptible, as he had already proved during his quaestorship (65 or 64), when he had put the Aerarium, the public treasury, in order, denouncing irregularities among scribes, corruption and forgery of documents. He had been elected as tribune for the year 62, thanks to strong popular support. In the consular elections, however, there had been widespread use of *ambitus*. Cato, true to character, helped the defeated candidate Servius Sulpicius Rufus (patrician and well-known jurist) to gather evidence against Lucius Licinius Murena, one of the two winners, with no concern that this might have put Catiline back in the running. Murena was successfully defended by Cicero, even though the latter had recently been the author of a law on *ambitus* which reinforced the penalties and clamped down on a long list of practices (including gladiatorial games). Against Cato he exploited the weapon of ridicule. In June 60 he would once again observe that, 'with the very best intention and in good faith, he works to the detriment of the *res publica*: he reasons and speaks as though he were living in the republic of Plato and not amongst the scum of Romulus'.[7]

Amid news of plots and public speeches by Catiline, Crassus brought Cicero letters carrying information about an imminent massacre of senators. On 21 or 22 October, a *senatus consultum ultimum* was therefore passed requiring the consul to keep watch over Rome, but he didn't act on it immediately. At a time when the spectre of a rebellion of slaves was already emerging, in a climate of fear that was mounting day by day, rumours then arrived that Manlius, on 27 October, had taken up arms at Faesulae. Several garrisons stopped the capture of the key stronghold of Praeneste; groups of soldiers – and companies of gladiators – were then sent to Faesulae, Apulia, Capua and Picenum, and the people were encouraged to tell on others.

Catiline stated that he was prepared to be held in detention by a senator; Cicero however, after other confirmations – and an assassination attempt against him – assembled the Senate once again on 8 November in the Temple of Jupiter Stator (the divinity that had protected the Romans against the Sabines of Titus Tatius), where he pronounced the *First Catilinarian Oration*, with its famous opening words: 'When, O Catiline, do you mean to cease abusing our patience?'[8] The accused escaped, heaping scorn on the 'new man' and claiming he was going to seek exile in Massilia (present-day Marseille). In fact, he went to join the rebels in Etruria.

In the *Second Catilinarian Oration*, delivered on 9 November before the people, Cicero portrayed the fugitive as a wild beast that could feel the city it was about to tear apart 'snatched from its jaws',[9] and described his accomplices as individuals made desperate through debts caused by an unsustainable lifestyle. Once his hostile intentions had been exposed – thanks to Catulus – Catiline was declared a public enemy and an army was sent against him under the command of consul Antonius Hybrida (whom Cicero, in turn, kept under secret surveillance through the quaestor Publius Sestius). In the meantime, Murena was acquitted.

Rome, however, was still not safe. The remaining conspirators – including the praetor Publius Cornelius Lentulus Sura – sought to persuade Catiline that slaves had to be enlisted as well, and they even tried to seek the aid of horsemen from the Allobroges (a Celtic population settled between the Rhône and Lake Geneva). It was through this that Cicero managed to discover the names of those involved in the plot. Through contacts, he persuaded the Allobrogian delegation, now in Rome, to pretend to take part. Having seized the signed and sealed documents, he brought the culprits into the Senate assembled in the Temple of Concord (dedicated years before by Lucius Opimius, the consul who had ruthlessly suppressed the insurrection by Gaius Gracchus). It was

3 December. The Allobroges indicated the leaders of the conspiracy, their plans, and unmasked Lentulus Sura, revealing what he had said: 'he, indeed, used to say that according to the Sibylline Books the sovereignty of Rome was destined to be held by three Cornelii: Cinna and Sulla had held it first, now he was the third whose fate it would be to govern the city'.[10] These were oracular utterances that harked back to the time of the last kings but had been pieced together after the fire that destroyed the Temple of Jupiter Optimus Maximus on the Capitolium where they had been kept. The conspirators were arrested and the Senate voted a *supplicatio*, the first of its kind for the action of a magistrate without an army.

It was the consul himself who informed the people, at the end of the session, with his *Third Catilinarian Oration*. He revealed the plan to burn down Rome, enough in itself to distance the city's plebeians, especially its shopkeepers, from the plot. In the opening words of this chapter, the historian Gaius Sallustius Crispus (86–c.34), better known as Sallust, confirms how public opinion changed.[11] Attempts to implicate Caesar were dismissed by the consul himself; there were also allegations against Crassus, but on 4 December the Senate declared them groundless. Years later, however, Cicero would no longer keep silent about the responsibility of the two.

The event that was to have the most serious consequences took place on 5 December. Fearing that the conspirators under arrest might be forcibly liberated, the consul recalled the Senate. Probably once again in the Temple of Concord, this time surrounded by armed knights, the most famous senatorial debate in the whole history of Rome took place. Reported by sources that often vary, it decreed that the prisoners should be put to death. The text of the *senatus consultum* was drawn up by Cicero, who seems to have had the whole session recorded by stenographers: he wanted it to be seen that the decision was the result of a common will. The consuls designated for the next year and the ex-consuls all proposed the death penalty. There was a dramatic turn of events when Caesar, *pontifex maximus* and praetor designate, stood up to speak. Appealing to the law of Gaius Gracchus on *provocatio*, he

46

argued it was more appropriate that they be sentenced to the confiscation of their property, to imprisonment in the most well-guarded strongholds of *terra Italia*, and to oblivion. Many agreed. The Optimates, led by Catulus, surrounded the seat of Cicero, who pronounced his *Fourth Catilinarian Oration*. He put forward ideas of undoubted force, which inevitably cast light on the events of that fateful year 49:

> they have tried to murder us, our wives, our children; they have tried to destroy the houses of each one of us, and all of this shared dwelling place that is the *res publica*; they have endeavoured to install a firm power of the Allobrogian people on the ruins of this city and on the ashes of the destroyed empire. [. . .] Threatened by the torches and arrows of vile conspiracy, our shared homeland – in supplication – stretches out its hands: to you it entrusts itself, to you the life of all its citizens, to you the citadel of the Capitolium, to you the altars of the household gods, the fortunes of all men, your homes, your hearths.[12]

The ex-praetor Tiberius Claudius Nero proposed to postpone the decision until the end of the revolt, and the author of the death proposal withdrew it. When leave to speak was given to Cato, who was just over thirty and about to become plebeian tribune, there was another dramatic turn. He argued that citizens who had taken part in the plot, calling for the support of the Gallic enemy, should be punished with death. Once he had ended his speech, all the consuls and most of the other senators agreed, attacking Caesar. When Caesar left the building – or, according to another version, was still inside – the knights on guard pointed daggers at his chest. Some days after, Cato proposed a more generous *lex frumentaria*, which abolished any limit to the number of those who had a right to grain at subsidized price. It was a move designed to dent the popularity of the *pontifex maximus*, strengthened by the position he had taken on 5 December: according to one source, when some time after he returned to the Senate to answer accusations relating to the Catiline conspiracy, the crowd surrounded the building in his defence. What is certain is that the fate of the prisoners was sealed that same night: they were strangled in the Mamertine prison, under the eyes of the consul. According to some sources, the people rejoiced when they heard news of the execution and Cicero was called 'Father of the Fatherland'. Soon after, Catiline and his army, after heroic resistance, were wiped out at Pistoria (present-day Pistoia) by the army of the consul Antonius Hybrida under the provisional command of his legate Marcus Petreius (ex-praetor).

The killing of prisoners, without trial or *provocatio*, after the sentence of 5 December (though backed by the *senatus consultum ultimum* of 21 or 22 October) caused much controversy. The tribune Quintus Cecilius Metellus Nepos, brother-in-law and former lieutenant of Pompey, stopped Cicero, at the end of his period of office, from giving an account of his actions. A later *senatus consultum* managed, however, to assure 'the impunity of all those who had taken part in that event'.[13] At the beginning of January 62, when the fate of Catiline's army was still in doubt, Metellus Nepos proposed that Pompey and his army be recalled. To many, the man who had defeated pirates and Mithridates seemed most able to resolve the situation. The Senate rejected the proposal, which the tribune took before the people, in the presence of Caesar. The two were standing at the entrance to the Temple of Castor, surrounded by armed gladiators and slaves. Cato refused to let the proposal be read out, and ended up injured: indeed a fight ensued, with stones, clubs and swords. Another *senatus consultum ultimum* followed; Metellus Nepos fled the city to join Pompey, while Caesar succeeded to remain unharmed.

Cicero was in a difficult diplomatic position: his letters were insufficient to comfort Pompey for the opportunity he had lost. Anxious not to worsen the situation, he then opposed the forfeiture of the magistracies of Metellus Nepos and Caesar, voted by the Senate. When Caesar handed in his resignation, the populace surrounded his house to support him (according to one version it was then that Cato proposed the grain law). Informants were still providing information. Regarding Caesar and his involvement in catilinarian events, there must have been at least two depositions, of which one – by a certain Lucius Vettius – was fiercely contested by the crowd; both were rejected by Cicero who would later allow documents to emerge that in a certain sense corroborated them.

Towards the middle of 62, still convinced of the popularity of his own action, Cicero recalled in his *In Defence of Publius Cornelius Sulla* how he had succeeded in 'freeing Rome from conflagration, its citizens from massacre, Italy from devastation', without a *tumultus* (the declaration of a state of emergency), without conscription, without arms, without troops; executing only five guilty men, 'I saved the life of all citizens, the peace of the entire world and, lastly, this city of ours, which is the dwelling place of all of us, the citadel of kings and of foreign nations, the light of all people, the abode of our empire'.[14]

THE *PONTIFEX* AND A RELIGIOUS SCANDAL

In that fateful year 49, Caesar, pontifex maximus, would repeatedly condemn the unlawful activities of his enemies. His first experiences in that sensitive appointment had not been easy: in 62 he had come under heavy attack from another patrician.

At the end of the same year, Rome was rocked by a religious scandal. Its main figure was Publius Claudius Pulcher, scion of the extremely powerful *gens Claudia*. In 68, little more than 20 years old, he had come into the limelight, leading the mutiny of Lucullus' troops at Nisibis, without legal consequences.

On the night between 4 and 5 December 62, the annual celebrations of the *Damia* were held to honour the *Bona Dea*. Worship of the Good Goddess was one of the many patrician cults in which religion and politics were closely bound. During the ritual, from which men were excluded – even to the extent of 'covering pictures of male animals'[15] – matrons and vestals offered sacrifices in the name of the Roman people, following secret ancient practices.

That year, the ceremony was performed at the house of Caesar, praetor and *pontifex maximus*. Claudius sneaked in, dressed as a woman, but his voice gave him away and the ceremony was stopped. What were his motives? To offend the owner of the house? Because he felt his *gens* was entitled to some role in the celebration? Because he was a lover of Caesar's wife? Out of pure folly? Or was it simply intended as a harmless gesture? One critic has even ventured to implicate, perhaps seeing rightly, 'the prurient fantasies of the Roman male, who tended to imagine that all women were promiscuous by nature'.[16] In any event, 'that same night, on their return home, the women told their husbands what had happened and next day word spread among the people: Claudius had committed a sacrilege and owed satisfaction not only to those whom he had insulted, but also to the city and to the gods'.[17]

On 1 January 61 the Senate gave power to the pontifices and vestals to investigate. They declared that what had occurred was sacrilege; so, the Senate recommended that an extraordinary tribunal be convened. But the tribal assemblies voted down the law that would have established the tribunal. Chaos broke out. Claudius' supporters, to be more certain of the outcome, occupied the *pontes*, the narrow passageways through which voting was carried out, and managed to annul many voting slips. The Senate at that point, refusing to deal with other matters, arranged for another law to be submitted to the *concilium plebis*. This required that the jury be set up along the same lines as the *quaestiones perpetuae* (the permanent tribunals). The penalty on conviction was death, which, according to long tradition, could be commuted to voluntary exile. Approval was granted between the end of March and early April despite further heated *contiones* by Claudius, who stressed the parallels between his own case and the events of 5 December 63.

The trial began in mid-April. In addition to the evidence about profanation of the rites and – as is not hard to imagine – the adulterous relationship, other allegations were made against Claudius. Lucullus gave evidence about the incestuous relationship between Claudius and his younger sister, Lucullus' ex-wife. There was also evidence from the women present at the night sacrifice: these included Caesar's mother and sister but not his wife, who was regarded more as an accomplice than a witness. The major absence was Caesar himself. Even though his triple role of *pontifex maximus*, praetor and injured party required him to take a stance, he had chosen to limit himself to disowning his wife; when asked why, he seems to have replied: 'I really thought my wife shouldn't even be under suspicion'.[18]

The defence sought to refute the allegations on the strength of a false alibi. Claudius, at the time of the night ceremony, was said to have been at Interamna Lirenas (near the present-day Pignataro Interamna), some 80 miles from Rome, guest of the knight – and witness – Gaius Causinius Schola. At that point Cicero – whom Claudius had supported in the recent episode involving Catiline – gave evidence, instead, that the defendant, three hours before the night sacrifice, had been to visit him. The defence lawyers began shouting, the judges surrounded him as protection. The Clodians besieged the court, which summoned an armed guard from the Senate. Once conviction was certain, the praetor suspended proceedings for two days, giving the defence time to corrupt the jurors, probably thanks to money from Crassus (between 9 and 12 million sesterces) and, it seems, the promise of 'nights with ladies and young boys of the aristocracy'.[19] Their vote, by secret ballot, acquitted the defendant. Cato proposed that the judges be placed under investigation, the Senate agreed, but the knights, having sided with Claudius, brought a halt to the proceedings. The response – a drastic one – was to stop the renegotiation of contracts for tax collection in Asia: the *publicani* there could no longer honour their financial commitments (that, with support from Crassus and later also from Cicero, they were pressing to be amended).

The elections that followed were characterized by wholesale corruption, triggered by the return of Pompey. Cato supported two senatorial decrees in this respect. Beside him was his powerful son-in-law Lucius

Domitius Ahenobarbus, perhaps the brother of the commander put to death by Pompey in Africa, who would play a key role in that fateful year 49. The decrees were aimed at *divisores*, the distributors of bribes. Candidates could no longer shelter them in their homes, which were now also liable to be searched. It seems, however, that this went no further than the law on *ambitus* that Cicero had had approved as consul in 63.

The general attention, however, was soon to be concentrated elsewhere.

3

THE ARRIVAL OF THE 'FIRST TRIUMVIRATE'

These three, who had the greatest power over all, exchanged mutual favours. A writer, Varro, in a book entitled *Trikáranos* [three-headed monster], exposed this agreement of theirs.

Appian, *Civil Wars*, 2,33

A MEMORABLE TRIUMPH AND THE FIRST STIRRINGS OF A THREE-HEADED MONSTER

In that fateful year 49, the pact that had bound Caesar and Pompey for a decade would finally break. The origins of this rift have to be sought in the spectacular but politically fraught return to Rome of the man who was the most powerful of his age.

Pompey, on his march towards Rome, was accompanied by a jubilant crowd. In September 61 he gave a public speech about his military campaigns and celebrated his third and greatest triumph for his victory over piracy and over King Mithridates. Cato alone – who had earlier supported a plebiscite that narrowed the criteria for awarding so great an honour – would say that this had been 'a war against little ladies'.[1]

Pompey had reached the peak of glory and had heaped Rome with riches. Appian's *Mithridatic Wars* devotes ample space to the account of his extraordinary triumph, celebrated on 28 and 29 September to coincide with his forty-fifth birthday.[2] Seven hundred ships were brought into port. The procession included two-horse chariots, litters filled with gold and others with sundry furnishings, the couch of Darius 'the Great', the throne of Mithridates himself, as well as his sceptre and an image eight cubits high[3] of solid gold and 75.1 million silver coins. They were followed by countless wagons heaped with weapons, ship rams, a multitude of prisoners and pirates, none of them in chains but all dressed in their traditional costumes. Then came the officials, sons and commanders of the kings, either as prisoners or hostages, 324 in all. Behind them were pictures of those absent: of Tigranes II of Armenia and his father-in-law Mithridates in fighting action, at the moment of defeat, and as they fled. There were also depictions of the siege, the night-time escape and death of Mithridates, with the virgins who had chosen to follow his fate, then the sons and daughters killed before him, as well as barbarian gods. A tablet bore the inscription:

800 SHIPS WITH BRONZE RAMS CAPTURED; 8 CITIES FOUNDED IN CAPPADOCIA, 20 IN CILICIA AND COELE SYRIA, IN PALESTINE PRESENT-DAY SELEUCIS WAS FOUNDED. KINGS DEFEATED: TIGRANES OF ARMENIA, ARTOCES OF IBERIA, OROIZES OF ALBANIA, DARIUS OF MEDIA, ARETAS OF THE NABATAEANS, ANTIOCHUS OF COMMAGENE.

Pompey followed on a chariot studded with gems, wearing what was said to have been the cloak of Alexander the Great found among the belongings of Mithridates. Then came Roman officers on horseback or on foot. When they arrived at the Capitolium, Pompey didn't have the prisoners killed but sent them back to their countries at the expense of the *res publica*, except for the two kings, one of whom was soon put to death, the other sometime later.

The Senate, nonetheless, impeded the victorious general, refusing to ratify the arrangement he had given to the eastern provinces and ignoring his demands for land for veterans. Behind these manoeuvres was his rival Crassus, who in turn was supporting the insistent and unheeded demand of the *publicani* of Asia. The Optimates, led by Cato – with whom Pompey had vainly sought a matrimonial alliance – and Lucullus, used obstructionist tactics that were hard to oppose. So Pompey appealed to the people. At the beginning of 60, the tribune Lucius Flavius proposed a distribution of lands for veterans. He went as far as imprisoning the consul Quintus Caecilius Metellus Celer, who was against it. But Celer called a meeting of the Senate in prison, until Pompey cautioned Flavius. Metellus Celer had won.

The solution came from Hispania Ulterior. Caesar had received the still unpacified province by lot. He had settled there the previous year, harried by the scandal of the *Bona Dea* and freed from many creditors thanks to guarantees offered by Crassus (almost 20 million sesterces). Proceeding with much energy and little pity, he had amassed victories and wealth. His soldiers, having also filled their pockets, had hailed him *imperator* and the Senate had awarded him a triumph.

Without waiting for a successor, in the spring of 60, he returned to Rome to stand, in July, for the consulship. The triumph, however, meant that he and his army had to remain outside the city. So he asked permission to stand as candidate *in absentia*. Cato at first said no, then played for time, speaking non-stop in the Senate until sunset. 'His voice was sufficiently loud to reach every listener, with an unshakeable and indefatigable strength and tone; he often spoke for a whole day without ever tiring'.[4] The Senate, already suspecting that Caesar would win the election, arranged that 'future consuls be entrusted with provinces that had lesser responsibilities: forests and pasturelands'.[5] Cato's son-in-law Bibulus also stood as candidate, with the help of much money. Caesar forewent the triumph and stood with him, supported by Pompey and Crassus; he obtained the majority: according to one version he won all the *centuriae*.

Pompey, who hadn't stood as candidate for reasons we don't know, needed Caesar. The pact soon reached between the two and Crassus (traditionally called the 'first triumvirate'), which was private, secret and only leaked out early the following year, could have been Caesar's idea, formed after the election and due to the hostility of the Senate. Caesar may also have wanted to involve Cicero, who refused. In April of the following year, Pompey would also marry Julia, Caesar's young and only daughter.

A 'POPULAR' CONSULSHIP

In the fateful year 49, Caesar, by crossing the Rubicon, would give a very undiplomatic response to those who obstructed his candidacy as consul for the second time. The results of his first consulship held in 59, had been welcomed by the people but obtained by infringing the rules.

Caesar, as consul, sought a broad consensus. He curried favour with knights, supporters of Crassus, veterans of Pompey, and with the people. For the knights, he proposed a law on the remission of a third of the sums due from the *publicani* of Asia. For all the others he arranged distributions of land, so that Plutarch was prompted to write that he behaved 'not as a consul but as a particularly audacious tribune of the plebs'.[6]

If the law on *publicani* passed unhindered, the approval of the two agrarian proposals was fraught with difficulties: every form of obstruction was used. The first proposal – which allocated public lands in *terra Italia* (excluding those in Campania), as well as lands available for purchase with Pompey's spoils of war, to Pompey's veterans and (perhaps) to the city populace – would be voted on before the end of January. In the Senate, Cato opposed it. Declaring that he wanted no innovations, he impeded the sessions with long-drawn-out speeches. Caesar threatened to imprison him, but when other senators followed the prisoner, he freed him: 'while he walked, he continued to speak'.[7] The consul then brought the question before the people, in a series of *contiones*. His colleague Bibulus, when asked, gave the same answer as Cato, snubbing public opinion. Caesar then led two eminent ex-consuls – Pompey and Crassus – into a *contio*. Pompey stated that arrangements should have been made for his veterans back in 70 and now there was all the more reason since, thanks to him, there was even more money. He concluded: 'if anyone dares to raise their sword, I will take up my shield'.[8]

Bibulus and three tribunes managed at first to stop the law from being passed, and Caesar had to fix another date. The night before the vote, his followers – among whom we can imagine many of Pompey's veterans – were already occupying the Forum. Some were armed. Bibulus, with his followers and two or three tribunes, then arrived at the tribune in front of the Temple of Castor from which Caesar had begun addressing the crowd early that morning. 'As soon as he was before the temple and tried to speak, he was dragged down the steps, his *fasces* [symbol of the coercive power of the magistrate] were broken, and blows and injuries were rained down on the tribunes and other followers'.[9] The attack was led by the tribune Publius Vatinius. According to one version, Bibulus received a 'basket of dung' on his head.[10] The law was passed, and Bibulus couldn't persuade the Senate to annul it. From that moment on, until the end of his mandate, he remained closed up in his house, devoting himself to studying celestial signs and holding meetings. The move was unprecedented, peaceful but also ineffective, causing some to say that the consuls that year were 'Julius and Caesar'.[11] Bibulus' edicts, displayed on the street corners, became notorious. Caesar required senators to swear to respect the agrarian law. Even those more hostile, like Cato, were convinced that this was now inevitable. At the end of April, the commission appointed to carry it out, headed by Pompey and Crassus, had already been elected.

Pompey's measures in the east were confirmed. The new provinces of Bithynia-Pontus, Cilicia and Syria raised Rome's tax revenues from 200 million to 340 million sesterces a year. A new agrarian law – on the public lands of Campania – was proposed and voted through in May, despite the opposition of Cato, who was dragged towards prison by one of the tribunes but set free by Caesar. The new project aimed at the city populace granted fertile lands in Campania to 20,000 men with families, giving precedence to those who had at least three children. Pompey consequently had the task of founding a *colonia* of Roman citizens at Capua – another factor that would have some relevance in that fateful year 49. But the commission ran into difficulties, both practical and economic (much land had to be repurchased), along with attempts to hinder it. A final settlement would not be reached until 46.

The following year, according to the rules, Caesar would have to be content with control over woods and fields in *terra Italia*. It was in fact standard practice to assign the provinces each year between March and July. The old military year began in March, which took its name from the god of war (that is, before the legendary king Numa Pompilius had introduced January and February, increasing the number of months from ten to twelve). In July, since at least the time of Sulla, the people elected consuls and praetors, whose yearly mandate in the city would run from the following 1 January. Even before the election was held, the Senate indicated the provinces that they would be able to govern, usually for another year, in their roles as proconsuls and propraetors, starting from January of the year after the next. The decision – which tribunes could not veto – was therefore made over seventeen months before the respective office, and was made before the election itself. This was to avoid allocations *ad personam*, which could have boosted the already widespread practice of corruption. To confirm the impartiality of the procedure, there was then a drawing of lots to determine the actual offices between those who had just won the elections.

For Caesar, however, the governorship of the provinces for the following year was granted by the plebeian assembly at the request of the tribune Vatinius, a procedure that also applied to Pompey but was highly irregular. For five years, up to 1 March 54, he would rule Cisalpine Gaul and Illyricum (which was under threat from Dacian tribes). He would have three legions and the right to appoint legates. On his side there was also his father-in-law, Lucius Calpurnius Piso Caesoninus, soon to stand as consul for the following year; Cato could therefore say that 'power was prostituted through marriage'.[12] At Pompey's suggestion, after the death of the governor designate Metellus Celer (poisoned perhaps by his wife Clodia, sister of Publius Claudius Pulcher), the Senate granted Caesar the apparently quiet province of Narbonese Gaul and a fourth legion.

To complete the picture, during this complex period there were not infrequent displays of public unrest. At the gladiatorial games announced by Gabinius, candidate for next year's consulship, the organizer was greeted by catcalls. In the theatre, during the *ludi Apollinares*, the celebrations for Apollo held in July, dissatisfaction about the three masters of Rome came into the open.

> the actor Diphilus made an insolent attack on Pompey exclaiming: 'For our poverty you are Great'; and he was obliged to repeat it countless times; amid a storm of applause from the whole theatre, then: 'A time will come when you will bitterly regret that power of yours', and so on. [. . .] Caesar's arrival was marked only by tepid applause; but the arrival of Curio the younger, who followed him, brought an enthusiastic welcome [. . .][13]

Caesar and his colleagues were furious. On that occasion they even threatened to abolish the *frumentationes*. And so, for the first time, we meet Gaius Scribonius Curio, who was then a very young Optimas. Nine years later, then on Caesar's side, he would play his own part in the precipitation of events towards war.

The year 59 marked another turning point. Just as Pompey was about to break his pact with his colleagues, Vettius – one of Cicero's informers back in 63 – declared in the Senate that he was involved in a conspiracy of senators, organized by Curio the younger, to kill Pompey. From then on, the 'triumvir' must have felt himself in danger of attack. This, in our view, must have heavily conditioned his choices and strategies.

But it is difficult now to understand to what extent the danger was real. The next day, when Vettius was taken by Caesar and Vatinius before a *contio*, he changed his version, adding the name of many Optimates, including that of Cicero. The crowd grew angry and surrounded Caesar to protect him. No judicial investigation took place: the witness was found strangled in prison and there were no consequences for any of those accused. The whole matter, ably manipulated by Caesar, reinforced the 'triumvirate'.

AN INCONVENIENT ALLY, THE ROMAN MOB, AN EXILE AND GRAIN

That fateful year 49 witnessed the ultimate consequences of an old rift, dramatically accelerated three years earlier by the death of Clodius. The events of 58–57 – when Clodius' political ascent was matched by an equally rapid fall – clearly demonstrate the enormous power of the Roman mob, the harshness of exile and how strategically important it was to control the city's food supplies.

In 59, to assure continuity, the elections for the following year's consuls were held without irregularities, though not until October. The two men elected – Piso, Caesar's father-in-law, and Gabinius, a Pompey supporter who had been tribune in 67 – were men of undoubted loyalty. Two praetors, Gaius Memmius and Ahenobarbus, opened an investigation into the legislative activity of the previous year. In spring 58, after a series of inconclusive debates in the Senate, Caesar was free to depart for his provinces.

The absolute – though equally unexpected – protagonist that year was Clodius, that same Publius Claudius Pulcher who in 62 had violated the ceremonies of the *Bona Dea*. He had renounced his family status and changed his *nomen* Claudius to the plebeian Clodius; he had then been made tribune, swearing revenge against Cicero, who had destroyed his alibi; and this – no less surprisingly – all thanks to Caesar. Cicero, in March or April 59, during his speech in defence of Antonius Hybrida, his ex-colleague as consul, had included various observations that were of no assistance to the defendant but managed to irritate the consul for that year. The reaction came just three hours later. Caesar had 'unexpectedly, with a *lex curiata*, given the go-ahead for that foul and abominable brute to pass to the plebeian order'; he had done so either because he was 'won over, as I believe, by his persistency or, as some think, out of bitterness towards me', but certainly 'without knowing nor foreseeing what infamies and what disasters would be heaped upon us': only 'Fortune, not personal strength, had allowed that tribune to turn the *res publica* upside down; and what strength, in truth, could exist in such a life, in a being depraved by obscenities with his brother, by incest with his sister, by every abnormal indecency?'[14]

Caesar had seemed more realistic; after Clodius' plebeian adoption and his election as tribune, he was prompted to offer Cicero a way out. This was the offer of a post that would guarantee him legal immunity in Rome – and, more precisely, a position on the agrarian commission or, alternatively, a legation in Gaul. Cicero refused both, misled by assurances from Pompey and by an excessive trust in his own 'allies'.

Once in office, Clodius felt immediately sure of support from the people, from the knights and (unlike Caesar) also from a section of the Senate. This was made possible thanks to the skilful use of various factors but, in particular, of four proposed laws, presented – unconventionally and perhaps unlawfully – all together, at the beginning of the year.

For the first time in the history of Rome, a plebiscite established the free distribution of public grain, giving the tribune control over the lists of those entitled, from which Cato had already removed any restriction in number. He had also made the freedman Sextus Cloelius superintendant of supplies and distribution. This onerous measure, according to Cicero, took up one-fifth of tax revenue (around 64 million sesterces for approximately 18 million *modii* of grain per year). The proposal, which was clearly demagogic, may also have upset Caesar's agrarian plan, to the delight of *publicani* and the landowning classes: those who had no property found a further reason for remaining in the city, which was becoming an increasingly attractive destination for migrant Roman citizens, and where slaves were being given their freedom.

A second plebiscite legalized corporations that had been abolished in 64, encouraging the creation of new ones; the tribune, according to Cicero, found these to be a useful instrument. Armed gangs, recruited at the Aurelian tribunal and the Temple of Castor, took control over the city's political life; their members included Populares, *liberti*, perhaps even slaves, and, according once again to Cicero, ex-followers of Catiline.

A third plebiscite limited the censor's power of expulsion from the Senate, a prospect welcomed by many ex-magistrates. A fourth limited the right to stop popular assemblies with the *obnuntiatio* or the veto, probably obliging the magistrate to give notification in person and at the beginning of proceedings, and increasing the number of days on which assemblies could be held. From that moment, in order to boost popular participation, Clodius had also ordered the closure of the *tabernae*, workshops and businesses (many of which were in the centre and in the Forum itself).

The tribune, with a further plebiscite, then reduced the wealthy island of Cyprus to the status of province and ordered the requisition of assets belonging to its ruler Ptolemy (brother of Ptolemy XII of Egypt, and accused of colluding with pirates): the proceeds would go to finance the grain law. He offered the task of carrying it out to Cato, either to distance a troublesome enemy from Rome or pursuant to some covert deal (the tribune of 62 also had an interest in matters relating to grain).

A further plebiscite – which had the support of the 'triumvirate' – concerned the killing of an unconvicted citizen: a clear reference to the patent violation, on 5 December 63, of the law of Gaius Gracchus on *provocatio*. Clodius went as far as to threaten the intervention of Caesar's army, still camped at the gates of Rome. The proconsul, questioned by him in a *contio*, said he regarded the execution of imprisoned followers of Catiline as an illegal act. The crowd that flocked to support Cicero was violently expelled from the Capitolium, and the public demonstrations of the knights proved worthless.

The clear impression is that the *nobilitas* had avoided the general accusation, sacrificing Cicero. He was advised by eminent figures to escape from Rome and from *terra Italia*, and this is what he did. A further plebiscite of Clodius, ratifying Cicero's status of exile, also accused him of having falsified the *senatus consultum* of 5 December: this, of course, relieved the entire assembly of its own objective responsibility. It was irrelevant, at that point, whether the provision was passed, as Cicero said, only thanks to the night occupation of the Forum.

The exile was also deprived of his properties. Possessions, slaves and lands were sold for the benefit of the people, under the direction of Clodius himself. His houses in Rome, Tusculum and Formiae (present-day Formia) were demolished (a gesture of powerful symbolic value from which, in 87, not even Sulla had been spared). The forfeiture of his residence on the Palatine Hill was accompanied by the expansion of Clodius' adjoining property. In it the tribune also built a small temple to *Libertas*, not before declaring the area to be 'sacred land', thereby preventing any future construction. As for Cicero, before his departure he had gone to the Capitolium with a statue of Minerva that he kept in his house, dedicated 'To MINERVA PATRONESS OF ROME'.[15] Over the following months he wrote a series of letters to Atticus and to his own family that give some idea of what it meant for a Roman politician to be forced to leave the city.[16] On 17 August 58, from Thessalonica, he confided to his friend: 'I grieve for having lost not only my belongings and my relatives but even myself. Indeed, what am I now?'[17]

Relations between Pompey and Clodius soon deteriorated: the tribune proposed measures on foreign policy that went contrary to directives that had guided the reorganization of the eastern provinces. During the height of the summer there was yet another major turn of events. A slave, caught in the Temple of Castor with a dagger under his tunic, declared that he had been hired by Clodius to kill his enemy: yet another attempt against Pompey. Pompey, instead of striking back, left the city – a move that many found surprising. He managed, however, to secure the return of Cicero. This happened after much wavering and public shows of violence from Clodius over a period that lasted more than a year (1 July 58–4 August 57). When, in January 57, eight tribunes proposed a plebiscite to recall Cicero from exile, a bloody conflict ensued, the likes of which had not been seen for years, evidenced by 'the Tiber filled with the corpses of citizens, the sewers choking, blood wiped up from the Forum with sponges', so that everyone was convinced that 'such a multitude and such great apparatus of war was not the work of private individuals and plebeians, but of patricians and praetors'.[18] The sequence of events is particularly disturbing. The eight tribunes occupied the *rostra* before dawn; Clodius and his men, mostly slaves, had already taken up their positions in the Forum during the night; Appius Claudius Pulcher, then praetor, also brought gladiators he had purchased for the games to assist his younger brother. Optimas Tullius Cicero, brother of Marcus, managed to save himself by hiding under corpses.

The violence and demonstrations continued, which is why Pompey had to resort to using gladiators recruited by the Optimas Titus Annius Milo, then tribune of the plebs. A Senate vote of 416 against one (Clodius alone) finally required the consul Publius Cornelius Lentulus Spinther to take control of the situation; the Centuriate Assembly endorsed the order on 4 August, with the assistance of a crowd that had rushed from every part of *terra Italia*, assembled also through special Senate decrees. Pompey himself, in his role as supreme magistrate of the *colonia* of Capua, had ordered the issue of decrees from that district, as he had from various other *municipia*.

Added to the political conflict was economic uncertainty. The year 57 saw worrying fluctuations in the price of wheat. The shortage had probably begun the previous year, at the time that Cicero had gone into exile. The fluctuations seem to follow the political events: a sudden drop on the day of the centuriate vote for Cicero's return from exile, then a tendency to rise and a crisis of major proportions with his triumphal arrival in Rome (on 4 September, at the start of the *ludi Romani*). On 7

September, when the Senate was debating how to deal with the shortage, a crowd hurried to the Capitolium, shouting that it was Cicero who was responsible; the consul Metellus Nepos (the tribune of 62 who, though once hostile to Cicero, had now changed his position) appeared in public to calm the situation but was greeted with stones. There were now open threats to kill the senators and burn them alive in the temple; the intervention of the Optimates and of Pompey's forces came just in time. Pompey was eventually given power, by a consular law supported by Cicero, to manage the supply and probably the distribution of grain, with a proconsular *imperium infinitum* lasting five years, and the right to appoint fifteen legates. He was also helped by Cicero and Cicero's brother Quintus, who that winter would be occupied in Sardinia.

There can be no doubt that Cicero was linked to the matter. He had been quaestor in 75, during another period of famine at Lilybaeum (present-day Marsala) in Sicily, winning favour both in Rome and on the island. So much so that the people of Sicily chose him to represent them in 70 against the corrupt governor Gaius Verres; in 69, while he held the office of aedile, he must have used 'whatever he received from the generosity of those people to lower the market prices'.[19]

After the proposal to put Pompey in charge, there was a return to plenty. Cicero claimed that the grain provinces were no longer sending supplies, due either to a shortage (poor crops) or because they were directing it elsewhere and 'were waiting for the shortage to occur so that they could take the credit for having helped Rome';[20] the main cause, he argued, was Clodius' grain law.[21] There was also some suspicion, on the other hand, about Pompey's conduct. Thanks to his relations with the governors (in particular with Gaius Vergilius, propraetor in Sicily in 58), he could influence the market.

In November and December 57, while Clodius was creating turmoil and unrest in Rome, attacking Cicero himself, as well as his residence and that of Milo, Pompey was involved in his new role. He visited Sicily, Sardinia and Africa, achieving, according to Plutarch, enormous success.

It was then, according once again to Plutarch,[22] that he had persuaded several timid boatmen with a phrase that was after translated in latin as *navigare necesse est, vivere non est necesse* (it is necessary to sail, it is not necessary to live); the first part of it was to be made famous by, among others, the Hanseatic League and Gabriele D'Annunzio, as well as being used as the title of a newspaper article by Benito Mussolini, written after a searing electoral defeat.[23]

Pompey knew just how necessary his work was for Rome, yet he preferred to keep his distance.

4

CAESAR, GAUL AND ROME

The Alps had once formed a natural barrier for Italy, and this was
not without some special divine will; for if that access had been
open to the barbarians and to the Gallic hordes, never would our
city have managed to become the centre or the seat of such a great
empire. Now they may come down if they wish: on this side of
those tall mountains and as far as the Ocean there is no longer
anything that Italy need fear. Still one or two more summers,
through fear or hope, punishment or rewards, weapons or laws, can
bind the whole of Gaul to us with everlasting bonds.

Cicero, *On the Consular Provinces*, 34

THE OBSCURE BEGINNINGS OF A GREAT CAMPAIGN

*In that fateful year 49, Caesar's recent conquest of Gaul would create a
strong apprehension. The whole uncertain, complex and, perhaps at first,
casual enterprise had immediately gripped the attention of Rome.*

While Clodius was causing unrest in Rome, the expedition to Gaul, by
dint of gamble and tactics of aggression, was producing its first results.
The conquest of that vast territory – which included not only present-day
France but also Belgium and the area of Germany and Switzerland west
of the Rhine – would bring an end to the nightmare of invasion from

Map 5 Caesar's conquest of Gallic territories, 58–50

the north, which had begun when Brennus sacked Rome and was dramatically revived at the end of the second century, when Marius, several times consul, had managed to halt the Teutonic hordes in Narbonese Gaul and the Cimbri in Cisalpine Gaul. It conjured a fear that was also used later – for propaganda purposes – against the Catilinarians, who were looking for the support of the Allobroges.

As happens even in major feats, it is not clear whether it all began by chance or by premeditated plan. In the first seven books of his *Commentaries on the Gallic War*, hurriedly written at the end of each military season (or between the end of 52 and the following year) and sent to the people of Rome, Caesar claims that the former was the case. What emerges from his writings is that he knew little at first about the country and its political circumstances. The fact remains that the complex system of alliances may have triggered a mechanism which then, under skilful management, became unstoppable.

In 121, west of the Alps, Rome had created an administrative district, Transalpine Gaul, or Gallia Ulterior, also known, after the foundation of the *colonia* of Narbo Martius (present-day Narbonne), as Narbonese Gaul. This last term generally identifies the 'Romanized' coastal area and, already by the time of Gaius Plinius Secundus, best known as Pliny the Elder (AD 23–79), it was considered 'more properly Italy than province'.[1] Transalpine Gaul, or Gallia Ulterior, can also indicate the larger area to the north, the area conquered by Caesar. Wedged into Narbonese Gaul was the territory of Massilia (the area that includes present-day Marseille), Rome's ancient ally. To the north Rome had established friendly relations with individual populations, above all the Aedui, inhabitants of the region between the river Loire and the Saône. But their position had been disputed by their eastern neighbours, the Sequani, who had looked for support beyond the Rhine among the Germanic tribes. A Suevian warrior prince, Ariovistus, having assembled a great army, had thus managed to settle in what is now Alsace. He had also defeated the Aedui, in 61. The Senate, uncertain what to do, had instructed the governor of Narbonese

Gaul to protect the Aedui. But then, in 59, with a signal that was ambiguous, and soon misinterpreted, the Senate referred to Ariovistus as 'socius et amicus' (ally and friend), one of the most significant declarations of support that Rome could make.

Caesar took to arms, for the first time, to hold back a westward migration of Helvetii from the area to the east of Genava (present-day Geneva, the last city of the Allobroges), a movement already viewed as imminent in 60 but which then came to nothing. Caesar blocked their passage through Narbonese Gaul, pushing them back also thanks to the construction of a line of fortifications. They were however allowed by Sequani to pass through their lands, heading into the region north of the Garonne estuary. Caesar then returned to Cisalpine Gaul, where he summoned three legions and recruited another two, which added to the one already in Transalpine Gaul. The Aedui and the Allobroges, under invasion from the Helvetii, called for his aid, and he defeated and massacred the enemy at Bibracte, the Aeduan capital (on present-day Mont Beuvray). Then, in an act hard to justify, Caesar turned against Ariovistus, who was also an enemy of the Aedui. He defeated him on what is now the plain of Ochsenfeld and drove him back beyond the Rhine. The following year saw his victorious expedition against the Belgians, for which, once again in Cisalpine Gaul, he recruited another two legions (including Legio XIII, which would cross the Rubicon with him in that fateful year 49). Following the report sent at the end of 57, the Senate decreed a *supplicatio* in his honour, the longest so far granted, of fifteen days. This extraordinary recognition was supported by Cicero and by Pompey himself. Rome also made more money available for his troops.

THE PACT FALTERS BUT DOESN'T COLLAPSE

In that fateful year 49 the bitter fruits of agreements relating to the provinces and finalized at the 'Luca Conference' would be reaped: the conference, born from the need to shore up the wavering pact of 60, led to

decisions again endorsed by the people and not by the Senate and which
were probably not very clear.

The successes achieved by Caesar in the first two years of war were insufficient. The situation was objectively complex. Nor did it all seem
enough from a political point of view: Caesar perhaps wanted even then
to prolong his command to ten years and then to stand again as consul.
Even more serious, in the background, were the tensions between the
'triumvirs' themselves.

In Rome, moreover, 56 began with a thorny question regarding
Ptolemy XII, the Egyptian king known as 'Auletes' (literally, 'the
Flautist'). Having been officially recognized by the 'triumvirs' in 59 after
he had paid them a huge bribe (144 million sesterces), he was overthrown by a revolt which had followed the Roman occupation of Cyprus
and the suicide of the Ptolemy who ruled there. The people of Alexandria
blamed him for the foreign interference and he took refuge in Pompey's
villa in the Alban Hills (outside Rome, near present-day Albano Laziale),
waiting to be restored to his throne. Those who stood to gain from that
lucrative mission became restless, as did the moneylenders, who had
lavished money upon the king and wanted the whole business to end
well. The Sibylline Books had also been consulted. It then emerged that
plans were already under way to hand the enterprise to Pompey; the
Senate were unhappy about too much power being held by the 'triumvir'
. . . even if, it need hardly be said, Egypt would have been highly important to the administrator of the *annona*, the grain supply.

Of disastrous effect, for Pompey, was a violent altercation that broke
out in court, for other motives. It happened during the trial of Milo,
who was being prosecuted by Clodius, then aedile, for the disorders of
the previous year. On 7 February 56, Pompey appeared as a witness for
the defence; the Clodians 'caused a great uproar and throughout his
speech he was constantly covered not by applause, but by insults and
curses'; then Clodius stood up, greeted by protests so noisy that 'all the

curses, all the most obscene expressions rang out against Clodius and Clodia'; and then, in fury, he 'asked his followers: "Who's the one that's starving the people?" And they answered: "Pompey!" – "Who wants to go to Alexandria?" and they: "Pompey!" – "Who do you want to be sent there?" And they: "Crassus!"'; then there was spitting; conclusion: 'the Clodians fled, Clodius thrown down from the *tribune*'.[2] The Senate put the blame on Milo's supporters and, to some extent, on Pompey. Decrees of censure were passed: and this was the end of his Egyptian ambitions.

Clodius – who failed to get the defendant convicted but was amply rewarded by the satisfaction of putting a spoke in the wheel of the 'triumvir' – was himself prosecuted. On 10 February, the Senate decreed 'the breaking up of secret societies and of various groups',[3] directed more at the bands of the aedile than at the *sodalicia*, the electoral associations that were still firmly in the hands of the Optimates. The response came without delay: that same day Clodius brought charges against Sestius, another rival tribune of 57, for *ambitus* and *vis* (political violence). During the trial, which proceeded on the basis of the second charge, the orators Cicero, Gaius Licinius Calvus (later a famous poet), Quintus Hortensius Hortalus (consul in 69) and Crassus defended the accused. Pompey was once again a witness for the defence, and Vatinius for the prosecution. Sestius was acquitted on 11 March. Cicero could then set out a true 'manifesto': his hope was that the fortunes of the *res publica* would be placed in the hands of the *boni*, the 'right-thinking people' at the centre of his political project.

Several scandals and even murders followed – commissioned by Ptolemy XII – against ambassadors sent by the people of Alexandria, which ended in criminal proceedings. One of them involved young Caelius, a figure of key importance for our understanding of the events of that fateful year 49. The defence case was entrusted mainly to Crassus. All we now have, however, is Cicero's speech *In Defence of Caelius*, answering the particular charges brought by Clodia, Clodius' vivacious sister, alias the 'Lesbia' celebrated by the poet Gaius Valerius Catullus.

The defendant was acquitted. The Egyptian question came to nothing; Ptolemy XII was restored by Gabinius in 55; he died, still firmly on his throne, in 51, leaving power to his children Ptolemy XIII and Cleopatra VII, who would play a major role, respectively, in the death of Pompey and in Egypt's final fall into the hands of Rome.

Looking once again at that fateful year 49, it is all the more interesting to recall that in mid-February 56 'Pompey's constant concern [. . .] is that of an attempt on his life'; he claimed he had to defend himself 'from a turbulent populace that has been alienated from him, from a hostile *nobilitas*, from a non-impartial Senate, from corrupt youth'; he prepared himself, summoning men from rural areas, while Clodius strengthened his gangs; 'we are much stronger already with Milo's troops; but substantial reinforcements are awaited from Picenum and Gaul'.[4] Men therefore ready to obey, and extraneous to local events: a common tactic in times of repression – and not just in the ancient world.

Clodius, as aedile, made numerous demonstrations of strength. Among these was the irruption of 'an immense, excited mass of slaves collected from all districts' onto the stage during a spectacle organized by him, with the result that 'they accosted every free man they pleased, [. . .] attacking them'.[5] The Clodian scribe Cloelius then had the Temple of the Nymphs (probably in what is now Rome's Largo Argentina) burnt down to destroy documents held there, probably relating to Pompey's *cura annonae* or Clodius' lists of those entitled to receive grain, which Pompey was having revised.

Clodius did not help the relationship between Caesar and Pompey. Pompey's men, supported by Cicero, were involved in a long campaign to boycott the law relating to the *ager Campanus* – the agrarian law relating to the publis lands in Campania. Eventually, on 5 April, there was a delay, due to lack of money: the Senate had recently paid out 40 million sesterces to fund Pompey's *cura annonae*. The assembly 'echoed with shouts almost like a *contio*: the shortage of money and the price of foodstuffs made the problem more difficult'.[6] The two measures for public assistance created conflict not just in objectives but also in terms of cost.

But this wasn't all. There had been several previous attacks on the 'triumvirs' by the consul Gnaeus Cornelius Lentulus Marcellinus. But an even greater threat was lying in wait. Ahenobarbus emerged as candidate for the consulship of 55. He was Cato's brother-in-law (having married his sister Porcia) and was so rich and influential that he could be described as 'consul designate from birth'.[7] He could also boast a kind of 'right' to Gaul – which the Senate could allocate to one of the consuls of 55 – through the achievements of his grandfather Gnaeus Domitius Ahenobarbus, consul in 122, victor over the Allobroges, founder of Narbo Martius and builder of the *via Domitia*, which crossed the province in an east–west direction. Suetonius writes:

> Since Lucius Domitius, candidate for the consulship, openly threatened to do as consul what he had been unable to do as praetor, and to take his army from him, [Caesar], in order to stop his election, having called Crassus and Pompey to Luca, the city of his province, persuaded them to stand a second time for the consulship and he succeeded, thanks to the influence of both, in having his military command extended for five years.[8]

After the debate of 5 April, Crassus went to Ravenna to talk to Caesar; the two (or Caesar alone) then travelled to Luca (present-day Lucca), in Cisalpine Gaul, before Pompey sailed from Pisa to Sardinia for the *cura annonae*. It seems that another 200 senators, accompanied by 120 lictors, had travelled to Luca (or to Ravenna), but the meeting was held in private. Peace was restored. Clodius stopped his attacks on Pompey and Pompey intimated to Cicero that those attacks on Caesar regarding the agrarian law would also cease. Quintus – who had been promised a command in Gaul and whom Pompey had met in Sardinia – helped to persuade his brother. Cicero, in his speech *On the Consular Provinces*, delivered before the Senate a few months earlier, eventually supported the extension of Caesar's command. By July, Caesar had wages for his troops, ten legates, and no successor.

We don't know when Pompey and Crassus decided to stand for the consulship of 55; but their decision came late: they were clearly the only two who could defeat Ahenobarbus. Cato had meanwhile returned from Cyprus. He arrived in Rome along the Tiber, on a royal boat with six rows of oars that preceded the fleet. The banks of the river were lined with cheering crowds, making it look like a triumph. Nor did he greet consuls and praetors until the fleet had been berthed at the dock. When, in the Forum, he displayed the goods confiscated from Ptolemy of Cyprus, the people were amazed 'in front of that great quantity of money'.[9] He clashed with Cicero over Clodius' tribunate, defending his right to guarantee his own actions in Cyprus. Regarding the consular elections, however, he declared that republican freedom was at stake, and was heeded. The consul Lentulus Marcellinus – who would have presided over the elections – was also hostile to the 'triumvirs'; Pompey and Crassus then, owing to the action of one tribune and popular violence unleashed by Clodius against the Senate, managed to have the elections postponed.

On 1 January of the following year, which opened without supreme magistrates, an *interrex* was appointed – a plenipotentiary senator, replaced every five days by one of his colleagues, who had the task of putting the electoral machine in motion. Pompey and Crassus then stepped forward as candidates and won, though not before using force to prevent Ahenobarbus from entering the Forum: 'they sent armed men who slew the slave who was leading with the torch and put the rest to flight. The last to retreat was Cato who, in defending Domitius, was wounded in the right arm'.[10] Fighting continued in the subsequent elections. Pompey would not allow Cato to be elected praetor, even though he had received the majority in the *centuria praerogativa*, and he dissolved the assemblies due to inauspicious signs. This must have increased the popularity of the 'conqueror' of Cyprus as well as public indignation. Vatinius was elected amid scenes of violence. At the elections for the aediles, Pompey's toga was stained with blood, a sight – it is said – that was misinterpreted by his wife Julia, who, seeing the vest carried in the house for changing it, became so alarmed for her husband's life that she immediately miscarried.

The two new consuls were free to divide power between themselves. Once again it wasn't the Senate but a plebiscite, requested by Gaius Trebonius, that allocated prominent commands for the next five years. Crassus had Syria, from where – by invading Parthia – he hoped to equal the military prestige of his colleagues. Pompey obtained four new legions and the two provinces of Spain, where central and northern tribes had rebelled. Being already engaged in the *res frumentaria*, he had permission to administer them through legates. Both he and Crassus were allowed to make decisions on matters of war and peace without accounting to the people and the Senate. The plebiscite didn't pass without disorder; in one *contio* Cato was first pushed away by Trebonius, then arrested, and eventually released due to popular violence. Before the vote, one tribune intending to use his veto was imprisoned in the Curia Hostilia, and the Forum was occupied during the night by Trebonius' men. Opponents, including Cato, declared there was an inauspicious celestial sign; they were then chased off in skirmishes that led to four deaths. A tribune – an inviolable figure – who displayed his wounds to the people was driven away by followers of Pompey and Crassus.

We don't have many details about the exact order of events, but there must have been great turmoil. The people at one point tried to demolish statues of Pompey and were stopped only by Cato's intervention; Crassus himself, during one argument – probably earlier in the Senate – had punched a rival colleague, Lucius Annalius, famous only for this episode, in the face, making him bleed heavily. A subsequent law of the two consuls, also passed with force and against the will of the Senate, gave Caesar – now with command over eight legions – a renewed mandate for five more years, but with time limits that were probably unclear (and have been the subject of much debate among scholars). Cato warned

Pompey that he was shouldering the responsibility of his father-in-law and would soon feel the whole weight. But Pompey wouldn't listen: he was too sure of his own superiority.

Crassus implemented another law on *sodalicia*, electoral associations organized to convince, corrupt or, worse still, to intimidate voters: the practice was condemned and probably placed on a par with *vis*.

Despite all these events, one of the most memorable moments that year for the population of Rome must have been the opening of the Theatre of Pompey, in the Campus Martius. With seating for 10,000, it was the first stone-built theatre – something thought to have been forbidden in Rome – and this, in one interpretation, only thanks to the construction, behind it, of a temple dedicated to Venus, patroness of Rome but also of Pompey. The building, surrounded by porticoes, also housed works of art, whose installation Atticus had helped to supervise. Fourteen statues represented the nations conquered by Pompey; one of Pompey himself was placed in a long hallway adjoining the portico, in which meetings of senators could be held (and where Caesar would be assassinated on 15 March 44). The opening was accompanied by recitals of poetry and music, athletics contests and wild beast hunts. Cicero, one of the spectators, confided to a friend in a letter written perhaps in September:

> [N]o one denies that the hunts – two each day for five days – are magnificent; but what pleasure can a person of good taste find in a human weakling torn apart by an extremely powerful animal or a splendid beast run through by a spear? In any event, if these are entertainments worth seeing, you've seen them often; and we, who have witnessed them, have seen nothing new. The last day was devoted to elephants. Great was the amazement among the rabble, but pleasure, none; indeed, there was a certain feeling of pity and a conviction that those monsters have something in common with human beings.[11]

It seems that Pompey himself – in his own way – had been half-hearted about the celebrations. Yet the Roman people must have enjoyed them.

ROME ON THE PATH TO ANARCHY

The dramatic events of that fateful year 49 would be triggered by the repeated violation of institutional regulations, which had become all the more apparent from 54, when Pompey began to nurture a dangerous ambition: dictatorship.

The consuls in 54 were Ahenobarbus, an opponent of Caesar, and the independent Appius Claudius Pulcher, older brother of Clodius, a patrician and an opportunist. This, along with Cato's success the previous summer in getting himself easily elected as praetor, was an indication of the power of the Optimates.

That summer, for the 'triumvirs', things took a dramatic turn for the worse with the death of Julia while giving birth to a daughter who died soon after. The people of Rome – now fearing a possible break in the 'triumviral' pact – then gave a powerful signal. Pompey's intention had been to bury his wife in the grounds of his villa on the Alban Hills, but after the ceremony held in the Forum, the crowd forcibly took the body to the Campus Martius. The consul Ahenobarbus protested in vain. The gesture of the people, it seems, pleased more the father than the widower.

The former, in emulation of the latter, planned a new forum, to the north of the Comitium, and a permanent electoral structure in the Campus Martius: a complex building with parallel corridors where the various voting units could enter in order. The first stage involved spending 60 million sesterces just for the purchase of private buildings to be demolished. Part of the sacred offerings accumulated over centuries in the temples of Gaul was used for this purpose.

Electoral corruption was even more rampant than usual. The shortage of money increased the rate of interest from 4 per cent to 8 per cent. The elections for the consulship of 53 had been postponed until September

CAESAR, GAUL AND ROME 🌐

due to the large number of candidates, investigations into each of them, the consequent debates in the Senate and the systematic use of the *obnuntiatio*. The consuls in office and two candidates were then embroiled in an incident that was likely to cause, even in a city addicted to corruption, further scandal. The four had come to an agreement. The two candidates, if they won, would be required to witness the passing of measures in reality never ratified but necessary for the ex-consuls to get to their provinces. Gaius Memmius, the anti-Caesarian praetor of 58 but now a candidate supported by Caesar himself – thanks to his soldiers and to Cisalpine Gaul – publicly revealed the existence of the manoeuvre. Since the agreement was not oral but – almost beggaring belief – written down, he took the document, on Pompey's advice, to the Senate. Upon which 'Appius didn't bat an eyelid, showed no sign of feeling the blow. But the other consul was numbed.'[12] None of this business seems clear. Pompey perhaps wanted to create some crisis in order to be appointed dictator, an idea that had already been rumoured in June 54. Six months later, a tribune would put forward a specific proposal, strongly opposed by Cato and ostentatiously rejected by Pompey himself.

Cato, who in July had already made himself guarantor of the election of the tribunes, persuaded the Senate at a certain point to propose a decree against *ambitus*: commissions chosen by lots would have to subject the candidates to secret investigation beforehand; but the popular vote was blocked by the veto of a tribune. Cato was also attacked with stones from the crowd, which was gaining considerable benefits through corruption.

Street violence increased at the same time that important trials were being held. Marcus Aemilius Scaurus, praetor in 56, ex-governor of Sardinia and now candidate for consul, was charged with extortion during the administration of his province (*de repetundis*), defended by Cicero, and was acquitted by a very large majority. Even more prominent was Gabinius who, on his return from Syria, was tried for *maiestas* (*lèse-majesté* of the Roman people, for having disobeyed the Senate and restored Ptolemy XII to the throne), as well as *de repetundis* and *de ambitu*. He was acquitted of the first charge thanks to Pompey, but risked being lynched by the crowd. He was defended on the second charge by Cicero, and supported by a letter from Caesar. The defendant was not helped by having Cato as president of the court, nor by a disastrous flood of the Tiber, which public opinion interpreted as punishment for the earlier acquittal. The crowd went as far as threatening the jury; the verdict was guilty. Gabinius went into exile, while Pompey spent the autumn dealing with the *cura annonae*, since the river had flooded the storehouses. And if that was not enough, there was even a fight between consular candidates that involved 300 gladiators.

Information about 53, on the other hand, is scant. The year began with no supreme magistrates. Ominous signs are recorded, even in Rome itself: 'owls and wolves were seen; prowling dogs howled; some statues exuded sweat and others were struck by lightning'.[13] For months Pompey, through the tribunes of the people, blocked the elections, and was asked on several occasions – at the specific request of the Senate – to keep order as proconsul until they could be properly held.

At that very moment the 'triumvirate' was shattered by terrible news. It concerned Crassus. At the end of 55 he had left for the eastern campaign, which ended in disaster in June 53 at Carrhae (the present-day city of Harran in Turkey). A Roman army of more than 30,000 men had been annihilated and his son Publius, and later he himself, had lost their lives. In 55, there had been considerable obstruction from rival tribunes, who had tried to prevent him from levying soldiers. One tribune, in particular, had raised the question of *bellum justum* (the respect of rules in beginning a war), had incited a crowd to prevent him leaving the city and hurled curses at the enterprise.

The chaos continued its course unabated. The consuls of 53, who took office during the summer, tried to hold the elections for the higher magistrates of the following year. On the list for the consulship were Milo, strongly supported by Cicero, and against him two names, Publius

Plautius Hypsaeus, an ex-praetor, and the illustrious Quintus Caecilius Metellus Pius Scipio Nasica, future father-in-law of Pompey. Pompey would marry Nasica's daughter Cornelia, widow of Crassus' son, probably the following year, refusing Caesar's proposal that Pompey should marry Octavia, Caesar's sister's granddaughter (and sister of the future Augustus), then 15 years old and perhaps already married to Gaius Claudius Marcellus (consul in 50), and that Caesar should marry Pompey's daughter Pompeia, then wife of Faustus Cornelius Sulla, son of the dictator. Cicero, meanwhile, had taken the place of the dead Crassus as augur (one of the experts that had to take *auspicia* for the magistrates).

Clodius, on the other hand, was standing for the office of praetor. His programme, according to Cicero, provided for *liberti* to be distributed no longer just among the four urban tribes but among all of them, which would work to his own advantage and perhaps drastically modify the relationships of power in the *comitia*. His only fear was that Milo would win, so that – once again in the words of Cicero and not without exaggeration – he went as far as organizing the electoral campaign of Milo's competitors 'in such way that he supported on his own his shoulders, as he used to say, all the assemblies. He gathered the tribes, acted as interlocutor, established a second Colline tribe by enrolling masses of wretches'.[14] The Colline was in fact one of the four urban tribes.

Violence was widespread, murders frequent and rival gangs now rampant in the streets and squares. Clodius' men attacked the consuls of 53 in a battle begun along the central *via Sacra* by supporters of Hypsaeus and Milo; at the consular elections there was fighting with swords and stones. Later news from Cicero reports that Marcus Antonius, better known as Mark Antony, then candidate for quaestor, had tried to kill Clodius: was this a personal matter, some slander against Antony, or, as some have suspected, an order from Caesar, who was secretly tired of such a troublesome ally?

The year 52 therefore began with no higher magistrates, creating the conditions for a situation of total anarchy. Milo, who after his praetorship had spent three whole inheritances on organizing games and corrupting the electorate, was pushing for an immediate vote. His two direct rivals consequently took a different view. To assist them, Pompey, through the veto of the new tribune Titus Munatius Plancus Bursa, prevented the Senate from appointing the first *interrex*. Only another turn of events could resolve the situation, though in the long run it tended to make it even worse.

CAESAR'S OTHER VICTORIES AND SHOCKING NEWS

The turn of events was so dramatic that Caesar, once informed in Cisalpine Gaul, sensed an important political shift that he frequently remembered during that fateful year 49.

> Since Gaul was calm, Caesar set out as he had planned for Italy to hold the provincial assizes. There he learned that Clodius had been killed; and being told about the Senate decree that all Italian inhabitants of military age should take the oath, he ordered a recruitment in the province. News of these events soon arrived in Transalpine Gaul. The Gauls, for their part, inflated the news with invented gossip, adding – as the situation seemed to require – that Caesar, detained by unrest in Rome, couldn't rejoin the army while the political conflicts were so intense. Urged on by this opportunity, the Gauls, who for some time resented being subject to the Roman people, started making plans for war more freely and more boldly.[15]

These are the opening words of Book VII of the *Gallic War*. Not only does it contain news of events in Rome but it describes above all the epic final rebellion of the whole of Gaul and its equally epic repression, in 52. The revolt, which threatened to thwart earlier achievements, was prompted – it would seem – by news of the death of Clodius. Gaul at that time, writes Caesar, was *quieta*, calm . . . a situation which, in fact, crops up too often, or at least, which he claims too often to exist. Let us take a step back in time.

On his return from Luca, the proconsul would have been in a position to deal more clearly with a complex situation. In 56 he had put down the revolt of the Veneti, a population from southern Brittany who controlled trade between Britannia and the continent. Venturing into the sea, he had won at the bay of Quiberon, killed the old people and reduced the rest to slavery; it was the first Roman naval success outside the Mediterranean. At the same time, the tribes of far-off Aquitania had also surrendered. In 55, he had then confronted the Germanic tribes which had crossed the Rhine near to its estuary. They had attempted an ambush and, in response, Caesar had captured a sizeable legation; now without their leaders, the tribes had been completely wiped out. He had then crossed the Rhine towards Germany, building an impressive wooden bridge in a very short time. Having burnt down several villages, he retraced his steps, demolishing the bridge behind him. Though it was late in the year, and having had to overcome the opposing fleet, he landed in Britannia on the eastern coast of what is now Kent. After two victories on land, he returned to Gaul. The Senate had voted a *supplicatio* of twenty days. Cato, in contrast, had proposed that Caesar should be handed over to the Germanic tribes, for war crimes. The two had exchanged furious letters. Colonial exploits, at any time, whet the appetites of the ruling classes. In this case many *nobiles* of varying ages had rushed to take part in the conquest of Britannia, which had been planned for the following year. Caesar could count on more than 800 vessels. The military ships were modified, made wider and more manoeuvrable; with them were private ships belonging to Roman traders. The fleet had terrorized the Britons, making it possible to land five legions and 2,000 horsemen; Gaul was left under the command of Labienus (tribune of the plebs in 63, who remained beside Caesar from 58 to 50 with the title of *legatus pro praetore*). Overcoming the obstacle of enemy war-chariots and scorched-earth tactics, Caesar had then managed to cross the Thames. Several tribes had surrendered. In July 54, Cicero sent Atticus various pieces of news he had received from his brother Quintus, who was there as legate, and from Caesar himself. The war was expected to end, since access points to the island had been blocked; it was also known that 'not a gram of silver is now to be found on it, nor is there any hope of booty other than slaves: and from them I don't think you can expect to produce poets or musicians.'[16] There was a similar tone in a letter of the same period to another friend: 'in Britannia I've heard it said there's not a scrap of gold or silver. If that's how things are, I suggest you take one of their war-chariots and get back here as quickly as you can.'[17] On 20 September, having imposed a tribute that would never be paid, Caesar ordered a return to Gaul.

Rebellion had broken out in the region not yet pacified. The Romans had lost one and a half legions in the Ardennes: famine had forced the proconsul to pitch the various winter encampments in different areas, making them more vulnerable. A truce was reached only through the direct intervention of Caesar, through the resistance of a Roman camp commanded by Quintus Cicero at what is now Namur, and after the victory of Labienus over the Treveri (in Belgic Gaul, in the area of the present-day Trier). The proconsul then spent the winter in the region, convinced he would have to stamp out the beginnings of a revolt in Belgic Gaul. In spring 53 he sent legates to make levies and had also asked Pompey – then in Rome – to send him those young men of Cisalpine Gaul who had already taken the military oath. Pompey had agreed 'in the interest of the *res publica* as well as the bonds of friendship that he had with him'.[18] So Caesar had secured three new legions, making a total of ten. He then carried out a series of raids in Belgic Gaul, also turning against the Germanic populations and crossing the Rhine for a second time, with another bridge (which this time, on his return, he ordered to be half-destroyed, leaving a garrison on the other half). Thanks to other expeditions, he had succeeded in pacifying the whole of Gaul. Leaving the legions in their winter camps, he had then returned for the provincial assizes in Cisalpine Gaul, where he received news of the death of Clodius.

All in all, returning to the opening passage of Book VII of the *Gallic War*, we tend to believe the account of the proconsul, despite his interest in loading responsibility for the revolt on his political rivals. In particular, Clodius must not have been unknown in Transalpine Gaul, having been there in 64, among the followers of the proconsul Murena . . . when, according once again to Cicero, he forged the wills of dead men, killed young men under his guardianship, agreed villainous pacts and formed criminal conspiracies.

Cicero's speech *In Defence of Milo* tries to put this into context: 'in a free city there can be no conflict between citizens that does not involve the *res publica*'; violence is sometimes necessary, as in the case 'of the killing of Tiberius Gracchus, of Gaius, or that in which the armed revolt of Saturninus was put down'.[19] The same speech nevertheless confirms the significance of the murder, though in a spirit quite different to that of Caesar: '102 days have gone by, I think, since the death of Publius Clodius. As far as the boundaries of Roman power extend, not only has news of it been broadcast but it has also spread joy.'[20] An event so important for the orator that one letter sent to Atticus on 22 July 51 is dated, half seriously, half in jest, the 560th day of the new era, now free from his worst enemy.[21]

Perhaps neither Caesar nor Cicero were exaggerating.

PART II
ROME IN CHAOS

5

FROM THE DEATH OF CLODIUS
TO A SOLE CONSUL

You dragged the bloody corpse of Publius Clodius out of the house, you flung it among the people, you left it stripped of ancestral images, of funeral rites, of the procession, of the eulogy, and, already half burned by a ruinous fire, you left it as food for stray night dogs.

Cicero, In Defence of Milo, 33

In that fateful year 49, the bitter fruits of a turmoil triggered by the death of Clodius would be reaped. The event led in this order to: a popular revolt, the burning of the Curia, an autocrat fearful of assassination and of the feelings of the city, a spectacular trial and, even worse, a devastating confusion over Caesar's command.

A POLITICAL MURDER, FLAMES AND
RUMOURS OF ASSASSINATION

Clodius was killed on 18 January 52, on the *via Appia*, by the gladiators of his enemy Milo. It is debatable what actually happened, due partly to the importance it played in the subsequent trial. Cicero's *In Defence of Milo*, a text intended for publication, which heavily reworks the speech he actually gave on 8 April 52, is not the most reliable source. The commentary on it by Quintus Asconius Pedianus (c.9 BC–AD 76), on the other hand, is extremely accurate. The grammarian and scholar had access to the speech actually delivered, but above all to the official records: thanks to his writings, the events of the early months of 52 are among the best known of the whole late republican period.

Milo, on the morning of 18 January, after a brief appearance in the Senate, left for his home town of Lanuvium (present-day Lanuvio), some 20 miles south-east of Rome, where the following day he was due to appoint a local priest. In the early afternoon, Clodius, on his way back from visiting the Senate at Aricia (present-day Ariccia, some 17 miles from Rome), met him just beyond Bovillae (present-day Frattocchie, some 12 miles from Rome), close to a shrine of the *Bona Dea*, the goddess that he had profaned years earlier. He was on horseback, accompanied by Schola – the false witness at his trial for sacrilege in 61 – and by two well-known plebeians and thirty or so slaves armed with swords, 'as was the custom for travellers at that time'.[1] Milo, on the other hand, was in a carriage with his wife and a friend, escorted by many slaves as well as gladiators who had taken part in the spectacular games offered by him in 54. After the other column had passed without incident, it was these gladiators, lingering at the back of their column, who began a brawl with Clodius' rearguard. Clodius turned round, throwing a menacing look . . . The famous gladiator Birria, quick as a flash, struck him on the shoulder.

Wounded, he was taken to a nearby inn. Milo then decided to finish off his worst enemy. According to another source, he hoped that, 'having immediately freed the slaves who had taken part in the crime, it would be easier to free himself from the accusation of murder once he had killed Clodius' than to deal with his reprisals had he lived.[2]

He therefore ordered the commander of the slaves, Marcus Saufeius, to drag the wounded man out of the inn and murder him. Since part of the escort had been slain and part had fled, the body of Clodius was left on the road – which had been built by his famous ancestor Appius Claudius Caecus, censor in 312. This coincidence would soon provide arguments for the supporters of Clodius. According to Cicero, his death was depicted as 'more atrocious because it happened along the *via Appia*';

it was enough to mention the name 'and here a tragedy worthy of the finest Greek theatre is suddenly unleashed! How many pathetic scenes when people talk about this *via Appia* – and they can do nothing else of late – bathed in the blood of a rogue and parricide!'[3]

Senator Sextus Teidius, on his way back from the country, placed the corpse in his litter and ordered it to be taken to Rome. He then retraced his steps: no one has ever questioned whether this was due to lack of space in the litter or out of prudence.

Before night-time the body had been carried to the Palatine Hill, into the atrium of the house the dead man had purchased just a few months earlier for the enormous sum of 14.8 million sesterces. His supporters among the populace and slaves crowded around. Fulvia fired their emotions by displaying the wounds that disfigured her husband's body.

Next morning an even larger crowd flocked there, along with well-known figures. First among them were the tribunes Plancus Bursa and Quintus Pompeius Rufus. Encouraged by them, the multitude took the body, still naked and covered in blood, to the Forum and placed it on the *rostra*. From there, the two tribunes could stir up an even larger crowd against Milo. Led by Cloelius – Clodius' right-hand man since 58 – the crowd carried the body into the Curia Hostilia, setting fire to it on a stack of seats, benches, tables and copyist manuscripts. Cicero, in the *Laws*, recalls the Law of the Twelve Tables which decreed that 'the dead shall not be buried, nor burned in the city (meaning inside the *pomerium*)', and comments: 'due, I think, to the danger of fires'.[4]

The fire that it caused was so vast that the flames engulfed the adjoining Basilica Porcia, a place of business conceived by Cato's most famous ancestor, Marcus Porcius Cato, the censor. The intended target, however, was the Curia Hostilia, the symbol of senatorial power, built, according to tradition, by the third king (from which it took its name) and enlarged during the dictatorship of Sulla (who, having first decimated the assembly by his proscriptions, had then placed it at the centre of his 'constitutional' reform and doubled its number to 600).

The body of Clodius, abandoned and only half burnt, was left prey to stray dogs . . . at least according to the passage from Cicero quoted at the beginning of this chapter.

The crowd moved on to the house of the absent Milo but was driven away by a barrage of arrows. It then headed towards the *lucus Libitinae*, just outside the Esquiline Gate, an area of *horti* (gardens) where undertakers also worked. There they collected *fasces* and carried them first to the homes of Scipio Nasica and Hypsaeus, then to the Pincian Hill, to the gardens of Pompey, each time proclaiming Pompey consul and dictator. The violence ended, it seems, only with the funeral banquet, begun around the ninth hour (about 3 pm). The crowd had acted, not 'through one of those impulses that sometimes takes hold of the popular masses, but through a clear determination'.[5]

The burning down of the Curia Hostilia 'caused even greater public indignation than the death of Clodius had done'.[6] Milo, who was now thought to be in voluntary exile – and who, according to some, had meanwhile committed other atrocities on his enemy's estate in the Alban Hills – returned, instead, on the evening of 19 January. Still wishing to stand for election, he tried to calm the people by having money distributed: 400 sesterces to each citizen.

On 19 January, or more probably the 20 or 21, the first *interrex*, (Manius Aemilius) Lepidus (probably the same Lepidus who was consul in 66), was chosen. He remained in office for the prescribed period of five days. Since he had no wish to call elections (this not being customary for the first *interrex*), the followers of Scipio and Hypsaeus, anxious to exploit Milo's unpopularity, pressed him by laying siege to his residence. They managed to storm it on his last day in office. They hurled his ancestral images to the ground, smashed up the bed belonging to his wife, a model of chastity, and vandalized the works she had produced on her loom in the atrium in accordance with ancient custom. Milo's band arrived just in time, there also to urge for elections: the two rival groups began fighting each other, and the siege came to an end.

Meanwhile, Milo requested a meeting with Pompey, offering to withdraw his candidacy. Pompey, feeling himself in difficulty, refused to see him. On 23 January, the tribune Pompeius Rufus, Clodius' closest ally, accused Milo, in a *contio*, of making an attack on the life of Pompey: 'he gave you someone to cremate in the Forum, and now he will give you someone to bury on the Capitolium'.[7]

Details of what took place on the *via Appia* began to filter out, distorted. On 27 January, in another *contio*, organized by Caelius (also a tribune at that time), at which Milo spoke – and maybe also Cicero – self-defence was raised: it was suggested that Clodius had attempted to ambush his enemy. The meeting ended in uproar. Some ran 'to the Curia and to the Temple of Castor holding firebrands or scythes', others 'armed with swords, protested throughout the Forum'; the assembly was thus 'disbanded by drawn swords, as it listened in silence to the speech of the tribune of the plebs'.[8]

Appian gives most detail.[9] While Milo was still speaking, and accusing Clodius of having been a desperate friend of desperate people who had set fire to the Curia, 'the other tribunes of the people, and that part of the people which had not let itself be corrupted, burst into the Forum armed'. Caelius and Milo escaped disguised as slaves. The others were slain: 'they no longer looked for Milo's supporters but killed those they came across, citizen or stranger regardless, and especially those who distinguished themselves for their robes and gold rings'. Since the disorder had arisen in a climate of lawlessness and mostly involved armed slaves, pillaging soon began: 'they ran amok, even broke into houses turning them upside down, looking they said for friends of Milo but, in fact, for whatever they could easily carry away; and for many days the name of Milo was an excuse for arson, stoning and, in short, for any crime'.

Was Milo really plotting against Pompey? Not necessarily, but the allegation was constantly being made, starting from the *contio* held on 23 January by Pompeius Rufus. Along with his colleagues Gaius

Sallustius Crispus (the future historian) and Plancus Bursa, he held other *contiones* each day. He also asked Pompey publicly whether he had evidence of the plot. Pompey replied that a certain Licinius – a plebeian priest who purified houses – had informed him that several of Milo's slaves were ready for an assassination attempt, and had given him their names. Pompey then sent to ask Milo whether those men under investigation belonged to him, and was told in reply that some had never been his, others he had set free. A certain Lucius, also a plebeian, had then sought to corrupt the informer; on being discovered, he had been placed in public custody, in chains. Cicero's version is much more spectacular:

> he even had to listen to the statement of a *popa*,[10] some Licinius or other in the area of the Circus Maximus, who said that in his tavern some slaves of Milo, totally drunk, had confessed to having hatched a plot to kill Gnaeus Pompeius; he said that one of them had then stabbed him so that he wouldn't go reporting them. Pompey is told of the matter in his gardens; I am one of the first to be called: on the advice of friends he refers the matter to the Senate. [. . .] The news goes round that for many hours of the night the house of Gaius Caesar had been under siege [. . .] No one had heard, despite it being a much frequented place, no one had been aware of it; nonetheless, people took it seriously.[11]

Rumours spread. Some reported the presence of 'a large number of shields, swords, javelins, even chains'; it was said there wasn't 'a single district or alley in the whole city in which a house hadn't been hired for Milo'; weapons were said to have been 'transported along the Tiber as far as the villa of Ocriculum [present-day Otricoli]'; even the house on the slopes of the Capitolium was 'stuffed full of shields and brimful of all kinds of incendiary missiles specially made for setting fire to the city'; such rumours, 'almost believed, were not rejected before being investigated'.[12]

The situation was certainly tense, and the safety of Rome was once again at the centre of attention.

A *SENATUS CONSULTUM ULTIMUM* AND AN UNPRECEDENTED DECISION

Between 3 and 10 February 52, a *senatus consultum ultimum* was passed. It was the first since the two relating to the Catilinarian conspiracy. In the absence of higher magistrates, the supreme assembly turned to the *interrex*, to the tribunes and above all to the proconsul Pompey, asking them to gather troops from the whole of Italy (and from Cisalpine Gaul, as Caesar recalls in his *Commentaries on the Gallic War*).[13] It was probably before Pompey's departure that the supreme assembly gathered under military protection outside the *pomerium* – to enable him to take part – and ordered the bones of Clodius to be dug up. In the *Laws*, Cicero would write that Clodius hadn't received 'funeral honours and burial';[14] in fact the Twelve Tables forbade the gathering of 'the bones of a dead man to then celebrate his funeral', with the exception of those who had died in war and far from home.[15] It also decreed that the Curia Hostilia be rebuilt. This last task went to Faustus Cornelius Sulla, son of the dictator (as well as quaestor in 54 and son-in-law of Pompey); it was decided to name the new building Curia Cornelia, recalling not only Faustus but also his father (Lucius Cornelius Sulla) who, after 82, had enlarged the previous building.

Pompey left on his mission. It was then that a version of events adverse to Milo was spread about. Scipio Nasica, Pompey's father-in-law, told the Senate that Clodius was clearly the victim. He had set out for Aricia with only twenty-six slaves. In the middle of the morning, when the Senate had adjourned, Milo had suddenly rushed upon him with more than 300 armed slaves, ambushing him beyond Bovillae. Clodius, wounded three times, had been taken to an inn – said Scipio Nasica – and then besieged; once dragged outside, he had ended up on the *via Appia*. As he lay dying, his gold ring had been slipped off his finger.

Hearing that his enemy's young son was at the villa on his Alban estate, Milo hastened there. The boy had been taken to safety, so Milo – he said – had tortured a slave, cutting him slowly to pieces. He had had the throats of the villa's manager and two other slaves slit. Of those who had tried to defend their master, eleven were said to have died, while only two of Milo's slaves had been injured. The following day, Milo had liberated his twelve most worthy slaves, distributing also 400 sesterces per citizen through the tribes, to calm the rumours. It was also said that he had sent word to Pompey that he was ready to relinquish his candidature. Pompey had answered that he had no wish to give advice on such a matter, so as not to limit the power of the people, and that through intermediaries he had sought to protect himself against further contact.

These were the rumours. Pompey quickly carried out the mission that the Senate had given him, returning to Rome perhaps before the military levy was complete. Not wishing to enter the *pomerium*, he remained in his gardens, on the Pincian Hill, guarded by troops. Once again, it seems, he refused to meet Milo.

At the end of February or the beginning of the intercalary month,[16] two young men, both called Appius, sons of Gaius Claudius Pulcher – another brother of Clodius (and praetor in 56) – started proceedings before Pompey to interrogate the slaves of Milo and his wife. Milo was supported by an impressive array of *boni*, including Hortensius, Cicero, Marcus Claudius Marcellus (consul in 51), Marcus Calidius (praetor in 57, who supported Cicero's recall from exile), Cato and Faustus Sulla.

Meanwhile, two factions had formed: one for Pompey as dictator, the other for the joint consulate of Pompey and Caesar. Despite the decree of the Senate, neither the tribunes nor the *interreges* had in fact been of much help.

On the twenty-fourth day of the intercalary month there was a debate.

Bibulus, a kinsman of Cato, made a proposal to the Senate that Pompey should be elected consul without a colleague: in this way, either the situation would benefit from his orders, or the city would be enslaved to its most powerful citizen. Contrary to all expectations, Cato stood up and supported that proposal, explaining that any form of power was preferable to anarchy. According to his predictions, Pompey would resolve the current difficulties for the best and would save the city, if it were entrusted to him.[17]

According to another version, the proposal was made by Cato himself. In any event, in 49 – in similar circumstances – he would observe that he who had prevented the elections and manipulated events would have the task of 'putting things right'. The *interrex* Servius Sulpicius Rufus (patrician, jurist, unsuccessful consular candidate in 63, then consul in 51) conducted the appointment. We don't know whether the Centuriate Assembly was called; one possibility is that, in the absence of other claimants, this wasn't necessary; it should also be said that the primary purpose seems to have been to avoid Milo's candidacy and therefore to enable the charge against him to proceed.

There had, of course, always been two consuls: 'there shall be two who hold sovereign power and, to "precede", "judge", "provide", they are called praetors, judges, consuls; they shall have supreme military power, they shall be subject to no one; their supreme law shall be the wellbeing of the people'.[18] The Senate declared that it would allow Pompey to choose a colleague, but only after two months. Was this to open the way for Caesar? As things turned out, no; only during the summer did the single consul co-opt his father-in-law Scipio Nasica, who was facing a charge of electoral corruption, which was withdrawn thanks to him.

The hated title of dictator was avoided, but on the basis of an entirely new procedure; Pompey, 'proud of the novelty and exceptional nature of the decree, was no longer concerned about earning the approval of the people'.[19] Having a single consul was not the only feature that was hardly orthodox. After 55, Pompey would not, in theory, have been entitled to hold the office for ten years; not only did he do exactly that, but he also remained proconsul. He was 'the first consul to have two very important provinces, an army and many resources, as well as absolute power by virtue of being sole consul'.[20] Caesar however – as recorded earlier – had remained loyal, helping him also to recruit men in Cisalpine Gaul and proposing another cross-marriage.

On the twenty-sixth day of the intercalary month, Pompey presented to the Senate two laws that would have major consequences. These introduced harsher penalties for *vis* as well as *ambitus*, drastically shortening the procedures. They regulated, first, the production of witnesses, and then, on the same day, the hearing of prosecution and defence, allowing two hours to the first and three hours to the second.

While the proposal on *vis* openly mentioned the murder on the *via Appia*, the burning down of the Curia Hostilia and the attack on the house of Lepidus, the *de ambitu* law was more far-ranging. It made it possible to accuse any person who had been a magistrate since the year 70, guaranteeing immunity to anyone convicted who secured the conviction of anyone else for a more serious crime. In other words, it raised the spectre of a purge.

> This covered a period of just under twenty years, during which Caesar too had been consul. So Caesar's friends suspected that he had fixed such a long period to cause offence and harm to their friend. [. . .] Pompey was indignant on hearing mention of Caesar, whom he considered above suspicion, given that his own second consulate also fell within that period.[21]

Among those who criticized the retroactive nature of the law was Cato, who refused to collaborate.

A debate arose. Hortensius, probably supported by Cicero, proposed that the killing of Clodius, the burning down of the Curia, the attack on the house of Lepidus should be declared as being against the *res publica*, claiming however that the existing laws were sufficient, though to be used *extra ordinem* (perhaps to accelerate the procedure). The Senate approved the first part of the request, but no decision was made on the procedure to be applied, due to a veto from the tribunes Plancus Bursa and Sallust. The former, who was 'completely mad', by obstructing the plans of the Senate, ensured there was 'a new procedure to follow'.[22]

Both of Pompey's laws were made public (*promulgatio*); Caelius threatened for several days to veto them, condemning the law on *vis* as being *ad personam* in nature, against Milo, and criticizing the rapidity of the new procedures. Pompey overcame this objection by declaring that, if he had to, he would defend the *res publica* by force.

Between the *promulgatio* and the vote[23] there were successive rumours and speculations that Milo would try to kill Pompey. One astonishing incident occurred. Plancus Bursa turned up at one *contio* with a freedman, a person well known, who claimed that – while travelling with four free men – he had witnessed the killing of Clodius. Because they had called out asking for help, they were kidnapped and imprisoned for two months in a villa belonging to Milo. It seems the allegation was believed and it caused a stir. Plancus Bursa and Pompeius Rufus also appeared on the *rostra* with one of the *triumviri capitales* – lower magistrates appointed to carry out executions – and asked him if he had arrested one of Milo's slaves caught in the act of killing. He replied that the slave had been arrested while sleeping at an inn and had been taken to him. They urged him not to free the man, but the following day Caelius and his colleague (Quintus) Manilius Cumanus – relying on their inviolability as tribunes – took him from the house of the magistrate and returned him to Milo.

Even Cicero became the target of Plancus Bursa's vitriol: the 'half-burnt tribune of the plebs' promptly 'each day railed bitterly against me, envious of my power, and claimed that the Senate did not decide according to its own beliefs, but according to my will'.[24] Bursa even declared his intention to prosecute him. Cicero, however, seemed irremovable.

A FAMOUS DEFEAT FOR CICERO, IN A TERROR-STRUCK FORUM

Pompey's two laws were approved by the Centuriate Assembly around 26 March. Under the provisions of the *lex de vi*, the people were immediately asked to choose a *quaesitor* – president of the court – from among former consuls, a choice that fell on Ahenobarbus. This, according to Cicero, followed the wishes of Pompey, who then – Asconius reports – proposed a register of judges comprising men of the most proven rectitude.

Milo was immediately summoned by the two young Appii under the new law *de vi* and in front of Ahenobarbus. They also made an allegation *de ambitu* based on Pompey's other new law. A third charge *de sodaliciis* was put forward by another person. Both *quaesitores*, Aulus Manlius Torquatus (possibly praetor in 70) and Ahenobarbus, ordered the accused to appear on 4 April. On the established day, Milo chose to face the trial *de vi* and the charge of the older Appius. From Torquatus he obtained the postponement of the trial *de ambitu*, with the same accuser, until the completion of the other trial.

Milo's slaves were called to give evidence (something that took place only under torture, because a slave was supposed to remain loyal with his master). Schola was called on the first day of the case against Milo. He said he had been present at the moment of the murder, which was particularly brutal; he emphasized that Clodius had not planned his route. Marcellus was unable to cross-examine him: terrified by the disorder caused by Clodius' followers, he had to take refuge on Ahenobarbus' high platform.

Marcellus and Milo himself asked Ahenobarbus for an armed guard. Pompey, who was at the Aerarium – at that time in the Temple of Saturn, inside the *pomerium* – was so disturbed by the uproar that he assured Ahenobarbus that he would return the following day with armed soldiers, as indeed he did. This was an infraction that Caesar would condemn several times, for his own purposes, in that fateful year 49.

On 5 and 6 April, Pompey managed to keep order during the hearing of the witnesses under interrogation from Cicero, Marcellus and Milo himself. Many inhabitants of Bovillae described what had happened: the killing of the innkeeper, the attack on the inn, the body of Clodius thrown onto the road. The Albanae Virgins gave evidence that an unknown woman came to them to fulfil a vow at the instruction of Milo, for the death of Clodius. Cicero's counter-attack served little purpose when he implicated Marcus Favonius, aedile at that time (and Cato, to whom Favonius had confided): 'you have heard from Marcus Favonius what Clodius said and you have heard, when Clodius was alive, that Milo would be dead three days from then; the deed happened three days after he had spoken'.[25]

Much more effective, however, was the conclusion of the evidence. Those present were moved by the tears of Clodius' mother-in-law and his widow. When the court was adjourned mid-afternoon, Plancus Bursa, in a *contio*, invited the people to turn up in large numbers the following day to prevent Milo from escaping but also to show their feelings to the judges – or, as Cicero put it, to 'dictate with their shouts the decree that you should issue'.[26]

On the last day of the trial, the *tabernae* throughout the city were closed, as had been Clodius' practice. Pompey posted armed guards in the Forum and at all its entrances and, like the day before, sat at the Aerarium surrounded by hand-picked soldiers. The eighty-one judges who would hear the arguments of the prosecution and defence were chosen by lot. Silence fell.

The prosecution – the elder Appius brother, Antony, and an otherwise unknown Publius Valerius Nepos – began to speak for the allotted two hours. Beyond the rhetoric about the *via Appia*, there was a statement of principle: 'divine law does not permit any man to contemplate the light of day who confesses to having killed a man'.[27]

Cicero alone responded. It seems that, out of fear, he had been brought by litter to the place of trial so that he could leave at the end of the prosecution speeches. He had just begun to speak when the Clodians burst out shouting, which couldn't even be contained by their fear of the soldiers.

> he saw Pompey seated on high, as though he were in an encampment, and weapons that flashed all around the Forum. He was frightened and could scarcely begin his speech: his body trembled, his voice reduced to a whisper. Milo, on the other hand, stood in the middle of the court defiantly, not in the least intimidated[28]

Cicero was unable to speak with his usual effect, and 'what he actually said remains written down even today; but the speech on which we are commenting he wrote so perfectly that it could rightly be considered his best'.[29]

What was his argument? He didn't want to follow a defence of murder in the public interest (as Marcus Junius Brutus – nephew of Cato and future assassin of Caesar – had meanwhile argued in an imaginary speech of his own). He argued instead that it had been Clodius who had planned to ambush Milo, thus choosing the line of self-defence, a concept that revolves – as it does today – around two key elements: aggression and reaction. We have only a scant idea of what Cicero actually said; the only thing of which we can be certain is that, in his reconstruction, Clodius had to die at the first blow.

The prosecution and defence were each then allowed to reject five judges from each of the three orders, to arrive at a final figure of fifty-one. Milo was convicted by 38 votes against 13. Among the senators, 12 against 6; among the knights, 13 against 4; among the 'tribunes of the treasury' (knights of lower standing), 13 against 3.

Everyone, Asconius observed, seemed to believe that Clodius had been wounded without Milo's knowledge, but that Milo had then ordered his murder. Some thought that Cato – who stated that Clodius' death had been a blessing, who backed Milo's candidacy as consul, who supported his defence and had given evidence about the threats heard by Favonius – had voted for acquittal. But since – as Asconius once again observes – the political elimination of the troublemaker Milo could itself be considered a blessing,[30] no one ever knew how Cato had actually voted.

This was Cicero's most sensational defeat. Other trials followed.

Milo, over the next few days, was also convicted in his absence *de ambitu* (under the presidency of Torquatus) and *de sodaliciis* (under the presidency of Favonius) and, lastly, once again *de vi* (under the presidency of Lucius Fabius and in accordance with the law prior to that of Pompey). He soon left for exile in Massilia. His belongings were sold for next to nothing to pay his heavy debts. When he saw a copy of Cicero's speech revised for publication, he apparently commented: 'it was lucky that these words had not been spoken in this form in court. Otherwise I wouldn't be enjoying mullets here in Massilia'.[31] From exile he would also complain how Cicero had managed the sale of his belongings, which ended up in the hands of a group of friends and went in part to Philotimus, one of his wife Terentia's freedmen.

Saufeius, the superintendent of Milo's slaves, was acquitted, Sextus Cloelius convicted; others, convicted either in their presence or absence, were mostly supporters of Clodius.

Pompey successfully intervened in favour of his father-in-law, accused of *ambitus*, entertaining in his own home the 360 jurors who had to hear the trial (according to Plutarch), or managing to dissuade the prosecutor (according to Appian).[32] He then appointed him fellow-consul for the rest of the year. Among other similar trials, a particularly violent one was that against Scaurus (praetor in 56 and already accused of extortion in 54, when he failed to win the consulship, but acquitted thanks to Cicero's defence). The crowd intervened to demand his acquittal; Pompey called in the army, resulting in deaths. Scaurus, defended once again by Cicero, was convicted.

Once Asconius' account comes to an end, we have much less information. Cicero's correspondence for 52 is silent, with the exception of two letters, and for the next two years, up to the summer of 50, it concentrates almost entirely on his new and undesired appointment as proconsul in Cilicia, granted by the Senate in March 51.

CORRUPTION, THE PROVINCES AND CAESAR'S CANDIDATURE

This moment marked the beginning of debates and measures, most of them obscure, which would lead to open conflict in that fateful year 49.[33] Caesar's future was decided against a more complex background: Pompey intended first of all to put a stop to the corrupt practices that seemed by then to be throttling the whole of Roman political life.

While the proconsul was busy safeguarding the future of the Gallic campaign against an increasingly ominous revolt, in Rome the debate over the timescale and procedures for his candidature to his second consulship had begun. In early 52, Caelius and nine other tribunes put forward a proposal.

According to Suetonius, when the Senate had already decided to elect Pompey as sole consul, Caesar persuaded the tribunes, who were proposing him as Pompey's colleague, to present an alternative request: that 'at the expiry of his mandate he be allowed to stand for a second consulship though remaining absent, in such a way that his candidacy did not compel him to abandon the province prematurely, before he had brought military operations to an end'.[34] It was then – again according to his biographer – that Caesar began funding his electoral campaign.

Pompey was in favour, fearing a colleague admired 'by soldiers and populace alike'; he therefore co-opted his father-in-law Scipio Nasica, over whom there 'was an impending charge of corruption'.[35] Caesar – whose friends had told him to beware of the law against corruption – may have been anxious to avoid being reduced to a private citizen. In addition to winning the plebiscite, he therefore asked the Senate for 'a small extension to his power over Gaul or at least over a part of it';[36] this final question had to be postponed.

Cicero may also have played some part; Caesar, who was at Ravenna in the first half of March 52, had asked him to intercede with Caelius; Pompey had urged in the same respect. Cicero, in 44, would say that not only had he advised Pompey 'not to extend Caesar's command for five more years' (in 56), but also 'to oppose the passing of the law that allowed Caesar to be candidate even if he was absent from Rome'.[37] Cicero had, in fact, been busy and Caesar, having obtained what he wanted, left for Gaul, noting 'that now in Rome the political situation was favourably settled through the energy of Pompey'.[38]

What history generally describes as the first rift between the two generals came about quite suddenly. In spring 52 a law passed by Pompey changed the rules for the assignment of provinces. By implementing a previous *senatus consultum*, the law introduced a compulsory interval of five years after the holding of a post in the (City) magistracy or (provincial) promagistracy. It therefore put a stop to the practice of politicians automatically running up debts during their electoral campaigns, certain that they could repay them soon afterwards thanks to their free and easy government of a province. Since the law allowed eligible proconsuls to be chosen from among old magistrates – *in primis* those who, like Cicero, had not yet held promagistracies – there were many more potential candidates for the provinces. Caesar probably couldn't even expect an extension from 1 March to the end of December 49 (justifiable only by not wanting to deprive the consuls of 50 of the first two months of their proconsular mandate). Above all, he could no longer expect a command immediately after his new consulship. Pompey's law, however, reintroduced the tribune's right to veto the assignment of provinces (a right which, as we shall see, was used systematically throughout years 51 and 50, until the *senatus consultum ultimum* of 7 January 49).[39]

Pompey secured 24 million sesterces a year from the Senate for his legions; nor did he even have any qualms, despite being the author of the law, 'about taking Spain himself soon afterwards for another five years'.[40] We know much less about the fate of his *cura annonae*.

A further, odd legislative move reaffirmed that candidates to magistracies had to present themselves in person, thus confusing Caesar's position. Pompey enacted 'a law contrary to the plebiscite'; he in fact, 'by proposing his law on the power of magistrates, in drafting the clause that forbade candidates to stand *in absentia*, had omitted to make an exception for Caesar'; however, he 'had the error corrected immediately after, but only when the law had already been engraved in bronze and registered'.[41]

There is something astonishing about this: would Pompey, in confirming an earlier prohibition, have forgotten Caesar and then falsified the official record so blatantly? Perhaps, having assured Spain for himself, he made a concession for Caesar, adding to the law 'the clause by which this was permitted to those who had been allowed by name and openly'.[42]

Events become less and less clear. Cato, while gaining increasing popularity thanks to games offered by the aedile Favonius, his loyal supporter, suffered a bitter defeat at the consulship election for 51.

What had happened? Cato had persuaded the Senate to require candidates to canvass the people in person, without the use of intermediaries (who frequently distributed money and favours). 'Thus he exasperated the people even further, because he deprived them not only of a source of earning but also of the opportunity to ask favours, making the people poor and, at the same time, despised.'[43]

There were, however, more interesting prospects in the air. At the end of 52, the Senate granted Caesar a *supplicatio* of twenty days, for a crucial turn of events beyond the Alps.

6

WINNER IN A TIGHT CORNER

Although it was not yet ten years that he had been fighting in Gaul, he captured more than 800 cities, subjugated 300 nations, fought 3 million men at different times, killed 1 million of them in battle and took as many prisoners.

Plutarch, *Caesar*, 15,5

In that fateful year 49, Caesar would launch an attack against the res publica *with an army that was now famed for its invincibility and ruthlessness. The events of the years 52–50 should have contributed more to its fame of ruthlessness, though it had come to the brink of disaster.*

SIEGES, SCORCHED EARTH AND AN EXTRAORDINARY VICTORY

Caesar had gathered a further contingent of men and returned from Ravenna to Transalpine Gaul. The revolt, stirred by rumours about his supposed political weakness, had begun in the territory of the Carnutes (between the Seine and the Loire), a political and religious centre where the assembly of the druids, the mighty priestly 'class', was held. It had then spread elsewhere. Vercingetorix, the 30-year-old son of a man so influential that he had once hoped to rule the whole of Gaul, had seized power as king of the Arverni (settlers in what is now the Auvergne) when news spread that the Carnutes had killed all Roman citizens at Cenabum (present-day Orléans).

> News soon reached all the nations of Gaul. Indeed when an event more important and more remarkable than usual occurs, they communicate it by shouting through the fields and countryside; those who receive the news transmit it in turn to their neighbours: this is what occurred then. So news of what happened at Cenabum at sunrise arrived before the end of the first watch (around 9 pm) in the country of the Arverni, some 160 miles away from Cenabum.[1]

Many tribes had joined forces, giving general command to Vercingetorix. Gallic armies had thus penetrated into the Roman province, heading for Narbo Martius.

Caesar arrived at the city. By reassuring and strengthening the area, he had deterred the enemy. He then took an army across the Cevennes – with snow up to 6 foot high – to lay waste the territory of the Arverni, who had imagined themselves out of reach during the winter, protected by the mountains as though by a wall. Caesar's movements had been many and various, helped by a Germanic cavalry; so too had been the movements of Vercingetorix.

Sieges had followed one after another. The siege of Avaricum (present-day Bourges), the largest and best fortified city of the Bituriges, was particularly tough. Caesar attacked it because it was in the richest region: he thought the whole population would surrender as soon as their main city had fallen. Vercingetorix had persuaded his followers to change strategy: to cut off Roman supplies and, following the example of the Britons, to set fire to the land. Flames sprang up suddenly and everywhere, but it was decided to spare Avaricum, contrary to the advice of Vercingetorix, who was thus compelled to march with his army to its defence. For twenty-five days the Romans proceeded with their siege works until they had built a great rampart, feeding themselves on meat alone for lack of corn but determined not to give up. Those under siege had planned to reach Vercingetorix's camp by night but the women, who were condemned to remain in the city with the children, had been able to signal their movement to the Romans. The Romans launched their attack during a sudden storm, killing some 40,000 defenders. The women's tactic proved useless: the soldiers 'stirred by the memory of the massacre of Cenabum as well as the effort that the siege works had cost them, spared neither the old people nor the women nor the children'.[2]

Once Caesar had settled various problems with his Aedui allies, he left Labienus with four legions to lead operations against the Senones and Parisii, and with the other six (including Legio XIII) he invaded the country of the Arverni, heading towards their main fortress, Gergovia (generally identified as a place 5 Roman miles south of what is now Clermont-Ferrand). The city, on top of a hill, couldn't be taken by attack. Vercingetorix set up camp nearby, occupying all the hills, and 'presented a formidable spectacle'.[3] Caesar nevertheless managed, by night, to capture a steep hill in front of the city from which he could cut his enemy's supply lines. The Roman camp had undergone a ferocious siege; several sorties had been successful, but a group of soldiers – against orders – had followed the Gauls as far as the city walls. Despite the arrival of reinforcements, disaster was averted only thanks to the containment operation of Legio X and Legio XIII. That day, just under 700 Romans, including 46 centurions, were killed in one of Caesar's heaviest defeats.

After other skirmishes it was clear that Vercingetorix didn't want open conflict. Caesar struck camp and left for the lands of the Aedui, which were now in turmoil. The garrison of Noviodunum (generally identified as present-day Nevers), on the banks of the Loire – where the Romans kept their hostages, grain, money, much of their baggage and a large quantity of horses bought in Italy and Spain – had been destroyed by the Aedui, who had also come to hear of a rebellion at Bibracte. They killed the grain merchants, shared out the money and horses and took to Bibracte the hostages that the Gallic peoples had offered to the

Romans; they then set light to Noviodunum, which they couldn't defend, loading as much grain as they could into boats and throwing the rest into the river or burning it. They then made forays in all directions to close off the supply lines. The revolt had spread, due to the (true) news about Gergovia and the (false) news about Caesar's retreat to the Narbonese Gaul. Labienus, after various conflicts of mixed success, had managed to rejoin Caesar.

Other populations and 15,000 horsemen had sided with Vercingetorix. Narbonese Gaul now had to be defended. It was garrisoned by twenty-two cohorts recruited there, under the command of the legate, Lucius Julius Caesar (consul in 64), whose son would also play a part in that fateful year 49.

Caesar found himself in the lands of the Sequani facing the army of Vercingetorix, who was now convinced that the right moment had come. There had been a heavy clash between cavalries; Caesar's Germanic one managed to win. Vercingetorix then retreated to nearby Alesia (generally identified as present-day Alise-Ste-Reine), in front of which Caesar, after a whole day spent slaying the enemy rearguard, had set up camp. Feeling sure that the enemy had been worn down by its defeats, he began siege works.

Alesia stood high on a hill. A plain some 3 miles long stretched out before it, while on either side were hills of similar height. The space beneath the walls, to the east, was occupied by Gallic troops who had dug themselves in with a ditch and a rampart. The perimeter of the wall begun by the Romans was some 10 miles long. Suitable ground had been chosen for the encampment. Watchmen stationed in twenty-three redoubts guarded it night and day.

In an initial clash between cavalries, Caesar's Germanic troops played a crucial role once again. At night, before the city had been cut off by the Roman siege works, Vercingetorix had sent cavalrymen back to their home territories to muster as many men as they could. He had 80,000 soldiers with him and just enough wheat for thirty days. Having ordered all grain to be handed over to him on penalty of death, he distributed the number of cattle that the Mandubii – the inhabitants of the region – had herded in, and divided the wheat into short rations. He ordered the troops to retreat inside the walls, and waited for help to arrive.

Using information from deserters, Caesar set about designing new and even more impressive fortifications, among the most famous – and most effective – ever recorded. It was a complex system of ditches filled with water specially diverted from a river, of ramparts, palisades, parapets with wooden battlements, pointed stakes and towers. A series of hidden ditches with pointed stakes of varying sizes made it possible for fewer soldiers to be employed. Expecting the arrival of an immense force, which might be capable of reversing the situation, Caesar had an identical defence line built facing the opposite direction, along a 14-mile perimeter, thus creating a defensive ring inside which he could hold his men.

It is worth noting – always with an eye on that fateful year 49 – that Caesar's account of his hability as besieger, once he had reached Rome, would stir apprehension.

Caesar's guess was only partly right. The assembly of Celtic princes decided that the enlistment of every able-bodied man would have caused too many leadership problems. The relief force therefore totalled 'only' 240,000 foot soldiers and 8,000 horsemen.

For those under siege, who had no idea what was happening, the wait had become unbearable. Some wanted to surrender while others, as long as their strength would allow it, urged an attack. Critognatus, noble and respected among the Arverni, proposed they should resist, eating the dead, as their ancestors had done in the war against the Cimbri and the Teutons (who had done so much damage to the Celtic populations before being stopped by Marius). At the end of the assembly, it was decided to send those who couldn't fight out of the city; if that was not enough, then Critognatus' proposal would be followed. The inhabitants were therefore driven out, including women and children. The defenceless mass then approached the Roman lines, pleading to be accepted as slaves and be fed. Caesar limits himself to recording the order to place guards along the ramparts; the result, easily imaginable, is reported by the 'anti-Caesarian' historian Cassius Dio (c.AD 155–c.235): 'being in the middle between the city and the Roman camp, they died miserably'.[4]

The relief force finally arrived. Its horsemen occupied the entire plain, while the foot soldiers were positioned on the hills, with manoeuvres that lasted days. A first cavalry battle once again saw the success of Caesar's Germanic cavalrymen. The rampart also successfully protected the Romans from a first coordinated attack; there, the legates Mark Antony (quaestor the following year) and Trebonius (tribune in 55) had distinguished themselves. There was then a second, similar clash, at a point of weakness in the fortifications. Fighting erupted contemporaneously in all points. For the Romans, occupied along such extensive lines, it wasn't easy to deal with simultaneous attacks, and the shouts that rose up behind them were unnerving: 'indeed on most occasions those things that are not seen disturb men's minds more deeply'.[5]

Caesar sent reinforcements where necessary. While he himself rushed to give support with horsemen and legionaries, Labienus, at the head of thirty-nine cohorts, emerged from the rampart, attacking the enemy with the cavalry and putting it to flight. There was massive slaughter. Hearing the signal to retreat, the relief force scattered. Vercingetorix finally surrendered. He would spend almost six years in prison before being executed during Caesar's Gallic triumph. Immediately after the victory at Alesia, Caesar had distributed one prisoner to each soldier. On reaching the lands of the Aedui, he secured their surrender. He then subdivided the legions over the territory, spending the winter at Bibracte.

ANOTHER TWO YEARS IN GAUL

The revolt in 52 must have affected Caesar's reputation among his soldiers, but probably also in Rome, good reason to rush to complete

Book VII of his *Commentaries on the Gallic War*, ending it with his epic victory at Alesia. When the Senate voted another twenty days for *supplicatio*, everyone probably imagined that his job was done.

The truth, once again, was quite different. The situation was still confused, as emerges from Book VIII of the *Commentaries*, written later and traditionally attributed to the close friend Aulus Hirtius, though the identity of the author is by no means certain. In particular, Caesar feared that the Gauls had realized they had to divide his forces and attack in different places. He began then to adopt even tougher tactics.

Having entrusted the encampment to Antony (now quaestor), he went while it was still winter to the lands of the Bituriges, where Legio XIII was garrisoned, with Legio XI not far away. He led the legions into fertile countryside, taking the farmers by surprise.

The population was forced to submit. For the hardships of that very cold winter, Caesar promised each soldier 200 sesterces, and 2,000 to every centurion. After other movements and clashes, particularly with the Bellovaci (settled between present-day Beauvais and the river Oise), he sent Legio XV to Cisalpine Gaul and moved towards the Carnutes, demanding the rebel Gutruatus, who had instigated the revolt. He was searched out and delivered to Caesar, 'who, contrary to his nature, was obliged to have him executed by the soldiers [. . .] so that he was beaten with rods and decapitated'.[6]

Caesar received news at this point about the resistance of the inhabitants of Uxellodunum (in 2001 officially identified, after long controversies, in the archaeological site of Puy d'Issolud). Their numbers were neglibile but he felt he had to punish them to stop the Celts imagining that all they needed was more determination; especially as he was well aware that 'it was known to all Gauls that his rule in the province would last only one more summer'.[7]

Arriving there unexpectedly, he cut off the water to those under siege, first by barraging missiles at those collecting supplies and then by diverting the spring with underground tunnels. The city surrendered.

Caesar, knowing that everyone was aware of his mildness and not fearing that a tougher act would be attributed to any natural cruelty, realizing moreover that his plans would come to nothing if a larger number of Gauls in different regions were to take similar initiatives, felt he had to deter others with an exemplary punishment. Accordingly he chopped off the hands of those who had carried weapons and spared their lives, so that the punishment inflicted on the wrongdoers would be better witnessed.[8]

Labienus also had a run of successes over the Treveri. Caesar at that point, judging that the remainder of the country had now been pacified, moved in autumn to Aquitania, where he had never previously been, though in 56 he had partially subjugated the region thanks to Publius Licinius Crassus (son of the 'triumvir', who would die at Carrhae in 53). The inhabitants spontaneously sent hostages.

He then left for Narbo Martius, sending his troops off to winter quarters. He made a brief visit to the courts of justice to obtain information on public matters and give out rewards on the basis of conduct during the revolt. He then visited the legions in Belgic Gaul and spent the winter at Nemetocenna (present-day Arras).

The *Commentaries on the Gallic War* devote just a few chapters to the year 50, during which little happened. Caesar, anxious to avoid rebellion among the Belgic people after his departure, gave out honorific titles and rewards, and imposed no levies. In the spring, contrary to his usual practice, he left for Cisalpine Gaul. He did so 'to visit the *municipia* and *coloniae*, to which he had recommended his quaestor Antony as candidate for the priesthood':[9] many people wanted Antony to lose so as to humiliate Caesar at the very moment when he was leaving office. Meanwhile he heard that Antony had been made augur, though he proceeded with the visit in order to return thanks and commend 'himself and his candidacy for the following year'; his opponents, however, were rejoicing over the election to the consulship of Lucius Cornelius Lentulus

Crus (Clodius' chief prosecutor in 61 and praetor in 58) and of Gaius Claudius Marcellus (brother of Marcus, consul of 51, and cousin of the consul of the same name of 50), who both wanted to strip him of every office and dignity. He was spurred on by another reason, the defeat of Servius Sulpicius Galba (praetor in 54), which occurred 'even though he was worth much more for popularity and votes, since he was bound to him through friendship and because he had been his legate'.[10]

Caesar was greeted in all *municipia* and *coloniae* with great rejoicing. He was brought before masses of people, sacrifices were offered and banquets spread out, anticipating the joy for the much-awaited triumph: the pomp of the wealthy was matched by the enthusiasm of the poor. Having crossed the whole of Cisalpine Gaul, he returned in great haste to Nemetocenna. Having assembled all the legions from the winter camps at the border of the Treveri lands, he inspected them. He handed command of Cisalpine Gaul to Labienus, 'to make it favourable to his own candidacy for the consulship'.[11]

The last four chapters of Book VIII describe what was happening in Rome. Let us briefly look at them.

Persistent rumours had reached Caesar that Labienus was being wooed by his opponents and that the Optimates were trying to persuade the Senate to deprive Caesar of part of his troops. But he hadn't paid much heed to the rumours concerning Labienus nor had he wanted to go against the authority of the supreme assembly: among the senators, if free to vote, his own cause would have triumphed. The tribune Gaius Scribonius Curio had often defended him, proposing that both Caesar and Pompey should discharge their troops, to restore freedom and independence to Rome. Curio had also pushed for a vote, but the consuls and Pompey's friends were opposed, delaying the matter until it ran out of time. This confirmed the feeling of the Senate and was in line with what had happened the previous year (in 51). Then, when, contrary to the previous law of Pompey and Crassus, the consul Marcus Claudius Marcellus had proposed to bring an end to Caesar's rule over the provinces before the end of its term, almost all the Senate had voted against. His opponents had therefore adopted more forceful means. The assembly had decided to send one of Pompey's legions and one of Caesar's to the Parthian war. But both legions had been taken from Caesar, since Pompey had provided Legio I, which had been recruited in Caesar's province and sent to him. Caesar, while understanding what was going on, had re-sent the legion to Pompey and also handed over Legio XV, then stationed in Cisalpine Gaul, filling its place with Legio XIII. He had also assigned the winter quarters, posting Trebonius among the Belgic tribes with four legions and posting the legate Gaius Fabius (praetor in 58) among the Aedui with another four, feeling that particular control was needed over both peoples. He then returned to Cisalpine Gaul, where he discovered that, by order of the consul Gaius Claudius Marcellus, the troops destined for the Parthian war had been entrusted to Pompey.

How many legions did Caesar then have under his command? From the *Commentaries*, there would seem to be nine. In fact, Suetonius reports that he had established Legio V 'Alaudae' in Narbonese Gaul to compensate for the loss of the troops who had gone back to *terra Italia*. A letter from Cicero of December 50 still attributes eleven legions to him, and so does the historian Lucius Annaeus Florus (c.AD 70–c.145), whereas Plutarch – like Suetonius – refers to ten. Caesar, in fact, also mentions twenty-two cohorts recruited in 52, perhaps forming the basis for the creation of Legio V 'Alaudae'.[12]

The *Commentaries on the Gallic War* come to a sudden end: 'after this gesture, even though no one could have any doubt about what was being prepared against Caesar, Caesar nevertheless resolved to submit to anything, so long as there remained some hope for him to dispute lawfully rather than to fight. He went . . .'[13] What followed – once again from Caesar's viewpoint – we can only infer, as we will do below, from the opening chapters of his *Commentaries on the Civil War*.

To gain a better understanding of what happened, let us now attempt to examine, briefly, the fraught institutional debate that went on during years 51 and 50.

SHADOW OVER THE FUTURE

The new consuls took office as normal on 1 January 51. The pair consisted of an incompetent enemy of Caesar and an indecisive advocate of peace. The first was Marcus Claudius Marcellus, praetor perhaps in 54, and a supporter of Milo in 52. The second was Servius Sulpicius Rufus, unsuccessful contender for the consulship of 62 and accuser of Murena but a great campaigner for the reinstatement of Cicero in 57, as well as the *interrex* who, in 52, had appointed Pompey as sole consul.

Marcellus began to attack Caesar indirectly. His victim was an inhabitant of Novum Comum (present-day Como), who 'was not a magistrate, that's true, but was yet an inhabitant of Transpadane Gaul' – a fact, it seems, that he 'got on the nerves' of both Pompey and Caesar.[14] This is what Cicero had written on his way to the post he so little desired as proconsul in Cilicia, awarded to him in March that same year. What had happened?

Versions vary. The most detailed account is that of Appian.[15] Caesar had founded Novum Comum, a *colonia* with Latin rights, 'and those who were its magistrates each year consequently became Roman citizens; this is a prerogative of the *jus Latii*'. At this point, in defiance of Caesar, 'Marcellus, with some excuse or other, beat with rods (a punishment not inflicted on Roman citizens) a citizen of Novum Comum who had been a magistrate in its city, and for this was regarded by law as a Roman citizen'; Marcellus angrily explained that 'the blows were the demonstration of his non-citizenship; he told him then to carry the scars to Caesar and show them to him'.

In short, an open challenge. Other remarks by Cicero reveal a broader underlying question: citizenship in the region. Back in May, Cicero had been told that the inhabitants of Transpadane Gaul – who had been granted Latin rights in 89 by Pompey's father, but which the censor Crassus, in 65, had not managed to transform into Roman citizenship – had received 'an order to create *quattuorviri*'.[16] Since these were the highest authorities of the *municipia* – therefore Roman political entities – the plan was clear: the inhabitants of the region were urged by Caesar to consider themselves fully fledged citizens. However, the voices faded towards the end of May, and the story of the Novum Comum magistrate came to nothing.

The Senate debate over Caesar's command, on the other hand, was long, complex and had much impact on popular feelings.

Officially it began between April and May of 51. The consul Marcus Claudius Marcellus demanded that Caesar should leave his governorship of the provinces by 1 March – probably of 50 – stating that he shouldn't be allowed to stand as candidate *in absentia*. The motion was not approved by the Senate or – more probably – it was vetoed by a tribune.

Marcellus seemed weak, as Caelius wrote to Cicero at the end of May: 'he hasn't yet put forward any proposal for succession in the Gallic provinces and – as he told me himself – has postponed his motion to 1 June'.[17] Attached to the letter was a whole volume, a *Commentary on Urban Matters*, that had been written to commission. It seems that opposition propaganda was rife: word was going round that Caesar had lost his cavalry and was 'under siege in the territory of the Bellovaci'; but these rumours were from the mouths of a small clique, 'who spread them around with an air of great mystery; though Ahenobarbus, as you might expect, was holding his hand to his mouth'.[18] Not even Cicero remained unscathed: 'on 24 May the gossips in the Forum had spread news of your death (if only it were theirs!). Throughout the city and in the Forum it was said you had been killed [. . .] on your journey.' The letter ends with another piece of important news which, in our view, helped decide Cicero's destiny in that fateful year 49: his *De re publica* brought him great universal success!

The situation was confused. Pompey had once again left Rome, as though he were off to Spain. But he remained in *terra Italia* to watch what was going on, feigning to be annoyed by the fact 'that Caesar would be stripped of his command'.[19] In the second half of May, Cicero, still on his way to his province, had happened to meet him at Tarentum (present-day Taranto).

Pompey's knowledge of Cilicia was invaluable. Equally valuable, for us, are the impressions that Cicero noted down for Atticus and Caelius. To Atticus he wrote that he had found 'a noble citizen, magnificently well-prepared to oppose the schemes that we all fear'.[20] To Caelius, who was about to stand for aedileship, he wrote that they had spoken long about matters that must remain confidential, but he could state that Pompey had 'a feeling for the institutions' and a wish to take the necessary steps, going as far as to advise: 'trust him: he will greet you with open arms, believe me. He now sees good and bad citizens in exactly the same way as we see them.'[21] The rumour that Pompey was heading for Spain – a move that Cicero didn't at all approve of – was still circulating in July. In October, when he was far away in Cilicia, he received further confirmation. Yet Pompey was still in *terra Italia*.

On 1 June, the question of Caesar wasn't mentioned. Caelius, sending another *Commentary* to his correspondent, wrote: 'Marcellus's outbursts have subsided, and not just through lack of energy but, it seems to me, through calculation';[22] according to Appian, Pompey played some role in this. In any event, Rome could enjoy a moment of peace.

Caesar didn't stand for the consular elections, which were held – it seems – at the usual time and without violence. Those elected – Gaius Claudius Marcellus (cousin of Marcus, consul in 51) and Lucius Aemilius Lepidus Paullus – were against him. With them was the resolute Curio: the 'most violent of tribunes'[23] and 'a man of keen intellect, an able speaker, much heeded by the populace'.[24]

The manoeuvring continued, as another of Caelius' letters records. On 22 July, the Senate raised the problem of the legion loaned to Caesar in spring of 53. 'Pompey then found himself forced to declare that he would recall that legion, but not at once under the urgency of that motion and not under the attacks of his critics.'[25] It was then arranged that Pompey should return to Rome as soon as possible so that the problem of succession to Caesar could be discussed in his presence; he was about to leave for Ariminum, to reach the army; the decision was planned for 13 August.

However it wasn't debated that day but postponed to 1 September due to a trial for *ambitus* against Gaius Claudius Marcellus, the newly elected consul for the following year. But on 1 September they couldn't reach the legal number (what that number was we do not know). Caelius predicted that 'the problem of succession' wouldn't be resolved.[26] Pompey – for the first time, so far as we know – gave a strong signal, opposing 'the election of Caesar as consul so long as he holds province and army', but advised delay; Scipio Nasica proposed that the meeting of the Senate on the following 1 March be fully devoted to it.[27]

In the first half of September, according again to Caelius, there was basically a stalemate: the matter would drag on for so long 'as to waste a couple of years or more'.[28] And so we reach the Senate meeting of 29 September 51. An extraordinary letter from Caelius reports what happened, setting out the texts of the Senate resolutions. Having finally established that Pompey was in favour of the suspension of his own command – and perhaps also that of Caesar – after 1 March 50, the Senate unanimously approved a motion of Marcus Claudius Marcellus, the consul of 51.[29] The consuls of the following year, on 1 March, 'SHALL BRING BEFORE THE SENATE THE QUESTION OF THE CONSULAR PROVINCES, AND SHALL NOT FROM THE I MARCH PRESENT TO THE SENATE OTHER MOTIONS BEFORE THIS OR AT THE SAME TIME'. For this purpose they could, among other things, 'HOLD MEETINGS OF THE SENATE AND VOTE DECREES ALSO ON COMITIAL DAYS' and together with the other magistrates and their successors, if appropriate, 'CARRY SUCH PROPOSALS BEFORE THE PEOPLE AND THE PLEBS'.

The succession to Caesar now had priority. Another three Senate resolutions were vetoed by pro-Caesarian tribunes. The first clearly went against the prerogatives of the magistrates, and of the tribunes in particular, by declaring that 'NO MAGISTRATE WHO HAS THE RIGHT OF VETO[30] OR OF VOTING IN OPPOSITION IS AUTHORIZED TO PREVENT QUESTIONS OF PUBLIC INTEREST FROM BEING BROUGHT BEFORE THE SENATE

AT THE FIRST POSSIBLE OPPORTUNITY AND A DECREE OF THE SENATE FROM BEING PASSED'; and again, 'ANYONE WHO VOTES IN OPPOSITION OR PLACES OBSTACLES SHALL IN THE JUDGEMENT OF THE SENATE HAVE ACTED AGAINST THE *RES PUBLICA*'.[31] The second resolution could have affected the size of Caesar's forces, declaring the view of the Senate, regarding soldiers serving in Caesar's army, 'THAT THE CASES OF THOSE WHO HAVE TERMINATED THEIR SERVICE OR HAVE VALID REASONS FOR BEING DISCHARGED SHALL BE BROUGHT BEFORE THIS ASSEMBLY, SO THAT THEY CAN BE RE-EXAMINED AND THE REASONS CAN BE KNOWN'.[32] Lastly, the third resolution, in relation to nine provinces governed at that time by ex-praetors, left open the possibility of 'ALL THOSE WHO WERE PRAETORS YET WITHOUT HAVING ANY PROVINCIAL COMMAND' to be assigned by lots for the office, and if 'THE NUMBER OF PERSONS WITH THE PREREQUISITES FOR BEING SENT INTO THE PROVINCES BY VIRTUE OF THE DECREE OF THE SENATE IS LOWER THAN THE REQUIRED NUMBER' it would be necessary to choose from among the members 'OF THE COLLEGE THAT COMES IN CHRONOLOGICAL ORDER IMMEDIATELY AFTER' those who did not have posts, 'AND SO ON, UNTIL THE COMPLETION OF THE REQUISITE NUMBER TO BE SENT INTO THE PROVINCES'.[33]

The first two resolutions also provided that, in the event of a veto – as indeed happened – the Senate had to return to them at the first possible opportunity.

Pompey declared that he couldn't take a decision on the provinces before 1 March without wronging Caesar. When asked what he would have done if anyone used their veto, he replied 'that it made no difference whether Caesar was prepared to obey the will of the Senate, or whether he sent someone to prevent the Senate from deciding'. Someone else immediately 'asked him: "And if that person wants to be consul and keep his army?"; at which he replied, with much good nature: "And if my son wants to start hitting me with a stick?" With these comments he gave everyone the impression that there was an agreement' between them.[34] Caelius concluded: Caesar could remain in Gaul, relinquishing his candidature for the elections in 50 for the consulship of 49, or relinquish Gaul, if his candidature were allowed.

In Rome, the Parthian advance across the Euphrates and beyond Commagene caused a great sensation and just as much unrest. In mid-November 51, Caelius wrote to Cicero: 'one man says that Pompey ought to be sent there, another that Pompey mustn't leave Rome; some talk about sending Caesar with his army, others the consuls; but no one wants to see private citizens appointed by a decree of the Senate'.[35] On the other hand, the consuls, fearful that the decree appointing them to military command might be approved and the task handed to others, didn't want the Senate to be called, 'to the point of raising doubt over their [the consuls'] institutional honesty'.[36] In October, however, Cicero had won a victory in the Amanus range (now Nur) that separated Cilicia from Syria. Afterwards, his troops proclaimed him *imperator*, thus entitling him to a triumph. Gaius Cassius Longinus, the quaestor who controlled Syria as a replacement for the absent proconsul Bibulus, had also succeeded – possibly thanks to help from Cicero – in extricating himself from the siege laid against him at Antiocheia (present-day Antioch). Soon after, Cicero would lead another victorious expedition against the fortress of Pindenissum.

ENTER CURIO 'WITH THE VENAL TONGUE'

The year of consuls Gaius Claudius Marcellus and Lucius Aemilius Lepidus Paullus had begun. They were, according to Caelius, two men who 'are truly scrupulous: so far they haven't got anything through the Senate apart from the *feriae Latinae*';[37] and the tribuneship 'of our friend Curio is completely frozen'; in short, 'it's impossible to describe in words the total immobility there is here'.[38] But Caelius, in the letter he had just written on an unnamed day in February, feels the need to add a note:

I wrote to you, above, that Curio is really cold; but now he's warm, so fervidly is he getting torn to bits by the critics. With a great about-turn, for not having obtained the inclusion of the intercalary month, he has moved to the people: he has started to talk in favour of Caesar and, with a certain ostentation, has presented a law on the road system, not unlike Rullus's agrarian law, and a law on foods, which requires aediles to oversee the distribution. He hadn't yet done it when I wrote the first part of the letter to you.[39]

Cicero had 'a shock. But what are you saying? Curio is now siding with Caesar? Whoever would have thought it, apart from me? For, on my life, I really did think it.'[40] In June, from Cilicia he was asking for advice from Atticus, since 'something unpleasant about Curio and Paullus' had reached him by letter; 'not that I fear any danger so long as Pompey remains standing . . . or even sitting, but in good health; but, heavens, the attitudes adopted by them, my good friends, I just don't like'.[41] The inactivity of the consuls, as well as Curio's about-turn, could be explained in various ways.

Let us start with the consuls. Caesar, who – according to Appian and Plutarch – was unable to influence Gaius Claudius Marcellus, bought off his colleague for 36 million sesterces: with this money 'Paullus commissioned for the Romans the basilica that bears his name, a beautiful building'.[42] Paullus was therefore able to complete a magnificent construction, begun in 55, during his appointment as curule aedile. Once again for the people. Appian reports that, in April or early May, as in the Senate resolution of 29 September 51, the consul Gaius Claudius Marcellus brought the question of the provinces before the Senate, but with no result; his colleague Paullus remained silent.

More difficult to explain is the behaviour of Curio, who had recently emerged on the political scene and was destined to become a key figure in this whole story. It happened quite unexpectedly. Through a rare circumstance (the lack of qualifications of one of those elected) he obtained the tribunate. He then changed his colours, in circumstances certainly not rare but nonetheless mysterious. The year before, Caesar – who generally allowed 'all those involved in politics to draw liberally from the wealth of Gaul'[43] – had refused him money for his electoral campaign. Caesar's allies, including Antony, had treated him with open hostility. The reason that Caelius gives is also odd: a squabble over the failure to introduce an intercalary month.

The historian Gaius Velleius Paterculus (c.19 BC–c.AD 31) gives his own assessment:

> At the outbreak of the civil war and of all the ills that followed it for twenty consecutive years, no one fanned its flames more greatly and passionately than Curio, a tribune of the plebs, a man of noble birth, eloquent and bold, prodigal of his own fortune and honour and that of others, a refined scoundrel with a persuasive tongue, for the public misfortune, whose nature could not be gratified by wealth or by any interest. He sided first with Pompey, that is to say, as it was then believed, on the side of the *res publica*; then, seemingly, against Pompey and Caesar, but in his heart in favour of Caesar. Whether he had done this for no ulterior motive, or, as people say, after having pocketed 10 million sesterces, is a question we shall leave unanswered. The advantageous peace treaties that already heralded a truce, which Caesar proposed with great spirit of moderation and Pompey with good heart accepted, were in the end thwarted and shattered by him, when Cicero alone was striving for public harmony.[44]

Plutarch, Suetonius and Appian also liken Curio's behaviour to that of the consul Paullus, referring to a bribe of enormous proportions (60 million sesterces, according to Appian). Appian adds that, by way of pretext, he had presented a road reconstruction project, claiming the right to supervise it for five years, though he was well aware it would be rejected by Pompey's allies. Cassius Dio takes a similar view: according to him, Curio had shammed at first, looking for an excuse for an about-turn; even the proposal for an intercalary month was a way of playing for time. But perhaps he was already convinced about the need for a compromise.

Between April and May 50, Pompey, from Neapolis (present-day Naples), where he was striving to recover from a recent serious attack of fever (probably malarial), made a proposal, supported by the Senate: 'that Caesar should leave his provinces on 13 November'.[45] But Curio was 'determined to submit to anything rather than allow this; and he abandoned the remainder of his programme'. And the others? 'Our people then, you know them well, they haven't the courage to push matters to extremes.' The picture was as follows: 'Pompey, appearing not to attack Caesar and instead to be proposing an arrangement that he considers favourable to him, claims that it is Curio who is stirring up trouble'; in reality, he was the one against, fearing that Caesar might be elected consul before he had relinquished his army and provinces. Curio, in response, was disputing every act of his opponent's third consulship. 'I assure you of one thing: if they use every means to try to be rid of Curio, Caesar will come to the aid of his tribune; if however, as seems likely, they are afraid, then Caesar will remain as long as he chooses.'

Why the deadline of 13 November? An interesting theory suggests that, by offering Caesar four months more than what he felt was right (30 July), Pompey wanted to dissuade him from standing as candidate *in absentia* during the summer of 50.[46]

But as June approached, the Senate came to accept this possibility. When the problem of the veto came up for debate, Marcus Claudius Marcellus (consul in the previous year), who had to speak first, proposed they should negotiate with the tribunes of the plebs, but a large majority of the Senate was against the idea. 'Our "Great" Pompey' now had 'such a delicate stomach' that he could scarcely find 'anything that he liked', and it was decided 'to accept the admission as candidate of one who intended to give up neither army nor provinces'.[47] Caelius ended: 'how Pompey takes it I shall tell you when I know; what will become of the *res publica*, whether he has no care about it or makes an armed resistance, will be a matter for you rich old men'.

Despite these developments, Caesar remained in Transalpine Gaul, moving to Cisalpine Gaul after the consular elections. There are many possible explanations: his determination to finish his work in Belgic Gaul, the hope of obtaining a similar privilege the following year, the need to reach an agreement over and above the consulship of 49, when – on the basis of the law conceived by Pompey in 52 – he would have found himself a 'private citizen' for five whole years.[48]

At the elections, Caesar's candidate for the consulship, the ex-legate Galba, was defeated. It is hard to understand the reference in the *Commentaries* to the injustice of the verdict; the winners, as already recorded, were Gaius Claudius Marcellus, certainly a supporter of Pompey, and Lentulus Crus, heavily in debt, who may well have been bought off by Caesar, and even 'could not survive if the *res publica* survived'.[49]

Antony, on the other hand, won the tribunician election for 49 and defeated Ahenobarbus for the augurate, which had become vacant after the death of the orator Hortensius. Plutarch claims that – as in the previous tribunician election – it was the work of Curio, who had brought his friend over to Caesar's side and now used his words and money on his behalf. As augur 'he took office straightaway and made himself most useful to those who supported Caesar politically'.[50] In early August, Caelius sent Cicero another letter from which the new climate emerged.

> Your eyes would never have been sore again if you had seen the face of Domitius [Ahenobarbus] at the news of his defeat. Those were crowded assemblies; and the support for the candidates was wholly consistent with party loyalties. Only very few gave their support in accordance with their personal relationships.[51]

The political struggle had become polarized according to party allegiances and not friendships: the game was getting tough, and the ruling classes had understood this. Caelius and a large part of the Roman populace were now on Caesar's side.

7

WINDS OF CIVIL WAR

Never has the city been in greater danger, never has the rabble had a more determined leader. Certainly, on our side too, very serious preparation is being made and this is being done under the firm and active leadership of our Pompey, who has begun to fear Caesar too late.

Cicero, *ad familiares*, 16,11,3

This chapter will take us to the start of that fateful year 49, when matters would come to a head with no turning back. Cicero's correspondence reveals the confusion, indecision and opportunism of many leading figures. In the background, as always, Rome and its fickle moods.

A PROPOSAL FROM CAESAR

War was now in the air. Caelius wrote to Cicero, again in August 50, that he saw no prospect of peace: Pompey was determined not to let Caesar become consul before leaving his army and provinces, whereas Caesar was convinced 'that he cannot protect himself if he relinquishes his army'.[1] Caesar, however, proposed a compromise: 'that both should give up their armies'. How could their own interests be best safeguarded? Caelius – sure that Cicero would face the same problem – reflected on his own position: he felt bound by gratitude and friendship to Caesar's followers; he detested the others while admiring their cause. He then added a few words of advice.

> It won't have escaped you – I imagine – that in civil disputes the more respectable side should be followed, so long as it is a political struggle, fought without weapons; but when it comes to armed conflict, then you have to choose the stronger side and prefer the party that is safer. In the present conflict, it is clear to me that Gnaeus Pompeius will have on his side the Senate and those who sit on the juries;[2] Caesar will be joined by all those who are torn between fear and hope for the worst; as for his army, there is no comparison. All in all, we have time enough to weigh their respective forces and to choose a side. [. . .] In short, you'll ask me how I think it's going to end. Unless one of the two goes off to the Parthian war, I see serious trouble ahead; and their decision will be down to the force of arms. Both are ready, physically and in morale. If only it could be accomplished without your personal risk, the spectacle that Fortune has in store for you is great and entertaining.[3]

Many others must have felt the same.

Caesar's proposal – that both should relinquish their armies – would be suggested again in autumn and winter. It may have been formulated for the first time between May and early summer. Appian in fact dates it after the meeting of the Senate in which the request of the then consul Gaius Claudius Marcellus was obstructed by the silence of his colleague Paullus. 'Curio [. . .] proposed that Pompey, like Caesar, should also abandon his provinces and army'; many were against it since Pompey's period of command had not yet ended, and the tribune himself knew that Pompey wouldn't have left office, and that the people were ill-disposed to him due to the trials for *ambitus*. The crowd praised Curio as the only person who tried to remove the enmity between the two and 'on one occasion followed him home showering him with flowers as though he were the victor in a great and difficult contest'.[4]

Appian goes on to record that Pompey, while convalescing, sent a letter to the Senate in which he praised Caesar's exploits, referred to his own, and stated that – once he had terminated the duties assigned to him – he would be happy to return the legions ahead of time.[5] Once back in Rome, he said he was sure Caesar would do the same, knowing that successors to Caesar would be chosen, while he could limit himself to a promise. Curio – again on an unspecified date – is said to have opposed him, saying that 'he should not be making promises but leaving office, nor depriving Caesar of his army before he too had become a private citizen'. He accused Pompey 'of aspiring to tyranny' and proposed 'to declare both as enemies unless they complied, and to muster an army to send against them'; in this way it didn't seem as though he'd been corrupted by Caesar. Pompey, angered and uttering threats, went off to an estate on the outskirts of Rome; before the end of the session, the senators voted only 'that Caesar and Pompey should each send one legion to Syria'. One doubtful but curious piece of news suggests that Pompey, to defend himself from Curio's eloquence, had gone to a school of rhetoric. In fact, during the previous months, over a period hard to identify, he had been away from Rome. In early November he was staying in Neapolis, where he received a visit from Atticus, who asked him what he thought about the request for a triumph made by Cicero (and meanwhile obstructed by many, including Cato).

Pompey seemed favourable, but he had other concerns. *Terra Italia* – not the city of Rome – had sent him what must have seemed like a clear judgement. During his illness, following the example of Neapolis, it had made votive offerings and had then rejoiced at his recovery. Plutarch recounts that, throughout Italy, 'every city, whether large or small, held festivals for many days'. The roads, the villages, the ports were thronged with people who feasted and made sacrifices. They greeted him with chaplets on their heads and lighted torches, strewing flowers over the ground.

It is said that this was one of the main causes of the civil war: Pompey 'was overcome with pride and with an immense joy, which gained the better over objective considerations that the situation required'.[6]

Meanwhile, during his absence, important decisions had been taken by the Senate, such as wages for his troops and the allocation of legions to Bibulus, who was fighting the Parthians. The second resolution, taken in May, put an end to the question that had dragged on since the previous year: having received rewards and wages, Caesar's two legions arrived in *terra Italia* led by Appius Claudius Pulcher, perhaps the elder of Clodius' nephews. Probably on Caesar's instructions, he claimed that all the troops of Gaul now hated their commander.

The ruling class remained uneasy. Another difficult question was the activity of the censors, Piso (consul in 58 and Caesar's father-in-law) and Appius Claudius Pulcher (consul in 54). The latter – far from 'censorious' when it came to his own previous lifestyle – had allied himself to Pompey when a daughter of his had married Pompey's eldest son, Gnaeus. He carried out his office with great severity.[7] His victims included knights and senators, and in this way 'he made all of them move to Caesar's party'; among these was the future historian Sallust. His colleague Piso, together with the consul Paullus, then intervened in defence of Curio. Appius Claudius didn't expel him, but said publicly in the Senate what he thought of him, 'so that Curio, in rage, tore his clothes'. The consul Gaius Claudius Marcellus, hoping to exploit the situation against Caesar, proposed that each express their view, but seeing that the majority was on the side of Curio, 'leaving the Senate he went to see Pompey, who was on the outskirts of the city. To him, on his own initiative, without there being any formal decree, he entrusted the defence of the city and the command of two legions of citizens'. These last events happened later and relate to quite a different matter, but the climate of tension is clearly apparent.

Cicero, now far away, wouldn't have scorned the compromise, but the news that reached him in October, if true, was 'really terrifying'; in short, 'Caesar is not prepared on any account to dismiss his army; three praetors-elect, the tribune of the plebs Quintus Cassius Longinus and the consul Lentulus are ready to side with him; Pompey intends to abandon Rome.'[8] What did he mean by this?

We must limit ourselves, for the moment, to observing that the question had grown very serious. In mid-October he admitted to his friend that he felt a 'sad surprise at the news you gave me about Caesar's legions'.[9] Prospects were grim: 'if that god who rescued us from a war against the Parthians more safely than we could have hoped doesn't turn his gaze to the *res publica*, I see an enormous struggle ahead, such as we have never had before'.[10] For Cicero, a personal difficulty emerges for the first time, which would long remain with him. He had recently approached the two contenders, receiving a letter from both: he would never have imagined that a rift could develop between them. Now, instead, a terrible conflict, 'and each of them thinks I'm on his side'.[11]

What to do now? Not in the extreme and hypothetical case of a war, which would have seen him on Pompey's side, but in that absolutely certain case of a debate in the Senate: 'can the candidature of an absent person be accepted? Does he have to dismiss his army? "Speak, Marcus Tullius". What can I reply: "Wait, I beg you, until I've spoken with Atticus"?'[12] In mid-October, he wrote to his wife Terentia that matters were now turning to war and that, once he was back, it would no longer be possible to pretend otherwise; he would return in haste, 'so that we can more easily decide together all that has to be done'.[13]

What was going on? A letter of 15 October confirms the – unfounded – rumour that Caesar would be arriving that day 'at Placentia [present-day Piacenza] with four legions'.[14] At the time of the 13 November deadline, we still have no information on the exact whereabouts of the conqueror of Gaul. Cicero landed at Brundisium on 25 November. Soon after, he wrote to his freedman Tiro, who had been left in Patrae (present-day Patras) recovering from an illness: 'at Rome I fear that from 1 January there will be serious disturbances'.[15]

THE CONTRADICTIONS OF THE SENATE

And so we come to the Senate meeting of 1 December 50. Not only was it tense but the sources often confuse it with the meeting that took place a month later, on 1 January 49, as well as with a *contio* held by Antony on 21 December 50.

According to the most reliable account, that of Appian,[16] the consul at that time, Gaius Claudius Marcellus, obtained the Senate's approval for the sending of a successor to Caesar. Curio did not exercise his veto because he wanted to present a similar motion in relation to Pompey. The consul Marcellus prevented him from doing so and asked if Pompey should abandon his command. The Senate said no. Curio then put forward a third motion: that both should give up their troops. The Senate approved, by 370 votes to 22. Marcellus broke up the assembly shouting that Caesar would become a tyrant. According to some sources, Curio was cheered as he left the hall and showered once again with flowers. Plutarch also reports that the Senate dressed itself in mourning.[17]

There was probably a new meeting of the Senate shortly after that one. The consul Marcellus proposed that the army stationed at Capua (the two legions mobilized for the Parthian war) be sent against Caesar. It was said that he had crossed the Alps in arms – according to Marcellus with 'ten legions'[18] – and would soon be invading Rome. Curio objected, stating that the news was false, at which point Marcellus and his colleague went to Pompey's villa on the outskirts of Rome and held out a sword, saying: 'I and my colleague order you to march against Caesar in defence of the nation; for this purpose we give you the army that is now at Capua and in the rest of Italy, and we authorize you to recruit another, as large as you wish.' Pompey obeyed the order, but added: '"If there is no better!", with some pretence or cunning, even then to make a good impression.'[19]

Who accompanied Marcellus? Appian appears to be referring to his colleague (therefore Paullus, but this seems unlikely, since he supported Caesar). According to Plutarch it was the consul-elect Lentulus Crus, whereas Cassius Dio indicates both consuls-elect (therefore Gaius Claudius Marcellus too).

Appian adds that Curio could no longer use his veto since his powers stopped outside the city boundary, but he publicly deplored what had happened and called upon the consuls (perhaps the consuls-elect) to tell their fellow citizens not to obey the military levy. By the time Caesar had reached the end of his mandate he was at Ravenna, on the border of *terra Italia*. The new college of tribunes, which had taken office on 10 December, as it did every year, had two of his supporters: Antony and Quintus Cassius Longinus (previously Pompey's quaestor in Spain in 54). Plutarch in this respect states that Antony opposed Marcellus when 'he wanted to let Pompey have the soldiers already recruited and to give him power to carry out other levies', demanding that the troops be sent to Syria and that those being recruited should not follow the proconsul;[20] yet we cannot give an exact date to this episode, which may have taken place in the early months of 49.

The gaps in historiographical accounts are once again filled out by Cicero's remarks during his journey to Rome – though he couldn't have entered the city if he wanted to receive the triumph (a move that would have lost him his *imperium*). Many questions rose in Cicero's mind. Why was Caesar's command extended? Why 'so much struggle to make ten tribunes propose allowing someone absent to stand as candidate'?[21] This had strengthened him to such a point 'that the hope of resisting him must now be placed in a single man: one whom it would have been better not to have let grow so much in power, instead of having to stand up to him now that he can do everything!' Caesar was a man 'of supreme daring, hardened to every risk' and:

I see that wavering towards his side are all those branded by some conviction or by dishonour, those who would deserve conviction or dishonour; and nearly all young men, and all the dregs of the city, and tribunes with influence added to whom is one Quintus[22] Cassius, and all those weighed down by debts, a band more numerous than you'd believe: his cause lacks only a cause, it has plenty of everything else. I see that everyone here is doing all they can to avoid an armed conflict, whose outcome is always uncertain and now also more dangerous for the opposing side.[23]

On 10 December, Cicero on his way to Rome, met Pompey, who was in Campania for the military levies. Pompey told him he was pleased he had returned from Cilicia and urged him to press his claim for the triumph. 'On the political situation he expressed himself in such terms as though war was already decided. No hope of agreement.'[24] He had been partly convinced of this by a recent event: Hirtius had been sent to Rome on Caesar's behalf but had not been to visit him. He had arrived on the evening of 6 December, was due to meet Scipio Nasica for discussions before dawn on 7 December, but had left during the night to rejoin Caesar. This seemed certain proof of a rift. The meeting had been arranged by Lucius Cornelius Balbus, an aristocrat from Gades (present-day Cadiz) who had gained Roman citizenship (later challenged in 56 but without success, thanks to Cicero's defence). He was now one of Caesar's main agents in Rome, in the role of financier and banker.

Cicero's concerns grew: 'honest men cannot reach agreement over what to think'.[25] Members of the order of knights and senators criticized Pompey and his journey. There was a need for peace; a victory would bring 'much trouble, but above all a tyrant'.

To avoid a war, Cicero, like many others, was in favour of letting Caesar have whatever he wanted. His demands were certainly 'shameless', but perhaps '[milder] than we expected'.[26] It was now too late to resist, and the earlier concessions had been far more damaging.

Someone, however, must have had a particular job in mind for Cicero. Before 19 December he had been told that Pompey and his advisers wanted to send him to Sicily, owing to the *imperium* that was still vested in him. He thought the decision strange: 'neither Senate decree nor popular mandate have granted me an *imperium* for Sicily'; if then the *res publica* delegated the choice to Pompey, 'why send me instead of any other individual?'[27] 'If this command becomes too onerous, I can always enter the first city gate I happen to see': a solution which, in formal terms, is unexceptionable but not very heroic – entry into the *pomerium* would have automatically put an end to his *imperium*.

Cicero also had an opportunity to consider the role of institutions and organized groups. 'Honourable men' existed individually, 'but in civil conflicts there is a need for parties and classes of decent people'.[28] Who, though? Could a Senate that left the provinces without governors and failed to keep control over Curio be said to have protected the public good? Could the *publicani*, never decisive but at that time 'most devoted to Caesar', have done so? Not to mention the bankers and farmers, never hostile to 'any form of government provided they are left in peace'.[28] There was nothing more to be done: 'we should have resisted him when he was weak, and it would have been easy; whereas now he has eleven legions, all the cavalry he wants: on his side are the Transpadanians, the city popu-lace, so many tribunes of the plebs, young men so desperate'.[30]

But what was Caesar doing? In Ravenna, perhaps after 13 December, he was due to meet Curio, who brought him the latest news from Rome: he thanked him and allowed him to join his council. The ex-tribune was urging him to march on Rome, but Caesar still wanted to negotiate.

One of his proposals, hard to date, is described by Suetonius (who, however, still places him in Transalpine Gaul) and confirmed by Plutarch and Appian. Suetonius also mentions a letter – perhaps connected – in which he is supposed to have begged the Senate 'not to deny him a priv-ilege granted him by the people, or to order the other generals to resign their command as well'.[31] Suetonius comments that, if the need arose, he counted on being able to mobilize his veterans more rapidly than Pompey could enlist new troops.

He had offered to leave Transalpine Gaul on condition that he kept Cisalpine Gaul with two legions or, alternatively, Illyricum and one legion (Suetonius), or Cisalpine Gaul and Illyricum and two legions (Appian); other versions suggest that Cicero himself, soon after his return, had proposed that Caesar kept Illyricum with two legions or had supported Caesar's proposal, namely Cisalpine Gaul and Illyricum with two legions (though Plutarch, in *Caesar*, refers to *tágmata*, cohorts), before then entering negotiations to persuade Caesar's followers to be content with two provinces and 6,000 men (Plutarch, Caesar).[32] Velleius Paterculus, meanwhile, talks in general terms about a legion and provincial governorship[33]. Pompey, in any event, was not averse to such conditions – a view not shared, however, by consuls and senators.

Pompey had already had another meeting with Cicero, still on his slow way to Rome, on 25 December; they travelled together to Formiae and had the opportunity for a long private conversation. Regarding a reconciliation, Cicero felt, 'he also lacks the will'.[34] Pompey thought that if Caesar became consul, even having disbanded his army, he would undermine the *res publica*. He predicted instead that, once he (Caesar) had heard what was being prepared against him, he would leave things as they were for that year, keeping his army and province. If not, Pompey wouldn't feel unduly upset. Cicero was reassured by that 'strong, able man of such authority who talked like a statesman about the dangers of a mock peace'.[35] They had the text of the speech given by Antony in a *contio* of 21 December: it was an attack on Pompey, from the very start of his career, with threats of war. Pompey concluded: 'what do you think Caesar himself is capable of doing when he seizes the *res publica*, if one of his quaestors without influence or resources has the courage to speak like this?'[36] Pompey seemed afraid of peace. 'In my opinion he is forced to that viewpoint by the fear of having to leave Rome.'

Cicero had also borrowed money from Caesar. This probably dated back to 51; it was an amount equivalent to 820,000 sesterces, for the return of which he had authorized his friend Atticus to incur a new debt with Gaius Oppius and Balbus, Caesar's bankers, at a higher rate of interest. He was now annoyed at having to pay, 'handing over for this what should have served for my triumph. But it is unthinkable to be indebted to an adversary.'

Other information is confused: Plutarch also mentions a letter read out by Antony to the crowd – but this is probably the one then taken by Curio to the Senate on 1 January 49 – relating to the difficulty Pompey had in recruiting soldiers, since everyone wanted peace.

At the end of the year, Cicero, still holding these opinions, sketched out all possible outcomes in the form of a *suasoria* – a rhetorical exercise that sought to discuss the options.

> Here are the cases that can be presented: either of Caesar being allowed to stand for consul and being authorized – by the Senate or the tribunes of the plebs – to keep his army; or that he is persuaded to relinquish his army and province to have the consulship; if he cannot be persuaded to do this, he shall accept that the elections be held without speaking about his candidature, but he shall keep command of the province; or, while remaining silent, he shall conduct his opposition by means of tribunes and there is an *interregnum*; or using the excuse of his candidature not being accepted, he mobilizes the army, and there is war. And will he start this immediately taking advantage of our insufficient preparation or when his supporters, in the election meetings, have attempted without success to have a law that allows his claim? And will he resort to arms only for that refusal, or for whatsoever reason; that, for example, a tribune censured for having been obstructive at the Senate and having incited the people, or even, by decree of the Senate, limited in his powers, or suspended, or expelled has fled to him protesting against his expulsion? And, when hostilities have begun, will it be better to defend the city or abandon it so as to prevent him having any supplies and other reinforcements? Of all those evils, one or other of which will have to be suffered, what seems to you the least?[37]

Cicero was talking of abandoning Rome. What did this mean?

THE DRAMATIC BEGINNINGS OF 49

Caesar's *Commentaries on the Civil War* open with the Senate debate of 1 January 49.[38]

A letter from Caesar had been delivered to the new consuls, Lentulus Crus and Gaius Claudius Marcellus, but it was only after much insistence from the tribunes that it was read to the Senate. However there was no discussion of its contents. Instead, the new consuls reported on the political situation. Lentulus Crus assured his support for the supreme assembly and the *res publica*, but only if the senators wanted 'to express their view with courage and determination'. If, on the other hand, they had regard to Caesar, as in the past, he would proceed alone, considering himself released from the authority of the Senate: he too could seek refuge in Caesar's favour and friendship. Scipio Nasica spoke in much the same way: 'Pompey has no intention of abandoning the *res publica* if the Senate follows him; if it hesitates and acts too half-heartedly, in vain shall they beg his help when they later need it.' The *Commentaries* observe that the speech seemed to come from the lips of his son-in-law, Pompey, who was at the city gates.

More prudent opinions were also expressed, such as that of Marcus Claudius Marcellus (consul in 51): 'the question should not have been put to the Senate until a general levy had been made throughout Italy and armies recruited'; only then could it be decided freely and with certainty. Marcus Calidius (who, as praetor in 57, pressed for Cicero's recall from exile) and Caelius (aedile in 50 and Cicero's correspondent), in putting forward similar arguments, suggested instead 'that Pompey should depart for his provinces, thus eliminating any cause for conflict': Caesar feared that the two legions taken from him were being 'kept by Pompey in the vicinity of Rome to be used against him'. But Lentulus Crus shouted and hurled insults at them, refusing to put Calidius' motion to the vote. Marcellus, in fear, withdrew his own. 'The clamours of the consuls, the dread of the army at the gates, the menaces of

Pompey's friends' convinced the majority of senators, who associated themselves against their will with Scipio's motion: 'BY A CERTAIN DATE[39] CAESAR SHALL DISBAND HIS ARMY; IF HE FAILS TO DO SO, HE SHALL BE DECLARED A REBEL OF THE *RES PUBLICA*.' The tribunes Antony and Quintus Cassius exercised their veto, and this was immediately debated. 'Violent are the opinions expressed: the more fierce and ruthless they are, the more they stir the applause of Caesar's enemies.' Yet it is interesting to note that, according to the *Commentaries*, senators, and perhaps also Caesar, thought, at that moment, that the two legions would be used by Pompey to guard the city.

The other sources provide other details.

While Caesar would later speak of 'very modest' requests, Cicero describes the letter as 'harsh and menacing'.[40] He later confirms, in a letter of August or September 46, that Marcus Claudius Marcellus (consul in 51) never had 'the slightest confidence in the way the civil war was conducted, nor in Pompey's forces, nor in the quality of his army', a view with which he would then agree.[41]

Other sources described how Caesar's letter was delivered and read, giving further and conflicting details. According to Plutarch, it was Antony who read it (in front of the people, in *Caesar* and in *Pompey*). Appian reports that it was delivered to the new consuls – on the first day of the year,[42] as they were entering the Senate (assembled not in the Temple of Jupiter Capitolinus, as usual, but in the *bouleutérion*, the Curia) – by Curio, on his arrival from Ravenna, 'after travelling 2,300 stadia in three days'.[43] It contained 'a proud list of all that Caesar had done throughout his career' and declared his wish to relinquish his office together with Pompey; but if Pompey 'retained power he would not withdraw and would come quickly to avenge the wrongs against his country and himself'. Once again according to Appian, all the senators 'shouted that it was a declaration of war and as his successor they appointed Ahenobarbus, who immediately left the city with 4,000 men recruited with the levy';[44] the tribunes Antony and Quintus Cassius, however, supported Caesar's proposal. Other details are given in Cassius Dio.[45] Curio did not deliver the letter 'to the consuls until they had reached the Senate, for fear that, having received it outside, they might hide it'. Even so, they hesitated and only made it public because they were forced to by Antony and Cassius. It proposed the discharge of the two armies. The Senate voted: no one wanted Pompey to dismiss his troops – stationed nearby – but everyone, except Caelius and Curio, voted for Caesar to dismiss his; the decisions were blocked however by the veto of Antony and Cassius.

The opposition of the tribunes created further problems. Once again, it is difficult to reconstruct what happened. Caesar himself condenses the events.[46]

Once the assembly had ended on the evening of 1 January, the senators – or, perhaps, only his supporters – were called by Pompey, who praised and encouraged those who stood firm and reprimanded and goaded the waverers. From every part, he summoned soldiers from old armies, promising them rewards and promotion, and drawing many from the legions handed over by Caesar. 'The city and the Comitium itself, close to the Curia, was crowded with military tribunes, centurions, recalled veterans.' Assembled in the Senate, moreover, were 'all the friends of the consuls, clients of Pompey and those who bore old grudges against Caesar'; the crowd put fear into the weak and encouraged the hesitant; most were deprived of any ability to express themselves freely. Piso (then censor and Caesar's father-in-law) and Lucius Roscius Fabatus (then praetor and Caesar's former legate) offered to go and visit Caesar, asking for six days to carry out their mission.

Some agreed in sending ambassadors to Caesar to inform him of the Senate's decision. But they were opposed by Lentulus Crus, Scipio Nasica and Cato, the last of whom bore an old grudge from his election defeat (for the consulship for 51). Lentulus Crus, heavily in debt, was moved by the hope 'of having in hand an army and provinces, of enriching himself with the gifts of candidates to various realms': he also bragged among his followers that he could become a second Sulla. Scipio Nasica was urged on by the hope of having a province and armies, to be shared with Pompey through their family ties, as well as his fear of criminal proceedings. Pompey too, encouraged by Caesar's enemies, unwilling to accept a power equal to his own, 'had broken every bond of friendship with him', joining with common enemies, 'most of whom he himself had drawn towards Caesar during the time of their kinship'. Furthermore, fearing dishonour for having taken over the legions destined for Asia and Syria, now 'an instrument of his own control', he saw war as the only solution. Everything now happened in haste and in confusion: Caesar's relatives couldn't keep him informed, nor could the tribunes ward off danger with their entreaties or retain 'their ultimate right of veto, which not even Sulla had touched'. Only seven days after their arrival in office, they had to think about their own survival, 'whereas the wildest tribunes until then had begun to protect themselves and be afraid only after seven or eight months in office'.

Other sources generally ignore this moment. Only Cassius Dio mentions an obstruction by Antony and Quintus Cassius that lasted from 2 January until they were expelled from the Senate. Let us try to reconstruct.

There were no sittings of the Senate on 3 and 4 January, which were comitial days. Meetings probably took place on 2, 5 and 6 January, and reached no conclusion.

Cicero finally arrived on 4 January, to be greeted by a large crowd, but 'fell into a true blaze of civil discord, or rather of war'. His desire to resolve the situation was hampered by many, on one side and the other, who wanted war. Caesar himself had 'sent a severe and menacing letter to the Senate and still has the impudence to retain his army and a province against the will of the Senate'.[47]

Cicero began negotiations, as he recalled in a letter sent to a friend in October 46. He had 'argued that Pompey should leave for Spain'; he had not insisted 'that Caesar should be lawfully entitled to stand as candidate in his absence', but that 'such candidature in fact be allowed, given that this was the will of the people upon pressure from Pompey himself, when he was in office as consul'; the excuse for war having presented itself, he had tried in every way to make his warnings heard, convinced 'that peace, even the most inequitable, was nevertheless preferable to the most just of wars'.[48]

What was his real involvement? We might detect it in the negotiations that had already begun over the number of provinces and legions that Caesar could retain. However, we should rule out the idea that, in order to take part in the meetings of the Senate, he had entered the *pomerium*.

These questions, as well as the proposal of a mission, might have been debated on 5 and 6 January, in a Senate already hampered by the veto of Antony and Quintus Cassius.

A *SENATUS CONSULTUM ULTIMUM* AND THE ORGANIZATION OF 'RESISTANCE'

A further, dramatic turn of events took place in the assembly of 7 January, which produced a *senatus consultum ultimum*. Caesar's version, despite its brevity, reports the wording:

> In the end it resorted to the extreme measure, to that Senate decree to which proponents never before had dared to stoop, except when Rome was so to speak under threat of conflagration and there was no further hope of general salvation: CONSULS, PRAETORS, TRIBUNES OF THE PEOPLE, PROCONSULS, WHO FIND THEMSELVES IN THE VICINITY OF ROME SHALL ENSURE THAT THE *RES PUBLICA* SUFFERS NO HARM. This is ordered by the Senate decree of 7 January.[49]

Once again, the decree – alluding to Pompey in its reference to proconsuls in the vicinity of Rome – was aimed first of all, in its original intention, at defending the city, as also emerged from Caesar's remarks to soldiers at Ariminum on 11 or 12 January. Caesar then recalls the tribunes who fled to join him. He was at Ravenna, waiting for an answer to his 'very modest requests, in the hope that human justice might re-establish the peace'.[50]

A more explicit confirmation of the unusual position of Pompey – a proconsul assisted in his delicate task by consuls – is provided by the *Periochae*, the ancient surviving summary of the lost books of Livy: 'the Senate entrusted the consuls and Gnaeus Pompeius with power to ensure that the *res publica* came to no harm'.[51]

Historiographical sources allow us to reconstruct other details about the unsuccessful opposition of the tribunes, though the order of events is not clear.

Plutarch mentions only a change of dress (the black of mourning, a mark of protest) by the Senate (in *Pompey*), and also the tribunes' expul-sion and escape (in *Caesar* and in *Antony* but not in *Pompey*), which gave Caesar his long-awaited opportunity.

Appian, despite a lively description, doesn't mention the *senatus consultum ultimum* and compresses events which took place in the period 1–7 January.[52] After the public reading of Caesar's letter, after the scandal it caused and Ahenobarbus' dispatch to Gaul, Antony and Quintus Cassius supported the proposal of the rebel proconsul; the Senate, 'with even greater resentment, declared Pompey's army as its own protector, and that of Caesar a public enemy'. The consuls then 'ordered Antony and Quintus Cassius to leave the Senate, lest, despite being tribunes, some harm might come to them'. Antony 'sprang from his chair shouting, and calling on the gods as witnesses to his magistracy which, sacred and inviolable, was being insulted', and to the tribunes themselves who, having made a constructive proposal, 'had been driven out with violence, they who had committed no crime nor any sacrilege'. Having left the building 'like a man possessed, prophesying war, slaughter, proscription, banishment, confiscation and the worst evils that were coming to them', he hurled curses against the perpetrators. With him went Curio and Quintus Cassius: 'soldiers from Pompey's army could already be seen around the Curia'. In great haste, 'that same night, disguised as slaves, they went secretly to Caesar on a hired wagon.'

Cassius Dio, having also recorded the tribunes' veto on 2 January, reconstructs the events as follows.[53] The Senate voted to change dress (into mourning); the tribunes opposed it, but the decision was officially recorded and carried out: 'everyone immediately left the Senate, changed dress and returned to deliberate on the punishment of the tribunes'. The tribunes sought to resist. Then, 'out of fear, provoked especially by the fact that Lentulus Crus had asked them to leave before the vote, they spoke at length and protested'. Now eliminated from the number of senators, 'they left for Caesar's camp, together with Curio and Caelius'. The defence of the city was then entrusted to the consuls and other magistrates, 'as was the custom'; having left the *pomerium* to visit Pompey, they declared a state of emergency (*taraché*) and entrusted the treasury and troops to him; at the same time they ordered Caesar to hand over command to his successors and dismiss his armies 'by a specific date, or else be considered an enemy, as one who was acting against his country'.

On the night of 7 January, Antony, Quintus Cassius and Curio left Rome to join Caesar. With them was Caelius, who a year later would write to Cicero: 'that night when on leaving for Rimini I came to see you, you behaved like the most courteous of citizens, entrusting me with a message of peace for Caesar'.[54]

The notion that the tribunes had been forced to flee – a version favourable to Caesar's propaganda – is rejected by Cicero in a letter sent to Tiro on 12 January: 'Antony and Quintus Cassius, without however being driven out by force, left, together with Curio, to join Caesar after the decision of the Senate to give consuls, praetors, tribunes and proconsuls the power to ensure the safety of the *res publica*'.[55] Who should we believe?

Most of the appointments over the next few days were made at meetings of the Senate held outside the *pomerium* so that Pompey could take part. Once again we start with Caesar's account, which continues however to condense the events of several days.[56]

Pompey confirmed what he had already communicated through the words of Scipio Nasica, praising the courage and firmness of the Senate and numbering his own forces. He stated that ten of his legions were ready and that he knew Caesar's soldiers were hostile to their commander. The Senate discussed making levies throughout Italy, sending the proquaestor or propraetor Faustus Sulla (Pompey's son-in-law) to Mauretania, funding Pompey from the public treasury. It was also discussed whether Juba I (king of Numidia) should be declared an ally and friend, a proposal opposed by the consul Gaius Claudius Marcellus. The tribune Lucius Marcius Philippus vetoed the sending of Faustus Sulla (who remained in Italy to muster troops before later joining Pompey in Epirus). Senate decrees were made on other questions; 'private citizens are appointed to the government of provinces, two are declared consular, the others praetorian'. Through the drawing of lots, Scipio Nasica was sent to Syria, Ahenobarbus to Gaul. Lucius Marcius Philippus (father of the tribune of the same name and consul in 56, a relative of Caesar) and Lucius Aurelius Cotta (consul in 65 and Caesar's maternal uncle) were left aside, 'following an agreement made in private, and their names were not even thrown into the urn for the draw'. Praetors were sent to the other provinces. 'Without waiting (according to the custom of previous years) for their investiture to be presented for the approval of the people, they put on their red cloak of command, celebrate the sacrifices and leave'. It is followed by remarks about the exceptional and unlawful nature of those events.

Appian – the only historiographical source to speak about these later meetings – adds further details.[57] The Senate, thinking that Caesar's army would arrive late and that meanwhile the rebel would remain where he was, ordered Pompey to assemble 130,000 Italic soldiers, choosing above all veterans, as well as mercenaries from neighbouring countries. For the cost of the war, it placed the whole public treasury in his hands, ordering that private and public assets be used for the same purpose, if need be; furthermore, 'with most urgent haste, it sent envoys into the cities to collect other money, with wrath and determination'.

Cicero, on the same 12 January, wrote to Tiro the words that appear at the beginning of this chapter; he added that, in the midst of such disorders, the Senate had voted by a broad majority to celebrate his triumph, but 'the consul Lentulus, to give greater weight to his good offices, said during the assembly that he would present a motion just as soon as the pressing problems of the *res publica* have been dealt with'; furthermore, Italy had 'been divided into military areas whose supervision is to be entrusted to each person. We have that of Capua.'[58] From several other sources we can infer that during those same days Pompey had sent ambassadors to Massilia to assure its loyalty and – perhaps less plausibly, seeing how events developed – had ordered the fortification of strongholds, even in Latium.

In any event, no one seems to have predicted the speed of Caesar's response.

PART III

FROM THE RUBICON TO THE SURRENDER OF ROME

8

THE RUBICON

Whoever you are bearing arms, leader, soldier, new recruit, stop, lay down your banner and your weapons and do not carry weapons and flags over this river! If anyone does so, he will be judged an enemy of the Roman people, as though he had taken up arms against his country and stolen the household gods.

Corpus Inscriptionum Latinarum, 11,30* (false inscription)

CAESAR'S VERSION

A couple of lightning moves made it clear how seriously the conqueror of Gaul had to be taken. The first move was his crossing of the southern boundary of Cisalpine Gaul at the head of an army (breaking the ban on leaving the province and, worse, entering *terra Italia* bearing arms, without the permission of the Senate). The second – and objectively more serious – was the capture of Ariminum, the first city on the road south.

Both took place on the same day, 11 or 12 January 49. There is no certainty about the date of these momentous events nor about what actually happened. The discrepancies among the sources require us to consider them one by one. We begin, of course, with Caesar's own account.[1]

On being told about the unprecedented flight of consuls from the city of Rome, about the military levies and seizure of money throughout

Italy, he addressed his soldiers – who, in his version, were still in Cisalpine Gaul (therefore at Ravenna) – recalling 'the injustices continually inflicted on him by his enemies', accusing Pompey of having been led astray by envy, whereas he had always supported him. He complained about the new precedent of armed repression of the tribunes' right of veto, which not even Sulla had challenged.

> The decree that ordered the magistrates to ensure that the *res publica* suffered no harm, this *senatus consultum*, in other words, which called the Roman people to arms, had been issued each time only to combat dangerous laws or in the event of violence by the tribunes, or plebeian secession, when temples and areas of high ground had been occupied; and Caesar shows how these former attempts were expiated by the ruin of Saturninus and the Gracchi. But nothing of this sort had then occurred, nothing had even been planned: no proposal of law, no attempt to call the assemblies, no secession.[2]

He then urged his soldiers to defend the reputation and honour of the general under whom, for nine years, they had gloriously served the *res publica*, had fought so many victorious battles, and pacified 'the whole of Gaul and Germany'. The men of Legio XIII were present: 'Caesar had sent for it as soon as the situation had become strained, the others hadn't yet been assembled.' They shouted in a single voice that they were ready to avenge the wrongs done to the general and to the tribunes. Caesar left with his troops for Ariminum and it was there that he met the tribunes, who sought his protection; he then summoned the other legions from their winter quarters, ordering them to join him.

From his account there emerge two disturbing silences and two probable fabrications.

There is no mention of crossing the Rubicon, an omission also shared by the letters of Cicero and the account of Cassius Dio, which both concentrate on his arrival at Ariminum; Cassius Dio notes only that

Caesar, in response to the assembly of 7 January, crossed 'for the first time the boundary of the region assigned to him'.[3] Caesar is also silent about the capture *manu militari* of Ariminum, referred to in the other sources (apart from Suetonius, who doesn't mention the city at all).

The two fabrications relate to the order of events. Caesar's *contio* before the men of Legio XIII took place, according to other authors, not at Ravenna, but after the crossing of the Rubicon (Suetonius) and more exactly at Ariminum (Lucan, Cassius Dio, Orosius), which at that time was occupied by troops acting in full complicity with their general. In some versions, the fugitive tribunes were also present (Lucan, Suetonius, Cassius Dio). In others, however, they were shown to the troops before the crossing of the Rubicon (Plutarch, *Caesar*), and probably at Ravenna (Appian). Orosius also states that the tribunes were already with Caesar at Ravenna, but Suetonius tells us that Caesar had been told about the *senatus consultum ultimum* before their arrival, whereas according to Caesar himself they joined him at Ariminum (as is confirmed by Caelius's letter to Cicero), even if he seems to indicate earlier that they were heading to join him at Ravenna.[4] What is more – and this fact is certain – the escape of the consuls from Rome and other associated measures were an effect, and not a cause, of Caesar's advance.

Despite what we might gather from Caesar, Cicero and Cassius Dio, seven other writers consider the armed crossing of the stream as a moment of transition from peace to war. Caesar's hesitation is said to have been accompanied by a series of supernatural events.

LUCAN'S VERSION

According to the poet Marcus Annaeus Lucanus (39 AD – 65 AD), better known as Lucan, author of the *Pharsalia*, an epic poem about the Civil War between Caesar and Pompey, Caesar 'leapt across the frozen Alps', conceiving 'his plan for great uprisings and the future war'. On reaching 'the narrow banks of the Rubicon' there appeared to him:

> the great image of his homeland
> in distress, clear in the dark night and with mournful face,
> and white hair flowing from her turreted head; she stood
> with torn locks and naked arms, and spoke between sobs:
> 'Where are you still heading, where are you carrying my flags
> O warriors? If you come lawfully, as citizens, you are allowed as far
>   as here.'[5]

Caesar shuddered, 'his hair stood on end and a torpor, which stopped him in his tracks, kept him at the bank of the stream'. Then, offering assurances of his peaceful intentions to Jupiter, god of thunder, who 'from the Tarpeian rock was watching over the walls of the great city', to the household gods of the *gens Julia*, Quirinus, Jupiter Latiaris, to the fires of Vesta and Rome itself, he 'broke the bonds of war and carried the flags swiftly across the swollen river'.[6] No information, though, about the size of his army.

The author at this point seems to move back, to offer the spectacular description of the crossing of the stream. The 'deep red Rubicon', which gushed from a modest spring and flowed with 'weak waves' in summer, was now strengthened by the winter, and 'the third moon with its crescent heavy with rain, and the thaw of the mountains [. . .] had swollen the waters'. At which:

> First the cavalry stood slantwise against the current to stop
> the waters; then the rest of the army could easily cross
> breaking the waves of the river already breached.
> Caesar, once over the waters, touched the opposite
> bank of Hesperia and paused on forbidden lands,
> 'Here' he said 'I relinquish peace and the violated laws;
> I follow you, O Fortune; pacts now vanish.
> We trusted in the fates, let the judgement of war prevail.'
> Having said this, the commander urges his men forward
> into the shadows of the night; he moves faster than the shot

hurled from a Balearic sling or the Parthian's arrow launched
behind, and marches menacing upon nearby Ariminum;
the stars, Lucifer now gone, were fleeing from the rays of the sun.[7]

Scholars don't seem to have noted that the cavalry manoeuvre described by the poet is hardly realistic. In reality, Caesar is said to have used a far more logical technique at least twice – in Gaul in 52, to cross the Loire, and in Spain in 48, to cross the Sicoris (the present-day Segre). Horsemen and pack animals, respectively, were used to create a 'corridor' – and certainly not a 'dam' – to prevent men crossing on foot from being swept away by the current.

Lucan also recounts that Ariminum, an ancient *colonia* established to resist attacks from Gaul, guardian 'of the gates of Latium',[8] was occupied in terror. Fortune helped the commander to legitimize the revolt: he was joined by the tribunes expelled from the Senate, accompanied by the 'impudent Curio with the venal tongue'[9], who urged him to act. Caesar assembled his soldiers and at some point recalled:

'Rome is shaken by a great tumult of war,
no less than if Hannibal the Punic had crossed the Alps:
they complete and strengthen the ranks of cohorts with recruits,
they cut down all the forests to fit a fleet, they order
that Caesar be hunted down by land and sea.'[10]

Among the unlawful acts of his enemies, he recalled the trial for the killing of Clodius, held while soldiers arrived inside the *pomerium*, 'camped out' in the 'terror-struck Forum', where 'the swords gleaming ominously encircled with a peculiar crown a tremulous courtroom', while Milo was surrounded by Pompey's banners.[11] After other accusations against Pompey, including his plan to become a dictator like Sulla (another constant theme), he refers to his soldiers' destinies. They should not be deprived of the just reward for their labours, even if he is robbed of his: 'these soldiers shall triumph, whoever leads them'; their 'tired old age' had a right to rest, nor would the pirates (of Pompey) become better colonists.[12] The reaction from the listeners, initially uncertain, was stirred by Laelius, the chief centurion of Legio XIII, who had been decorated – like Caesar himself – with oak leaves for saving a comrade's life. He went as far as claiming that he was ready, if so commanded, to kill his closest relatives and even:

> 'If you have me despoil the gods and burn down the temples,
> the army mint would melt down the statues of the gods;
> if you have me pitch camp by the banks of the Etruscan Tiber,
> I'll advance like a fearless marker of frontiers
> on Ausonian fields. Whatever walls you want flattened,
> the ram propelled by these arms will shatter its stones,
> even if the city you have ordered to destroy
> is Rome itself.' At which all cohorts shouted their assent,
> and with hands raised high, they pledged themselves
> to whatever war he summoned them.[13]

Was the siege of Rome – which then had 500,000 inhabitants – a real possibility? Did Lucan's historical sources – Livy and Lucius Annaeus Seneca 'the Elder' (c.54 BC – c.39 AD), grandfather of Lucan and author of a now lost *History of the Civil Wars* – contemplate it? Or was this only the late poetic reconstruction of a fervent 'republican', a young poet who lived and committed suicide under his hated master Nero? What did the soldiers who had crossed the Rubicon and occupied Ariminum really feel and expect? Did the men of Legio XIII – a legion recruited in the winter of 58/57 in Cisalpine Gaul, which had played a key role at the siege of Gergovia and probably in the victory at Alesia – really imagine they were ready for such an exploit, even with the reinforcements that were on their way? And, above all, were the Romans fearful that this could happen?

In our view, this plan must be categorically excluded, even if, unfortunately, later sources don't help us with the answer. Attention, indeed, is always focused on the protagonist or, at most, on the main antagonist. It is interesting, however, to note the many references to earlier 'marches on Rome'.

PLUTARCH'S VERSIONS

Between *Caesar* and *Pompey* there is no shortage of discrepancies.

In the first of these we read that Caesar's best pretext was offered by Antony and Curio (not Quintus Cassius), who were presented to the soldiers – it is not specified where, but would seem to be before the crossing of the Rubicon – as 'men of great prestige and magistrates who had fled in servile clothes on hired carts'.[14] Caesar had no more than 5,000 foot soldiers and 300 horsemen; a large part of the army was still on the other side of the Alps, waiting to be marched down by officers sent for that purpose. Relying on speed and surprise, Caesar ordered military tribunes and centurions to occupy Ariminum, using swords alone and seeking to limit the number of casualties. Having entrusted the army to his lieutenant Quintus Hortensius (perhaps son of the great orator), he spent the day in public, watching gladiatorial exercises. Just before evening he took a bath and 'then went into the banqueting room where he remained for a while with those he had invited to dinner, and rose from the table when it was getting dark'.[15] He spoke to everyone and told them to wait, as though he would be returning. However, he had ordered a few to follow him, by different routes. He climbed onto a hired cart 'and moved first in one direction; then changed road and went down towards Ariminum'.[16]

When he reached the river that marks the boundary between Cisalpine Gaul and the rest of Italy (this is the Rubicon) and began to reflect, now that he was closer to danger and was troubled by the magnitude of the venture he was about to carry out, he checked his speed; then he stopped and in silence, for long, he pondered for and against. At that moment he often changed his mind and considered many problems with his friends who were present, among whom was Asinius Pollio: he reflected upon the nature of the evils that such a crossing would bring for all men, and how much fame it would leave for posterity. Finally, on impulse, as if moving from reason he were hurling himself towards the future, uttering this which is a common saying to those who are preparing for a bold and difficult venture: 'Let the die be cast', he hastened across the river and then beyond, proceeding with great speed, before daybreak he fell upon Ariminum and captured it. They say that the night before crossing the Rubicon he had a monstrous dream: he thought he was having incestuous intercourse with his mother.[17]

Here, Gaius Asinius Pollio (76 BC–AD 4 or 5) makes his one and only appearance. He would later write an influential work of history in seventeen volumes – all now lost – which began in 60, covered the period of the civil wars and continued as far as the battles of Philippi (October 42) or Actium (September 31). There is no reference here, however, to the presence (presumably implied) of Caesar's army at the crossing of the stream; other sources date the dream to his time as quaestor.[18] The account then continues by describing how panic spread through Italy and to Rome, with no mention of his speech in Ariminum.

The same time period in *Pompey*:[19] immediately after referring to the breakdown of negotiations in the Senate, attempted also by Cicero, news reached Rome that Ariminum had been captured; it was also said that Caesar was marching 'directly on Rome with all his army'. This was false: 'for he was marching with no more than 300 horsemen and 5,000 foot soldiers', not having waited for the rest of the troops, who were still beyond the Alps, and preferring to fall suddenly upon his enemies and to surprise them. At the Rubicon he stopped and waited in silence, reflecting 'on the greatness of his daring'. Then, 'like those who throw themselves from a precipice into a deep abyss', he put an end to his reasoning and, 'closing his eyes before that unprecedented action, shouted only these words in Greek to those who were standing nearby: "Let the die be cast!" and he ordered his army to cross the river'.

Compared with *Caesar*, we have no mention of the tribunes meeting the soldiers, nor of the presence of Pollio, but instead that of the army that follows Caesar across the Rubicon. There is another piece of information – given nowhere else – that the famous phrase (found moreover in Greek comedy) was spoken in Greek. But there is no reference to the previous night's dream. It is followed by the panic unleashed in Italy but especially in Rome; and once again, there is no speech in Ariminum.

In *Antony*, however, the intervention of the tribunes is emphasized as a *casus belli*: as soon as they arrived before Caesar – it doesn't say whether in front of soldiers – they began to shout 'that in Rome there was no longer any constitutional order, since not even the tribunes of the people had any freedom of speech, but anyone who spoke in defence of justice was persecuted and placed his life at risk. Upon this, Caesar invaded Italy with his army.'[20]

Plutarch strongly influenced the later version of the twelfth-century Byzantine historian Joannes Zonaras, who describes the arrival of the tribunes, the outrage they caused in front of the soldiers, the famous phrase and Caesar's dream.

SUETONIUS' VERSION AND CAESAR'S REASONS

In comparison with the others, Suetonius' version is rather different. He also places the crossing of the Rubicon after the failure of negotiations with the Senate, preceding everything with an interesting background thought.[21]

The pretext – contrived by the proconsul who had crossed into Cisalpine Gaul and stopped at Ravenna after having terminated the judicial sittings – was to avenge his tribune allies. But there were probably a variety of other reasons. Pompey 'often repeated that Caesar had deliberately wanted to overturn and disrupt everything', being unable 'to bring to completion, at his own expense, the monuments already begun and to satisfy the hopes he had raised in the minds of the people for his return'; others said that he feared having to account for the illegalities of his first consulate. Cato, indeed, had said and sworn on several occasions 'that he would denounce and drag him to trial as soon as he had discharged his troops', and the people claimed that 'if he had returned as a private citizen he would have had to defend himself, like Milo, before the judges, surrounded by armed guards'. This would seem the most reliable version, since, according to Pollio, after the Battle of Pharsalus (or, more properly, of Pharsalia), on observing his dead opponents, he is supposed to have said: 'It was their choice! If I, Gaius Caesar, after having completed so many campaigns, had not resorted to the help of my soldiers, I would have seen myself condemned!'[22] Others thought that, having weighed up the forces in the field, he had seized the opportunity to take power, as he had wanted to do since his youth. This, continues Suetonius, must also have been the opinion of Cicero, who in the third book of *On Duties* relates how two lines of Euripides were always on Caesar's lips: 'If you have to violate justice, do it in order to govern; for any other motive respect the law.'[23]

The fear of a trial as Caesar's motivation to act has been seriously discussed by scholars: in particular it has been emphasized how, apart from declarations by Cato and Ahenobarbus, Cicero's correspondence never mentions this eventuality and, above all, that Caesar had the means to resist it. So it is generally felt that the insult he suffered – his humiliation by Pompey, mentioned several times also in the *Commentaries* – is sufficient reason to explain his action.

Let us return to Suetonius' account. On being warned that the tribunes' veto had been rejected and that they had quit Rome, Caesar ordered his cohorts 'to go ahead of him secretly so as not to arouse suspicion', then:

he went, so as to further divert attention, to watch a public spectacle and to examine the project for a school of gladiators that he intended to build. Then, as was his custom, he ate in much company and later, after sunset, having had the mules from a nearby mill harnessed to a cart, he set off in greatest secrecy and with a weak escort. But, in the darkness, he lost the road and wandered for a long time, until when, at dawn, having found a guide, he resumed on foot along narrow paths. Having reached his cohorts on the path of the Rubicon, a stream that marked the boundary of his province, he stopped for a moment and, meditating on the importance of that decision, he exclaimed to those who stood nearby: 'For the moment we can still turn back but, once across this bridge, all will have to be decided by arms!' While he was still hesitating, he had a vision. A man of wondrous beauty and stature suddenly appeared, sitting nearby playing his flute. Several shepherds ran up to hear him, and even a troop of soldiers and some trumpeters left their posts. That man, having taken a trumpet from one of these, rushed towards the river and, sounding the battle signal with a mighty blast, crossed to the other bank. Caesar then ordered: 'Onwards, along that road on which we are called by the wonders of the gods and the injustice of our enemies. [Let] the die [be] cast!'[24] Accordingly, having crossed with his army, and taken with him the tribunes of the people who, expelled from Rome, had joined him, he assembled the troops and, tearing the robes on his chest and crying, he pleaded for their loyalty. A rumour spread that, on that occasion, he had promised a knight's wealth to every man, but this belief is based on an incorrect interpretation. For during the course of his speech, he raised his left hand several times, showing the ring on his finger and saying: 'With joy I will relinquish even this ring, to satisfy all those who are ready to defend my honour!' At this gesture, the soldiers in the last rows, who saw the orator better than they could hear his words, thought he had said what his gesture suggested, and the rumour spread that he had promised everyone the right of the ring plus 400,000 sesterces.[25]

Here, for the first and only time, a small bridge is mentioned – hardly spectacular but very reasonable, bearing in mind the winter season.

Later on, he also makes the only reference to a herd of horses conse-crated by the proconsul for a vow expressed at the time when he crossed the Rubicon.[26]

Nevertheless he fails to specify where Caesar spoke in the presence of the tribunes of the plebs (we might imagine Ariminum, a place whose occupation Suetonius never mentions, perhaps taking it for granted).

This seems the most credible version. The vision of the giant has there-fore been interpreted as an invention by Caesar for the benefit of soldiers exasperated by his delay and perhaps acted out with the help of a Gallic prisoner of impressive stature; perhaps not even the promise of the ring was the result of a misinterpretation.[27] It was the symbol of membership of the order of knights, guaranteed by a wealth of at least 400,000 sesterces.

APPIAN'S VERSION

Appian provides yet another account, which needs to be looked at in its entirety.[28] Caesar had just returned from Britannia (where, in reality, he had last been in 54); moving from Gaul across the Rhine, he had crossed the Alps with 5,000 foot soldiers and 300 horsemen, reaching Ravenna, 'the last city of his province, at the boundary with Italy'. There was then – in the following order – the arrival of Curio and his pleas for war, an attempt at compromise, the Senate meeting of 1 January, the subsequent expulsion of Antony and Quintus Cassius, and their arrival (together with Curio) to join Caesar. To the troops he displayed the tribunes, still dressed as slaves and on the cart they had hired. In Rome, meanwhile, the Senate was in debate, believing that Caesar would remain where he was.

Appian moves on to describe the crossing of the Rubicon. Caesar had sent word for his army to join him, 'but since he always liked to cause surprise and awe from his speed and courage more than from the strength of his resources', he decided to begin the war 'with only 5,000 men and to occupy the key points of Italy'. So he sent the centurions ahead with a few of the bravest men, 'in peaceful manner, so that they entered Ariminum and immediately occupied it: this is the first city in Italy for anyone who arrives from Gaul'. Then, that evening, as if feeling unwell, he retired from dinner leaving his friends at table, and climbed onto a cart towards Ariminum, followed at a distance by horsemen.

> Having then arrived in haste at the river Rubicon, which marks the boundary of Italy, he stopped, and remained staring at the current, reflecting on each of the troubles that would occur if he crossed that river bearing arms. Then, recovering himself, he said to those present: 'Friends, if I refrain from crossing this river, my misfortunes will begin; if however we cross it, there will be troubles for all.' After these words, as if possessed, all of a sudden he crossed the river adding this famous expression: 'Let the die be cast!' From here moving swiftly, he captures Ariminum at daybreak, and advances further, establishing garrisons in suitable places, subjugating whoever he finds, either with force or with mercy. From each place the people ran off in confusion, as happens in situations of panic: not having accurate information, everyone thought that Caesar was advancing at full force, with a vast army.[29]

This confirms many details of previous versions: Ariminum is said to have been taken by surprise (Plutarch, *Caesar*); Caesar is described as hesitant when he sees the stream (Lucan, Plutarch, Suetonius). We must also conclude that, in addition to the horsemen, all of his 5,000 men had followed him; the tribunes must have been displayed to them earlier (at Ravenna). But there is no reference to the *contio* at Ariminum: attention here is centred on the panic created in Rome and on subsequent events.

VELLEIUS PATERCULUS, CASSIUS DIO, EUTROPIUS, OROSIUS AND THE LOST LIVY

Velleius Paterculus states that 'Caesar, having decided to fight, crossed the Rubicon with his army', adding no further details.[30]

Cassius Dio – who doesn't mention the crossing of the stream – states, however, that at Ariminum, having assembled the troops, he ordered Curio and 'the others who had come with him' to relate what had happened in Rome; he then 'stirred the anger of the soldiers with a speech fitting to the circumstances';[31] finally he set out for Rome.

Flavius Eutropius (fourth century AD), in his *Breviarium historiae Romanae*, says only that Caesar 'marched with his army against his country from Ariminum, where he had assembled his soldiers'.[32]

A noteworthy variant is found in the *Histories Against Pagans* of Paulus Orosius (c.AD 375–c.420), who refers also to Livy's lost text. He records briefly that Antony and Quintus Cassius joined Caesar at Ravenna, accompanied by Curio and Caelius. Caesar then crossed the Rubicon and, as soon as he reached Ariminum, 'he explained his plan to the five cohorts, which were the only ones he had at that time and yet with which, as Livy says, "he attacked the world".[33] While deploring the insults that he himself had suffered, he guaranteed that the purpose of the civil war was to restore the tribunes to office'. We must therefore assume that Livy, in Book CIX, spoke of only five cohorts, around 2,500 men. His *Periochae* don't allow us to confirm this information, but scholars have suggested that Caesar might have regarded the other five cohorts as unreliable, due to the influence of Labienus.

A CONTROVERSY, A FAKE, MONTESQUIEU AND NAPOLEON

In addition to the variations among ancient sources, the Middle Ages marked the beginning of a long controversy – not just parochial in-fighting – over the exact whereabouts of the 'real' Rubicon. Late ancient cartography – passed down to us by the *Tabula Peutingeriana* – indicates, on two separate occasions, a single river, the Rubicon, situated 12 miles from Ariminum and 3 miles from Ad Novas; it was 11 miles from Ad Novas to the River Savio, and another 11 miles from there to

Ravenna. Along the *via Aemilia*, 12 miles from Ariminum in the direction of Bologna, was the village of Ad Confluentes, and 8 miles from there, Curva Cesena (present-day Cesena). It has proved difficult to identify the exact positions of Ad Novas and Ad Confluentes, but today it is believed that they are to be found on a Roman coast road, along the path of the *via Popilia*, on which Caesar's legions probably passed.

Three water courses are potentially identifiable with the ancient Rubicon: the Pisciatello or Urgòn (at Cesena), the Fiumicino (at Savignano) and the Uso (which flows near Santarcangelo, nearest to Rimini).

The controversy began with a thirteenth-century boundary dispute between the inhabitants of Cesena and Rimini, and was fuelled by a vast body of scholarly work. We shall limit ourselves to stating that Giovanni Boccaccio identified the Rubicon as the Pisciatello. The solution – though only a political one – came during the Fascist period. The *podestà* of Savignano di Romagna, following a resolution of the Rubiconia Accademia dei Filopatridi, took legal steps to change the name of the town to Savignano sul Rubicone: this was ratified by Royal Decree no.1190 of 4 August 1933, which therefore identified the Fiumicino as the ancient Rubicon. And it was here that Federico Fellini filmed the scene of schoolchildren crossing the water with their headmaster in his film *Roma* (1972).

The actual situation seems more complex. This is due not just to Caesar's night wanderings, the divergent ancient texts, the scarce detail of the *Tabula Peutingeriana*, boundary disputes and parochial fervour.

According to a well-substantiated explanation,[34] the course of the Rubicon changed over the centuries. The stream that rises at Strigara, in the district of Sogliano al Rubicone, is thought to correspond – at least as far as Calisese – with the Rubicon of Roman times. This is said to be proved by the nearby church of San Martino in Rubicone, recorded in documents from the eleventh century, and the fact that the stream is still known today as Urgone or Rigone, Rugone or Rubigone. Between AD 400 and 750 the route of the historic Rubicon is said to have altered, at

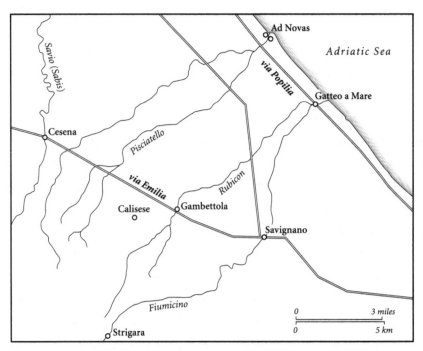

Map 6 The course of the Rubicon before the hydrographical changes of the fourth century AD

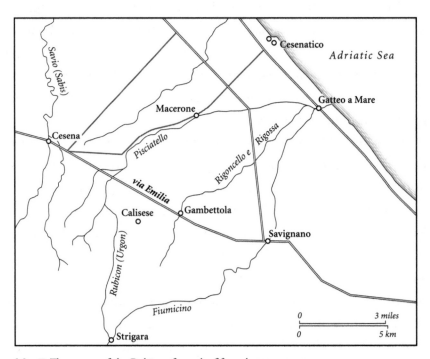

Map 7 The course of the Rubicon from the fifteenth century AD

Calisese, from flowing towards Savignano to flowing in the direction of Cesena. Having joined the Pisciatello, it then formed the new Rubicon-Pisciatello, which flowed down to the district of Cesenatico. But the course of this also changed, so that its mouth moved to the district of Gatteo a Mare (where the historic Rubicon originally reached the sea). The bed of the Rubicon during the Roman period would therefore have been transformed into a drainage channel that follows the course of the present-day Rigoncello.

Uncertainty, as often happens, has inspired creativity. And so a *decretum Rubiconis* appeared, a fake document devised by the humanist Ognibene Bonisoli and published in 1475 in his commentary to Lucan's *Pharsalia* (one of the most popular Latin poetical works until the early nineteenth century). The text – set out at the beginning of this chapter – was later inscribed on a plaque that was once on the bridge of San Lazzaro, which crossed the Pisciatello some 2 miles from Cesena, and is now conserved in the archaeological museum in Cesena.

Both Montesquieu, in chapter 11 of his *Considérations sur les causes de la grandeur des Romains et de leur décadence*, and Napoleon Bonaparte, in chapter 9 of his *Précis des guerres de Jules César*, refer to it as genuine.

9

THE ESCAPE FROM ROME

> What do you think about Pompey's plan? I mean, his plan to leave Rome. I'm bewildered. But it's an absurdity! Are you going to leave the city? Just as if the Gauls were about to turn up?
>
> Cicero, *ad Atticum*, 7,11,3

PANIC WITHOUT PRECEDENT, BETRAYAL AND NEGOTIATION

What happened after the occupation of Ariminum? Caesar is reticent, perhaps because of the fabrications we have pointed out. The lack of helpful information in Cicero's correspondence and the speed of what happened means that there are few firm pointers to the order of events. Let us look at them.

It must have taken three days at most for news of the occupation of Ariminum to reach Rome along the 213 or so miles of the *via Flaminia*.[1] It would be followed by the occupation of other places further south. Caesar's aim was clearly to control the *via Cassia* (which passed through Arretium [present-day Arezzo]) and the *via Flaminia* (to Rome from Fanum [present-day Fano] on the Adriatic coast as well as an alternative southern route from Ancona).

'Caesar sends Mark Antony from Ariminum to Arretium with five cohorts. He remains at Ariminum with two cohorts, stops and decides to hold a levy there. He occupies Pisaurum (present-day Pesaro), Fanum, Ancona, each with one cohort.'[2]

Caesar, perhaps with a further manipulation of the facts, suggests that these events happened after – and not before – the breakdown of further negotiations.[3] It is certain, however, that news of the occupation of Ancona had reached Rome by 17 January at the latest, when Pompey informed the Senate; Arretium would also have been taken by then: Rome was abandoned when 'Caesar had occupied Ariminum, Pisaurum, Ancona and Arretium'.[4] And on 21 January, Lucius Scribonius Libo (perhaps ex-praetor, and father-in-law of Pompey's younger son Sextus), having left Etruria, was already at Formiae. There is just one letter, of 8 February, which raises a doubt over Cicero's understanding of Caesar's speed. This describes an event on 22 January as being 'prior to his impetuous march', unless these words relate to what happened after the failure of the second mission of Lucius Julius Caesar.[5]

Other sources record a wave of panic that started from the northeastern borders of *terra Italia* and engulfed the seven hills of Rome. They create a vivid picture but one that is little noted by scholars; once again, for this reason, it is worth following the various accounts.

According to Lucan, Caesar, now certain of his troops' support, had sent word from Ariminum for other forces to arrive. The poet creates an exaggerated picture of armies spread across the whole Italian peninsula, but it is interesting to note the false rumours about barbarians who had come south with Caesar.[6] Following him were 'peoples settled between the Rhine and the Alps', with orders to sack 'Rome, under the gaze of the Romans'; the rumours were strengthened by fear: nor was it only 'the people shaken with vain fear, but also the Curia'. Then 'the fathers themselves leapt down from their benches, and the Senate fled, entrusting to the consuls the odious decrees of war'; each was unsure where to escape, and 'wherever the urge to flee is carrying him, there he is followed by a stampeding crowd, and dense columns burst forth in long series'.

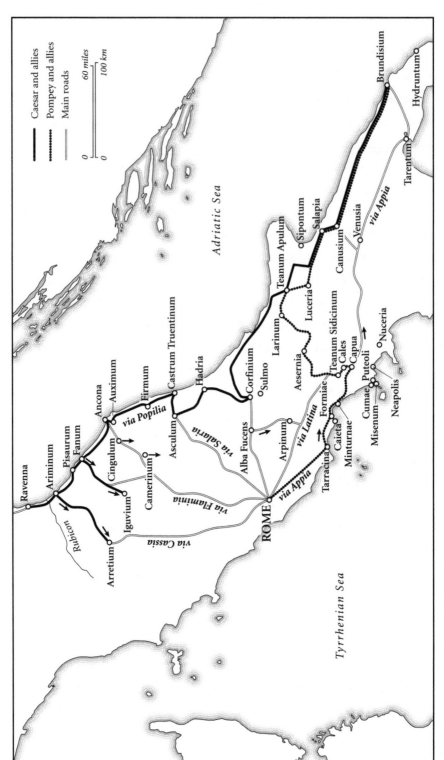

Map 8 Caesar's advance through Italy and Pompey's escape

These last reactions might be dated to a time after 17 January, but references to the Gallic peril – which in reality Caesar himself had repelled – remains a constant presence, especially in Lucan. Ariminum had been built to hold back the Celts;[7] Pompey would also later compare the crossing of the Rubicon with the Gallic invasion[7] and Lentulus Crus legitimized the 'Senate in exile' with the illustrious precedent of the flight to Veii.[9] These last two claims therefore presuppose a tradition different from that handed down by Livy: in those years long before, Rome would fall entirely into the hands of the enemy, and Pompey – as Appian also records[10] – would recall it to his own advantage.

Plutarch's *Caesar* reflects upon the entirely new nature of the situation.[11] It wasn't a matter of individuals wandering around Italy in a state of shock, as had happened previously, but of whole cities passing 'one through another'. Rome was filled with people escaping from the countryside, with no inclination to obey authority or be held under control. This mass was on the verge of 'destroying itself by itself'. Passions became violent: the different factions clashed. Panic prompted the senators to accuse Pompey, who himself was distraught: they attacked him for having given too much support to Caesar or, alternatively, for having allowed Lepidus (but more probably Lentulus Crus) to insult him at the very moment he was making concessions. Unprecedented confusion and fear are confirmed in Plutarch's *Pompey*.[12] Those who lived outside Rome were hurrying to get there, while its inhabitants were anxious to get out. The disorder was so great 'that the healthy part of the city was weak, while the rebellious part was full of passion and difficult for the magistrates to control'.

Panic is also the key aspect in Appian's account.[13] In the absence of accurate information 'everyone believed that Caesar would advance at full force with an immense army'. The consuls would not allow Pompey to take decisions, persuading him to leave the city to raise troops: Rome, according to them, was about to be taken. The senators, ill-prepared, in the grip of terror, regretted their earlier choices. There were many prodigies: 'blood rained from the sky, statues sweated, lightning struck several temples, a mule foaled; many other disturbing signs foretold the end and the transformation of that political constitution'. Public prayers were offered; the people, remembering the massacres of Marius and Sulla, demanded that both Caesar and Pompey lay down their commands.

Cassius Dio adds other interesting details.[14] Caesar advanced at first towards Rome, capturing cities without resistance, 'since the soldiers that defended them abandoned their posts having fewer forces, or they moved over to his side'. Pompey was afraid because the deserter Labienus had told him about his opponent's secret plans. Caesar had always held Labienus in great esteem – to the extent of giving him command of Transalpine Gaul whenever he went to Italy – but he had become arrogant and for this reason the proconsul had taken a dislike to him.

It is worth recording that Caesar had already heard rumours about Labienus. The man who resolved the situation at Alesia, a man born at Cingulum (present-day Cingoli) in Picenum, is thought to have begun his military career under the patronage of Pompey. Official news of his defection was probably given at the meeting of the Senate on 17 January.[15] Labienus in reality had managed to take with him only one troop of Celtic and Germanic horsemen; Caesar had his money and baggage sent back to him.

Cassius Dio continues by recording that Pompey, since he no longer had an army, and since the population, and in particular his supporters, remembering Marius and Sulla, wanted peace and were 'strongly inclined to abandon him', sent out as 'voluntary messengers' Lucius Julius Caesar (son of the consul of 64 of the same name) and the praetor Lucius Roscius Fabatus, his old legate, who had already offered to mediate.[16]

We don't know exactly when they left. Indeed, on the basis of Caesar's *Commentaries*, we can't even be sure they carried out the whole of their assignment together. Caesar also states that the negotiations took place between the capture of Ariminum and later occupations, but Cicero had met Lucius Caesar, who was on his return from the mission, at Minturnae (present-day Minturno) in Campania on 23 January: everything suggests a departure prior to 17 January. We don't even know the terms of the proposal he was carrying with him. Caesar records that the young man, on his arrival – he doesn't specify where – declared that he had a private commission from Pompey, which required Caesar not to regard what he had done 'for the *res publica*' as a personal matter.[17] Roscius repeated the same, 'clearly demonstrating that he was spokesman for Pompey'.

We shall see the results in due course. Here we observe merely that Cassius Dio describes an interesting though less probable sequence of events:[18] the mission, according to him, took place when the senators were still in Rome, and was wrecked by Pompey. After a first return of the ambassadors, fear spread that Caesar's demand to talk directly with his opponent might lead to a personal agreement. The ambassadors prevailed and were allowed to return to Caesar to propose the immediate discharge of both armies. Pompey was afraid: 'Caesar was in a far stronger position if they were to face the judgement of the people.' Before the two ambassadors had returned he therefore left for Campania. In reality the first mission would not come to an end until 23 January (at Teanum Sidicinum, present-day Teano), and it would be Caesar who severed negotiations.

Meanwhile, in the Senate, something most unlikely happened.

THE DRAMATIC MEETING OF 17 JANUARY

On the eve of the third anniversary of the killing of Clodius, the *res publica* suffered a severe blow. Rome, which had already been abandoned ten days earlier by the tribunes Antony and Quintus Cassius, suddenly lost a large part of its ruling class, who were forced to leave. Unlike what had happened during the then distant Plebeian Secessions, the city was abandoned not by those at the bottom, but at the top. Unlike what had happened in 82, during Sulla's first arrival in the city, this was not a desperate population that opened its gates to the 'enemy'. Caesar makes the most of pointing out the extraordinary nature of the situation (though he dates this before the time of his speech to the troops): 'The consuls, in an act until then unprecedented, [. . .][19] leave the city, and private citizens have lictors[20] in Rome and on the Capitolium, breaking all ancient traditions. There are levies throughout Italy, arms requisitioned, money exacted from the *municipia* or seized from the temples, all divine and human laws are thrown into confusion.'[21] How could such a thing occur?

Lucan would also write: 'O gods, generous in granting high rank, but stingy in preserving it! [. . .] you, Rome, at the mere sound of the word war, are left abandoned; your walls are not trusted even for a night. Yet so much terror must be forgiven. They are afraid, if Pompey also flees.'[22]

Only Cassius Dio gives a rational explanation: Pompey feared that the negotiations would be successful.[23] He therefore ordered the senators and those who held positions of office to follow him, granting them impunity (for having abandoned the city) through a decree, and 'warning that he would judge those who stayed behind in just the same way as enemies'; he then ordered them to decree 'that the whole treasury and all the votive offerings that were in the city be taken, hoping to be able to recruit a large number of soldiers with these resources'. The public votive offerings given by towns throughout Italy for his return to health – an unprecedented privilege – had convinced him that he was much loved . . . but he felt uncertain about whether he might be abandoned 'out of fear for the one who was stronger'.

Plutarch seems to suggest an error in calculation: 'while Caesar with only 5,300 men took a single Italian city, he [Pompey] fled from Rome in panic, yielding perhaps through cowardice before so few enemies, or perhaps imagining (and he was wrong) that they were more'.[24]

Even less rational, according to other sources, is the sequence of events leading to the decision at the end of a dramatic session of the Senate, which probably took place in the Curia Cornelia.

Pompey seemed to be in a corner. Cicero writes: 'I saw him on 17 January, gripped by fear, and on that day I had a clear feeling about what he was plotting'; from that moment all he did was 'add mistake upon mistake', thinking only of escaping; and what 'threats to the *municipia*, to men of honour in person, and lastly, to all those who wouldn't follow him! How many times did I hear him say "Sulla could do it, why can't I?"?'[25] This means that he saw Pompey on 17 January, in a place unspecified, though probably outside the *pomerium*. A collective madness about the war seems to have seized 'not only criminals, but also those who pass for honest men'; and so, 'while Caesar, gripped by some kind of madness, forgetting his name and the offices held', occupied Ariminum, Pisaurum, Ancona and Arretium, 'we have left Rome'.[26] Not only did the move go against tradition but also against the most recent declarations, as Caesar emphasizes in *Civil War*. Pompey had indeed claimed, at a Senate meeting sometime after 7 January, that he had ten legions at the ready and knew Caesar's soldiers were hostile to their commander. Cato too, before fleeing from Sicily, had publicly declared that Pompey had waged a useless war without preparation and that 'in the Senate, when questioned by him and others, he had given assurances that everything was in full readiness for the war'.[27]

Other sources report astonishing attacks, which may in fact date back to meetings held in the days immediately before 17 January, when news arrived that Ariminum had been captured. When questioned by Lucius Volcatius Tullus (consul in 66) about the state of the army, Pompey replied timidly, and after some hesitation, that he held ready those soldiers that Caesar had sent back and believed 'he could quickly assemble the 30,000 men recently levied'. Tullus then cried out: '"Pompey, you have deceived us!" and proposed sending ambassadors to Caesar.'[28] Caesar would recall, in the speech he gave in Rome on 1 April 49, that Pompey had declared in the Senate that 'the sending of envoys to somebody meant acknowledging that person's authority and revealing the fear of the senders'.[29]

Another critic was Marcus Favonius, a praetor at that time, close friend of Cato, 'an impulsive man who exploded at any argument, lacking in control, as if strong wine had gone to his head'.[30] In response to an unfortunate but also famous declaration, 'he invited Pompey to stamp his foot on the ground and send out the armies he had promised'.[31] This was a reference to what had happened when, after the votive offerings of the cities for his recovery from illness, Pompey was so elated that he mocked anyone who was frightened about the war and the lack of military forces to fend off any attack by Caesar on Rome. 'He smiled and, with a casual air, made a plea for calm, adding: "In whatever part of Italy I stamp my foot, there will spring up armies of infantry and cavalry."'[32] His claim, though, couldn't have been entirely untrue: Plutarch, in *Caesar*, observes that at that time, 'for number of soldiers', he was superior to his adversary.[33]

The proconsul calmly endured Favonius' sarcasm; 'to Cato, who reminded him what he had once said about Caesar', Pompey acknowledged that he had proved to be the best prophet; to which Cato recommended he be appointed 'general with full powers, adding that it was for those who had caused the worst wrongs to repair them'.[34] Plutarch continues by stating that, after this exchange and his recommendation – confirmed also in *Cato the Younger*[35] – Cato would travel to Sicily, the province awarded to him by lot, as others would also do (in reality, Cato would take up the position later on). But from that day onwards he dressed in mourning, 'he no longer cut his hair or his beard, no longer wore garlands, and until the end, whether his side won or lost, he kept the same appearance, being pained, dejected, oppressed by the misfortunes of his country'.[36]

Cato's recommendation certainly had no immediate effect. Only Velleius Paterculus claims that 'the consuls and the Senate entrusted supreme power to Pompey's forces'.[37] It cannot be ruled out, however, that this decision was taken at the end of the year, which would be confirmed by various sources. The dynamics of the first months of conflict might raise doubts over the ability of the proconsul to give orders to other magistrates and promagistrates. Plutarch once again, in both *Caesar* and *Pompey*,[38] also asserts that, prior to leaving the city and asking those on his side to go with him, he proclaimed the *taraché*, a state of emergency. But this, being required for military levies, must already have been in operation. We don't even know whether Caesar was ever officially declared a public enemy, as would seem to emerge from later references by Appian and Cassius Dio. What did Pompey actually say? Cicero, in a letter of 19 January, mentions and comments on some unguarded declarations.

> He says: 'Cingulum is in our hands; we've lost Ancona. Labienus has broken away from Caesar.' Are we talking about a general of the Roman people or of Hannibal? [. . .] What do you think about Pompey's plan? I mean, his plan to leave Rome. I'm bewildered. But it's an absurdity! Are you going to leave the city? Just as if the Gauls were about to turn up? He says: 'The *res publica* is not closed off by walls.' But is preserved in the temples and in the hearths. 'Themistocles did just the same.' But one city couldn't sustain the avalanche of all the barbarianism: but Pericles, fifty years or so later, didn't do this when he had nothing else left but the walls: and our people, when all the rest of the city had been taken, they held on firmly to the Capitolium. [. . .] On the other hand, from the distress in the *municipia* and from the comments of those I've had occasion to approach, I reckon this decision will produce one result. The protests that Rome is being left with no magistrates, with no senate, is causing a great outcry here (where you are, I've no idea, but do let me know). In short, Pompey with his flight has put everyone in great alarm.[39]

Together with the story of the sack of the Gauls, here are two now 'classic' models of defence, those of the *strategól* Themistocles and Pericles. Themistocles, in 480, had saved the people of Athens from

Persian invasion by persuading them to let the city be sacked but defeating the enemy shortly after in the naval battle at Salamis. Pericles, in 431, had resisted the Spartan invasion of Attica by making the population take refuge in the walls of Athens, though destined, a year later, to be victims of a terrible epidemic.

Only Appian reports Pompey's answer to Favonius' demand for soldiers. He does so after having recorded the opposition of the consuls, who urged the proconsul to 'move across Italy and recruit an army, convinced that the city was now about to be taken',[40] as well as describing the panic of the senators, the omens and the prayers of the people, and finally the proposal by Cicero (or rather Volcatius Tullus) to send mediators:

'You will have them,' he said, 'if you follow me and do not think it a disaster to leave Rome, and after Rome also Italy, if need be. Indeed, for men, strength and freedom do not exist in lands and in houses, but men themselves, wherever they may be, have these with them, and if they defend themselves they shall recover their lands and houses as well'. This is all he said, and having threatened those who stayed back if through love of personal property they failed to fight for their country, he immediately left the Curia and the city to join the army at Capua: the consuls followed him.[41]

According to Appian, Pompey made a further speech, probably after his arrival in Thessalonica, echoing the words already spoken almost a year before, on that fateful 17 January 49, giving a further answer to his critics. In front of all the senators, knights and the whole army, he said:

The Athenians too, O citizens, abandoned their city to fight against invaders in defence of freedom, believing that the city was made not of houses but citizens; and with this action they re-conquered it and made it still more famous. So too did our forefathers leave the citadel on the arrival of the Gauls, and Camillus re-conquered the city moving from Ardea. All sensible men believe that country means liberty, wherever they may be. We too, thinking in the same way, have come here, not abandoning our country but to prepare ourselves well for it, and to defeat one who has spent much time laying traps against it, and who in an instant has occupied Italy with the help of corrupt people. You have decreed that he be considered an enemy, and he even now is sending magistrates into your provinces, he places some in charge of the city, others he sends throughout Italy: such is the audacity with which he deprives the people of their power. And if he does this while he still fights and is afraid and, with the help of the gods, will suffer the consequences, what cruelty or violence is to be expected in the event of him winning? While he does this against his country, certain men gather together, bought off with the money that he has procured from our Gaul, men who choose to be slaves rather than benefit from the same rights as his.[42]

The remark about Marcus Furius Camillus would become of central importance: he is said to have returned from Ardea in 390 to re-conquer Rome which, as Lucan states, was completely defeated; Caesar, on the other hand, had appropriated gold from the Celts themselves to corrupt his fellow citizens.

The parallel between Lucan and Appian – Caesar as a new Brennus, for whom Rome was completely abandoned – leads us to wonder whether there may have been a powerful debate or, at least, an effective propaganda campaign surrounding the historical 'precedent' to Pompey's escape in that fateful year 49. It seems that scholars haven't given this much consideration. We will venture a theory. A crucial point would have been the defence of the citadel against Brennus. Livy thinks this actually happened, so much so as to make us suspect that the figure of his Camillus – often identified with that of Augustus – might represent that 'ideal' Roman leader that even the much-admired Pompey had failed to epitomize.

EXODUS AND A SECOND WAVE OF PANIC

The wave of panic that started at the Rubicon and broke upon the city of the seven hills, then surged back, submerging *terra Italia* and the shores of the whole Mediterranean.

Caesar displays little interest in any of this, suggesting that Pompey's flight from Rome was a result not of his crossing the Rubicon and the capture of Ariminum – as in fact it was – but of the collapse of negotiations and his advances as far as Auximum (present-day Osimo).

> On news of these events, terror ran instantly through Rome; the consul Lentulus, who had gone to open the Aerarium to carry the money to Pompey in accordance with the provisions of the Senate decree, immediately after the opening of the most sacred and most secret treasury fled the city. Indeed the false news had spread that Caesar was ever closer, that his cavalry was at the gates. Lentulus was soon followed by the other consul, Marcellus, and most of the magistrates. Pompey had left Rome the day before, heading towards the legions handed over to him by Caesar, which had been camped in winter quarters in Apulia.[43]

And so the consuls, according to him, had fled the day after Pompey.

Many other sources report the outbreak of panic on 17 January. This, once again, is a matter on which scholars haven't placed much attention, and is worth examining in detail.

Lucan, having described the hordes that had rushed blindly out of the city once crowded with inhabitants and subjugated populations, reports how celestial prodigies and gloomy oracles spread among the people. The ghosts of Sulla and Marius were seen; Arruns, an Etruscan soothsayer, ordered the burning of monsters that had in the meantime been generated, 'that the terror-struck citizens should skirt the vast *pomerium* along the outer boundaries, thus purifying the walls with a solemn procession'.[44] However, when a bull was sacrificed, its entrails were found to be completely putrid, a sign of disaster. There were those who, on seeing the stars, predicted a world revolution. The population was gripped with fear and foreboding. Matrons thronged the temples and altars.

Plutarch, in both *Caesar* and *Pompey*,[45] writes that the consuls followed Pompey – he doesn't say whether at once – without performing the ritual sacrifices. In *Caesar* he tells us that the senators 'took whatever possessions they could, as if they were snatching the property of others', while in *Pompey* he records that the proconsul was criticized for his strategy, but not personally, and indeed 'it was noticeable that those who fled because they felt unable to abandon Pompey were more numerous than those who fled out of love of freedom'.[46] Some of Caesar's followers also lost their heads, dragged along 'by the current of that impetuous river'; the city was a miserable spectacle, 'like a ship that, in the surge of a great tempest, is carried by desperate helmsmen to be dashed against the first obstacle'; still 'they regarded exile as their country because of Pompey, and left Rome as if it were Caesar's camp'.[47] So Pompey 'fled taking his wife and children with him, and leaving the wives of other citizens undefended, when he should either have won fighting for his country or have accepted the conditions imposed by the one who was stronger, since he was a fellow citizen and a kinsman'.[48]

Appian doesn't describe the second wave of panic, except to record that, after Pompey's departure and that of the consuls – meaning, therefore, at the same time and not a day after, as Caesar's *Commentaries* state – the senators 'remained undecided for a long time, and passed the night together in the *bouleutérion* (the Curia). At daybreak, however, most of them left and joined Pompey.'[49]

Cassius Dio goes into much detail.[50] After Pompey's order, 'the decree on the treasury and on votive offerings' was made; but nothing was touched, since meanwhile it had been learned that Caesar, in annoyance, had not given a peaceable reply to the messengers (information that could be linked to Caesar's *Commentaries*).[51] There were many rumours about the numbers and the cruelty of his soldiers, 'who would cause damage of every kind (it is known that in such circumstances the reports are always worse than the reality)'; everyone was frightened and left in haste.

This is followed by a spectacular description of the exodus.[52] The 'most eminent members of the Senate, of the equestrian class and also of the people' left the city. They left for the war but in reality suffered the fate of captives, compelled to leave their country and to think of foreign soil as being safer than their own. Those who went off with their families 'left the temples, houses and land of their ancestors' at the mercy of their enemies. Aware of Pompey's plans – which already seem here to be public knowledge – 'they knew that, even if they were saved, they would end up living in Macedonia and in Thrace'. Those who left their children, their wives and dearest possessions seemed to retain 'some hope for their country' but in reality their plight was sadder due to their separation and because, having yielded their dearest possessions to their foes, they were unable to act freely. They could find an enemy in Caesar, because they hadn't stayed in Rome, but also in Pompey, because they hadn't taken their families with them. Conflicting sentiments afflicted those who stayed behind, defenceless, at the mercy of the enemy and of the 'future master of the city', fearing violence and massacres, 'as if they had already happened'.

The multitude who remained, though of no kinship to those who were leaving, worried about acquaintances, friends, their uncertain destiny, but even more about themselves. Witnessing the departure of 'magistrates, senators and all those who had some power', they realized these would not have left 'if they hadn't seen the city exposed to so many and such terrible dangers'. And with no 'leaders and allies', they felt like orphans and widows. Thinking about 'ancestors (indeed some had suffered personally, others had heard from victims about all the havoc caused by Marius and Sulla)' they expected no moderation, but feared the worst: Caesar had an army consisting mainly of barbarians. Even those who regarded him as a friend feared he might change attitude.

The confusion and grief brought by the departure of the consuls – therefore supposedly after that of Pompey – and their followers was unimaginable. Throughout the night 'they made a great racket, packing their baggage and running here and there'; at daybreak everyone uttered 'a long lament at the temples': wandering about, they invoked the gods, kissed the ground, listed the dangers they had overcome, 'and were crying because they were leaving their country (something they had never imagined)'. There was lamenting at the gates. Most 'hurled curses, feeling themselves betrayed'. Those who remained and those leaving expected nothing but misery: anyone who saw them 'would have thought that one single city had become two, and that one was leaving and escaping, while the other remained captive'.

Much less dramatic but no less extraordinary is the testimony of a very special observer. This helps us understand how, from this moment, the *nobilitas* and the ruling class, in the broadest sense, had really begun to break into factions. Supporters of Caesar were perhaps the minority, though nonetheless significant, along with those 'without allegiance'. This also helps us understand how, in Pompey's camp, heroism was not the norm.

CICERO'S ESCAPE

Cicero had stayed on the outskirts of the city waiting for the celebration of his triumph. He met Pompey on 17 January – we don't know where – then suddenly left, before dawn next day, for Formiae.[53] This was to avoid 'encounters and gossip, easy on sight of my lictors, crowned moreover with laurel'.[54] According to him the decisions had been foolish, and Pompey remained 'in his fortresses, in a stupor. If he stays in Italy, we'll all stay with him; if he leaves, we'll have to think about it.' Once again the prospect of retreat . . . but this time from Italy.

Having stood the risk of being allotted the mission to Sicily, Cicero had at some point received and accepted a position that he considered much less onerous: 'Pompey wants me to be inspector for the whole of Campania and the coast, and wants to put me in charge of levies and appropriate preparations: so I don't think I'll be fixed in one place.'[55]

At that time he was probably in the company of his son, his brother Quintus, and his brother's son. His wife Terentia, his daughter Tullia – then pregnant, shortly after her third marriage, to the young Publius Cornelius Dolabella, a patrician and keen supporter of Caesar – and sister-in-law Pomponia were still in Rome. How did he deal with the situation, and the separation?

His main concerns centred around the fate of the city, the spectre of pillage and violence, but also the reputation of the women, and consequently his own. On 22 January, from Formiae, he wrote to them:

> you should carefully consider and reconsider what to do: whether to stay in Rome or stay with me or in some safe place. [. . .] You could stay in Rome safely thanks to Dolabella, and this could be of help if violence or pillaging were to start up; on the other hand, I am concerned to see that all respectable people are far from Rome and keep their women with them. As for the region in which I am now staying, all of it – *municipia* and countryside – is completely bound to me; and so you could spend much time with me and live here, and, in my absence, without danger, also in my properties. [. . .] Tell Philotimus to take steps to fortify the house and keep it well guarded. I advise you again to organize a service of trusted messengers, so that I can receive a letter from you each day.[56]

Next day the tone had already changed. The women could stay at home – perhaps the residence on the Palatine Hill that he had recovered with difficulty in 57 after his return from exile – but if Caesar allowed the city to be sacked, not even Dolabella could have protected them. They were also at risk of being trapped. They had to be sure there were still women of their own rank in Rome: otherwise, some way had to be found 'so that you can remain there without compromising your reputation'.[57] The coastal area controlled by him seemed safe: if nothing changed 'you could very well stay with me and in my properties'. Another major problem: Rome would soon be left 'hungry'; on this point too, they ought to consult Atticus and anyone they think appropriate. One positive note: Labienus had improved the situation. So too had Piso, who had abandoned the city 'condemning the criminal conduct of his son-in-law'.[58]

Cicero also sent a number of questions to Atticus: was it better for the women to remain in Rome, or to come to him, or alternatively to find 'some safe corner'?[59] Dolabella would protect them, but how would he (Cicero) face the criticisms about having left them in Rome 'when all worthy people are leaving'?[60] What about his son and nephew? Send them to Greece? Returning to the women, since 'others of the same social rank' had gone, he told his friend that he had already written to them, and asked him to speak to them: the coast under his command offered 'farms where, all things considered, they could be comfortable'.[61] If Cicero had received criticisms with regard to his son-in-law Dolabella, his wife and daughter's stay in Rome would have increased them. But already, on 28 January, a greater trust in Pompey seemed to reduce the urgency for them to be moved, at least until 'we have a clearer picture about how things develop'.[62] This would prove particularly difficult.

THE CHAOS SEEN FROM FORMIAE

The turmoil that gripped Pompey's camp must have been immense. Caesar, having described the flight of the magistrates from Rome, continues:

> Military recruitments around Rome are stopped; the whole region on this side of Capua is considered by all to be in danger. At Capua

they are beginning to take heart and to assemble, they decide to recruit the colonists established there in accordance with the *lex Julia*.[63] Lentulus meanwhile orders certain gladiators kept by Caesar at a school there to be brought into the piazza, he encourages them by raising the hope of freedom and, having given them horses, commands them to follow him. But he then yielded to the advice of his followers (since that form of action drew general disapproval) and he distributed them, so that they were held among the various groups of slaves of the Roman community in Campania.[64]

It was naturally unseemly to require slaves to fight in wars between Romans: Cinna felt it appropriate to do so, but not Catiline.

According to one interesting piece of information, which cannot however be dated, once Pompey had left Rome, he hurried to recruit soldiers among citizens, to gather money and send out patrols in every direction. Caesar, on being told of this, 'did not march against Rome (for he knew the city lay as a prize for the victor and stated that his action was aimed, not against it, almost as if it were an enemy, but in defending it against its political adversaries)'. Instead, he sent letters throughout Italy, in which he challenged Pompey to appear with him for judgement and urged the populations to have trust and 'to remain in their own places, promising many benefits'.[65]

But, above all, it is from the correspondence of Cicero – who remained at Formiae for most of the following months – that we catch a glimpse of the chaos during that period, though from the limited viewpoint of Campania. The perpetual exchange of news, the flow of thoughts and lack of certainty make these pages extraordinarily vivid.

Besides – as he wrote on 22 or 23 January from Minturnae – not even Pompey seemed to have a clear idea about what to do. Had he reached any decisions? 'I don't think he himself knows them; certainly, none of us do.'[66] This impression was widespread. Libo – whom Cicero had met on 21 January, together with the consul

Lentulus Crus – had already stopped trying to gather troops in Etruria. While Lucan speaks of flight, describing Libo as 'cowardly',[67] Florus states that he was 'driven out'.[68] He stopped in Campania, still busily recruiting.

'Fear and uncertainty' everywhere; Pompey was on his way to Larinum (present-day Larino), where several cohorts were camped; others were at Luceria (present-day Lucera), Teanum Apulum (near to present-day San Paolo di Civitate) and in other parts of Apulia; whether 'he intends to settle himself in some place or cross the sea, no one knows'.[69] Cicero was convinced, however, that from Caesar they had to expect every excess. The suspension of business dealings, the departure of the Senate and the magistrates, the closure of the Aerarium wouldn't stop him. But what should he himself do if Pompey left Italy? Shouldn't he follow him, as several important figures he met had told him? Cicero, personally, felt hampered by his lictors.

His thoughts proliferated. Labienus' defection would certainly have been more beneficial if, in Rome, he had found magistrates and a Senate capable of welcoming his gesture. What – he asked Atticus – was the mood in Rome? Did they feel any 'regret about Pompey or animosity towards Caesar'?[70] It was the latter who was to blame for the war: strengthened by an army he kept 'much bound with hope and promises, covetous in all and everything'.[71] Having been handed 'a city bare of defenders and overflowing with every other thing', he would have considered temples and houses as ripe for plunder; yet in the absence of a senate and magistrates he would not be able to 'give life to any semblance of government'. Pompey, however, didn't reply to Cicero's letters and was perhaps even unaware of what was taking place in 'his' Picenum. As for recruitments, nothing good: no defence contingent, for the organization of which Pompey 'was detained in the vicinity of Rome'; all hope was placed upon 'two legions held through deception and almost hostile'; the new recruits indeed had no wish to fight.[72]

On the many questions still unanswered, Cicero waited for news from Atticus: what Caesar would do about the defection of Labienus, what the proconsul Ahenobarbus would do among the Marsi, and the propraetors Quintus Minucius Thermus in Iguvium (present-day Gubbio) and Publius Attius Varus in Cingulum, what was the feeling among the people of Rome and what was his own prediction: 'I would like you to write to me often, also about what you think is best for my women and what you intend to do yourself.'[73]

PEACE EVER MORE DISTANT

Cicero was sure about one thing: Lucius Caesar was not to be taken seriously. He met him at Minturnae on the morning of 23 January, 'the bearer of absurd proposals'.[74] Either Caesar was playing games with the Senate by sending Lucius on such a delicate mission, or he was quite simply an impostor.

Cicero must soon have realized that the situation was quite different. The mission was not only genuine, and suggested by Pompey, but was also of great importance. On 23 January, at Teanum Sidicinum, Lucius had informed the proconsul and consuls of Caesar's counter-proposals, receiving a reply: the Senate would return to Rome to decide, on condition that Caesar withdrew 'his garrisons from the cities occupied outside his province'.[75] According to Cicero, Caesar was about to retrace his steps.

What had he told the ambassadors? Caesar himself claimed to have declared that, though angry with Pompey and though having always placed honour before everything else, he sought to remove major discords and 'free all of Italy from fear'.[76] His enemies had deprived him of a benefit granted to him by the people – to stand as candidate *in absentia* – and had stripped him of 'six months' command'. For the sake of the *res publica*, he had been prepared to accept that the generals should relinquish their command, but the Senate had not even accepted the proposal he had made by letter. Instead, they were recruiting troops throughout Italy, they were keeping two legions taken from him, using the Parthian war as their excuse, and Rome was in arms. Although he understood that everything was directed towards his ruin, he was ready to reach an agreement for the good of the *res publica*. He therefore proposed:

> Let Pompey leave for his provinces, let both disband their armies, let everyone throughout Italy lay down their arms, let Rome be liberated from terror, let free assemblies and political freedom be granted to the Senate and to the Roman people. For this to be more easily achieved and sanctioned, having established clear conditions, by oath, let either Pompey approach or let Caesar approach: all disagreements shall be settled through talks.[77]

Caesar continues in this way.[78] Roscius and Lucius, having reached Capua (according to him, though it was in fact Teanum Sidicinum), met the consuls and Pompey. In their written reply, Caesar was required 'to return to Gaul, to quit Ariminum, to disband his armies'; if he did this, Pompey would go to Spain, but until that moment the levies would continue. According to Caesar it was unjust to require him to retreat and to disband his army while the other held his provinces, and legions that were not his own, and continued levying troops. Pompey made promises without fixing a date for his departure. There was therefore no guarantee for Caesar that, once he had laid down his command, Pompey would respect his side of the bargain. He hadn't even offered any proposals in relation to talks, leaving therefore 'no hope of peace'.

According to the *Commentaries*, it was then that Caesar sent Antony to Arretium, organized a levy at Ariminum and occupied Pisaurum (present-day Pesaro), Fanum and Ancona. In reality, he had moved his troops much earlier.

During those same days, Cicero had received other messages. Pompey asked him to move to Capua, to step up the levies, 'to which the colonists of Campania respond half-heartedly'. He received more accurate news about the gladiators: Pompey, advisedly, had 'distributed them without much difficulty in twos among the various heads of families'; [1,000][79] shields had been found at the school of gladiators and rumours circulated that they were to fuel an insurrection.[80] Caesar's account, as already seen, is different.

But Cicero, in his own small way, was being untruthful, as emerges from a comparison between two accounts of what he saw at Capua. In the 'official' account, sent to Pompey from Formiae on 15 or 16 February, we read that Titus Ampius Balbus (praetor in 59) 'was very actively involved in recruitment' and Libo helped him 'with equal diligence for the great authority he enjoys in that colony'; Cicero himself had stopped at Capua so long as there were consuls there, and on their orders he had returned on 5 February for three more days.[81]

But in the 'unofficial' account, sent from Capua on 26 January – which makes clear to us, as if this were needed, the value of his correspondence with Atticus – Cicero complains about the shameful lack of preparation, even at a financial level; 'the private wealth of the City and the public money in the Aerarium' had been left for the enemy.[82]

While most people were convinced that Caesar was only playing for time, Cicero was strangely optimistic about negotiations. 'On reaching Capua on the 25th, which was yesterday, I met the consuls and many of our order'; all hoped that Caesar, once he had withdrawn the garrisons, would respect the proposals he had put forward; Favonius alone would not accept conditions, but he wasn't heeded.[83] Even Cato preferred 'servitude rather than having a civil war', saying that he wished to take part in the meeting of the Senate that would discuss the agreement in the event of Caesar withdrawing his garrisons. And so 'he doesn't want to go to Sicily, which would be most necessary, and wants to be present in the Senate, which could be most damaging'. Moreover, (Lucius) Postumius (perhaps a quaestor), whom the senators had ordered to hurry to the island to replace Titus Furfanius Postumus (perhaps also a quaestor), declared that he wouldn't move without Cato. As a stopgap, Gaius Fannius (a tribune hostile to the 'triumvirate' in 59, and later praetor) was to be sent with *imperium*.

The government of Sicily would prove – in our view – to be of central importance: we limit ourselves here to observing that Cato was openly calling for peace. Pompey had, however, left Teanum Sidicinum on 23 January with Labienus, who had joined him the previous day, heading for Larinum, to join 'the Appian legions'.[84]

A letter from Cicero, sent to Tiro on 27 January, once again from Capua, contains a different version of the conditions put forward by Caesar (who apparently wanted to keep Illyricum) and of the senators' reply:

> that Pompey should go to Spain, the enlisted troops and our garrisons be disbanded; on his part, he will hand over Gaul to Domitius [Ahenobarbus], Hispania Citerior to Considius Nonianus (this was indeed established by lot) and he will come in person for election to the consulship without any further demand that his candidature be considered even if he is far from Rome; he will also be present for the twenty-four days of the electoral campaign. We have accepted his conditions, but provided he withdraws his garrisons from the places he has occupied: only in this way can the Senate meet without fear in Rome to discuss the terms imposed by him.[85]

This, however, as we have seen, annoyed Caesar.

From one of Cicero's letters from Formiae, sent on 2 February, it can be seen what degree of vagueness had now been reached. Pompey, he writes, was an elegant writer, but the reply of the senators who had met at Capua, a public document destined to be made known to all, was drafted by Publius Sestius (tribune for 57, Cicero's ally and later praetor); the result was a document 'decidedly in the style of Sestius'; which however refused nothing to Caesar.[86] Cicero hoped that Caesar, having put forward such insolent demands – 'who are you to say: "when he has left for Spain, when he has recalled the garrisons"?' – would now accept. Everything was being conceded to him, and more ignominiously, now that he had 'violated the *res publica*' and was threatening war against it. But something was puzzling: if Caesar had wanted to reach a settlement 'he ought to have kept calm and waited for the answer; it is said, on the contrary, that he is more arrogant than ever'.

Cicero's letters sent from Capua the previous week had had, in other respects, a clear tone of optimism. To Tiro, indeed, he had written that if Caesar rejected the conditions put forward then he wouldn't be in a position to carry on with the war (above all in the face of public opinion); in such case, all they had to do was block his 'march towards Rome', hoping that this were possible.[87] It has to be said that the whole letter is at odds with what he had written to Atticus. He continued by saying that the military levies were producing 'good results', that Caesar would not march towards Rome for fear of losing the Gallic provinces, 'both extremely hostile, apart from the Transpadanians'; behind him he also had six legions and the auxiliary troops of Spain, commanded by the legates Lucius Afranius (consul in 60) and Petreius (who had defeated Catiline in 62). Behaving 'as a madman, he could perhaps be crushed, so long as Rome comes to no harm'; besides, he had received a hard blow from Labienus, whom many were about to copy. Cicero was also optimistic about his own situation: from Formiae he controlled the coast, refusing better offices in order to be more credible in his efforts for peace with Caesar; in the event of war, however, he would have command 'of an encampment and of specific legions'.[88]

Why so great a difference – though barely mentioned by scholars – in comparison to what he had written to Atticus? Ought we to reduce everything to a matter of self-esteem in relation to his freedman? In our view, no. Someone could have intercepted the letter on its long journey towards Patrae, where Tiro was still convalescing. Or it could have been intercepted by someone where he was staying, such as Pompey's ally

Aulus (Terentius) Varro (Murena). Another possibility is that, in the meantime, good news had arrived.[89]

Prior to 28 January, Pompey had written to him that in a few days he would have 'a good army'; Cicero hoped to go back to Rome if Pompey moved to Picenum.[90] Labienus, moreover, was reassuring him about Caesar's weak position; and Cicero himself had been ordered by the consuls to be at Capua for 5 February. He had given serious thought to the possibility that Pompey might leave Italy; if so, he planned to go to Spain and send his sons to Greece. On 2 February, however, he advised Atticus to remain in Rome, but without feeling any fondness for Pompey, 'since no one has ever so devalued the city's properties! Can you see I even want to joke about it?'[91]

Cicero's personal situation, nevertheless, was becoming more complicated. At that very moment he discovered that Caesar, on 22 January, had asked the jurist Gaius Trebatius Testa (who had served under him in Gaul) to write asking him to remain in the vicinity of Rome. Cicero, with a certain presumption, had inferred that the rebel proconsul was concerned about the general exodus. He replied to his friend Trebatius emphasizing his difficulty in meeting the request, but explaining that he was 'on his farm', and hadn't taken on any official responsibilities.[92] He confided to Atticus, however, that he wanted to stall for time until there was open war; only then, having sent his sons to Greece, would he take a stance. He was waiting for his wife and daughter (and perhaps also his sister-in-law Pomponia): he had heard there was 'a new wave of panic in the city'.[93]

The women, having arrived on 2 February, stayed at the villa in Formiae, together with Cicero's son and nephew. He and his brother left for Capua. A positive note: Pompey's peace proposal – clearly circulated for propaganda purposes – was welcomed by the population of Rome. But it remained uncertain how well prepared the army was and what was actually happening. Conflicting rumours were doing the rounds: that Quintus Cassius had been 'driven from Ancona',[94] but also that

Caesar, having opened negotiations, was stepping up recruitment and military activities. What should he do? Perhaps go with Pompey to Spain, all the more since it seemed Curio had 'poured scorn' on the mission of Lucius Caesar.[95]

While hopes of peace were fading, in Pompey's camp there seemed no limit to how bad things could get. Cicero reached Capua on 4 February 'under a torrent of rain'; the consuls had already arrived but were waiting, 'undecided, unprepared'; Pompey was said to be 'at Luceria to make contact with the Appian legions, not the most dependable'; Caesar's arrival was said to be imminent, 'not to give battle (against who?) but to cut the escape route'.[96]

Lentulus Crus arrived late in the evening of the 5th; Claudius Marcellus 'still hadn't appeared on the 7th'; no prospect of hope from them, 'not a word about levies'; those responsible for recruitment 'dare not show themselves', seeing that Caesar was close at hand and 'no one knows where our leader is, or what he is doing; nor do they even transmit the lists of names'.[97] Pompey, lacking courage, strategies, resources, author of a 'shameful flight from Rome', of abject speeches in the citadels, knew nothing about his adversary's forces or his own. This new situation was disturbing: it was indicative of Pompey's short-sightedness (but also, in our view, of the inaccessibility of Rome).

The tribune Gaius Cassius Longinus reached Capua on 7 February with an order from Pompey for the consuls: 'go to Rome, take delivery of the money in the sacred Aerarium and return with it at once'.[98] Having abandoned the city, how could they go back? 'With what escort? Return with it! And whoever would allow it?' The consul (Lentulus Crus, the only one present) 'sent word to him that first he should go to Picenum' (evidently, to divert Caesar from Rome). That region, however, was lost, as Cicero discovered in a letter from Dolabella. 'Caesar will very soon be in Apulia and our Gnaeus on a ship.' Besides, Caesar was asking Cicero, by letter, to return to Rome, as already asked by Caelius and Dolabella.

It seemed as though *terra Italia* was now all lost; if Pompey hadn't taken refuge on a ship, he would have been captured: 'what lightning speed!'[99] By 10 February, Capua was now resigned to the worst: 'they are all fleeing, unless Pompey, with the help of some divinity, can join his forces with those of Domitius [Ahenobarbus]'.[100]

Ahenobarbus. Cicero's hopes were now concentrated on him. He had heard that Ahenobarbus had an efficient army, that his forces had been joined by cohorts led from Picenum, and that Caesar was now frightened of 'being caught in the middle', while decent people in Rome were feeling more hopeful.[101] Certainly, the contrary was also to be feared, 'namely that we can all consider ourselves his prisoners and that Pompey is on the point of leaving Italy'; perhaps Caesar was in pursuit, maybe to kill him.

So, at least, Cicero made a decision. He wouldn't allow his wife and daughter to go back to Rome: someone might have interpreted this as the prelude to his own return.

10

CAESAR'S 'LONG MARCH' AND POMPEY'S FLIGHT TO BRUNDISIUM

Am I, a man hailed for so many years as the preserver, father of
Rome, to lead bands of Getae, of Armenians, of Colchians against
it? Am I to starve my fellow citizens, devastate Italy? That man
[Caesar], I first thought, is after all a mortal being, subject
moreover to death in many possible ways; but this city of ours,
this people of ours must be preserved, so far as possible, for
immortality

Cicero, *ad Atticum*, 9,10,3

A RELENTLESS ADVANCE

Caesar was advancing. But in what timeframe? While Cicero's perspec-
tive is 'distorted' by his viewing of events from Campania, both Appian
and Cassius Dio, having described the flight from Rome, continue with
what happened later in Corfinium; Plutarch does the same in *Caesar*
(whereas in *Pompey* he has the rebel consul go straight to Rome). The
main source is Caesar's long description of events after he had dispatched
Antony to Arretium, and occupied Pisaurum, Fanum and Ancona.[1]

Caesar was informed that the propraetor Thermus was occupying
Iguvium with five cohorts, fortifying its citadel, even though its population was against him. He sent Curio with the three cohorts he had
stationed at Pisaurum and Ariminum. Thermus, once informed, beat a

hasty retreat. His soldiers deserted him during the march, returning to their homes, while Curio, 'amid general enthusiasm', took Iguvium.[2] Caesar then, sure of the support of the *municipia*, sent out the cohorts of Legio XIII and moved on south to Auximum, which was held by a number of cohorts under the command of the propraetor Varus, who was levying troops throughout Picenum. Auximum was of strategic importance: a *municipium* under the patronage of Pompey, some 10 miles from Ancona, which could have been used as the base for a counter-offensive on the *via Flaminia*.

But when news came of Caesar's arrival, many members of the local Senate went to Varus, unwilling to refuse entry to a general 'who had well served the *res publica*, after such great exploits'; they also advised him to consider the judgement of posterity and his imminent danger. Varus lost his nerve and fled with his troops. Part of Caesar's vanguard pursued him. In the skirmish, he was deserted by his men, most of whom returned home. Others went over to Caesar, who gave them an honourable welcome. He also thanked the population, promising not to forget what they had done. The gates of Picenum, Pompey's traditional fiefdom, had been opened to him: the Italic people were taking their positions.

Caesar's *Commentaries*, perpetuating his false account of the order of events, then describes the consuls' flight from Rome, in terror at these latest events, and the interruption of levies north of Capua.

They go on to say that the smaller towns gave Caesar an enthusiastic welcome on his march from Auximum, providing him with supplies. Ambassadors from Cingulum, a town laid out and completed by Labienus at his own expense, arrived to request his orders: he asked for soldiers and was given them. Meanwhile Legio XII joined him (too speedily, we note, since supposedly in early January 49 it wasn't yet in Cisalpine Gaul). Lentulus Spinther (consul in 57, who supported Cicero's return from exile), on news of Caesar's arrival, fled from Asculum; he attempted to take his ten cohorts with him but most of them deserted. Now with few men, he met Lucius Vibullius Rufus, commander of the military engineers, who had been sent by Pompey to raise morale in Picenum. Vibullius, on being briefed, took the soldiers under his own control and discharged Lentulus Spinther. He assembled thirteen cohorts, including new recruits and six cohorts led by Gaius Lucilius Hirrus (tribune in 53 and at that time probably a legate), retreating from Camerinum (present-day Camerino). By forced march, heading south, they reached Ahenobarbus at Corfinium (present-day Corfinio). He announced that Caesar was not far behind, with two legions. Ahenobarbus had assembled his twenty cohorts from Alba Fucens (near to present-day Massa d'Albe in the Abruzzo) and from neighbouring regions. Caesar, having accepted the surrender of Firmum (present-day Fermo) and driven off Lentulus Spinther, ordered retreating soldiers to be rounded up, and organized a levy. He stopped for just one day to replenish supplies, then marched on towards Corfinium.

Lucan also records this frantic moment.[3] Once 'the Etruscan people, left defenceless by Libo's cowardly flight, and Umbria, having driven out Thermus, lost their independence', Faustus Sulla too, 'turning his back at the mere sound of Caesar's name, did not conduct the civil war with the good fortune of his father'; so 'once the cavalry beat upon the gates of Auximum,' people fled 'by woods and crags'; Lentulus Spinther was 'driven from the fortress of Asculum', fleeing without any cohort to lead. This is the only evidence that Faustus Sulla was present at Auximum, and was perhaps taken from Livy; Florus himself merely records, among Caesar's successes after Ariminum and before Corfinium, that 'Libo was driven from Etruria, Thermus from Umbria'.[4]

By 11 February, Cicero, at Formiae, had already heard that Vibullius was hurrying from Picenum to join Pompey, pursued by Caesar, that Ahenobarbus' troops totalled only 6,000 men and that the consuls had left Capua; it was now certain 'that Gnaeus is retreating'.[5] Yet in the days immediately after, other news set his mind at rest: Pompey had 'an efficient army';[6] there was also good news about the cohorts from Picenum and about Ahenobarbus, even 'splendid' news about Afranius in Spain.[7] Cicero therefore assured his friend he would be at Pompey's side in the event of war . . . but exactly what kind of war?

Between 15 and 17 February he received a first answer, followed by advice which, after so much waiting, he would have preferred not to have received:

Gnaeus Magnus greets Marcus Cicero *imperator*.

Quintus Fabius [Vergilianus] came to me on 10 February. He tells me that Lucius Domitius [Ahenobarbus] with his 12 cohorts and with the 14 led by Vibullius is marching to join me. He reckoned in fact to leave on the 9th. Gaius Hirrus will follow him with 5 cohorts. I think you ought to come to Luceria. Here you will be completely safe.[8]

He replied to Pompey's request on 15 or 16 February, playing safe: until then he had remained on the coast over which he had charge, 'making sure to keep a vessel at the ready'; the serious news that he received in the meantime caused him to think he ought to be ready to follow 'whatever plan of action you have prepared'; but since there was now a more solid hope, 'if you think that Tarracina (present-day Terracina) and the coast can be held, I will remain there, despite the lack of garrisons in the citadels'.[9]

Cicero described what he had seen at Capua in very positive terms; he repeated that he did not know what decisions Pompey had made, or his plan of war, but guaranteed that if he wanted to keep control of the coast – strategic not only geographically but also politically, 'endowed with excellent citizens' – this would be possible by keeping a command there; if however 'a massive concentration of military forces' were needed, he would join him immediately, as he had told him 'on the day I left the City'.[10] Cicero had in fact seen Pompey the day before, on 17 January. What had he told him? We can only suppose that he gave an assurance of loyalty.

One letter to Atticus offers a very valuable indication. The report of Vibullius and news of the levies of Ahenobarbus, attached to a letter from Pompey[11] and now lost to us, were considered less encouraging. The invitation to Luceria, in Pompey's own handwriting, indicated how he intended 'to abandon these cities and coastline, which doesn't surprise me: he has relinquished the head, there is no reason why he should save the other limbs'.[12] Cicero wanted to reassure Pompey: he wasn't looking for a safe place; if summoned to Luceria he would go immediately; he urged him 'to keep hold of the coastline if he wanted to assure himself of provisions of grain from the provinces'.[13] This is another aspect to which scholars seem not to have given much consideration:[14] why doesn't this final, important comment appear in the letter that Cicero sent to Pompey? Was it something that it was better to keep quiet about, or something the general would have considered obvious, or, on the other hand, a matter particularly dear to Atticus, who was still in Rome, a place more at risk of famine than anywhere else?

Cicero clearly understood how pointless his words were: the concentration of forces at Luceria was for the purpose of escape; soon 'Rome will be swarming with those *boni*, with those rich and upstanding men', thanks also to the desertion 'of the *municipia* that are found in these parts'.[15] He himself would have joined the group, if he hadn't had 'the annoying escort of these lictors'; nor would he have felt humiliated by the company of these characters, 'no one more foolish than a Lucius Domitius [Ahenobarbus] or more inconstant than Appius Claudius'. Note here that Ahenobarbus, on whom he was pinning all his hopes, is described as *stultus*. The only thing holding him back, he concluded, was his respect for Pompey, which would have led him even to Luceria.

Yet this noble sentiment hadn't prevented him from sending 'just one letter' to Caesar from Capua, around 5 February, in reply 'to what he wished to know about his gladiators';[16] brief, highly deferential but praising Pompey and urging harmony, such as to make him hope it would also be read by others . . . followed then by another letter, written that same day, 17 February, a copy of which was sent to Atticus. Both now lost.

His remarks about Pompey became more critical. In 'no nation, at no time do I find any head of the *res publica* or leader that has made as many blunders as our friend', abandoning 'the City, which means his country, for which, and in which, it would have been glorious to die'.[17] But something was spurring Cicero to believe that Atticus underestimated the magnitude of the catastrophe. In our view, this aspect should be considered very carefully. 'We are wandering about with wives, with children, without resources', with all hope in the life 'of a single man increasingly threatened year by year by diseases', people not driven from their country but called upon to leave it, not to return to it but to leave it exposed to pillage and arson.[18] Many, instead of joining the fight, remain 'in their country houses or in their gardens on the outskirts, not in Rome'; meanwhile, Cicero would have to abandon Capua and the coast to go to Luceria, waiting for news about the Spanish victories of Afranius and Petreius, since Labienus was given little consideration; in any event, the most important military actions were those of Vibullius, who scorned Pompey.

It appears, then, that Atticus was placing 'all hope of salvation' in this man alone, and that he was urging his friend to follow him, even outside *terra Italia*, though expressing, according to Cicero, a view 'quite different to his earlier assertions'.[19] Another baffling note: having written the letter 'by the same lamp on which I have burned yours', Cicero set out to join Pompey. Why burn the letter? Had Atticus asked him to? Did the rest of his correspondence share the same fate? Yes and no, seeing that afterwards he still had the messages his friend had sent since 21 January, but they had been copied into a *volumen*, a papyrus roll.[20] Another question inevitably arises: why did Atticus and all those left in Rome seem so unworried?

On 17 February, Cicero set off for Luceria in Apulia, 'the region of Italy most wretched, most far away from the attacks of this war'.[21] He continued to explain to his friend the reasons for his recent choices. While Pompey was preparing his escape by sea, he had accepted the appointment at Capua with indifference, pessimistic about a cause not supported by decent citizens: 'the great mass and the worst were inclined to the other side'. On realizing this, he had told Pompey that without money and forces he would achieve nothing. He had recognized that 'from the start people thought only of escape'; but how could he join Pompey, now that Caesar was occupying new districts, making it dangerous to travel to Luceria?[22] Sail on the Tyrrhenian sea in winter? With his brother? With his son? Caesar would also avenge himself on the property of those absent! If he didn't depart, provided he were left 'some small corner', he would behave like those who, under Cinna, preferred apathy 'to an armed march against the walls of my home town'.[23] And the complications caused by the lictors? And if Caesar wanted instead to grant him his triumph? Would he refuse it? He needed Atticus' advice: 'I'm keeping a ship ready at Caieta (present-day Gaeta), one at Brundisium.'

That very night, between 18 and 19 February, spent at Cales (near present-day Calvi Risorta in Campania), he received an important message. 'Caesar is before Corfinium, Domitius [Ahenobarbus] inside Corfinium with a worthy army, eager to fight'.[24] He didn't want to believe that Pompey might abandon Ahenobarbus, even if he had already sent Scipio Nasica with two cohorts to Brundisium and had told the consuls by letter that one of them would have to lead the legion recruited by Faustus Sulla to Sicily.[25] It was hoped that (Gaius) Fabius (praetor in 58) might pass over to Pompey's side with his cohorts, and that Afranius, having defeated Trebonius in the Pyrenees, would arrive in strength, as had been rumoured: only on these conditions could they remain in Italy. Uncertain how and when Caesar's advance would happen, 'unclear whether he is heading for Capua or Luceria', Cicero, to avoid falling into a trap, finally decided to send Pompey a letter – now lost – and return to Formiae.

On the evening of 19 February he had an opportunity to read a further message brought by the praetor Gaius Sosius to his neighbour

Manius Aemilius Lepidus (consul for 66, who had also retired to Formiae awaiting developments), with a copy of Pompey's letter to the consuls (the same he had heard about or read at Cales). In it he urged them to concentrate all forces 'in one single point as soon as possible' and join him as soon as they could, 'leaving at Capua just a garrison, as many as you shall think sufficient'.[26] There was now no further mention of Sicily (which indicated an abrupt change of strategy). Attached was the copy of the dispatch that Pompey had received from Ahenobarbus on 17 February (already known to Cicero the previous day but now unfortunately lost). Cicero, we read, then felt his limbs shudder.

Over the next few days he became convinced that Pompey would abandon Ahenobarbus, 'unless I am entirely blind'.[27] He kept a ship ready but waited for advice from Atticus. He then discovered that Gaius Attius Paelignus (a knight) had opened the gates of Sulmo (present-day Sulmona) to Antony, inside which were five cohorts, and that Quintus Lucretius Vespillo (a senator) had managed to escape; 'Pompey, now alone, is going to Brundisium. It's all over.'[28] By 23 or 24 February news had arrived that Ahenobarbus, on being told this, had surrendered: 'the pain prevents me from writing any more'.[29]

But what had happened at Corfinium?

THE SURRENDER AT CORFINIUM AND
A REMARKABLE CORRESPONDENCE

The wave of conquests that had brought panic in Rome was followed by a slower pace of action, useful to both sides. Around 3 February, however, Caesar was joined by Legio XII and was once again on the move.

Ahenobarbus, Caesar's old enemy and now lawfully the governor of Transalpine Gaul, had set up camp at Corfinium (present-day Corfinio), a *municipium* that controlled access to Rome from the Adriatic coast as well as routes to Samnium and Campania. In addition to his own cohorts – between twelve and eighteen, some of which were at Alba Fucens (commanded by the praetor Lucius Manlius Torquatus) and at Sulmo (commanded by Vespillo and by Attius Paelignus) – there were also fourteen to nineteen cohorts retreating from Picenum, led by Vibullius.

Corfinium, in its mountain position, could have easily resisted, as the Italic insurgents had shown during the bloody Social War, when they had made it their capital and renamed it Italica. Caesar must have been well aware of this. Ahenobarbus, for his part, believed – probably rightly – that he could hold out by joining untrained but loyal troops with those of Pompey . . . feeling confident of his support.

Pompey was at Luceria, at least a 130-mile march from Corfinium, with fourteen of the twenty cohorts that formed the two legions once commanded by Caesar; the other six had been garrisoned at Canusium (present-day Canosa di Puglia) and were now in Brundisium itself, commanded by Scipio Nasica. Luceria was an important stronghold, but on a hill surrounded by a plain. Unlike Corfinium, it couldn't defend itself alone. Finally, between Luceria and Capua, the consuls had assembled cohorts of new recruits; but it is not known where they were between 5 and 18 February, after they had left to join Pompey.

No one went to aid Ahenobarbus. Why? This is explained by an extraordinary correspondence of four messages written by Pompey to the consuls and to Ahenobarbus between 11 and 18 February. Equally extraordinary, they have survived as an attachment to a letter sent by Cicero to Atticus on 28 February.[30]

Around 5 February, Pompey urged Ahenobarbus to join him with all his troops, or at least to send him the cohorts retreating from the north; at the same time, as we have seen, he asked the consuls to go and take the treasury from Rome, to be met by the refusal of Lentulus Crus, apparently unaware of the fall of Picenum.

Ahenobarbus informed Pompey that he would be leaving Corfinium on 9 February to join him at Luceria, an intention known also to

Cicero.[31] But something made him change his mind. This may have occurred on 8 February with the arrival of Vibullius and his cohorts and the news that Caesar had only two legions.

Pompey was annoyed when told about the change of plan, not by Ahenobarbus himself but in a letter from Vibullius, which probably reached him on 11 February. It was probably that same day that he wrote to Ahenobarbus urging him to make haste so as not to be obstructed by the forces that Caesar was amassing. Ahenobarbus gave a trivial explanation for his change of strategy, stating that Caesar had left Firmum and was now at Castrum Truentinum (present-day Martinsicuro). 'If then there are those who want to keep you back to defend their villas,' replied Pompey, 'I have every right to ask you to send me the cohorts that have come from Picenum and from Camerinum, leaving all their possessions behind'.[32] In reality, Castrum Truentinum was a place of strategic importance, the point on the Adriatic coast where the *via Salaria* headed inland for Asculum and Rome.

It may have been 13 or 14 February, but no later than the morning of 15 February, when Pompey instructed his friend Decimus Laelius (tribune in 54) to tell the consuls[33] that one of them would have to go 'to Sicily with the troops recruited in and around Capua and with those assembled by Faustus Sulla'; Ahenobarbus, with his twelve cohorts, was to meet up with them; the remainder of the troops were to join him at Brundisium, then to sail to Dyrrhachium (present-day Durrës in Albania).[34]

Pompey then received another letter on the 16th, probably in reply to his instructions. Ahenobarbus declared that he wanted to remain to keep an eye on Caesar's movements: if the enemy were to move along the coast against Pompey, he would join his ally in Samnium; if Caesar marched on Corfinium, however, he would try to hold out.

Pompey, in a message written the same day, praised Ahenobarbus but was anxious to point out the dangers: their forces should not be scattered, bearing in mind that those of Caesar were growing every day, and

Curio would soon be joining them with those gathered in Umbria and in Etruria.

> When all the troops are together, even if one part will be sent to Alba Fucens, even if the other on approaching you doesn't attack but remains on its defensive lines, you will be immobilized and, being alone, with your forces you won't even be able to support yourself in front of such a multitude when you go out to forage. I therefore persist in my advice, come immediately with all your forces. The consuls have taken this decision too. I have sent Marcus Tuscilius[35] to warn you that it is absolutely essential to avoid putting my two legions in front of Caesar without being backed up by the cohorts from Picenum. If therefore you hear that I'm moving back on Caesar's approach, don't be alarmed: I have to be careful not to be surrounded and immobilized. I cannot put myself on the field due to the season as well as the fairly low morale of the soldiers; nor can I recall the garrisons from all the strongholds so as not to be left without the possibility of retreat. And so I have assembled at Luceria no more than fourteen cohorts. The consuls will either send their garrisons to me or will go with them to Sicily. In short, I need an able-bodied army with which I can hope to break through the enemy lines or occupy regions that can be held; but neither the one nor the other possibility is available at the moment, because Caesar occupies the major part of Italy, and because I don't have an army as strong and numerous as his.[36]

It is interesting to note the vagueness of Pompey's plans for Sicily. Just as he was finishing his letter, another arrived from Ahenobarbus, to which he replied immediately: 'I don't think I can do what you are urging me, namely to come to join you: I cannot rely too much on these legions of mine.'[37]

Even before this last message had reached its destination, the inevitable had happened. On 17 February, Pompey received another letter from Ahenobarbus saying that Caesar had set up camp near Corfinium. He was therefore compelled to reply: what 'I had thought and warned you about has happened'.[38] Caesar would not attack him:

> he'll hem you in with all his troops together to close off the road and prevent you being able to unite those troops formed of excellent elements and these legions of mine that give me so little confidence. Your letter therefore much disturbs me, because the scant faith that I have in my troops dissuades me from involving myself in a battle crucial for the fate of the *res publica* and, what is more, the new soldiers recruited by the consuls haven't yet arrived. If it is still possible for you to extricate yourself in some way, try to get down here immediately, before the enemy has gathered all his troops. It's not possible to concentrate new recruits here rapidly; and even if it were, you can understand how little trust can be given them, who don't even know each other, against legions of veterans.[39]

Pompey then, between 17 and 19 February, wrote a long letter to the consuls reporting what had happened and giving new instructions. The experience of Ahenobarbus demonstrated the need to concentrate troops in a single place. Pompey had urged him to join him, or at least to send him his nineteen cohorts from Picenum, but he was now surrounded, with insufficient forces 'to gain strength in the field since he holds my nineteen and his twelve cohorts divided in three different places (some are in Alba Fucens, some in Sulmo)'.[40] Pompey, with his two legions, didn't feel up to tackling the enemy, 'especially as I only have fourteen cohorts, having sent two to Brundisium, nor can I leave Canusium without a garrison during my absence'.[41] Due to the lack of reinforcements from Ahenobarbus, he changed strategy. Both consuls were to join him at Brundisium – with no further mention of Luceria or Sicily – and were to leave a garrison at Capua. Pompey emphasized that this order had been approved by Lucius Caesar, Marcus Claudius Marcellus and all senators present there. The soldiers could be sent armed, and the remaining arms carried on pack animals.

The suspicion remains that if Ahenobarbus had known about Pompey's true plans he would have been more prudent.

How are the events recounted by Caesar? He describes what happened in much detail.[42] His troops further ahead encountered five cohorts sent by Ahenobarbus to cut the bridge over the river some 3 miles from Corfinium. They were attacked and driven back into the city. Caesar set up camp close to the walls. Ahenobarbus had already sent messengers to Pompey, begging him to come to his assistance. 'It would be easy,' he wrote, 'with two armies, and taking advantage of the difficulties of the terrain, to surround Caesar and cut off his supplies. Unless this is done, he himself would be in danger, and with him more than thirty cohorts and a great number of senators and Roman knights.' Ahenobarbus therefore sought to encourage his troops, positioned military engines along the walls and assigned to each man the sectors of the city to defend; he also promised 'from his own private property [4] *jugera*[43] for each man and proportional increases for centurions and troops recalled to service'.

Caesar was then told that the inhabitants of Sulmo, 7 miles from Corfinium, wished to receive his orders but were prevented by Vespillo and by Attius Paelignus, who occupied that city with seven cohorts. He then sent Antony with five cohorts. On seeing the flags, the towns-people and soldiers threw open the gates to welcome them. Vespillo and Paelignus climbed down from the walls but were captured. Paelignus asked to see Caesar who, having enlisted his cohorts in his own army, set him free. Caesar then fortified the camp and was joined, over the next three days, by Legio VIII, by twenty-two cohorts of new levies from Gaul, and by around 300 horsemen sent from the king of Noricum (reinforcements that had arrived little more than a month after the crossing of the Rubicon, and too speedily for it to be imagined they weren't already in Cisalpine Gaul in early January 49). He then set up a second camp under the command of Curio on the other side of Corfinium and continued to encircle the city with siege works.

By the time Caesar finished most of the works, messengers arrived with the reply for Ahenobarbus. Ahenobarbus read it carefully. Pompey wrote that he would not put his own forces at risk: it had not been his advice to close himself up in Corfinium. If possible, he should reach him with all his troops. But this was no longer possible owing to the siege works (which, we can hardly avoid noting, had nevertheless allowed the messengers to get through). Ahenobarbus kept Pompey's reply secret even to his chief officers, announcing, on the contrary, that Pompey was on his way; only to a few intimates, in secret, did he communicate his intention to escape. His demeanour, however, betrayed him. His soldiers therefore decided to mutiny.

Having dragged their commander before the people and imprisoned him, they sent word to Caesar that they wished to open their gates and hand him over. Caesar, though impatient, was afraid his men might plunder the town and sent the messengers back, delaying the matter until the next day.

Just before dawn on 21 February, Lentulus Spinther called out to the sentries from the walls, saying he wanted to talk to Caesar. Welcomed into the camp, he asked for pardon. Caesar interrupted him, saying that he had left his province only to defend himself from the insults of enemies, to restore authority to the tribunes driven out of Rome, to restore freedom to himself and to the people of Rome who were oppressed by a meagre faction. Lentulus Spinther, now reassured, returned to the town to relay Caesar's words. When the senators (including Ahenobarbus and Lentulus Spinther), sons of senators, military tribunes and knights – many also from neighbouring *municipia* – were brought before him, Caesar offered them unconditional freedom. He also asked members of the local senate for the 6 million sesterces deposited there by Ahenobarbus and returned them to him, even though this was public money. That same day, 21 February, after receiving the oath of loyalty from the troops that had surrendered,[44] 'having spent a total of seven days below Corfinium', he left, heading for Apulia.

What do the other sources say? Velleius Paterculus and Suetonius give little detail. Plutarch, in *Pompey*, leaves it out, while in *Caesar*,[45] though giving just a summary, he offers one detail. Ahenobarbus, having ordered a poison from his physician, a slave, drank it, but then regretted the gesture on hearing of Caesar's benevolence. The physician at that point revealed that it was only a sleeping-potion and 'then, overjoyed, he got up, went to Caesar, shook his right hand and went back once more to Pompey'. This news, when it reached Rome, 'reassured its citizens; some of those who had fled came back'. The story about the slave physician – which certainly doesn't place Ahenobarbus in a good light – is also recorded in *De Beneficiis*[46] by the philosopher Lucius Annaeus Seneca (4 BC – AD 65), son of Seneca the Elder and paternal uncle of Lucan, and in Suetonius.[47]

Appian states that Ahenobarbus 'did not have with him all the 4,000 soldiers that had been assigned to him'; he is then said to have been captured by the townspeople 'near the gate' and set free by Caesar, with his money, perhaps in the hope – which did not materialize – that he would remain with him.[48]

Among the historical sources, the picture of a contemptible Ahenobarbus is contradicted only by Cassius Dio. According to his version, the soldiers captured him since they had no intention of fleeing, as Pompey had demanded; Ahenobarbus, on the other hand, was just obeying an order, though he had a strong and faithful army: 'he had earned the favour of the soldiers in many ways and had also won them over with the promise of land (since he had fought on Sulla's side and had acquired a large amount under that regime)'.[49]

The later actions of Ahenobarbus – his defence of Massilia and his death at the Battle of Pharsalus – do nevertheless demonstrate his 'republican' zeal.

Lucan would also seem to point to his 'absolution': he was 'pugnacious', Corfinium 'surrounded by strong walls' and his army formed of recruits 'opposed at one time to the assassin Milo'.[50] And the attempt to pull down the bridge would have served little purpose: after the Rubicon, Caesar would never have stopped at the sight of a river. Ahenobarbus would then hasten to fortify the city:

> and here, impiety of war!, the besieged, throwing open the gates,
> drag out their commander, a prisoner: back
> at the feet of his proud fellow citizen; but with threatening look
> and head high, noble Domitius demands death by sword.[51]

Caesar, instead, would pardon him, humiliating him.

It is interesting to note how only Caesar and Appian mention the return of the money. A letter from Cicero, however, would suggest the contrary . . .[52]

CICERO AND AN INTERMINABLE WAIT

In a previous section, we left Cicero on 23 or 24 February, at Formiae, now certain about the fate of Corfinium. Such fate, as we have seen, was in fact decided on the 21st. Cicero then received other news, from Caesar's supporters as well as from Pompey.

Lucius Cornelius Balbus (nephew of Caesar's agent of the same name) went to see him on the evening of the 24th. Balbus' mission, on Caesar's behalf, was to search – far off the beaten track – for the consul Lentulus Crus, in order to deliver a letter, instructions and 'the promise of a province to induce him to return to Rome'.[53] The envoy claimed that Caesar wished to make contact with Pompey for a reconciliation; Balbus senior made the same claim by letter, which indeed stated that the rebel proconsul's only desire was to 'live in safety under the princedom' of the other. But Cicero thought some sinister objective lay behind the display of clemency. According to his calculations, Pompey must already be at Brundisium, having left Luceria on 19 February with a light escort, ahead of the legions . . . but the other was 'an extraordinary "monster" of vigilance, of speed, of decision'.

Cicero, on 27 February, seeing how far Pompey had fallen short of the ideal statesman he had described in *De re publica* and ever more convinced that his escape was premeditated, made some grim predictions.[54] The two rivals had sought power, but Pompey 'had no concern about giving happiness or dignity to the people'. He hadn't abandoned Rome because he was prevented from defending it, nor had he left Italy because he had been driven out. On the contrary, 'from the very beginning he developed the idea of throwing all lands and seas into turmoil, of rousing barbarian kings, of bringing wild armed people to Italy, of putting together vast armies'. His objective, shared by many followers, was an autocracy like that of Sulla. Between the two contenders, as in the past, there was still a possibility of agreement, but they were only interested in *regnum*. The following summer would see 'unhappy Italy trodden under foot and shaken by the violence of both men with a mob of slaves'; most to be feared was not so much 'the proscriptions that were frequently and openly talked about at Luceria, as much as the complete ruin of the *res publica*, so vast will be the forces that the two shall hurl into the conflict'.

Was Cicero really convinced of this? Scholars seem divided between those who associate such utterances with his more general failure to understand what was really going on and those, on the other hand, who see this as revealing Pompey's true strategy. We regard a third possibility, so far not considered, as more likely. The apocalyptic scene would seem more rational if Cicero's primary aim was to unsettle Atticus who was too trustful of Pompey – to whom he was also related – and perhaps to justify a possible rapprochement with Caesar. We cannot but observe that Cicero, in that same letter, was informing his friend about a message written to him by Caesar, who was grateful for his neutrality, and about a similar oral message to him from Balbus iunior. He attached to the same letter to Atticus several equally valuable documents: two letters from Pompey and his replies; the last exchange, in particular, had been recent and also insistent.[55]

> Gnaeus Magnus proconsul greets Marcus Cicero *imperator*.
>
> If you are well, I am glad. I was pleased to read your letter; in it I found your undiminished valour still in the common cause. The consuls have joined my army in Apulia. In the name of that unique and continuing devotion of yours to the *res publica*, I urge you to join me soon, so that we can by joint accord bring help to the battered *res publica*. I advise you to take the *via Appia*: you will soon be at Brundisium.[56]

The sarcasm in his road direction is, in our view, inescapable – there was only one direct route to Brundisium.

Cicero, that same day, gave Pompey a series of explanations. While he was writing the previous letter he hardly imagined that Pompey intended 'for the wellbeing of the *res publica* to cross the sea'.[57] On the contrary, he was thinking of either an agreement or defence.

He followed it with an account of his own activities, filled with extraordinary justifications. Even before the previous letter had reached Pompey, Cicero, recognizing the tone of the instructions – written or not, we do not know – that Pompey had given to Laelius for the consuls, had decided not to wait for a reply and set off 'immediately, with my brother Quintus and our sons' for Apulia.[58] But on reaching Teanum Sidicinum he was told by Gaius Messius (a pro-Pompeian, tribune in 57, supporter of Cicero's return from exile, aedile in 55) and many others that Caesar was marching on Capua and would reach Aesernia (present-day Isernia) that same day. Worried, he saw himself being taken prisoner. So he headed for Cales to await news from Aesernia. There, however, he received a copy of the letter Pompey had sent to Lentulus Crus. It referred to the message received from Ahenobarbus on 17 February – with a copy attached – and emphasized the importance of immediately concentrating armies, leaving a garrison at Capua. Having read it, 'I, and everyone else, were convinced you would march with full force to Corfinium, to which place I did not think there was a safe road for me', since Caesar was there.[59] During the anxious wait, two pieces of news arrived. These related to events in Corfinium and Pompey's departure for Brundisium. 'Without a moment's hesitation', he and his brother decided to make their way to Brundisium but many people coming from Samnium and Apulia advised caution: Caesar had the same destination but was faster. At that point neither he nor his brother wanted to take the risk of 'an ill-advised act being detrimental both for us and for the *res publica*'.

And on that same day, the 27th (at Formiae, where they had returned), the letter Pompey had sent on the 20th from Canusium arrived, containing the invitation to head for Brundisium. But at that point – wrote Cicero to Pompey – he should already have been there, whereas their route was now cut off and they were about to be captured, like those at Corfinium. 'Prisoners', Cicero stressed, are not only those 'who fall into the hands of fighting men but also those in isolated places who find themselves midway between their own defences and enemy lines.'[60] The letter continues, predictably, with other justifications and assurances of loyalty and friendship.

Cicero wrote to Atticus again the next day. He felt he had no cause for concern: he hadn't accepted the command at Capua nor obstructed the negotiations of Lucius Caesar and Roscius nor – indeed! – had he suspected that Pompey would abandon Corfinium. He asked his friend's advice, and for information about Ahenobarbus and Lentulus Spinther: Pompey placed all the blame on the former, 'as can be seen from his letters of which I send you copies'.[61]

On 1 March, while awaiting news, he observed that all hope now laid in an encounter between the contenders; but if Pompey 'has already crossed the sea, nothing is left but the fear of a disastrous war'.[62] Caesar was perceptive, alert, proficient, and 'if he doesn't deal out death sentences, if he abstains from confiscation, those who most feared him will most adore him'; the inhabitants of the *municipia* and of the countryside are worried, after all, only 'about their fields, their homes, their money. If you knew how their minds have changed! Now they fear the one they had so trusted, and they love the one they had feared.'[63]

The wait dragged on: Caesar left Corfinium on the afternoon of 21 February. That same morning, Pompey moved off from Canusium but Caesar was so quick that he arrived 'at Brundisium before he should have done'.[64] Cicero continued asking for news about Ahenobarbus and Lentulus Spinther. Ahenobarbus was thought to be at the villa of Manius Aemilius Lepidus at Tibur (present-day Tivoli), or near Rome, still with Lepidus, though Lepidus claimed he had taken some back roads to an unknown locality in order to hide himself or get to the sea (as indeed he would then do); nor was it known what happened to his son. Lepidus then added 'a very disagreeable detail' regarding Ahenobarbus: 'a very considerable sum that he had at Corfinium' was not returned to him.[65]

On 3 March, Cicero supposed that the consuls were also already across the sea. With the exception of Appius Claudius Pulcher (who was still a censor), all Pompey's men held an *imperium*, and consuls 'by traditional right may visit any province'.[66]

At that very moment he received a letter from Balbus senior from Rome, asking him to take part in negotiations between Caesar and Pompey: 'your involvement in inducing my dear consul Lentulus to remain was appreciated by Caesar, then by me, sincerely, most appreciated'.[67] And in conclusion:

> I know you will fully approve of Caesar's conduct at Corfinium, that in such a situation nothing better could be hoped for than a solution without bloodshed. I am very pleased that the arrival of Balbus, my friend and yours, has cheered you. Whatever he has told you from Caesar, whatever Caesar has written to you, I know that through his deeds he will prove, however Fortune turns, the sincerity of what he has written to you.[68]

Cicero knew that the Optimates were now openly criticizing him, they 'who now, oh how they rush to meet, how they sell themselves to Caesar! Those in the countryside, yes, they are making a god of him; but at least they are sincere, as they were when they made votive offerings for the sickness of the other'; they are frightened of course, and also of Pompey and of 'goodness knows what threats' uttered by that one at Luceria.[69]

Always the same problem: what should he do? The wait was nerve-racking: Pompey 'left Canusium on 21 February and I am writing on 6 March, which is fourteen days later'.[70] No one knew the whereabouts of Lentulus Spinther and Ahenobarbus, but Rome was 'crammed full of important people' and justice was being administered by the praetors Publius Rutilius Lupus and Sosius, whom Pompey had thought 'would arrive at Brundisium before him'; there was a 'general exodus' even from Formiae. But Cicero had another plan: to remain at Formiae where news arrived more quickly, then move to Arpinum and reach the Adriatic by a quieter road, leaving behind or discharging his lictors. 'The *boni*, the solid pillars of the *res publica*, now and in the past, find fault in this delay of mine and do not spare me from severe comments in their untimely banquets.' So leave, and, 'to be good citizens, let us bring war to Italy by sea and land, let us reignite against us the already spent hatred of the disloyal, let us follow the advice of Lucceius and Theophanes'.[71] The two characters named here are Lucius Lucceius (praetor in 67, orator and historian, friend of Cicero) and Gnaeus Pompeius Theophanes of Mytilene, an intellectual who, after the Mithridatic War had followed Pompey to Rome, where he had also adopted Balbus senior. The two would remain among Pompey's most faithful advisers, which, in the case of the Greek Theophanes, caused scandal among Romans.

Atticus' advice now seemed vague. He had always been against leaving, but not in his last letter: 'is this some small amnesia of yours, or have I not understood or have you changed your mind?'[72] Worst of all was Pompey. He had delayed informing him about his plans until after the loss of Corfinium, and couldn't complain about not being joined at Brundisium, 'when Caesar was already between me and Brundisium'.[73] Cicero had seen more clearly on many matters: *municipia*, levies, terms of peace, abandonment of Rome and the public treasury, occupation of Picenum.

At Formiae, there was a continual arrival of people and news. Marcus Curtius Postumus hurried to join Caesar, who, according to him, had Spain, Asia, Sicily, Africa, Sardinia in his grasp: 'he will follow him [Pompey] at once to Greece'.[74] The son of Ahenobarbus also made a rapid visit on his way to Neapolis, to his mother. He informed Cicero that his father was on the outskirts of Rome, while others were saying he was on his way to join Pompey, or to Spain.

All the more reason for Cicero to ask: what should he do? Pompey must have realized it was not so easy to leave Italy when it was wholly occupied, and in wintertime: at another time of the year he could have sailed from the Tyrrhenian coast but now the only option was to cross the Adriatic, access to which was all but blocked. No news, 'and we've reached the 9th, the day by which, according to my calculations, Caesar ought to have reached Brundisium, or perhaps even by yesterday, given that on the 1st he spent the night at Arpi (5 miles north of present-day Foggia)'.[75] Postumus, unlike Cicero, thought that Caesar might pursue his enemy even by sea: 'the prodigality of the man is well known to the masters of ships'.

A letter arrived, instead, from Caelius, who was probably on his way to Albintimilium (present-day Ventimiglia, on the border with France) to quell a revolt among local populations. He described Pompey as 'heedless', Caesar as 'quick as lightning'; he referred to matters that had to be discussed face to face, and soon: he would indeed be returning to Rome once Pompey had been driven from Italy; 'the strongest reason I have for hurrying to return is impatience to see you and to share my innermost thoughts with you; and how many thoughts I have!'[76] What was he talking about? About a mysterious 'Caelian plan' that scholars have struggled with but failed to unravel.

While Atticus was still offering advice about the various routes to take, Cicero was pondering. Their ancestors 'wanted to consider the day of the battle of Allia as more inauspicious than the day when the city was captured, since the second evil was a consequence of the first, so that the first is still cursed whereas the second is generally ignored'; in the same way one could recall ten years of Pompey's blunders, as well as 'the rashness, incompetence, carelessness in the present moment'.[77] 'The acclamations of the *municipia* for the recovery of that other one' were nothing 'compared to the congratulations to Caesar on his victory'; but '"Are they afraid?" you ask. They say that even then they did it out of fear.'[78]

On about 11 March, Cicero received a letter from Balbus senior: the consul Lentulus Crus, he said, had already made the crossing before Balbus iunior had managed to meet him; moreover 'the six cohorts at Alba Fucens have joined [Vibius] Curius[79] along the *via Minucia*': Caesar himself had written to say he would soon be arriving in Rome.[80] Finally, news also of Ahenobarbus, at his estate at Cosa, about to set sail: 'bad if it's for Spain, good if it's to reach Gnaeus'.[81]

Cicero had only just finished writing this when he received a message from Capua.

> Pompey has crossed the sea with all the forces he had available, around 30,000 men, with the consuls, and two tribunes of the plebs, the senators that were with him, all with wives and children. He set sail, so it is said, on 4 March: from that day winds are blowing from the north. It is also said that he made the ships he didn't need unserviceable or set fire to them.

This news had been sent to Capua, to the tribune Lucius Caecilius Metellus, from his mother-in-law Clodia, who also embarked.[82] This was news indeed, and devastating (though in fact it was written in advance): only the consuls would leave on 4 March, or at least before the

9th, the date of Caesar's arrival at Brundisium, whereas Pompey and the rest of the army would set sail on the 17th.

All was lost: Cicero reflected on how inopportune it had been to lay himself open . . . even if, according to him, he had been urged on by his family and his brother. His source of anxiety was the arrival of a letter, probably that same day, written by Caesar on 5 March.

> Caesar *imperator* greets Cicero *imperator*.
> [. . .] I'm on forced march, having already sent the legions ahead, but don't want to miss writing to you and send you [Gaius] Furnius himself [tribune in 50] and thank you, though this I have already done many times and promise still to do many times, being so much in your debt. I ask you above all to arrange, given that I hope soon to be in Rome, that I might see you there, and thus profit from your advice, from your reputation, from your authority, from your help in general.[83]

His room for manoeuvre was diminishing.

Atticus advised him not to join Caesar but rather to obtain his agreement to maintain a similar attitude towards Pompey. Mediation, however, was not appropriate: Cicero felt that Pompey had a strong desire to establish a despotism 'like the reign of Sulla'. A just cause would have been supported in the worst way. 'First plan, to throttle Rome and Italy with hunger; then to devastate the countryside, to set fire to everything, not to keep their hands off the possessions of the rich'; but the same was to be feared from Caesar's side.[84]

Once again we have to point out one aspect that scholars seem to have overlooked: the horrifying picture about Pompey's plans he had drawn for his friend Atticus coincides with a moment when Caesar was apparently seeking his support.

Meanwhile, Balbus senior and Oppius had written to him: during the uncertainty over Caesar's movements, they were advising him 'not to take sides against one or against the other, most friendly as you are with both'.[85] But immediately, with another message, Balbus senior wrote to say that Caesar wanted a reconciliation with Pompey and abhorred cruelty: Cicero should place himself under his protection, just as 'in the times of Milo' he had placed himself under the protection of Pompey.[86] Attached was a letter from Caesar: an out-and-out 'manifesto' on the benefits of clemency.

> Let us try therefore, if possible, to attract the minds of all people and through such means to obtain a lasting victory, since others, by using terror, have not managed to avoid hatred nor to keep victory in their grasp for long, if we exclude Lucius Sulla, whom I never wish to imitate. Let this be the new rule of victory: to equip ourselves with tolerance and generosity. As for the means for achieving such a purpose, I have already thought of some, but many others may be devised. Indeed I urge you to think about them yourselves.[87]

He then recalled how he had immediately released Numerius Magius of Cremona, Pompey's chief engineer, in the hope that he would urge Pompey 'to prefer my friendship to that of those who had always been his and my bitter adversaries'.[88] On 14 March it was being rumoured that Caesar would be at Formiae by the 22nd. How should he approach and greet him? 'I have never had a more difficult problem to solve.'[89]

On 17 March, Cicero expressed his scepticism to Atticus about the words of Clodia: she had doubled the number of soldiers and given false 'news about the unused ships'.[90] The flight of the consuls had made the prospect of peace more remote. On receiving news of it, Cicero returned Atticus' copy of the treatise *On Concord* by Demetrius of Magnesia – a work now lost – which he had been insistently requesting over the previous weeks, hoping to obtain useful ideas from it for a public speech. 'We have a disastrous war looming, and it will begin with our being starved', in the peak of impiety: 'these leaders of ours are contemplating killing with hunger the most ancient and most sacred mother, our country!' He had heard their discussions: the whole fleet 'from Alexandria, from Colchis, from Tyros, from Sidon, from Aradus, from Cyprus, from Pamphylia, from Lycia, from Rhodus, from Chios, from Byzantium, from Lesbos, from Smyrna, from Miletus, from Coos' had been assembled 'to intercept supplies to Italy and to occupy the provinces that give us grain'. Pompey would return furious, even more so towards those who had worked for his safety, after having attacked Epirus (where Atticus had enormous estates) and Greece: he promised his soldiers in fact that he would beat Caesar even in generosity. Ahenobarbus was perhaps at Cosa.

Atticus advised Cicero not to be too submissive towards Caesar. The institutional question was certainly not unimportant. The rebel proconsul was claiming that the Centuriate Assembly for electing the new consuls could be presided over by a praetor: this was what he meant when he said 'that he wished to avail himself of my advice', but it is decreed in the books 'that not only consuls, but not even praetors can be invested by a praetor', something that had never been done.[91] 'Before long Caesar will be wanting to resolve the question through me.' Cicero's embarrassing position was also due, in our view, to the success of his *De re publica*. He then promised his friend that he would give him the names of those who had crossed the Adriatic. To guarantee the supply of grain, new taxes would be imposed on the provinces, as Atticus was arguing. It was pointless concentrating on the purchase of estates, which had all now 'gone down in value due to the shortage of ready money' and were in any event doomed 'to pillage'.[92]

The following day, having recalled the panic felt by Pompey and his countless threats, he made some interesting remarks about the abandonment of the city, once again examining the past, not only of Rome. Tarquinius and Coriolanus had called on external enemies to take arms against their country. Hippias of Athens, son of Pisistratus, had done the same.[93] On the other hand, Sulla, Marius and Cinna, while winning disastrous victories, 'perhaps didn't go outside the law'.[94] As we can see in the passage at the beginning of this chapter, Cicero himself wondered with what spirit he, hailed as the preserver and father of Rome, would have led barbarian armies against it: Rome and its people had to be preserved for immortality. He reread the messages sent to him by Atticus between 21 January and 9 March, which had been copied on a roll; they expressed conflicting ideas, especially about what to do if Pompey fled from Italy. But the general's decision had clearly not been taken on the spur of the moment: 'our Gnaeus has been pondering this disgrace for two years, so much so that he is minded to ape Sulla, so that all he has thought about for so long is proscriptions'.[95]

Should we really believe him, as most scholars have done? Wasn't this a rather more effective way of reproaching his friend, to whom both he and Pompey were related, for his patent incapacity to predict the future and for his positions strongly hostile to Caesar? (During this same period Atticus referred to Caesar's followers with the Greek term *nékyia*, the procession of 'summoned' ghosts.)

While there was still no news about Caesar's return, a bizarre discovery was made around 20 March.

> Our friend Lentulus is at Puteoli: did you know? The news came from a traveller who was sure he recognized him on the *via Appia* just as he was peeping through the curtain of his litter; it seemed unlikely to me; in any event I sent some slaves to Puteoli to find him and, if possible, to give him a letter. They tracked him down with some difficulty in his gardens, where he keeps himself hidden, and he let me have a letter in which he shows himself full of gratitude for Caesar[96]

Meanwhile Gaius Matius Calvena, a friend both of Cicero and Caesar and a staunch advocate of peace, had arrived; Cicero showed him the letter that Caesar had sent him a few days before;[97] he interpreted it as an invitation to take part in negotiations. Others confirmed that Pompey, on 8 March, was still at Brundisium. And all 'the same old story: speeches full of threats, hatred against the Optimates, war to the *municipia*; nothing else but proscriptions, veritable Sullas; and what big words Lucceius has to say, and the whole Greek rabble, and Theophanes'.[98] What crimes would a Scipio, Faustus or Libo escape, 'whose creditors are already in agreement?'; and what can be said about the 'small-headedness of our Gnaeus', who is said to be thinking 'of Egypt, of Arabia Felix, of Mesopotamia', scorning Spain?[99]

Cicero then wrote to Caesar: he explained he would work for reconciliation and for the *res publica*, as he had done previously with Pompey and in the Senate (not gathered, we suppose, inside the *pomerium*); he confirmed that he had taken no part in the war, regarding it as contrary to Caesar's right, 'since men who were hostile and jealous were striving against a privilege that had been granted by the Roman people'.[100]

But then there was another turn of events. On 20 March, a message from Quintus Paconius Lepta (who had been Cicero's prefect of military works in Cilicia) informed him that Pompey was stuck at Brundisium and even the route out of the port was closed by barges. 'Alas, tears prevent me from thinking or writing any more.'[101] What should he do? An army of the Roman people was surrounding Pompey, 'enclosed by a ditch and by an embankment,' cutting off his escape; 'and we continue to live, Rome is still standing, the praetors deliver judgements, the aediles organize games, decent people take out loans, I, I myself remain inert!' Go there like a madman and invoke the loyalty of the *municipia*? 'Honourable men will not follow me, the indifferent will scoff, those who dream about revolution will turn to violence, especially now that they are victors and armed.' What should he do? Kill himself?

News filtered through slowly. In a letter sent from Brundisium on 13 March, Dolabella thought that Pompey was in flight and waiting only for a 'favourable wind to put out to sea'; Cicero was convinced that on 18 March, a magnificent day, 'he would have made the most of it'.[102] What should he do? Leave without any hope of return? Caesar was 'strengthened with Gallic foot soldiers, horsemen, ships, auxiliary troops'.[103] He would then have the property of his fellow citizens at his disposal. In the end, however, by showing himself more moderate than expected, he won all sympathy, 'and the other one who enjoyed it everywhere no longer has it'; indeed the Roman *municipia* and countryside feared him, worshipping Caesar, so much so that 'even supposing that he cannot win, it's still hard to see how he could be defeated'.

What was going on at Brundisium? Lentulus Spinther, then at Puteoli, feared a turn of events like that at Corfinium. Pompey had sent Magius for peace negotiations, but 'meanwhile the siege continued'.[104] This is confirmed by a letter from Caesar dated 9 or 10 March and copied into a letter from Balbus senior, received probably on the 23rd.

> Caesar to Oppius and Cornelius
>
> On 9 March I reached Brundisium and camped before the walls. Pompey is inside Brundisium and has sent Numerius Magius to me to negotiate peace. I gave the answer that I thought appropriate; I wanted you to know at once. When I see the prospect of being able to determine the change towards a compromise solution, I will keep you immediately informed.[105]

Balbus senior was also worn down by the wait, hoping for an agreement. On 24 March, Cicero received the copy of a letter that Caesar had sent on 14 March to Quintus Pedius (a nephew, who had not been elected as curule aedile for 53).

> 'Pompey is still in Brundisium. I have set up camp before the gates. We await a work of great proportion and which will require many days due to the depth of the sea, but, on the other hand, I see nothing better. Between the two furthest points of the port we are forming

a barrier of rocks to force him to set sail as soon as possible with the forces he has at Brundisium, or to prevent him from leaving'. Where then is that peace for which Balbus was saying he was on tenterhooks?[106]

Another person, who had left Curio on 13 March, reported some disturbing comments from Caesar: he was promising to avenge Carbo, Brutus and those who had been victims of Sulla with Pompey's complicity; he was claiming that Curio – perhaps already at Rome – was behaving no differently than Pompey in the times of Sulla in carrying out orders; he threatened to recall those who had been banished in violation of the ancient laws, pointing out that Sulla had indeed rein-stated those who betrayed their country; he condemned the violent methods with which Milo had been banished; he guaranteed, finally, that he would act only against 'those who had taken arms against him'.[107]

The final turn of events: 'I have only just finished writing, and here arrives, before daybreak, a letter that Lepta sends me from Capua: Pompey left Brundisium on 15 March, Caesar will be at Capua on 26 March.'[108] This news was correct, apart from the date: Pompey had fled from the city on the 17th, though the boarding of the last troops could be started two days earlier.

What had happened at Brundisium? What would become of Rome?

11

IN CAESAR'S HANDS

I cannot believe you are about to cross the sea,
you who are so attached to Dolabella and to that most noble woman
who is your Tullia, you who are held in such high esteem
by all of us [. . .] I would like to persuade you that no one is dearer
to me than you, apart from my Caesar [. . .] for which purpose
I deliver this letter to my dearest friend Calpurnius, so that you
may know how close your life and your dignity are to my heart.

Antony, *tribunus plebis pro praetore*, to Cicero: *ad Atticum,*
10,8A,1–2

POMPEY AND THE FLIGHT FROM ITALY

With the fall of Corfinium, the road south was finally open. The
surrender of Ahenobarbus' cohorts had certainly set an example. Here is
Caesar's own version.[1]

Pompey – once informed of Ahenobarbus' surrender – moved from
Luceria to Canusium and then to Brundisium. He mustered new recruits;
he armed slaves and shepherds, forming a body of some 300 horsemen.
The praetor Torquatus escaped from Alba Fucens with six cohorts, the
praetor Lupus from Tarracina with three; in fear, they moved across to
Vibius Curius. Other cohorts fell in with Caesar's army and cavalry in
later stages; Numerius Magius was captured and taken to Caesar. Caesar

sent him back to Pompey asking for direct talks: his communication with ambassadors was producing no results. He reached Brundisium with six legions, three of veterans and the others completed during the march; he had sent Ahenobarbus' cohorts to Sicily. He was told that the consuls had sailed for Dyrrhachium with a large part of the army and that Pompey was still at Brundisium with twenty cohorts, but it wasn't clear whether he had stayed there to keep better control over the Adriatic or due to lack of ships.

Fearing that Pompey didn't intend to leave Italy, Caesar decided to blockade the port. He had an embankment built out from both sides at the point where the mouth of the bay was narrowest. Further in, where the sea was deeper, he extended the dam with double floats of timbers, 30 feet square,[2] which were fixed with four anchors and covered with earth, to facilitate the movement of soldiers. The fronts and sides were protected with hurdles and wicker covered with hides, and every fourth float had a two-storey tower. Against these preparations, Pompey fitted large cargo boats taken from the port of Brundisium with three-storey towers, war machines and missiles which he hurled each day against the works. Caesar, though surprised that Magius had failed to return,[3] didn't want to abandon negotiations. He sent the legate Gaius Caninius Rebilus to urge his friend Libo (now Pompey's legate) to act as intermediary to seek an interview with his adversary. Libo agreed, but Pompey answered that, in the absence of the consuls, negotiations were not possible.

Caesar therefore focused on war. Nine days later (on 17 March), when half of the siege works were complete, the ships that had transported the consuls and part of the army to Dyrrhachium returned. Pompey, either alarmed by Caesar's siege works, 'or because he had decided from the very beginning to leave Italy', made preparations to depart. To prevent Caesar's soldiers from invading the city at the moment of boarding ship, he blocked the gates, raised barricades in the streets and in the squares, cut ditches across them and planted poles and pointed sticks. He levelled and disguised them all with light hurdles and earth, closed off access routes to the gate and the two roads that led outside the walls, planting enormous pointed beams. Then he ordered his troops to embark in silence, posting lightly armed soldiers at wide intervals along the ramparts and on the towers. He would call them, with a prearranged signal, as soon as boarding was complete, and left them with fast boats in a place easily accessible. The inhabitants, however, tired of being bullied by Pompey and his soldiers, when told of their departure, signalled to Caesar's men from the roofs in every part – once again, as at all times, civilians were the great uncertainty in urban conflict.

Caesar ordered ladders to be prepared and his soldiers to be armed. Pompey weighed anchor at nightfall, boarding his legions and calling the guards. Caesar's men climbed the walls, but, on being warned by the inhabitants about the barricade and ditches, they stopped; the people led them by a circuitous route to the port. There, with lances and rafts, they stopped two ships full of soldiers, who were trapped in Caesar's barrage.

What do the other sources say? Velleius Paterculus and Suetonius are very brief. Lucan provides two particularly interesting details. He confirms that messages had already been sent to foreign allies from Brundisium (reported in Plutarch's *Pompey* and by Appian), putting the following words onto the general's lips as he turns to his elder son Gnaeus:

'I order you to probe the remotest places of the world;
go up the Euphrates and the Nile, to as far as the glory
of our name extends, and all the cities where Rome
became known through me, its general; bring
to the coast the Cilician colonists scattered through the lands
[. . .]
but why do I talk on? O son, you shall carry the war
throughout the East, and raise in all the world the cities
conquered; let all my triumphs return to the field.'[4]

Lucan, referring to the events at Brundisium, also writes that 'here two ships were stopped, hooked by the harpoons prepared for the fleet, and here for the first time Nereus was reddened with fraternal blood in the struggle back on shore'.[5] So there must have been fighting.

Florus,[6] after mentioning events at Corfinium, observes that 'the war would have ended without bloodshed if Caesar had managed to defeat Pompey at Brundisium'. He had caught up with him, but Pompey had escaped at night from the beleaguered port: 'O shame! – He who a little earlier was prince of the Senate, the arbiter of peace and war, fled on a battered and almost helpless ship through the sea on which he had triumphed! – Nor was Pompey's flight from Italy more heinous than that of the Senate from Rome.'

Plutarch, in *Caesar*, having mentioned the capture of Corfinium, records that the victor, having taken Ahenobarbus' soldiers and whatever he managed to obtain among those enlisted for Pompey, with 'substantial and threatening' forces moved against the enemy, who did not join in battle but escaped to Brundisium; from there he sent the consuls to Dyrrhachium, setting sail 'soon after, on Caesar's arrival'.[7] In *Pompey* – where events follow the arrival of Caesar's troops in Rome, as in *Antony*[8] – the description is more detailed, and indeed the final evacuation of Brundisium seems to have lasted two days.[9] Caesar set out in pursuit of Pompey, to 'drive him from Italy before the arrival of his army from Spain'. Pompey occupied Brundisium and found an abundance of ships; he ordered the consuls to precede him to Dyrrhachium with thirty cohorts. He sent Scipio Nasica and his son Gnaeus to Syria to raise a fleet, then closed himself inside the city. He barricaded the gates, sent soldiers onto the walls with light armour, ordered the population to stay in their houses, had ditches dug and barricades built in the streets, except for the two that went down to the sea. Two days later, most of the soldiers had embarked. After a swift order for the guards to join him, he set sail. Caesar, on seeing the walls deserted, understood. Wishing to pursue him, he risked running into the poles and ditches. Warned by the inhabitants, he made a circuit of the city, discovering that all ships had put out to sea except for two, with few soldiers.

The remarks that follow are very interesting. 'Everyone regards this escape of Pompey by sea as one of the best strategies of war,' whereas Caesar was astonished that he, though holding a fortified city, awaiting troops from Spain, and 'having control of the sea, should have abandoned Italy and handed it over to him'. Even Cicero criticized Pompey for having imitated Themistocles rather than Pericles, even though his situation resembled more that of the latter than the former. Caesar 'showed by his actions that he feared the passage of time might work against him'; having captured Magius, he had sent him to Brundisium to seek an agreement.

Appian recounts that, while Corfinium was under siege, Pompey hurried from Capua to Nuceria (though more probably Luceria) and then to Brundisium before going to Epirus and there he made preparations for war, writing then 'to all peoples, kings and cities, to generals and rulers, to send promptly the necessities of war whatever each of them could'; his description of the siege is short, and concludes: 'late in the evening he set sail, leaving the defence of the walls to the bravest soldiers; these too sailed off with a favourable wind, as night came'.[10] There is no mention of the ships captured by Caesar.

Some interesting confirmation comes from Cassius Dio.[11] Before mentioning the capture of Ahenobarbus at Corfinium, the historian observes that Pompey had decided to cross over to Macedonia, Greece and Asia, 'much encouraged by the memory of his exploits there and the affection that its kings and populations held for him'. Though Spain was equally favourable, he couldn't get there safely, since Caesar controlled Gaul. He also believed that if he went by sea no one would pursue him 'due to shortage of ships and the approach of winter (autumn was already far advanced)', whereas he had been able in the meantime to collect money and troops from subject peoples and from allies. Caesar's plan, on the other hand, was to fight in Italy, attacking Pompey while he was still at Brundisium '(in fact, not having enough ships, Pompey had ordered only certain divisions to board: to these he had added the senators, to prevent them, while remaining there, from contriving anything new)'. But seeing that the place was difficult to capture, he invited his opponent to talks; Pompey, having informed the senators, replied that they 'had decided not to open negotiations with an armed citizen'. Caesar then attacked the city. Pompey defended it for several days, until the ships returned. Having blocked and closed off access routes to the port so that no one could attack him as he was leaving, he set sail at night without too much difficulty, but two ships full of soldiers fell into the hands of the enemy.

The next remark is also interesting. Pompey left Italy after he had decided and carried out exactly the opposite of what he had done before, and hence 'he ended up with an entirely opposite fate and reputation'. Having first arrived at Brundisium by boat, he had discharged his army to avoid any harm to his fellow citizens, and now at the same city he was leading another army against those same citizens. Having first carried the riches of the barbarians to Rome, he was now taking them away and, suspicious of every Roman, he was planning to use as allies the people he had once conquered. Previously he had arrived steeped in glory, now he was humiliated by his fear of Caesar, 'and in place of the great fame he had acquired for having expanded the power of his country, he was proving to be the most wretched of citizens for having abandoned it'.

AN IMPOSSIBLE PURSUIT

The 'victor' now found himself wrong-footed, as emerges from his own words, which anticipate what happened later regarding the provinces.[12] He would have liked to assemble a fleet, cross the Adriatic and get to Pompey before he could strengthen his forces on the other shore, but Pompey, 'having requisitioned all ships, had taken away the possibility of an immediate pursuit'. Caesar's only option was to bring in 'ships from the farther coasts of Gaul and Picenum and from the Strait of Messina', a task that was 'long and difficult, given the season'. He also feared that Pompey's old army and the two provinces in Spain, including Hispania Citerior with which Pompey had close links, would be strengthened, that auxiliary troops and cavalry would be organized, and that, in his absence, those still loyal to Pompey would try to win back Gaul and Italy. He therefore decided to leave for Spain.

He ordered the magistrates 'of all the *municipia* to find ships and send them to Brundisium', he sent the legate Quintus Valerius Orca (praetor in 57) to Sardinia with a legion; he also sent the propraetor Curio to Sicily with three legions, ordering him to send his army on to Africa once he had conquered the island. The inhabitants of Caralis (present-day Cagliari), when told this news, and before Orca had even left Italy, overthrew the governor Marcus Aurelius Cotta (praetor in about 54). Cotta escaped to Africa, knowing 'that the whole province nurtured the same feelings'. In Sicily, however, Cato 'had old war ships repaired, ordered new ones from the cities' with great diligence. Through his legates he recruited Roman citizens in Lucania and Bruttium (present-day Calabria), from the cities of Sicily he demanded horsemen and foot soldiers. When preparations were almost complete, he learned of the arrival of Curio, who had been appointed by the Senate in April: in a *contio*, he accused Pompey of betrayal and fled the island.[13] Orca and Curio, finding their provinces ungoverned, landed with their armies. Caesar's follower Lucius Aelius Tubero – sent, according to one account, 'not to fight but to acquire grain'[14] – having landed there, found instead Pompey's follower Attius Varus. Having lost his cohorts around Auximum, he had fled and taken control of that vacant province on his own initiative, where he had been governor several years before, assembling two legions with a levy. Tubero, on reaching Utica (close to the present-day town of Kalâat-el-Andalous in Tunisia), couldn't enter the port or the city; he wasn't even allowed to put his sick son ashore, and had to leave again. Other sources confirm this account. Caesar, being unable to pursue Pompey, turned his attention to Rome, to the islands and to Spain.

Lucan, having recorded Caesar's disappointment at having allowed Pompey to get away, continues as follows,[15] thinking – in our view – also about Rome's policy of 'bread and circuses' in his own time, during the early years of the Roman empire. Caesar began to move for peace, knowing how to 'stir the vain enthusiasms of the people': anger and transferences of favour are brought about by need. 'Hunger alone is taking over the cities, and those in power buy up fear when they feed the idle mob: the starving populace knows no fear.' For this reason, he sent troops to occupy Sicily and Sardinia, both 'famous for their rich corn-fields', which had poured their plenty sooner and more abundantly 'than distant harvests on Hesperia and the granaries of Rome', scarcely outdone by Libya when 'through its abundant rain' it has a good year.

Plutarch, with a similar account both in *Caesar* and *Pompey*,[16] states that Caesar would have liked to set off in pursuit, but had no ships. Having become master of Italy 'in sixty days, with no bloodshed', he then headed for Rome (in *Caesar*) or directly to Spain, to 'draw to his side the troops that were there' (in *Pompey*). In *Cato the Younger*,[17] Plutarch gives more detail about what happened in Sicily. Cato, now in mourning, came to hear that Asinius Pollio had arrived at Messana (present-day Messina) with an army. He sent to ask the reason for his journey, but knowing that Pompey had abandoned Italy he lamented her fate. He could have driven Pollio out of Sicily, he said, but 'since another army, larger than the first, was on its way, he did not wish to involve the island in a war and cause its destruction. He advised the people of Syracusae [present-day Syracuse] to join the stronger side and think of its own safety; and he lifted anchor'.

Appian also considers the strategic aspects.[18] Caesar 'saw that people everywhere liked Pompey'. If he had pursued him he feared that the numerous and well-trained army in Spain would have attacked him from behind, so he decided to destroy it first. 'He thus divided his troops into five parts and left one in Brundisium, a second at Hydruntum (present-day Otranto), a third at Tarentum, to guard Italy'; he then sent another with Quintus Valerius Orca to occupy Sardinia 'which supplied provisions (in fact the island was already occupied), and Pollio to Sicily, governed at that time by Cato'. When Cato asked if he was coming to a province not his own with a decree of the Senate and of the people, Pollio replied: 'I have been sent by he who commands Italy to do this business.' At which Cato 'said only that he would not oppose him at that time so as not to place the life of his subjects at risk, and he set sail for Corcyra [also present-day Corfu]'. And so, according to Appian, like Plutarch in *Cato the Younger*, it was Pollio and not Curio who 'conquered' Sicily.

Cassius Dio, having devoted much space to events at Brundisium and Pompey's escape – accompanied by ominous signs at sea, in Rome and throughout Italy – recalls that Caesar made no attempt to cross to Macedonia: 'he was short of ships and concerned about Italy', as he feared that Pompey's men might occupy it from Spain. He left a garrison at Brundisium, to prevent the return of those who had left, and went to Rome.[19]

Cicero, however, made another erroneous prediction. On 25 March he wrote: 'it is clear he wants to stop all access to the sea, and one would say he has his eyes more on Greece than on Spain':[20] Lepta had in fact written to him that Caesar had left three legions, respectively at Brundisium, Tarentum and Sipontum (not Hydruntum).

When it was known what had happened at Brundisium, Cicero's doubts about what to do remained: Caesar would be passing through Formiae on the 27th and Cicero intended to meet him, then go to Arpinum.

Just as he had finished writing, another message arrived, from Matius and Trebatius: Pompey had set sail from Brundisium with all his troops on 17 March. Caesar had entered the city next day and had spoken to the people. He had then left for Rome 'where he expects to arrive before 1 April, to remain there just a few days then leave for Spain'.[21] In the meantime, Caesar had also written to Cicero.

Having congratulated him for his leniency after the capture of Corfinium, he replied to me in these terms:

'Caesar *imperator* greets Cicero *imperator*.

'You, who know me well, rightly say that my actions are quite devoid of any form of cruelty. This in itself already gives me great satisfaction, but I am exultant with joy at your approval. And I am not worried if it is said about those I have set free that they have been released to fight me once again. I desire nothing better than to be consistent; let them do likewise. I would be very happy to have you with me, in Rome, to have the benefit of your advice, of your approval on each occasion, as I have always had. Be assured that your Dolabella is as dear to me as anyone. And I will be most thankful for his understanding, his affection towards me, nor is it possible that he would act otherwise, such is his courtesy.'[22]

Caesar had commanded 'publication of the order that the Senate shall hold a full assembly on 1 April' to be made at Formiae as well.[23]

Then, at last, their meeting took place. The rebel proconsul proved even less moveable than expected. Cicero explained that if he were to return to Rome, he would be forced to speak against the offensive in Spain and the sending of troops to Greece, as well as on the fate of Pompey. Caesar then invited him to think it over. 'I'm sure he wasn't very pleased with me, but I, I was pleased with myself, which hasn't happened for a very long time.'[24]

He then went to Arpinum to the ceremony – probably on 1 April – at which he gave his son his *toga virilis*, after his sixteenth birthday, marking his official passage into manhood. There too, everyone was in low spirits. He was even keener to join Pompey: not for the *res publica*, now in pieces, but out of personal gratitude. Since the Adriatic was closed, he would sail from the Tyrrhenian coast: 'if Puteoli is difficult, we can continue on for Croto [present-day Crotone] or Thurii [near Sibari]; and we, honest citizens, shall roam the sea like pirates. I can see no other way of fighting this war of mine. And I'll hide myself away in Egypt.'[25]

A CITY MORE OR LESS AT PEACE

Caesar finally arrived in Rome, after a march which, despite initial esti-
mations, had become much longer. He ought to have been there by the
last day of March; he had summoned the Senate for 1 April.[26]

Caesar himself describes the events.[27] Having led his soldiers to the
nearest *municipia*, he left for Rome. Once the Senate had assembled, he
recalled the wrongs committed against him, declaring that he had never
sought special offices but, having waited the prescribed time for the
consulship, had contented himself with a right available to every citizen.
Despite the opposition of his enemies and the violent resistance of Cato,
'who, following his old practice, managed to spin out his speeches for
days and days', the ten tribunes had permitted him to stand as candidate
in his absence, during the consulship of Pompey. If Pompey had disap-
proved, why had he let the motion pass? On the other hand, if he
approved, why had he prevented him from enjoying a benefit granted by
the people? He had been prepared to discharge his army, risking his position and prestige, while his enemies preferred to disrupt everything
rather than relinquish power and disband their armies. He complained
of the insult caused by the removal of his legions, the harshness and arro-
gance in limiting the powers of the tribunes, he listed the requests for
talks that had been refused. He urged the senators to assume government
of the *res publica* and to administer it with him; otherwise, he would do
it alone. Ambassadors had to be sent to Pompey, without fear of what
Pompey had said not long before in the Senate, namely that 'the sending
of envoys to somebody meant acknowledging that person's authority and
revealing the fear of the senders': these were sentiments of a weak spirit.

The Senate approved, but no one dared to go; indeed Pompey, 'on his
departure from Rome, had declared in the Senate that he would hold
those who had stayed behind on the same account as those who were in
Caesar's camp'. Three days were spent in debate; Caesar's opponents
managed also to 'corrupt the plebeian tribune Lucius Caecilius Metellus

in order to drag out the project and impede other plans'. Caesar, on being told of this, having wasted several days, left for Transalpine Gaul without completing what had been previously planned. Control of *terra Italia* was now left to Antony, as propraetor.

Other sources are brief; others still, talking about Metellus, give a very different account: the tribune – and quaestor in Sicily in 52 – had opposed the requisition of the treasury, stopping only when threatened with death.

According to Florus,[28] Caesar, having arrived at the city, which was 'almost empty due to fear', and having proclaimed himself consul (although this is wrong),[29] broke open 'the locks of the secret Aerarium, since the tribunes delayed in opening them, and before taking power he took possession of the tributes and the wealth of the Roman people'. Also, before pursuing Pompey, with his 'lieutenants he occupied Sicily and Sardinia, which guaranteed his supplies'.

Lucan, having described the organization of the provinces, tells of Caesar's arrival in Rome at the head of a peaceful army, marching through frightened cities.[30] Catching sight of the distant walls of Rome, he uttered: 'You, seat of gods, could men desert you when not compelled by any war? For what city will they fight?' And again: 'O Rome, Fortune has saved you – with so vile a leader! – giving you a war among citizens.' He then entered the terrified city. 'For men believe he seeks to topple the fire-blackened walls of conquered Rome and scatter the gods. Such is the measure of their fear: they think he wants whatever he can get.' At the meeting of the Senate, he would be granted all he wished; fortunately he was prudent. Freedom nevertheless exploded into anger: 'defiant Metellus, seeing how with a rock they were trying to break open the Temple of Saturn', slipped through the ranks and stood before the doors, but in vain.

Then the Tarpeian rock echoes and with a great crash
vouches that the doors are opening; then they carry off

the Roman people's wealth, held in the recesses of the temple,
and intact for countless years, furnished from the Punic wars,
from Perseus, from vanquished Philip's plunder, left
to you, O Rome, by Pyrrhus in headlong flight
(this very gold Fabricius wouldn't take to sell you to a king),[31]
and whatever thing you saved, or sober customs of forefathers
and the rich peoples of Asia sent in tribute,
delivered from Minoan Crete to the victor Metellus
or carried by Cato by the long routes from Cyprus.
They carried away the riches of the East and the last treasure
of captive kings paraded in the triumphs of Pompey;
the temple is stripped bare by a sinister thievery, and then
for the first time Rome was poorer than Caesar.[32]

In Plutarch's *Pompey*,[33] Caesar's arrival in Rome and the appropriation from the treasury occur immediately after the crossing of the Rubicon and Pompey's flight from Rome.[34] In Plutarch's *Caesar*,[35] the 'victor' of Brundisium 'found Rome more tranquil than he had expected, and many senators in it'. He addressed them with a conciliatory speech and urged them to send envoys to Pompey, but found no volunteers, either through fear or because they were not convinced that Caesar meant what he said. Metellus, appealing to particular laws, sought to prevent him drawing from the public treasury, but Caesar retorted that 'the time of arms is not the same as that of laws'. He explained that war had no requirement of free speech and that Metellus and his opponents were in his power. He then went up to the door of the treasury (an unlikely detail, since the Aerarium of Saturn was inside the *pomerium*) and, as the key was missing, he ordered smiths to break open the door. Metellus, backed up by others, objected once again. Then Caesar, raising his voice, threatened to kill him: '"You know, young lad," he said, "that it's more difficult for me to say it than do it."' The tribune drew back and Caesar took what he required for the war.

Appian's account is also very interesting for its 'Gallic' interpretation.[36] Caesar, having hastened to Rome, finds a population terrorized by the memory of Marius and Sulla, and reassures it with promises. Only one speech is recorded, to the people and not to the Senate, in which he recalled his mercy towards Ahenobarbus, released unharmed with his possessions. He then broke open the doors of the Aerarium, threatening to kill Metellus, the only one who dared oppose him, and took the untouchable treasure. It was said to have been deposited there 'at the time of the Gauls, with the sacred public obligation that it should not be taken for any reason, except in the imminence of war against the Gauls'. Caesar claimed he had fulfilled the obligation, for he had defeated the Gauls 'to guarantee Rome an absolute tranquillity'. He then entrusted the city to Marcus Aemilius Lepidus (patrician and praetor, son of the consul of 78 of the same name), and *terra Italia* with the army that guarded it to Antony (tribune appointed propraetor). He chose Curio (he too with an appointment as propraetor) for Sicily, and Orca for Sardinia; he sent Gaius Antonius (brother of Mark Antony and legate) to Illyricum, and Marcus Licinius Crassus (son of the 'triumvir' and legate of the same name) to Cisalpine Gaul. He ordered two fleets to be built speedily, for the Ionian and the Tyrrhenian seas, and appointed Hortensius and Dolabella to command them. And so, with Italy now safe from attack, he left for Spain.

Cassius Dio relates that Caesar, in Rome, delivered 'a lengthy speech fitting to the circumstances to senators assembled outside the *pomerium* by Antony and Longinus', who less than four months earlier had been driven from the city.[37] He wanted to encourage them to be calm, at least for the duration of the war; he censured no one, but railed against those who threatened Rome, and proposed sending messengers to the consuls and to Pompey. He then said the same things to the people, 'who had also gathered outside the *pomerium*'.

Then an aspect that emphasizes the attention that Cassius Dio and his sources paid to the 'urban' situation. He sent for grain from the islands and promised 300 sesterces to every citizen.[38] But the Romans were suspicious, recalling the promises of Marius and Sulla; Caesar needed help and his soldiers were to be seen in large numbers throughout the city; the envoys hadn't left and Piso, Caesar's father-in-law, had been rebuked for having once mentioned them. In the end, not only did the Romans not receive the sum promised, but they had had to give Caesar 'all the money in the public coffers to maintain those soldiers whom they feared'. For all these facts, as if these had been propitious, they wore the clothing of peace (which they had not hitherto worn). The tribune Metellus, having failed in his opposition, stood guard at the building, but the soldiers 'cut the bolt (the consuls kept the key, as if someone could not use the axe in place of the key) and carried away all the money'. The same method was used in all other matters: voting and actions were done in the name of the people (indeed the tribune Antony presented most of the proposals) but were based on power. 'Both Caesar and Pompey called their opponents enemies of the people and claimed they were fighting to defend the community: but in reality both looked after their own interests and were likewise ruining the country'. Sicily and Sardinia had been abandoned by their Pompeian commanders, and Caesar occupied them unopposed.

Orosius quantifies the amount taken from the Aerarium: Caesar, having broken open the doors, 'dragged out 4,135 pounds of gold and around 900,000 of silver'; then 'having returned to his legions in Ariminum, he had soon crossed the Alps and reached Massilia'.[39] A different account is given by Pliny the Elder,[40] who refers to 15,000 ingots of gold, 30,000 of silver and 30 million sesterces in coinage, as well as 1,500 pounds of Cyrenian silphium (an extremely valuable spice and medicine, taken from a plant now extinct).

'DEPARTURE' FOR ANOTHER TWO MONTHS

Cicero, in one letter after another, recalled how many people had returned to Rome over the previous days. Among these, perhaps, were

Terentia and Tullia. He, however, had slowly headed down from Arpinum towards the coast, stopping many times and reaching Cumae (present-day Cuma) by 14 April.

On 3 April he already supposed that something had been decided 'in the conference of senators, which, for me, is not the Senate'[41] (and this, of course, due to the large number of those who were with Pompey). His friend had told him that Flavius (perhaps Lucius, praetor in 58 and an ex-Pompeian) had been offered the command of a legion and of Sicily (an appointment in fact given to Curio) and Caesar's followers were already committing crimes, part of which were planned and part determined by the circumstances. Cicero had decided to stay far from Rome, not wanting to take part in negotiations nor to be an ambassador for false proposals. Preparations for his 'escape' were going ahead.

On 7 April he asked for other news: whether Caesar had departed and in what situation he had left Rome; who had been 'put in charge of the individual regions and of the affairs of Italy itself' and who were they thinking of sending, in accordance with the Senate decree, to negotiate with Pompey and the consuls.[42] Indeed Atticus – he was informed – had been seen 'in the house of the *pontifex* [Caesar]', who had written again to Cicero alone, and not to others, excusing him for 'not having come to Rome'.[43]

Cicero's endless care for his public position was undermined by a brutal and unforeseeable family circumstance. The young son of Quintus – and nephew of Atticus – had written a letter to Caesar, 'such a painful blow for us that we have kept it hidden from you; I think it has embittered his father for his whole life'.[44] After a visit to Hirtius, the nephew had told Caesar about 'my [Cicero's] own unyielding opposition to his policies and my plan to leave Italy'.

On 14 April, at Cumae, he met Curio, on his way to Puteoli. Curio said it was certain that all who had been banished under the law of Pompey would be called back; he would make use of their services in his own government in Sicily. He was also certain that Caesar would take

Spain, before then going on to hunt down Pompey until he was dead. He then referred to events in Rome: Caesar had been on the point of killing the tribune Metellus and starting a massacre; many were urging him to do so, but he had been deterred by the fear of becoming unpopular. As soon as he had understood that the business of the Aerarium had caused ill-feeling among the people, 'although he had firmly intended to address the people before leaving, he no longer wished to risk it', and departed with a sense of unease.[45] Curio's only fear was about Pompey's fleet: if it put to sea, it would force him to abandon Sicily. Cicero asked him if he could pass through his province in order to reach some solitary spot, in Greece. Curio agreed but revealed to him that Dolabella had informed Caesar of his wish that Cicero might return to Rome, and that Caesar had approved: 'I heave a sigh of relief, for it frees me from suspicion about that domestic treachery and the meeting with Hirtius'; for the moment, 'no danger in the city'.[46]

While Cicero was once again delaying his departure, due to bad weather, until 'not before the new moon',[47] he thought it certain that Pompey was on his way 'to Gaul through Illyricum'.[48] He wrote to his friend that he himself wanted to retire 'to Malta or some similar spot or even in a fortress': Dolabella was making enquiries about sailing conditions in the Adriatic, Curio about the Strait of Messina.[49] On 22 April, Curio was still sure of Caesar's unpopularity and the dangers he himself would face in Sicily if Pompey were to put to sea. Cicero meanwhile had also written to Servius Sulpicius Rufus, an advocate of peace, and to his own former quaestor in Cilicia, informing them of his wish to leave.

On 2 May, he told Atticus it was now perhaps the time to 'exclude from our correspondence all those arguments that might be dangerous if they were intercepted'; news from Spain would of course be important but only to a certain point: Pompey now held 'the same view as Themistocles and believes that the master of the sea is without question the master of everything else'.[50] This is the reason for his lack of interest in Spain: 'his constant concern was for the fleet. He will take the sea at the appropriate moment, therefore, with a multitude of ships and will land in Italy'.[51] The only hope is that Caesar falls by himself, 'when six or seven days were enough – popular as he was and new – to attract the most ferocious hatred of a hungry and corrupt populace', unmasked by his threats to Metellus and by the appropriation of the treasury.[52] Caesar, he predicted, wouldn't manage to stay in power for more than six months.

Antony, with whom Cicero would have had to negotiate the crossing to Malta, had meanwhile sent him a blunt letter, which began with the words: 'I cannot believe you are about to cross the sea',[53] quoted at the opening of this chapter. Another letter had arrived that same day from Caesar, written on 16 April as he marched towards Massilia, written in a similar tone:

> Caesar *imperator* greets Cicero *imperator*.
>
> While I know that you don't act lightly or imprudently, prompted however by the rumours that are going round, I felt I ought to write and ask you in the name of our mutual affection not to move off, now that the outcome is close, along a road that you decided not to take when the contest was undecided. You would in truth commit a more serious offence against our friendship and would be acting with little respect to your own interests if it could be said that you had not bowed to Fortune (now everything turns in our favour and against our enemies), and that you have not followed an idea (which is still the same as when you rightly thought not to take part in their projects), but that in reality you condemn some part of my own action: for me, nothing on your part could be more serious. I beg you therefore, for the bonds of our friendship, not to do it. In the end, what can be more fitting, for a man of noble and peaceful mind, for a good citizen, than to keep away from civil strife?[54]

Cicero realized the following day that much of the news needed to be checked out: the speed of Caesar's advance, the situation in Spain,

Pompey's plans to move north. 'I think therefore it is better to go to Malta.'[55]

Another letter from Caelius begged him not to do anything before receiving further information: Caesar, after a now certain victory, would no longer be what he had been before. So far as Spain was concerned, 'Caesar's arrival will be enough to make it ours. What the others can then hope for after the loss of Spain, I really don't know.'[56] A last piece of advice: to search for a secluded spot where he can wait for the end of the conflict.

Cicero reassured him: he wasn't 'so short-sighted as to abandon the rising star for one that is on the decline and indeed about to set';[57] he felt impeded only by his lictors. Another brusque letter arrived from Antony, whose duty it was 'not to allow anyone, in any way, to leave Italy': Cicero would have to ask Caesar directly for permission.[58] He now felt trapped; the only positive note was news of the resistance at Massilia. But the prospect of a sea voyage was becoming intolerable: to trust himself and his children to a small boat in that adverse weather? 'Just imagine how I'd feel in a boat!'[59]

Yet on 5 May he seemed to have decided to leave in secret for Sicily, from where there was reassuring news: the inhabitants, en masse, had 'hurried to welcome Cato' and he, enthusiastic, had begun enlistments: 'the province could be held'.[60] The resistance at Massilia also brought hope for nearby Spain; an incident that occurred in Rome, at the theatre – about which we have no details – was also indicative of resent-ment towards Caesar; morale was low among the legions Caesar had recruited in Italy as well. It would be necessary therefore 'to attempt some action with the spirit of Caelius and, let us hope, with more success'.[61] Caelius' mysterious project, whatever it was, was falling apart; Antony, meanwhile, was making a poor show of himself.

Listen to this act of diplomacy. He had sent round a message to summon the *decuriones* [the members of the local Senate] and the *quattuorviri* of the *municipia*. They arrived at his villa early in the morning: and he slept on until the third hour [around 9 am]; then, on being told of the arrival of men from Neapolis and Cumae (with whom Caesar is furious), he orders them to return next day, since he had to bathe and purge himself. This was how he spent the whole of yesterday.[62]

Cicero didn't find support even from Servius Sulpicius Rufus, in whom he had laid much hope. When he came to see him on 8 May, he had no plans and was distraught: he didn't know who to choose between the two contenders 'amid such a rain of tears that I don't know how they hadn't run dry over such a long period of misery'.[63]

On 10 May, however, Atticus, in two letters written that same day, sent good news, which seems to have involved exploiting the discontent in Caesar's army and 'the "Caelian" plan'.[64] Meanwhile, preparations for departure were going ahead: 'while supplies and the rest are being boarded, I'll rush off to my villa at Pompeii'.[65] But he heard from Curio that Cato, though able 'without difficulty to hold out in Sicily (and if he had done so he'd have had all good men with him)', had sailed from Syracuse on 23 April: 'let's hope at least that Cotta stays firm in Sardinia, for there's a rumour going round! What a disgrace for Cato, in such case!'[66]

Then a bizarre problem arose. Cicero, travelling to Pompeii in order to allay suspicions about his departure, was told that the centurions of the three cohorts stationed there wanted to see him the following day to 'place themselves and the city' in his hands.[67] The solution came immediately: 'I left the next morning, before dawn, so as not even to be seen.' What guarantee could three cohorts offer? And if there had been more, with what resources? Even Caelius – as Atticus wrote – had taken a similar position; furthermore 'it could have been a trap, and I took away all suspicion'.

The 'Caelian plan', as already mentioned, has been the subject of many theories: one of these is that a force led by the proconsul Cicero would take over command in Sicily or Africa, perhaps to impose a general peace.

On 16 May, from Cumae, Cicero wrote that he had found Hortensius very courteous and that he now intended to make use of Serapio (a person whom Atticus had sent, about whom we know nothing else) and his ship, to sail with him, but 'the equinox, being very stormy, is still delaying us'.[68] He also mentioned a mysterious safe-conduct which he thought Atticus had in his possession: 'you had written to me that you planned to leave the country, and, having heard that no one can leave without it, I thought you had it, also because you had obtained it for your slaves'.[69]

There is an interruption in the correspondence. Cicero's letter of 19 May would be the last to his friend until the following year. In it he writes that Tullia, that very day, had given birth to a child in the seventh month; the birth had gone well, but the child was very weak. It would die soon after. 'A period of exceptional calm forces me again to wait and it is an obstacle more serious than the sentries that watch over me.'[70] He would go to Formiae and would write as soon as he had reached his final destination, which was not however Malta.

He set sail from Caieta on 7 June, as emerges from the next letter, sent to Terentia.

> I hope that our ship is indeed good. I am writing this letter to you having just climbed on board. [. . .] if you think it appropriate, keep yourself in those properties most out of the way from soldiers. The farm at Arpinum might be just right for you and for all the city servants, if prices become too expensive. Our sweet Cicero sends you his most affectionate wishes.[71]

Hunger was still viewed as a real danger.

With these words, Cicero's news was, for the moment, interrupted. Many of his predictions would not come to pass.

12

THE BATTLE FOUGHT, THE *RES PUBLICA* AND THE CITY

having seen how events turned out, it is more surprising that they were possible, than that we hadn't seen them coming and hadn't managed, as human beings, to forecast them.

Cicero, *ad familiares*, 15,15,2[1]

The situation degenerated into the longest and cruellest civil war the Romans had ever known, dragging the whole of the Mediterranean into it until Caesar's final victory in March 45. Very little of what Cicero had hoped or feared during the early months of 49 would actually occur. In particular, Rome and terra Italia *were saved from conflict and from the dreaded naval blockade. This was thanks to Cato's flight from Sicily, and to Caesar's speed and Pompey's relative lack of response, sending no fleet to attack the Italian coast. . . and perhaps undermining the remarkable decision taken on that fateful 17 January 49. All in all, it brought an end to the* res publica, *but saved Rome itself and the whole of* terra Italia.

THE SILENCE OF A SPECIAL WITNESS

Cicero, now on his ship, was still awaiting news from Massilia and from Spain. We don't know when it reached him: there's an unfortunate gap in the surviving correspondence until January 48.[2] This means we don't have any direct knowledge about his views during Pompey's councils of war. But even when his correspondence with Atticus resumed – from

Epirus, then from Pompey's camp and from Dyrrhachium – caution prevailed, as indeed the situation required. With his correspondent far away and Cicero in the theatre of war, there was a greater risk of their letters being intercepted, above all by 'friends'. The first letters – from a man who must have seen and heard much – concentrate entirely on personal and financial concerns: he urged Atticus to take care of his affairs at the very time when his wealthy wife Terentia seemed to be holding the purse strings. Another possibility is that the letters for this period had, understandably, been subjected to a thorough editing process by Cicero himself, or by Atticus or later editors.

In a letter sent around mid-April 46 to another friend, Cicero would seek to defend his actions, describing the difficult situation at Pompey's camp when he arrived:

> firstly the troops, few in number and hardly in fighting mood; then, apart from the commander and a few others (I'm talking about the leaders), all the others so greedy in war and so ruthless in speech that even the prospect of victory made me shudder; finally, the enormous quantity of debts among those in highest position. In short, nothing good, apart from the cause. At such a sight, despairing of victory, I first set about recommending peace, which I had always advocated; then, on seeing Pompey so disgusted by that proposal, I began to suggest dragging the war out as much as possible. There were moments when he seemed to share this point of view and prepared to adopt it; and perhaps he might even have done so, if from a certain battle he hadn't gathered confidence in his troops. From that moment on, this great man stopped being a general. With recruits and a motley army he opened battle against perfectly trained legions; shamefully defeated, having lost even his encampments, he escaped alone. I decided at that point that, for me, the war was over. If we hadn't been on a par when our forces were intact, I couldn't believe we would succeed in winning once thrashed. I therefore withdrew

from a war in which all that remained was to die on the battlefield or run into an ambush or fall into the hands of the victor or seek the protection of Juba or choose a place in which to live some kind of exile or voluntarily kill myself.[3]

There are also plenty of references to his own pacifist stance in his speeches *In Defence of Marcellus* and *In Defence of King Deiotarus*, delivered in October 46 and November 45.

A still less heroic picture emerges from other sources. Cicero was immediately criticized by Cato for having taken sides, thus ruling out the possibility of mediation. To the 'republicans' he offered ironic words of praise, which entered history but didn't help him at the time. The situation was improved only by a loan of 2.2 million sesterces to Pompey. For health reasons he played no part in the battles at Epirus and Thessaly. After Pompey's defeat, on reaching Corcyra he refused to continue the 'struggle', even though, according to one source, Cato proposed he should lead what was left of the army and the fleet, later defending him from the threats of Pompey's elder son when he refused. Cicero then returned to Italy, after an equally dramatic rift with his brother Quintus.

From October 48, for almost a year, he remained at Brundisium, waiting for Caesar's 'pardon' and for the outcome of events which seemed ever more distant and unclear to him. In his correspondence with Atticus he was troubled not so much by the fate of the *res publica* as by his family: the deterioration in relations with his wife, his daughter's matrimonial problems, the hostility of his brother Quintus and his nephew. He never regretted having returned, due in part to how events turned out but also for an ethical reason, which he stressed to his friend as soon as his suspicion arose:

there was such savagery in that environment, so much mixing with barbarians, that the plans for proscriptions were no longer aimed at individuals, but at the mass, and they had determined by common accord that the possessions of all of you would be the spoils of that victory of theirs: 'of all of you', I say, since inhuman plans were being devised for you too.[4]

Having at last obtained Caesar's 'pardon' at their meeting at Tarentum on 25 September 47, he returned immediately to Tusculum, and only at the end of the year to Rome.

He spent almost the whole of 46 there, which explains the infrequency of his letters to Atticus (also there). That year began with his divorce from his wife Terentia, and he continued his writings and the preparation of a funeral eulogy for Cato, who had recently killed himself at Utica (Caesar would reply to that eulogy the following year in his *Anticato*). In October, after another series of approaches to the ruling faction, he returned to public life. He thanked Caesar in the Senate for the pardon granted to Marcus Claudius Marcellus, the consul for 51 who, after Pharsalus, had gone into voluntary exile at Mytilene of Lesbos. He then supported Quintus Ligarius, an equestrian who had supported the Pompeian cause in Africa and was accused of high treason. The year ended with his daughter Tullia's divorce from Dolabella and reconciliation with his brother Quintus.

The year 45 was much worse. It began with the death of Tullia while giving birth to a son. The loss of his daughter left Cicero with a deep wound that would never heal. After further months, spent writing letters from his many villas at Astura, Tusculum and Arpinum, he soon separated from the young Publilia, his new wife whom he had married, it seems, for her rich dowry. Having returned to Rome in November, he defended the Galatian king Deiotarus before Caesar, at the house of the absolute master of the *res publica*. Deiotarus, accused of having planned, in 47, the murder of Caesar, had joined Pompey's cause, had taken part at the Battle of Pharsalus and even accompanied his defeated ally as far as Lesbos; he had then extended his control over the region, taking advantage of the Civil War; he had been pardoned by Caesar in person, in 47, but deprived from some possessions, that he, in 45, had asked

Caesar to regain, when an enemy embassy from the region accused him of the attempted murder. Caesar's judgment was probably a wait-and-see one. Then, at the end of December, at his villa at Puteoli, recently inherited from a banker, Cicero entertained the dictator and his retinue, and had the opportunity to make a welcome discovery.

> O guest so unjustly deprecated! He was indeed most pleasant. [. . .] He was massaged, then took his place at table. He used some emetics, then ate and drank heartily and without concern. The hospitality was rich and sumptuous: not only this, but all well cooked, made more hearty by a fine conversation, and, if you wish to know, most cordial. [. . .] No deep discussions; much literature. Need I say more? He enjoyed it and was at ease.[5]

Other sources give more detailed accounts of the complex and countless events after June 49.[6] We will cover all of this in a cursory manner, and look only at the more obvious consequences of the extraordinary flight from Rome, determined on that fateful 17 January 49.

THE CAMPAIGNS OF 49: SPAIN, MASSILIA AND AFRICA

Despite Cicero's hopes, Spain and Massilia were subdued in just a few months. Caesar dealt with the complexity of the situation thanks to his speed and ability to manage the problem of supplies. Meanwhile, Pompey's great fleet was almost totally absent in the western sector of the Mediterranean. Let us look at the key moments.

Caesar marched towards Spain in early April 49. His legate Gaius Fabius had gone ahead from Narbonese Gaul; other legions would then come down from Belgic Gaul to join the proconsul at Massilia; the three veteran legions quartered at Brundisium would also sail to meet him. Massilia, formally free and allied to Rome, retained its ambiguous position until Ahenobarbus – new and lawful governor of Transalpine Gaul

– arrived there, but with only seven ships, requisitioned from private citizens on the island of Aegilium (present-day Isola del Giglio) and in the district of Cosa. Ahead of Ahenobarbus, young men of the area had been sent as ambassadors in January by Pompey, just before his flight from Rome. Massilia handed over its command to Ahenobarbus and the city prepared to hold out against Caesar's siege. To this end, Caesar sent three legions commanded by Trebonius and a fleet of twelve ships, built in a single month at Arelate (present-day Arles) on the orders of Decimus Junius Brutus Albinus (who seven years before had commanded Caesar's Atlantic fleet against the Veneti, and would be one of his assassins).

His other legions moved on towards Spain, to block the Pyrenean passes guarded by Afranius, on whom Cicero had placed much hope. News wrongly reported 'that Pompey was making his way with his legions through Mauretania [in northern Africa] and would be arriving in Spain'.[7] The finance and logistics were no less worrying. To pay his soldiers, Caesar had to borrow money from the military tribunes and centurions. At Ilerda (present-day Lleida) there was a shortage of grain, whose price had risen to 200 sesterces per *modius*, 'a heavy increase that usually occurs not just through current shortage but also through concern about the future':[8] the sources record a price of 3 or 4 sesterces during the previous twenty or so years. Meanwhile, false information sent from their adversaries persuaded those in Rome that the war was over: a crowd then poured upon the house of Afranius and many left for Pompey's camp. Ahenobarbus' meagre fleet at Massilia was instead defeated by Caesar's fleet; and so 'Brutus, winner on the sea, added to Caesar's arms the first naval victory'.[9] Perhaps it was also because of this that the situation in Spain turned: the rumours about enemy legions arriving from Mauretania stopped, Caesar found himself pursuing his opponents, preventing their passage into 'Pompeian' Celtiberia. Once again he demonstrated his clemency, allowing the enemy commanders Afranius and Petreius to leave the province and discharge their armies.

Pompey's only reaction, as the siege of Massilia worsened, was to send just sixteen ships. The fleet had an initial success along the way. Taking advantage of the fact that Curio was about to set sail for Africa, it made a surprise crossing of the Strait, raiding Messana. But once it had reached Massilia it was defeated by Caesar's fleet.

Pompey's faithful supporter Varro, governor of Hispania Ulterior, tried to help but to no avail. Encouraged by the resistance at Massilia and reassuring news from Afranius, he sought to concentrate his fleet and army at Gades in order to prolong the war. Caesar continued unde-terred, 'though many necessary matters called him to Italy'.[10] He sent other legions to Hispania Ulterior and assembled the magistrates of every city at Corduba (present-day Cordova), gaining their support. Varro, deserted even by his soldiers, had to surrender himself and his money. Since Ahenobarbus had fled by sea, Massilia capitulated too, after a very heavy siege. There, Caesar was informed 'by the praetor Marcus Lepidus of his appointment as dictator'.[11] He returned to Rome in December to take office.

While controlling Sicily and Sardinia, he hadn't yet managed to get his hands on Rome's other grain province, Africa. For this purpose, Curio had sailed from Sicily on 8 August 49 with two of his four legions and 500 cavalry, conducting a campaign that was poorly planned. It is enough here to observe several interesting remarks by Caesar. Curio, at some point, declared to his soldiers – the ones who had surrendered at Corfinium – that they had 'set the example for all *municipia*, one after the other', and that Pompey, unbowed, had left Italy 'moved only by the foreboding' that he saw in their surrender. Caesar, he said, had entrusted to him 'the provinces of Sicily and Africa, without which he cannot defend Rome', trusting in their loyalty.[12] Curio laid siege to Utica, but through miscalculation and unreliable information he was defeated and killed on 20 August at the River Bagradas (the present-day Medjerda), fighting the army of King Juba. The poor planning continued, matched by an evident naval inferiority: those who remained on the field hurriedly embarked for Sicily but, in the crush, only a few managed to reach the small boats lined up to transport the soldiers; the fleet and the merchant ships had already fled. It was a total disaster and most of the men surrendered.

Caesar, having briefly returned to Rome (from 2 to 12 December 49), exercised his office of dictator – awarded during his absence in mid-October – for an equally brief period. He did not appoint a commander of the cavalry but presided over assemblies in which he was at last elected to the supreme magistracy, in the year 'in which he could formally become consul',[13] along with Publius Servilius Isauricus (praetor in 54). It seems his father-in-law Piso had urged him to negotiate further with Pompey but that Isauricus, to please him, had persuaded him against the idea.

POMPEY'S DEFEAT

Cicero, in his more dramatic letters at the beginning of 49, had speculated about a naval blockade and an Italian invasion, which he thought would begin the coming summer. Neither of the two events would actually take place; among the possible reasons for this – without ignoring Cicero's own exaggerations – were Caesar's speed, Pompey's political calculations, and excessive optimism among Pompey's followers.

In the meantime, Pompey had built up an enormous army in the east. Even at that time, as Appian points out, figures differed, but we can imagine a force, at its finest, of eleven legions and 7,000 cavalry, plus the militias of non-Roman allies. Pompey's fleet, according to the sources, had a maximum of 600 ships assembled from throughout the east, subdivided into six commands, under the supreme leadership of Bibulus. He, favourite to Cato, was strategically positioned with over 100 ships at the port of Corcyra, the eternal gateway to the Adriatic and only a day's journey from Italy. The financial situation was also looking good, thanks to levies from the provinces, from eastern allies, and even from the *publicani*. Furthermore, the supply network guaranteed provisions of every kind.

Pompey's fleets managed to fend off several of Caesar's attacks on the Adriatic. In 49, the legates Marcus Octavius (aedile in 50) and Libo had secured the surrender of Gaius Antonius, Caesar's legate in command at Liburnia (in Illyricum), and had destroyed or captured the ships led by Dolabella (while he was still Tullia's husband). Octavius would keep control of the area – apart from a few places – until May 47, when Vatinius (tribune in 59 and praetor in 55, legate at that time and soon to be consul), sailed from Brundisium with his fleet, and defeated him.

A partial explanation for Pompey's inactivity could be his belief, still firmly held at the end of 49, that Caesar wouldn't make a sudden move. This was his spirit when he laid out his naval strategy (assuming of course that this is not a duplication of the speech given in Rome on that fateful 17 January 49). In Thessalonica, the 200 senators who had assembled there declared a piece of land chosen for the *auspicia* to be public property, 'so that their acts might demonstrate a certain appearance of lawfulness, and it might be believed, in that way, that the people and the whole city of Rome were present there'.[14] Despite this, they did not elect new magistrates – contrary to what was taking place in Rome – since the consuls had not proposed the *lex curiata* (which the ancient curiate assembly, represented at that time by lictors, had to endorse). They therefore appointed proconsuls, proquaestors and propraetors, and finally gave Pompey supreme command. Cato may have persuaded the council to respect certain rules: not to seize any city that was subject to Rome and not to kill any Roman 'except on the field of battle'.[15] Cato, for his part, once he had left Sicily, had one single aim: 'to drag out the war'.[16] He hoped there could be a peaceful solution and wanted Rome to remain unscathed.

Caesar left for Brundisium on 12 December. We don't know what the situation was in Rome, though it did have properly elected magistrates. He set sail from Brundisium on 4 January, at the earliest opportunity. Once again having to deal with a shortage of ships, he boarded only seven of the twelve legions he had mustered, who moreover were already afflicted with illness and had difficulties over supplies. He managed to cross the Adriatic with no loss of boats, escorted by only twelve warships. The others were still guarding Sardinia and Sicily, since Africa was still held by Pompey's forces. He secured the surrender of the main towns of northern Epirus. Bibulus stepped in late, but managed to destroy the fleet on its return – burning thirty ships, according to Caesar, together with their crews – and set up garrisons along the Adriatic.

Caesar records that he had tried to negotiate, through Pompey's prefect Vibullius: the conditions of peace, he said, 'ought to be sought in Rome from the Senate and the people'.[17] All to no avail. And so there was stalemate, which saw the two rival armies facing each other on opposing banks of the River Apsus (the present-day Seman). For a long while the contingents still at Brundisium were unable to reach Caesar. Once, when they had already set sail, they were ordered to turn back so as not to fall prey to Bibulus. Pompey's legate Libo, with fifty ships, then managed to occupy the island in front of the port of Brundisium which, however, was liberated by Antony. Caesar made countless pleas for reinforcements and an unsuccessful attempt to return in disguise to Italy, during which, at the mouth of the River Apsus, he revealed his true identity and is said to have encouraged a frightened helmsman with another celebrated phrase: 'Brave the tempest with a stout heart: you carry Caesar and Caesar's Fortune!'[18] Then came the turning point.

The fleet, commanded by Antony (as propraetor) and by the legate Quintus Fufius Calenus (praetor in 59) set sail on 10 April – probably after Bibulus had died of sickness and his command had passed to Libo – and was able to land four legions at Lissus (present-day Lezhë in Albania). Over and above the outcome of the campaign, it is interesting to note that Antony, having sent the ships back to bring over the remaining troops, left barges at Lissus for a crucial purpose: if Pompey, 'believing Italy to be defenceless, should decide, as rumour had it, to transport his army there', then Caesar would have some chance of pursuing him.[19] Caesar eventually managed to join up with Antony's armada, despite attempts by Pompey to intercept it. But Caesar's problem over supplies continued: nothing arrived by sea, 'since Pompey had absolute control of it'.[20] Added to this were partial successes by Pompey's elder son, at the command of the Egyptian fleet, at Oricum (in the bay of Aulona) and Lissus, where he also sank the barges.

The main action took place at Dyrrhachium, where Pompey had his base, his stores of food and weapons, and easy access to supplies. The two great strategists began to lay siege upon each other. Pompey built a 15-mile line of defence with twenty-four redoubts, while Caesar, still short of grain, found himself having to encircle, from outside, a stronger army with full reserves, around an even larger perimeter. Caesar made another unsuccessful attempt to negotiate, this time through Scipio, who was in Macedonia. Favonius, it seems, was the one who opposed it.

At one point Pompey managed to break the blockade, placing his besiegers in difficulty, but he failed to take advantage of it, fearing an ambush. Caesar himself declared that 'the enemies would have put an end to the war that very day if they had had someone capable of winning'.[21] The partial success brought on an insane confidence in Pompey's camp. Caesar encouraged his men with the following reasoning:

> It is Fortune that must be thanked, since they had managed to take Italy without losses, they had pacified the two Spains against generals of great skill and ability, leaders of warriors, they had subdued the neighbouring provinces, rich in grain: lastly they must remember with what turn of fate, in the midst of opposing fleets, while not only the ports but also the coasts were full of enemies, they had crossed the sea without losing a single man. If not everything was as successful as they hoped, they had to endeavour once more to revive Fortune.[22]

The war turned into a chase, spread over days and with mixed success. Caesar's remarks about potential plans of action are most valuable.[23] If Pompey had headed off towards Gnaeus Domitius Calvinus (consul in 53, whom Caesar had sent with two legions to Macedonia, against Scipio Nasica), 'he would have found himself far from the sea and cut off from Dyrrhachium, which was his supply base for grain and all other provisions', and so would have to fight on an equal footing. If, on the other hand, he had sailed to Italy, 'he, Caesar, would have joined up with Domitius and would have set off to give help in Italy passing through Illyricum'. Lastly, if Pompey had attempted 'to attack Apollonia [near the present-day Pojan] and Oricum and drive him from the whole coast, he would have besieged Scipio and forced Pompey to rush to his aid'.

Caesar marched rapidly towards Thessaly through Epirus and Athamania. There was ruthless pillaging at Gomphi (the greek Gomphoi), where his men behaved shamefully, 'especially the Germans, who when they get drunk are most ridiculous'.[24] At that point all the cities in the area surrendered, except for Larissa, where Scipio Nasica had led his legions. Caesar, finding himself in an area where the corn was ripening, decided to stop and wait. He was at Pharsalus (or, more accurately, the plain of Pharsalia).

Pompey, having joined his army with that of his father-in-law Scipio Nasica, shared command. Caesar's *Commentaries* describe the impatience of the enemies, the accusations of slowness against their commander and the premature in-fighting over the division of honours and spoils. Would Hirrus be allowed to stand for the office of praetor in his absence? There were daily squabbles between Ahenobarbus, Scipio Nasica and Lentulus Spinther over Caesar's office of *pontifex*; Afranius was accused of betrayal by retreating from Spain; Ahenobarbus was already proposing, once the war was over, to set up a court to judge those senators, one by one, who had stayed in Rome or who, finding themselves in territories occupied by Pompey, had not collaborated: the penalties would be death or, in less serious cases, a heavy fine. Pompey presented his tactical plan, promising an easy victory with almost no losses thanks to his superiority in cavalry; Labienus agreed with him, declaring that Caesar's famous legions were now manned with new recruits.

Other sources describe, in more or less the same terms, a much earlier debate about what to do, which took place in Pompey's camp at Dyrrhachium at the time of Caesar's defeat.

Plutarch records Pompey and Cato's desire for peace, the impatience of Favonius, the attacks against Afranius – accused of having sold the Spanish army to Caesar – and against Pompey, accused, especially by Ahenobarbus, of wanting to drag out the war so that he could retain control over the senators. Afranius proposed returning to Italy, 'the greatest prize of the war';[25] whoever ruled it would immediately have Sicily, Sardinia, Corsica, Spain and the whole of Gaul as well; Plutarch then observes that Italy was holding its hands out to Pompey, who felt, however, that he couldn't run away from Caesar or abandon Scipio Nasica, convinced that 'the best way of looking after Rome was to fight as far afield as possible, so that the city might await the winner without suffering the evils of war, indeed not even knowing about them'.[26] Cato, who had urged his men on before the conflict, wept for his country after the victory at Dyrrhachium, 'seeing so many good citizens had killed one another for that fatal and abominable lust for power'.[27] When Pompey set out to follow Caesar to Thessaly, Cato had been charged with the defence of Dyrrhachium – where his weapons, money, relatives and friends were – with fifteen maniples (or, in other versions, fifteen cohorts and 300 ships).

Appian also devotes a long section to this period of uncertainty.[28] Afranius urged that they should send their fleet against Caesar, 'in which they were much superior, and, by keeping a firm control of the sea, to cause him difficulty in moving about': Pompey should personally lead his army in all haste to Italy, which is 'well disposed towards him and in which there were no enemies'. Having once become master of Italy, Gaul and Spain, he could attack Caesar once again 'from the land that was the seat of power'. Appian observes that Pompey was not persuaded by such helpful words of advice but preferred those who told him that Caesar's army was hungry and it would be shameful to run away. He had succumbed to the idea of a battle on the field out of respect for his eastern allies, so that he could go to Scipio Nasica's assistance in Macedonia, and because he was convinced about the power of his own army. Caesar had problems over supplies and Pompey would have preferred to wear him down, but the 'great mass of senators of equal dignity that surrounded him, the most illustrious knights, and kings and princes', disregarding military questions, had urged him to act. He succumbed to the officials who were now calling him 'king of kings and Agamemnon, given that he too commanded other kings while the war continued'. And so he prepared for battle. The others, certain of victory, behaved improvidently, so that they were already crowning their tents with laurels, ordering sumptuous meals and vying for Caesar's office of *pontifex*.

Cassius Dio reports that Pompey, after his victory at Dyrrhachium, certain that the war was now over, had assumed the title of *imperator*, but hadn't wound laurel around his *fasces* so as not to displease his fellow citizens. For much the same reasons he hadn't sailed to Italy, whose inhabitants were not hostile, or at least were unarmed, 'for he could easily conquer all of it; indeed, with 500 fast ships, his fleet was far superior, so that he could land everywhere at the same moment'.[29] He didn't want to give the impression, however, of having triggered the conflict for the sole purpose of conquering Italy. Nor did he want to strike terror into the Romans: for this reason, he hadn't even sent news of events to Rome.

And so 9 August 48 arrived the decisive battle, 'great and unparalleled by any other', fought out between the most illustrious commanders 'not just among the Romans, but among all men of that time', having been trained for war since their boyhood. The 'prize was Rome and the whole of its empire, which was then vast and powerful'.[30]

The battle is well described by the sources. It is enough to record here that Caesar claims to have led a total of 22,000 men against more than 45,000 on the opposing side. Pompey's superiority in cavalry was even clearer. Then, when Caesar's cavalry was put to flight, six cohorts appeared, hidden behind the far right of the formation, who used javelins as spears to lunge at the faces of the young cavalrymen. Being thus exposed on the left flank, the Pompeians scattered, while their front began to collapse. When the field was won, Pompey fled. Of Pompey's own troops, 15,000 – according to Caesar – lay on the battlefield, probably including Ahenobarbus (even if Caesar says he was killed after, during an attempt of escape). Another 24,000 were taken prisoner. The casualties on Caesar's side – once again, according to his own account – were little more than 200. When Caesar went to view the luxurious tents in the enemy camp, now abandoned, he declared: 'It was they who wanted this.'[31] Plutarch observes that Pompey regretted too late having fought the battle 'without gaining any advantage from the fleet, which was unquestionably his best force'.[32]

CAESAR'S VICTORIES AFTER POMPEY

Cicero seems to limit the war to a conflict between two leaders, from which the *res publica* would emerge in tatters; this is confirmed by his refusal to involve himself in public life after Pharsalus. In particular, he wrote to Atticus on 17 December 48 that he was opposed to the concentration of forces in Africa, to 'defend the *res publica* with the help of those barbarian populations, people totally untrustworthy, especially against an army almost always victorious'.[33]

The sources agree about the chaos created by Pompey's escape, heading east by whatever means he could find; some accounts say he first thought of seeking protection from the Parthians of Juba; but with the persuasion of friends, particularly Theophanes, he opted for Egypt, placing his trust in the very young Ptolemy XIII, whose father he had put on the throne and who had recently sent him a fleet. Many had begun to leave in the second half of August to join Cato, who was now at Corcyra, at the head of an army and 300 ships.

It is not clear what happened then, but it seems the fleet withdrew from other engagements, such as the blockade of Brundisium. According to Plutarch, when Cato was given command, he thought at first that if Pompey died he would return the troops to Italy and go into exile; he then tried to offer the command to Cicero, saving him – when he refused – from the vengeance of Pompey's elder son. He hurried to Africa, where he thought Pompey would take refuge, while another group headed for Spain. In the Adriatic there was still one fleet, which remained active over the following years.

On 2 October, Caesar landed on Egyptian soil in pursuit of Pompey. He didn't get there in time: some days earlier, his enemy had been assassinated on the orders of the young king's advisers. When Caesar received Pompey's decapitated head and his ring, he appeared – more or less sincerely – bereft. He would later punish the culprits with death.

At the end of October, Isauricus named him dictator, for a whole year. Antony meanwhile became commander of the cavalry. Cicero, from Brundisium, still encumbered by his lictors, wrote to Atticus on 27 November that he never doubted what would be Pompey's end. So much mistrust had entered 'the mind of all kings and all peoples [. . .]. I cannot but lament his fate: I had found in him an upright, temperate, serious man.'[34]

Caesar remained in Egypt, embroiled in a lengthy conflict. His arrival at Alexandria – a city that vied with Rome for the title of the most populous Mediterranean city – with few men but with his consul's *fasces*, triggered rebellion. This wasn't helped by his demand for sums of money promised by Ptolemy XII (in full, or at least 40 million sesterces) nor by his interference in the dynastic conflict between Ptolemy XIII and his sister Cleopatra VII, who had been kept away from power. She managed to reach Caesar, remaining with him during the siege from urban guerrillas and from the army of Ptolemy XIII. It was a long while before Rome had any idea what was happening; a letter from Cicero of 14 June 47 states that 'there have been no letters from him since 13 December', apart from the 'story of a letter of his of 9 February'.[35] The situation was resolved only when reinforcements arrived. With help from the armies of Mithridates of Pergamon and Antipater I the Idumaean (Pompey's former client in Judaea), Ptolemy XIII was defeated in battle and died in the Nile. Cleopatra and Ptolemy XIV, even younger than her, were placed on the throne.

But Caesar didn't return to Rome even then. At the end of June, leaving a garrison of Roman troops in Egypt, he went to Asia Minor to fight Pharnaces, son of Mithridates, whom Pompey had installed on the throne of the Cimmerian Bosporus and who then tried to extend his lands at the cost of his neighbours, defeating Caesar's legate Calvinus. On 2 August 47, during a surprise attack, Caesar beat Pharnaces at Zela (the present-day Turkish city of Zile). Later – in a letter to his friend Amantius or on a triumphal inscription – he used the famous phrase 'I came, I saw, I conquered.'[36]

Afer having 'pardoned' Deiotarus, he was called back to Italy to tackle the urgent problem of debt and disorder in Rome, but the greatest challenge came from the mutiny of several legions. He landed at Tarentum on 24 September 47 and was greeted next day by Cicero before returning to Rome, where Antony had been governing with a rod of iron. Having resolved the disorder, and proposed reforms, he agreed to the election of two consuls – Quintus Fufius Calenus and Publius Vatinius – for the remainder of the year. For the next year, he himself was to be elected, along with Marcus Aemilius Lepidus.

Not waiting even to take office, he reached Lilybaeum, on the western coast of Sicily, on 17 December 47. He sailed on the 25th for Africa, boarding six legions and 2,600 cavalry on transport ships: once again, the fleet was inadequate.

What was going on in the Roman provinces? Months before, news of Pompey's death had reached Cato and his men when they had already reached the port of Cyrene (in present-day Libya). They had crossed to Africa, placing their reliance on Varus and Juba. Their whole force totalled ten legions, to which were added four Numidian legions with elephants, auxiliary divisions and around 15,000 horsemen, among which were Labienus' Gallic and Germanic contingents and Berber light cavalries. The coast was patrolled, and abundant supplies were assured from requisitions of food. Cato once again refused supreme command, offering it to Scipio Nasica. He then established a garrison at Utica, where the 300 men 'whom they had for much time made counsellors of war and called senate' were installed.[37]

Caesar, like Curio before him, had no information to help him decide where to put ashore. Only a small part of the fleet was with him when he sighted land on 28 December. He landed close to Leptis Minor (present-day Lamta in Tunisia) with 3,500 legionaries and 150 cavalry. The city welcomed him but there were problems over supplies; he had to send orders to other provinces, including Sardinia, to collect grain and send it to him urgently. He barely survived a cavalry attack led by Labienus and Petreius, taking shelter in the small town of Ruspina (present-day Monastir). Three weeks later, the rest of the fleet arrived. Caesar formed an alliance with Bocchus I, king of Mauretania. Once the forces led by the praetor Sallust had arrived, he found himself at last at the head of ten legions. At Thapsus (close to present-day Bekalta) he forced the enemy army into battle and defeated it, on 6 April 46. Petreius and Juba killed themselves, as did Scipio Nasica, who had escaped by sea but was cornered by part of Caesar's fleet at Hippo (present-day Annaba in Algeria). Afranius and Faustus Sulla were captured and executed. Labienus and Varus fled to Spain, joining Pompey's sons Gnaeus and Sextus. Cato committed suicide at Utica: he hadn't taken part in the battle, having refused to fight against Caesar.

In less than three and a half years from the crossing of the Rubicon, most of Pompey's faction had been wiped out. Caesar returned to Rome in late April 46, where he was given a third dictatorship, this time for ten years, with Marcus Aemilius Lepidus as commander of the cavalry, and celebrated his fourth triumph. But the warring wasn't over.

Spain, over the previous year, had seen military and civil rebellion against the injustices of Quintus Cassius Longinus, which not even his successor had been able or willing to quell. The situation had enabled Pompey's sons to organize another rebel army, which had grown to thirteen legions and was under the capable command of Labienus.

Caesar, dictator and sole consul for the following year, set off in November 46, reaching Obulco (present-day Porcuna) in less than a month. Gradually he put the enemies under pressure. On 17 March 45 he attacked them at Munda (traditionally regarded as close to present-day Montilla), though from a position of disadvantage and with a smaller army. Caesar found himself fighting for his life but managed to crush his enemies: they suffered 33,000 deaths, including Labienus and Varus, with a loss to Caesar of only 1,000 men. The troops hailed him as *imperator*. On 5 May 45, Cicero wrote to Atticus from one of his villas: 'Hirtius has written to me that Sextus Pompeius has quit Corduba and taken refuge in Hispania Citerior, that Gnaeus Pompeius has fled I don't know where: nor do I much care.'[38]

Gnaeus was wounded, and would be killed and decapitated a few weeks later. Sextus, having assembled those who had escaped, was able to sail away with a small fleet; he stayed 'well hidden and moved from place to place, living by piracy'.[39] This man, whose death ends the last surviving book of Appian's *Civil Wars*, would carry out a sporadic naval blockade between 41 and 36 in pursuit of the 'republican' campaign against the 'triumvirate' of Caesar's heirs: Antony, Lepidus and Octavian.

Once he had secured the surrender of Hispania Ulterior, Caesar returned to Rome to celebrate another triumph in October 45, this time over Roman citizens.

ITALY AND ROME

What happened in Rome between April 49 and October 45? The information is scant but most valuable. In the early months of 49, Cicero was contemplating the possibility of a rebellion by Caesar's troops, as well as by Rome itself. Neither of these took place, though the army almost did rebel. There was discontent among the four or so legions stationed near Placentia. The reason is not clear: troops were claiming the reward promised back at Brundisium (according to Appian), or even the right to sack the country (according to Cassius Dio). Caesar, having hurried back from Massilia after capturing the city and taken up his appointment as dictator, calmed the rebels. Only twelve were put to death, chosen by lot among the leaders of the mutiny. The *Commentaries* make no mention of this episode but, according to Cassius Dio, he told his men that Romans who resorted to pillage would be behaving 'like Celts'.[40]

Once back in Rome as dictator, one of the major problems he had to tackle was the level of debt among citizens. By autonomous decision or a comitial law, instead of the much feared remission of debts, he ordered the appointment – or selection by lots – of arbiters to value the assets of debtors prior to the civil war. One way of satisfying creditors was to force sales, even at the prices before, to repay the debts. He then revived what he claimed to be an earlier law, which prohibited the holding of securities worth more than 60,000 sesterces in gold or silver. Appian also records distributions of grain 'to the hungry people', which are generally regarded as different from those distributions made on his first entry to Rome in April 49 (referred to, moreover, only by Cassius Dio). He also allowed the return of exiles who had been convicted for *ambitus* under the *lex Pompeia*, with the sole exception of Milo. In particular, followers of Clodius returned, as well as Sallust and Gabinius. The children of citizens proscribed by Sulla were also rehabilitated. Transpadian Gauls were given Roman citizenship, while Cisalpine Gaul remained a province.

As consul for the following year, Caesar left for the Balkan campaign. Cassius Dio, a hostile source who keeps a particular eye on the 'urban' repercussions of the conflict, notes that on this occasion he had collected all the votive offerings – also from the Capitolium – and that the sooth-sayers, interpreting a series of prodigies, had concluded: 'if he remained in Rome, he would have ruin; if he crossed the sea, safety and victory'.[41]

Cassius Dio also provides an extraordinary description of the con-flicting moods from the period before Pharsalus up to Caesar's return in autumn 47.[42]

So long as uncertainty remained, everyone appeared to support Caesar, fearing the soldiers camped in the city and the consul Isauricus. Many were shamming: when news reports arrived, often numerous and contradictory, 'arriving in the space of a day or even an hour', feelings ran hot and cold. The news from Pharsalus was received at first with disbelief. Caesar hadn't told the Senate and, given the disparity between the two forces, there was great surprise. Later, the statues of Pompey and Sulla were pulled down from the *rostra*, though no more than that, for fear that Pompey might still be alive. But when his ring was brought to Rome, the victor was granted every possible honour: senators competed in proposing, in voting, 'in shouting and in gesticulating, as if Caesar were there to see them'. Honours, statues and unprecedented political privileges – including consulships and dictatorships lasting years – not to mention those he turned down. There is then a long section dealing with what happened to Marcus Caelius Rufus, beginning in the early months of 48.[43] We will now consider this, also looking at other sources.

Caelius, as we have seen, like most *boni*, initially allied himself with Caesar through his friend Curio. His cynical words of August 50 indi-cate a choice that was convenient but nevertheless problematic. Curio's death in August 48 had distanced him from Caesar, who hadn't awarded him the honours he had expected. Indeed, having been elected praetor for that year in the assemblies held by the dictator at the end of 49, he had been appointed by him – and not, as was customary, by lot – to a praetorship of lower rank than that of urban one, which was awarded to Trebonius (tribune in 55 and formerly Caesar's legate in Gaul). He also seemed convinced that the tide was turning, as he had written to Cicero at the end of January:

> here, apart from a few capitalists, at this moment there is not a single man or a single class that is not Pompeian. Thanks to me, the lower classes in particular, but generally all the people, who were previously with us, are now on your side. You will ask why. Wait instead for what is to come; I'll make you win even if you don't want to.[44]

At first Caelius vetoed the actions of Trebonius, who had introduced a new system for the valuation of assets. He was unsuccessful. This, according to Caesar, was because of the fairness of the urban praetor's decisions, but one suspects it was also because debtors were content to redeem their debts with overvalued property. He then proposed a general moratorium on debts for six years, with the cancellation of interest: this, by freezing the situation, was welcomed by both debtors and creditors. Due to the opposition of the Caesarians, and above all from the consul Isauricus, he withdrew the proposal, proceeding with two others that were more radical and popular. He perhaps wanted to make the most of a housing problem that was far from simple. Many lived as tenants in a city which, four years after the flooding of the Tiber (in 54), had been devastated by fire – 'how it began is not known', but it had been the worst of its kind until then.[45] An earthquake had brought further damage and conflagration the following year. Caelius proposed the remittance of rent for a year, together with a vaguely defined law on the cancellation of debts.

Isauricus then called back a group of soldiers who were marching to Gaul – suggesting, contrary to what Cassius Dio claims, that no troops were stationed in Rome – and, having convened the Senate under their protection, put forward motions that were nevertheless vetoed by the tribunes. He then ordered his messengers to destroy the tables recording Caelius' proposals. Caelius drove these men out, 'causing a tumult that involved the consul himself'.[46] The Senate, meeting once again under military protection, decreed an end to Caelius' magistracy and voted a new *senatus consultum ultimum* – the first since that of 7 January 49 – entrusting the city's defence to Isauricus. Caesar, unlike Cassius Dio, doesn't mention the *senatus consultum ultimum*, stating only that, after acts of violence against Trebonius (not Isauricus), the assembly decreed that Caelius be dismissed, at which 'the consul refused him admittance to the Senate and had him pulled down from the *rostra* while he was trying to address the people'.[47]

According once again to Caesar, Caelius left the city, claiming that he wished to go and explain his reasons to him; instead, through messengers, he summoned Milo, who was exiled in Massilia – where he may have played a part in the resistance against Caesar – but who still had gladiators in his service. Caelius sent Milo ahead into the area of Thurii (on the eastern coast of Calabria) to stir a revolt among the shepherds. As we have seen, Caelius had strongly supported him during his trial in 52. According to Cassius Dio, however, Milo, the only exile not to have been allowed to return, was nevertheless back in Italy and had gathered 'many men, some with no means of support and others fearful of punishment', who began sacking country areas and 'raiding towns, including Capua'.[48]

It seems very likely that Caelius and Milo were together at a later stage. Milo had, in fact, sent a letter to the *municipia* stating that he was acting by order of Pompey, on the instructions of Vibullius. The actions of the two are not at all clear and, probably, not entirely linked. The sources also record the mobilization of fugitive slaves, gladiators or shepherds. The first areas affected by the attempted rebellion were in Campania, but the plan must have altered following the resistance of Roman citizens at Capua, a failed surprise attack on Neapolis and the reaction of Isauricus. The two rebels were finally killed: Milo probably at Compsa (present-day Conza della Campania), Caelius at Thurii. Caesar observes: 'these beginnings of serious unrest which, given the excessive duties of the government and the difficulties of the times, brought unease to Italy, came to a quick and easy end'.[49] From Cassius Dio, however, we get some feeling of the extent of the revolt, which was enough to justify the massive intervention of Caesar's forces.

There seems to have been a clear attempt to capture strategic maritime ports as the shipping season approached, when the more favourable weather would have enabled Pompey's fleet to set sail. And we know from Cicero that the idea of controlling access to the Peninsula was aired in Rome also after Pompey's death. On 17 December 48, he wrote to Atticus from Brundisium that he had read a copy of a letter from Caesar in which he mentioned:

> having heard that Cato and Lucius Metellus had returned to Italy with the idea of living openly in Rome; that he did not allow it for fear of disorder; entry to Italy must be forbidden to all those whose case he has not personally examined; the tone of the letter was very severe.[50]

Cicero wrote to Atticus again from Brundisium in January 47, when Caesar was still stuck in Alexandria, saying not only that concrete preparations were going on in Africa and that Spain was following suit, but also that 'Italy can be considered lost, the legions less powerful and less enthusiastic, in Rome the situation is desperate.'[51]

Cassius Dio gives a more detailed account.[52] Even after the death of Milo and Caelius 'many dreadful events occurred, as the prodigies had already foretold' at the end of 48. A swarm of bees had settled on the Capitolium beside the Temple of Hercules during a sacrifice to Isis and Serapis; the sacred enclosure of the two Egyptian divinities was then demolished but, by mistake, also a shrine to Bellona, the goddess of war, unearthing jars full of human flesh. The first months of 47 were marked by other prodigies, including an earthquake, thunderbolts on the Capitolium, on the Temple of Fortuna Publica and on the gardens of Caesar. The birth of infants with their left hands to their heads prompted the soothsayers to predict a rebellion against the upper classes, '(and the people believed what they said)'. Fear was increased by the spectacle of a city which, in the early months of 47, had no consuls and praetors, while Antony 'with the sword that hung from his side [. . .] very clearly announced the monarchy'. The Romans, on seeing him, also began to be suspicious of Caesar.

On top of this were the quarrels between two tribunes. Dolabella – who, like Clodius, had had himself adopted by a plebeian in order to become a magistrate – ended up quarrelling with his Optimate colleague Lucius Trebellius. He proposed the remission of debts and equally popular measures on the renting of property. Because of these two, there were 'many armed men everywhere', though the Senate had put a stop to public activities prior to Caesar's arrival, and Antony had declared 'that no private person could carry arms in the city'. Their quarrel continued, however, and Antony took advantage of it to 'keep soldiers inside the walls and watch over the safety of the city as well as the tribunes'. There were in fact many rumours that Caesar was dead, fuelling unrest also among soldiers back in Italy from Pharsalus, who rioted and killed several officials. Antony put Lucius Julius Caesar (consul in 64) in charge of the city but he failed to gain the respect of the tribunes.

Back from his mission to the soldiers, which proved fruitless, Antony came up against new difficulties. In searching for consensus, he wavered between supporting Dolabella and Trebellius. The two tribunes were at war, 'occupying in turn the most advantageous parts of the city', committing crimes and arson, 'to such an extent that on one occasion the vestal virgins had to carry the sacred vestments and vessels from the Temple of Vesta'. The Senate ordered Antony to restore order, and almost every district was packed with soldiers. On being told that Dolabella had fixed the date for the vote on his proposals, 'the multitude, having built barricades around the Forum and wooden towers in various places, showed they were ready to attack anyone who acted against them'. At which point Antony, coming down from the Capitolium with soldiers, broke the tablets that contained the text of the laws and threw several rioters down from the cliff.

Caesar makes no reference to this event, but what survives of Livy's account is quite remarkable:

> In Rome, with riots being provoked by the tribune of the plebs Publius Dolabella, who had presented a proposed law for revision of the registers of debtors, following the rebellion of the populace, the master of the cavalry Mark Antony brought military divisions into the city and 800 plebeians were killed.[53]

Calm only returned when Caesar came back from an absence of over twenty months, for six of which he was almost totally cut off in Egypt. Dolabella – no enemy of Caesar – was rewarded with the consulship rather than being punished. Following in Curio's footsteps, Dolabella must have been very popular: to this end he had probably tried to exploit the memory of Clodius, planning even to erect a statue to him. Things had, in any event, degenerated, so that urgent measures were needed. Let us follow Cassius Dio.[54]

Caesar, 'a formidable gatherer of money', returned from Bithynia through Greece, having received loans and enormous sums, including those promised to Pompey, convinced that power was based on money and military strength. He didn't go straight to Africa because he'd been told about the disorder in Rome and 'feared that the situation could become dangerous'. In Italy he punished no one, limiting himself to collecting money from everyone – private individuals and cities – in every form. The 'loans' were levies, always compulsory and never paid back: 'he said he had spent everything he had for the people and this was why he had to incur debts'; this upset many people but was of no concern to him.

The sources record other tax and financial measures that are difficult to date accurately but were introduced almost certainly after those of 49. There was a move to curry popular favour by reducing rents for a year, down to 2,000 sesterces in Rome and 500 in Italy, and to reduce debts by the amount of interest already paid from the beginning of the war. Added to this was the obligation for creditors to invest part of their wealth in lands in Italy and some limitation on interest rates, though we don't know what. Many people were given public appointments, to be exercised during the remainder of that year and the next, increasing the number of praetors and priests. Various rewards went to rebel soldiers. The largest group was in Campania: it had not received what had been promised after Pharsalus and was protesting against the extension of military service (in view of the forthcoming campaign in Africa).

The praetor designate Sallust almost lost his life; a horde of soldiers followed him to Rome, killing two senators. Caesar allowed them to stay in the city, but unarmed except for their swords. As a precaution he kept another of Antony's legions on guard around his house and along the roads that led from the city (he knew well that Rome had to be defended, even from a group of protesters). He therefore went among the agitators, in the Campus Martius. He persuaded most of them to back down on their demands, promising to pay part of the money immediately, part later. To those agitators he didn't want in the army he gave public land, or his own land, but in places far apart, so as not to cause danger to neighbours or disorder. To the greatest troublemakers he granted land outside *terra Italia*.

Cassius Dio gives us similar detail about the events of 46.[55] Caesar returned to Rome on 25 July after his victory in Africa, travelling via Sardinia and having sent troops to Spain. The Senate had voted forty days of *supplicatio* for Thapsus. His speech before the assembly was one of reassurance. He didn't intend to follow the example of Marius, Cinna and Sulla. The soldiers would be left to guard the empire, and this – as well as the adornment of the city – was why taxes were necessary: 'we are in continual need of arms, since without them it is impossible for a people who live in so great a city and rule so vast an empire to live in safety'. According to Plutarch, when Caesar returned to Rome from Africa 'he boasted before the people that by his victory he had subdued a region so vast that it would furnish the public treasury each year with 200,000 Attic *medímnoi* of grain and 3 million pounds of olive oil'.[56] The victorious general could therefore celebrate four separate triumphs – all in April, but on four non-consecutive days – over Gaul, Pontus, Egypt and Africa, immortalized in the cycle of paintings by Andrea Mantegna (1485–1505) now at Hampton Court Palace in London.

Cassius Dio also gives a detailed account of these triumphs, though they are described by many other authors. Of most interest is not just the killing of Vercingetorix and the display of pictures of those Romans who had been defeated (except for Pompey, whom many still mourned) but also the quantity of riches carried in procession: coins worth over 360 million sesterces, more than 2,800 gold crowns weighing nearly 20,500 pounds. Some 22,000 tables of food were laid out for the population. Gifts went, in proportion, not just to officers, centurions and soldiers but also to individual citizens, who each received 10 *modii* of grain and 10 pounds of olive oil; in addition to the 300 sesterces already promised were another 100 for delay in payment.

After the triumph, Caesar inaugurated the Forum Julium and the Temple of Venus Genetrix, dedicated to his daughter Julia. It was probably then that he offered entertainments with horses, music, war re-enactments – including naval battles in an artificial lake dug in the Campus Martius – and games featuring gladiators and elephants. There were countless numbers of participants, and victims – something that, according to some sources, people didn't enjoy. 'These shows were watched by vast throngs who had come from every part, so that many outsiders slept in tents pitched in the streets and at crossroads, and many, including two senators, were crushed and suffocated in the crowd.'[57]

There are interesting details about the city populace as well. Caesar 'discovered from a census of citizens, so it is said, that their number was half of what it had been before the war: by so much had the city been reduced through the dispute between these two men'.[58] In reality, it seems the situation can be explained on the basis of Caesar's decision to reduce the number of those benefiting from the *frumentationes* from 320,000 to 150,000 – a reduction caused not only by a drop in population but also by putting a stop to false claims, 'as is common in times of political strife'.[59] In practice, it seems that this had been possible thanks to a census of the occupants of the *insulae*, carried out by the landlords. At the same time, a colonization programme involving 80,000 citizens brought order to the *ager Campanus* as well as Narbonese Gaul, Spain, Africa, Macedonia, Greece, Asia, Pontus and Bithynia. The *collegia* were disbanded, except for those in existence since earliest times. Numerous urban planning projects went ahead, but it is difficult to say how many poor citizens were employed in them. On 13 July 45, Cicero wrote from Tusculum to his friend Atticus: 'How disgraceful! Your compatriot wants to expand the city that he saw for the first time two years ago and which he thinks is too small, though it has been big enough to hold him.'[60]

In October 45, on his return to Rome from Munda, he held another celebration, after his victory over Roman citizens. The comments of Cassius Dio are particularly interesting.[61] Caesar 'again offered a solemn banquet to all the people, as if a great fortune had occurred'; three splendid triumphs were celebrated, and thanksgiving ceremonies to the gods lasted fifty days. But before that, on 21 April, 'the Parilia was celebrated with a chariot race, which then became yearly, not in honour of Rome, which had been founded on the day of the celebration, but for Caesar's victory, because news of this victory had arrived the previous day, in the evening'. Yet the victory itself had occurred on 17 March. We cannot rule out, as one scholar has observed, that this extraordinary coincidence had been created through a calculated delay. Caesar knew he had to make Rome feel it was once again playing a central role.

ROME AT THE CENTRE, FROM OCTAVIAN TO
NAPOLEON

The die thrown symbolically across the Rubicon had scored a win. Yet no one, not even Caesar, could have predicted it. Crucial – and in reality more fateful than the famous crossing – was the unexpected evacuation of Rome, ordered by Pompey on 17 January and followed, two months later, by his retreat from Italy.

What were his reasons for leaving? History has offered theory upon theory, which we will now try to summarize. First of all, there is the one about 'panic', which would prompt moves aimed at remedying the initial errors but carried out when resistance was still possible (Mommsen). It has also been observed, on the other hand, that Legio XII and Legio VIII, the twenty-two cohorts of new recruits and the 300 or so horsemen from Noricum must already have been in Cisalpine Gaul in early January 49, much closer than Caesar's *Commentaries* would have us believe (Ottmer). There were then interpretations of a political kind, which suggest a strategy perhaps inevitable but certainly useful also for Pompey's assertion of supremacy, which he actually achieved in early 48 (Meyer). It has also been observed that, for this reason, the retreat may have been long thought out, as is shown in particular by the events at Corfinium (von Fritz, Burns). Lastly, the great potential of Pompey's 'naval strategy' has been emphasized and, in particular, of a maritime blockade (Pocock, Powell, Welch). This would later be achieved by his son Sextus, the surviving defender of the 'republican' cause, whose fleet would cause serious difficulties for Rome's supplies . . . even though the objective by then would be more limited: to create chaos, to force Octavian to negotiate.

The evidence of Cicero's correspondence, so valuable in reconstructing the climate of the moment, seems less helpful for an understanding of Pompey's strategy. In particular, one suspects that the extraordinary references to the use of the fleet against Rome and *terra*

Italia all appear as provocations directed towards Atticus. A similar – and perhaps even more revealing – impression emerges from Caesar's *Commentaries*. They report that Calidius, on 1 January 49, was convinced that Caesar feared that the two legions taken from him were being 'kept by Pompey in the vicinity of Rome to be used against him', continuing then to describe the unexpected and unprecedented flight from the city.[62] Would a politician like Caesar, so aware of public opinion, have failed to mention his enemy's plan to strangle Rome through starvation or at least to adopt a strategy of 'piracy'?

Many years later, in his *Res gestae*, Octavian, already Augustus, would portray the war against Sextus Pompeius – though without even naming him – as a battle against a common pirate.[63] Florus, in the same vein, would write: 'what a difference there was between him and his father! Pompey had wiped out the Cilician pirates, this one defended himself with a horde of pirates.'[64] Lucan would also describe him as 'a son unworthy of his father's name "Great", that Sextus who then, exiled and banished in Scylla's waters, a Sicilian pirate, dishonoured his father's naval glory'.[65]

Was Pompeius' criminal strategy perhaps impeded by Cato, with his abandonment of grain-rich Sicily? He certainly fled the island to avoid creating innocent victims, among whom we might include the inhabitants of Rome: he had once helped them thanks to a generous grain law and now they risked starvation. His recommendations, along with the other events of the following year, especially the victory at Dyrrhachium and the rejection of Afranius' advice, also played their part in keeping the Pompeian fleet ostensibly inactive.

So let us look at events from the opposite viewpoint, starting from the remarks of an eminent 'Caesarian' who couldn't have been present at the dramatic meeting of 17 January 49. This was Napoleon Bonaparte, who among other things had a deep understanding of the mood of a capital city and the limits of a naval blockade. Now banished to St Helena, this is how he summarized Pompey's errors:

1. Pompey was wrong about the mood of the people: he was misled by the opinion of important men, of senators, who spoke out against Caesar. The people felt an irresistible inclination towards Caesar.
2. The six legions that he had in Spain could have reached Rome in a few weeks, embarking at Cartagena, Valencia and Tarragona and landing at Naples or Ostia.
3. It is Rome that he needed to keep; it is there that he should have concentrated all his forces at the start of the civil wars; troops have to be kept together, so that they become charged and familiar with the power of the cause; they are attached to it and remain faithful to it. If the thirty cohorts of Domitius had been camped before Rome with Pompey's first two legions; if the Spanish legions, those of Africa, of Egypt, of Greece had been brought by a combined movement on Italy by sea, Pompey would have rallied against Caesar an army stronger than his.[66]

We, like Napoleon, are convinced that the defence of Rome might have avoided the domino effect that was triggered, on that fateful 17 January 49, by a traumatic decision that could easily be interpreted as a sign of extreme weakness. If Pompey 'has relinquished the head, there is no reason why he should save the other limbs', Cicero reminded Atticus; 'they are afraid, if even Pompey himself escapes', Lucan would later observe, referring to the desertion of Rome by its citizens.[67] With what hope – but above all for what reasons – should the *municipia* of *terra Italia* have held out against Caesar, who had arrived not at the head of barbaric hordes but was seeking to act with the greatest clemency, to safeguard the sacrosanct rights of the tribunes and, at most, to resolve a personal vendetta for an equally personal insult? Not even the land-owners, Cicero's 'right-minded' supporters – no longer even an integral part of the army – would have wished to involve themselves in defending the *res publica*, an ideal rendered increasingly abstract by the constant spectacle that Roman politicians had managed to create over the preceding years.

Unlike Napoleon, we doubt that Pompey was unaware of the feelings of the people. He certainly hadn't grasped those of the Italian *municipia*, which he probably thought he had understood through the assurances of local magistrates and the unprecedented rejoicing after his recovery from illness. But he made no mistake about Rome. In the city which, according to Cassius Dio, constituted the 'prize' of the conflict,[68] having once reached the fateful 17 January 49, he had long experienced the feelings of mistrust, at various levels – of the *nobilitas* and the whole Senate, without doubt, but also of the people. He feared attempts on his life and revolts. The *senatus consultum ultimum* of 7 January 49 entrusted him with the desperate mission of defending a heavily populated urban centre, which now adored Caesar (though even he, from the outset, would have had to be extremely cautious of its moods, in a relationship made up of long absences and major social reforms). Yet for reasons politically understandable but never entirely clear, Pompey, according to Cicero, had never 'worried about giving the population happiness or dignity'.[69] The fight against corruption might itself have backfired.

In any event, in our view, there was a real risk in 49, as Caesar approached, of an unmanageable revolt breaking out and the Romans eventually opening their gates to the conqueror of Gaul, as had happened after the first of Sulla's two 'marches' in 82, when hunger gained the upper hand. From Pompey's point of view it must have been a desertion that was forced upon him and was unavoidable. The rather unsubtle game of precedents – from Themistocles to the sack of the Gauls – was a way of justifying the shock produced by it. This, as we have seen, was quite clear to Caesar, Cicero, Lucan, Plutarch, Appian and Cassius Dio. It was also probably apparent to Livy, as emerges perhaps from his description of the celtic sack.

Rome, however, demanded something else. This was very clear to the Populares, and above all to Caesar. It was probably also clear to his adopted son Octavian, initiator in 43 of another 'march' on the city – which opened its gates to him – and also, in 32, of a skilful and, in our view, eloquent propaganda exercise. At the height of tension with Antony (Caesar's tribune of 49, now ruler of the eastern provinces and husband of Cleopatra), he would publicly reveal the contents of his enemy's will while he was still alive. This patent impropriety would succeed in transforming, in the eyes of the Romans, a battle for power into a battle between two worlds. Cassius Dio records:

> The content of the will was such that the Romans made no reproach to Octavian for his highly irregular behaviour. For Antony solemnly affirmed that Caesarion was indeed the son of Caesar; he stated that he had given splendid gifts to Cleopatra's children and wished to be buried in Alexandria by her side. Outraged by this, the Romans thought the other rumours must be true, namely that, if he were victorious, he would give Rome to Cleopatra and move the seat of the empire to Egypt.[70]

Italy and the western provinces would then swear allegiance to Octavian. Rome should remain at the centre. Forever.

GLOSSARY

aedilis Magistrate appointed to oversee building works, public games and city life. Two plebeian aediles were created in 493 BC, joined in 367 BC by two curule aediles.

ambitio Activities connected to candidacy for elections.

ambitus Crime of electoral corruption.

annona From the name of the Italic divinity of abundance, supply and distribution of grain.

augur Priest who, from the observation of celestial signs, established the will of the gods in relation to matters of public importance. After Sulla, the college of *augures* had fifteen members.

auspicia Enquiry ordered by the magistrate and carried out by the *augur* to ensure that the divinities were favourable to a certain decision.

bellum justum The 'just war', primarily a war declared according to pre-established formalities.

bonus Literally 'good man', 'gentleman'. An expression used by Cicero to indicate a social category wider than *optimas* but loyal to traditional values.

censor One of two magistrates elected every five years to carry out the *census*, namely the registration of citizens of various classes according to property, and the *lectio senatus*, revision of the list of senators based on moral criteria. The *censores* were given responsibilities for managing the assets of the Roman people.

centuria One of over 190 units that constituted the *comitia centuriata*.

clientela Institution that originally indicated the *patronatus* of a patrician *gens*; it was then extended over time to the more wide-ranging category of political allegiance in exchange for advantages of varying nature.

collegium Association relating to a cult or profession.

colonia Urban settlement under Roman or Latin law which presided over a particular area of territory or offered land to be cultivated by particular groups (city plebs, military veterans). After the Social War the colonies of *terra Italia* gradually became *municipia*.

comitia centuriata Electoral or legislative assembly of the Roman people, organized according to the census classes, subdivided in turn into more than 190 *centuriae*.

comitia tributa Electoral or legislative assembly of the Roman people, organized according to the thirty-five *tribus*.

concilium plebis Electoral or legislative assembly of the Roman plebs, organized according to the thirty-five *tribus*.

consul One of two magistrates appointed annually to exercise supreme power in Rome or, with *imperium*, in *terra Italia* or in the Roman provinces. From Sulla's time, after the end of their mandate, they were appointed as *proconsules* in governing the provinces.

contio An assembly, neither electoral nor legislative, in which the people were informed by the magistrate on a particular matter.

cursus honorum The succession of public offices during a political career: quaestor, tribune and/ or aedile, praetor, consul, perhaps censor. A minimum age was set for individual offices and intervals between each office.

dictator An extraordinary magistrate invested with enormous power, nominated by consuls and by the Senate in times of greatest danger, and assisted by a *magister equitum*. He could not remain in office for more than six months. The dictatorships of Sulla and Caesar were 'anomalous'.

discessio Method of open voting in the Senate, carried out by moving position inside the hall.

eques Literally 'knight', representative of the equestrian class, originally a member of the city's cavalry but in the late republican times mainly an economic and social distinction.

extra ordinem Outside the *ordo*, in other words extraordinary. It can refer to commands or particular legal procedures.

fasces Bundles of wooden rods and an axe, symbols of the magistrate's coercive power. They were carried by *lictores*, officials who accompanied magistrates.

feriae Latinae Festivities of ancient origin celebrated in April, in the presence of the consuls, at Monte Albano.

frumentatio Distribution of grain to the Roman population at a subsidized price or even free of charge.

gens One of the original great families, 'clans' established in Rome during the Roman monarchy and early republican period; members of the *gens* had a shared *nomen*, whereas the families that formed part of them were distinguished by their *cognomen*.

imperator Title given to the magistrate who had won an important military victory.

imperium The power of a magistrate to lead an army. A magistrate had *imperium infinitum* when his sphere of responsibility extended to all Roman provinces.

insula A block of apartments, often rented.

intercessio A magistrate's veto against the actions of a colleague, a lower magistrate or (in the case of *tribuni plebis*) a higher magistrate.

interrex Senator appointed to enable elections to be properly conducted in the event of there being no consul. *Interreges* carried out their duties in turn for very few days.

jus Latii The right relating to Latin citizenship, lesser than Roman law at that time, but greater than the status of allies or foreigners.

legatus Person appointed by a magistrate for a particular mission.

legio A legion whose infantry at that time was divided into ten *cohortes*, with a theoretical maximum of 5,000 men.

lex publica Law approved by an assembly of the Roman people; a proposal that is voted by the *concilium plebis* is generally described by the sources as *plebis scitum*.

libertus Slave freed by his master; he took Roman citizenship and voted in one of the four city *tribus*.

libri Sibyllini Texts according to the tradition dating from the Roman monarchy and entrusted to a college of fifteen priests, appointed by the Senate to consult them.

lictor An official who accompanied magistrates and carried the *fasces*.

ludi Games and public entertainments held generally during major religious festivals.

magister equitum Master of the cavalry, assistant to the *dictator*.

maiestas Crime committed by someone who diminishes the majesty and dignity of the Roman people in some way.

municipium Pre-existing urban centre to which Roman citizenship was extended. After the Social War the *municipium* became the structural basis for the urban settlements of *terra Italia*.

nobilitas Literally 'renown', indicated the limited group that could claim to have a higher magistrate among their close ancestors.

obnuntiatio Declaration of an unfavourable *auspicia*, for the purpose of invalidating the deliberations of a popular assembly or the Senate.

optimas Politician who described himself as 'the best'; *optimates* were *nobiles* of more conservative tendency.

patricius Belonging to the patrician class, the ancient line of aristocracy of blood, but now in the minority among the *nobilitas*.

penates Divinities that protected the family.

perduellio Crime of high treason.

plebeius Belonging to the plebs. In ancient times plebeians were deprived of many rights but were now in the majority, even among the *nobilitas*.

plebis scitum Vote of the *concilium plebis*, binding on the entire citizenship from 287 BC.

pomerium The furrow cut by a plough to mark the boundary of the sacred area originally identified by Romulus for the city of Rome and then extended over time. Inside, among other things, it was forbidden to carry arms, and the magistrate lost his military *imperium*.

pontes Literally 'bridges'. Narrow wooden structures that voters had to cross to deliver their voting *tabella*.

pontifex Priest who upheld the legal and religious traditions of the city; after Sulla the college of *pontifices* consisted of fifteen members, headed by the *pontifex maximus*.

popa Priest of lower rank, often not free, who performed sacrifices.

popularis Politician of popular tendency.

praefectus classis Fleet commander responsible to a magistrate with *imperium*.

praetor Magistrate with a lower *imperium* to that of the *consul*, whose main task was to administer justice; Sulla increased the number of *praetores* to eight; from that moment, after the end of their mandate, they were appointed as *propraetores* in governing the provinces.

promulgatio Official publication of the text of a *rogatio* to be submitted for voting.

provincia Originally the responsibility of a magistrate, then a territorial area entrusted to governors chosen at first from among the annual magistrates and then, after Sulla, generally from among the *proconsules* and *propraetores*.

provocatio Appeal to the people which a Roman citizen could make in the event of a death sentence.

publicanus A member of the *equites* who, having formed a company, exercised functions under contract with the *res publica*, primarily the collection of taxes in the Roman provinces.

quaestio Court judging serious crimes, presided over by a *quaesitor*, usually a praetor, and formed, depending on which period, by senators, *equites* and *tribuni Aerarii*.

quaestor Magistrates with responsibilities over finance, elected by *comitias tributa*. This was the first step in a political career; from Sulla they reached twenty in number.

quattuorvir Member of a college of four people; after the Social War, the higher magistrates of the *municipia*.

regnum Ancient power of the kings, outlawed by the *res publica*; aspiration to *regnum* was a frequent accusation against anyone too powerful.

repetundae Crime of extortion by the governor of a province.

rogatio Proposal of law to be decided by public vote.

senatus Assembly of former magistrates for life, which had the role of directing the policy of serving magistrates.

senatus consultum A politically binding deliberation expressed by the Senate at the request of a summoning magistrate. The *senatus consultum ultimum* was extraordinary and final in its nature, made where there was some danger to the *res publica*.

sodalicium An electoral association; *crimen sodalicii* related to illegal practices of electoral manipulation.

spectio Observation of the *auspicia*, during which the deliberations of a popular assemblies or the senate had to be suspended.

suasoria Rhetorical exercise in the form of a soliloquy where a historical figure is impersonated in the act of reflecting on a decision of major importance.

supplicatio Official thanksgiving to divinities; it was decided by a *senatus consultum* following a successful military campaign.

terra Italia From the period of Sulla, the Italian peninsula south of the line from the Arno to the Rubicon.

tribunal A wooden platform that had various functions.

tribunus Aerarii Originally a financial overseer of the *tribus*, the name still appeared in the census to indicate someone of rank immediately below the *equites*.

tribunus militum One of the tribunes elected by the people to manage the *legiones*.

tribunus plebis One of ten magistrates of the *plebs*, who enjoyed inviolability and the right of veto (*intercessio*) against all other magistrates and the Senate itself.

tribus One of the thirty-five territorial tribes (four city and thirty-one rural) into which Roman citizens were divided.

triumphus Solemn procession of the *imperator* in the city of Rome; it had to be authorized by the Senate.

triumvir capitalis One of three lower magistrates responsible for carrying out death sentences.

tumultus State of emergency, with consequent military levy.

vestalis One of the priestesses who looked after the Temple of Vesta, keeping the sacred flame alight. Chosen from among patrician girls aged between 6 and 10, they remained in service for thirty years, preserving their chastity.

vis Crime of public violence.

Glossary of Place Names

Basilica Porcia A building north-west of the Forum and adjoining the *Curia*, constructed by Marcus Porcius Cato the Censor in 184 BC.

Campus Martius The Field of Mars, outside the *pomerium*, an area where legislative and electoral assemblies, and particularly the *comitia centuriata*, were held.

Capitolium The Capitoline Hill, or, most properly, its southern summit, on which the Temple of Jupiter Optimus Maximus stood.

Comitium Political meeting place north-west of the Forum.

Curia Main meeting place of the Senate. Originally called *Curia Hostilia* since, according to tradition, it had been built by Tullus Hostilius, the third king. Rebuilt after 52 BC and called *Curia Cornelia*.

lucus Libitinae The 'sacred grove' dedicated to Libitina, the goddess of funerals and burial, on the Esquiline Hill.

rostra The tribune for orators in front of the *Comitium*. It took its name from the rams of warships captured at Antium in 338 BC.

tabernae Shops of various kinds, from grocers to moneychangers, located also in the Forum.

via Sacra The main road in Rome, from the Capitolium and through the Forum.

villa publica Building in *Campus Martius*, originally used for census operations.

CHAPTER NOTES

A Note on the Text

1. Cf. Suetonius, *Caesar*, 40,1–2.
2. Cf. Nino Marinone, *Cronologia ciceroniana* (ed. Ermanno Malaspina), Pàtron, Bologna, 2004, 2nd edition, pp. 291, 295, 431.

A Note on Sources

1. Emanuele Narducci, 'Cicerone, i suoi amici e i suoi nemici. L'epistolario nel giudizio dei posteri', in Alberto Cavarzere (ed.), *Cicerone: Lettere ai familiari*, I, Rizzoli, Milano, 2007, p. 15.
2. Nepos, *Atticus*, 7,1–3.
3. Plutarch, *Cicero*, 37,1–4.
4. Cicero, *ad familiares*, 8,14,4.
5. In Cicero, *ad Atticum*, 10,8B,1.
6. Cicero, *ad familiares*, 7,28,3.

1 The Stage and Its Main Characters

1. Cicero, *De re publica*, 1,39.
2. Ibid., 2,10.
3. Ibid., 2,11.
4. *Penates* were spirits that protected a family or a whole community.
5. Cicero, *Laws*, 2,3–5.
6. Cicero, *ad Atticum*, 7,11,3.
7. Suetonius, *Caesar*, 77,1.
8. Cicero, *De re publica*, 2,40.
9. The Roman *modius*, a measure of volume for dry quantities, was equivalent to just under 8.7 litres.
10. Cicero, *In Defence of Murena*, 36.
11. Cicero, *In Defence of Sestius*, 106.
12. Cicero, *Laws*, 3,24.
13. Ibid., 3,27.
14. Cicero, *In Defence of Sestius*, 96.

15. Emanuele Narducci, *Processi ai politici nella Roma antica*, Laterza, Roma and Bari, 1995, p. 6.
16. The Roman mile was equivalent to just over 1,480 metres.
17. Cicero, *In Defence of Sestius*, 137.
18. Cicero, *Laws*, 3,29 and 3,28.
19. Ibid., 3,40–1.
20. Sallust, *Conspiracy of Catiline*, 29,3.
21. Livy, *History of Rome*, 1,60,2.
22. Tacitus, *Annals*, 4,34,3.
23. Livy, *History of Rome*, 6,1,3.
24. Ibid., 5,37,1.
25. Ibid., 5,39,5.
26. Ibid., 5,39,10.
27. Ibid., 5,46,7.
28. The Roman pound was a measure of weight equivalent to just over 327 grams.
29. Livy, *History of Rome*, 5,48,9–49,7.
30. Aelianus, *On the Nature of Animals*, 12,33.
31. Pliny, *Natural History*, 29,57.
32. Livy, *History of Rome*, 5,50,3.
33. Ibid., 5,50,4.
34. Ibid., 5,54,3–7.
35. Ibid., 5,55,2.
36. On the depreciation of land values in 49, see chapter 10 (sub-section on 'Cicero and an Interminable Wait').
37. Plutarch, *Fabius Maximus*, 18,1.
38. Diodorus Siculus, *Bibliotheca historica*, 37,13.
39. Appian, *Civil Wars*, 1,4.
40. Dionysius of Halicarnassus, *Roman Antiquities*, 8,16,1.
41. Ibid., 8,22,1.
42. Livy, *History of Rome*, 2,40,7.
43. Ibid., 7,39,16–17.
44. Ibid., 7,40,2.
45. Appian, *Civil Wars*, 1,8.
46. Ibid., 1,258.
47. Ibid., 1,259.
48. Ibid., 1,316.
49. Ibid., 1,406.
50. Ibid., 1,427.
51. Gaius Velleius Paterculus, *Roman History*, 2,27,1–2.
52. Plutarch, *Sulla*, 29,6.
53. Appian, *Civil Wars*, 3,365.
54. Ibid., 3,373–5.
55. Plutarch, *Pompey*, 1,3.
56. Cicero, *Against Verres*, II, 5,77.
57. Plutarch, *Pompey*, 1,2.
58. This is how Ronald Syme, *The Roman Revolution*, Oxford University Press, Oxford, 1939, p. 31, described Pompey's followers.
59. Cicero, *In Defence of the Manilian Law*, 30.
60. Valerius Maximus, *Memorable Deeds*, 6,2,8.
61. Plutarch, *Pompey*, 12,7.
62. Plutarch, *Crassus*, 2,1.
63. Ibid., 2,6.
64. Suetonius, *Caesar*, 6,1.
65. Ibid., 7,2.

66. Michel Reddé, *Mare nostrum: Les infrastructures, le dispositif et l'histoire de la marine militaire sous l'empire romain*, École Française de Rome, Rome, 1986, p. 463.
67. Cicero, *In Defence of the Manilian Law*, 32–3.
68. Cassius Dio, *Roman History*, 36,23,1.
69. Plutarch, *Pompey*, 25,2.
70. Cicero, *On Duties*, 3,107.
71. Plutarch, *Pompey*, 25,12.
72. Ibid., 26,4.
73. Ibid., 27,2.
74. Cassius Dio, *Roman History*, 36,42,3.
75. Plutarch, *Pompey*, 30,4.
76. Ibid., 39,1.
77. Pliny, *Natural History*, 7,99.
78. Plutarch, *Pompey*, 43,1–2.

2 Plots and Scandals

1. Bertolt Brecht, *Die Geschäfte des Herrn Julius Caesar. Romanfragment*, Gebrüder Weiss, Berlin-Schöneberg, 1957.
2. Appian, *Civil Wars*, 1,132.
3. Cicero, *Catilinarians*, 1,12.
4. Cicero, *In Defence of Murena*, 51.
5. Appian, *Civil Wars*, 1,145.
6. Anonymous, *de viris illustribus*, 73,12.
7. Cicero, *ad Atticum*, 2,1,8.
8. Cicero, *Catilinarians*, 1,1.
9. Ibid., 2,2.
10. Sallust, *Conspiracy of Catiline*, 47,2.
11. Ibid., 48,1–2
12. Cicero, *Catilinarians*, 4, 12–18.
13. Cassius Dio, *Roman History*, 37,42,2–3.
14. Cicero, *In Defence of Sulla*, 33.
15. Seneca, *Letters to Lucilius*, 16,2[97],2.
16. W. Jeffrey Tatum, *The Patrician Tribune: Publius Clodius Pulcher*, University of North Carolina Press, Chapel Hill and London, 1999, p. 86.
17. Plutarch, *Caesar*, 10,5.
18. Ibid., 10,9.
19. Cicero, *ad Atticum*, 1,16,5.

3 The Arrival of the 'First Triumvirate'

1. Cicero, *In Defence of Murena*, 31.
2. Appian, *Mithridatic Wars*, 568–78.
3. The Roman cubit was just over 44 cm, the Greek cubit over 46 cm.
4. Plutarch, *Cato the Younger*, 5,4.
5. Suetonius, *Caesar*, 19,2.
6. Plutarch, *Caesar*, 14,2.
7. Plutarch, *Cato the Younger*, 33,2.
8. Cassius Dio, *Roman History*, 38,5,4.
9. Ibid., 38,6,3.
10. Plutarch, *Cato the Younger*, 32,3.
11. Suetonius, *Caesar*, 20,4.

12. Appian, *Civil Wars*, 2,51.
13. Cicero, *ad Atticum*, 2,19,3.
14. Cicero, *In Defence of Sestius*, 16.
15. Plutarch, *Cicero*, 31,6.
16. A total of thirty-four letters from Cicero, *ad Atticum*, 1,3 (March–April 58, while travelling) to 3,27 (January–February 57, from Dyrrhachium, present-day Durrës in Albania).
17. Ibid., 3,15,2.
18. Cicero, *In Defence of Sestius*, 77.
19. Plutarch, *Cicero*, 8,2.
20. Cicero, *De domo sua*, 11.
21. Ibid., 25.
22. Plutarch, *Pompey*, 50,2; *Moralia*, 204 C.
23. *Il Popolo d'Italia*, 1, 1 January 1920.

4 Caesar, Gaul and Rome

1. Pliny, *Natural History*, 3,31.
2. Cicero, *ad Quintum fratrem*, 2,3,2.
3. Ibid., 2,3,5.
4. Ibid., 2,3,4.
5. Cicero, *On the Response of the Haruspices*, 22–4.
6. Cicero, *ad Quintum fratrem*, 2,5,1.
7. Cicero, *ad Atticum*, 4,8a,2 BL.
8. Suetonius, *Caesar*, 24,1.
9. Plutarch, *Cato the Younger*, 39,3.
10. Plutarch, *Pompey*, 52,2.
11. Cicero, *ad familiares*, 7,1,3.
12. Cicero, *ad Atticum*, 4,17,2.
13. Cassius Dio, *Roman History*, 40,17,1.
14. Cicero, *In Defence of Milo*, 25.
15. Caesar, *Gallic War*, 7,1,1–3.
16. Cicero, *ad familiares*, 4,17,6.
17. Ibid., 7,7,1.
18. Caesar, *Gallic War*, 6,1,4.
19. Cicero, *In Defence of Milo*, 13–14.
20. Ibid., 98.
21. Cicero, *ad Atticum*, 5,13,1.

5 From the Death of Clodius to a Sole Consul

1. Asconius, *On Cicero's Orations*, p. 31 C.
2. Cassius Dio, *Roman History*, 40,48,2.
3. Cicero, *In Defence of Milo*, 18.
4. Cicero, *Laws*, 2,58.
5. Cassius Dio, *Roman History*, 40,49,3.
6. Asconius, *On Cicero's Orations*, p. 33 C.
7. Ibid., p. 51 C.
8. Cicero, *In Defence of Milo*, 91.
9. Appian, *Civil Wars*, 2,82–3.
10. An attendant for sacrifices.
11. Cicero, *In Defence of Milo*, 65–6.
12. Ibid., 64.

13. Caesar, *Gallic War,* 6,1,4.
14. Cicero, *Laws,* 2,42.
15. Ibid., 2,60.
16. An extra month, generally added every two years, had the purpose of making up for the astronomical lag in the pre-Caesarian year, officially subdivided into 12 months (one of 28 days, seven of 29 days and four of 31 days), making a total of 355 days. The additional month of 27 days was introduced, on alternate years, after the 23 or 24 February (which was therefore reduced by 4–5 days), and extended the current year to a total of 377 or 378 days.
17. Plutarch, *Cato the Younger,* 47,3–4.
18. Cicero, *Laws,* 3,8.
19. Cassius Dio, *Roman History,* 40,50,5.
20. Appian, *Civil Wars,* 2,85.
21. Ibid., 2,87–8.
22. Cicero, *In Defence of Milo,* 14.
23. A period called *trinum nundinum,* literally 'after three *nundinae*'; the *nundinae* were the market days held every eight days; the *trinum nundinum* therefore varied between 17 and 24 days.
24. Cicero, *In Defence of Milo,* 12.
25. Ibid., 44; cf. 26.
26. Ibid., 3.
27. Ibid., 7.
28. Plutarch, *Cicero,* 35,5.
29. Asconius, *On Cicero's Orations,* p. 42 C.
30. Ibid., pp. 53–4 C.
31. Cassius Dio, *Roman History,* 40,54,3.
32. Plutarch, *Pompey,* 55,7; Appian, *Civil Wars,* 2,93–95.
33. We rely mainly on Lorenzo Gagliardi, *Cesare, Pompeo e la lotta per le magistrature: Anni 52–50 a. C.,* Giuffrè, Milano, 2011, with modifications indicated in the Bibliography and Further Notes section.
34. Suetonius, *Caesar,* 26,1.
35. Cassius Dio, *Roman History,* 40,51,1–2.
36. Appian, *Civil Wars,* 2,97.
37. Cicero, *Philippics,* 2,24.
38. Caesar, *Gallic War,* 7,6,1.
39. Gagliardi, *Cesare,* pp. 101–2, sees a possible compromise in the introduction of the veto itself.
40. Cassius Dio, *Roman History,* 40,56,2.
41. Suetonius, *Caesar,* 28,2–3.
42. Cassius Dio, *Roman History,* 40,56,3.
43. Plutarch, *Cato the Younger,* 49,5.

6 Winner in a Tight Corner

1. Caesar, *Gallic War,* 7,3,2–3.
2. Ibid., 7,28,4.
3. Ibid., 7,36,2.
4. Cassius Dio, *Roman History,* 40,40,4.
5. Caesar, *Gallic War,* 7,84,5.
6. Ibid., 8,38,5.
7. Ibid., 8,39,3.
8. Ibid., 8,44,1.
9. Ibid., 8,50,1.
10. Ibid., 8,50,3.

11. Ibid., 8,52,2.
12. The twenty-two cohorts would form the basis of the future Legio V, which in 51 would take the total of Caesar's legions to eleven (cf. Caesar, *Gallic War*, 8,24,2). On the establishment of Legio V 'Alaudae', see Suetonius, *Caesar*, 24,2; eleven legions in Cicero, *ad Atticum*, 7,7,6; Florus, *Epitome of Roman History*, 2,13,5; ten legions in Plutarch, *Pompey*, 58,10; Suetonius, *Caesar*, 29,2; on the twenty-two cohorts, see Caesar, *Gallic War*, 7,65,1. Cf. H.-M. Ottmer, *Die Rubikon-Legende: Untersuchungen zu Caesars und Pompeius' Strategie vor und nach Ausbruch des Bürgerkrieges*, Boldt, Boppard am Rhein, 1979, pp. 15–38.
13. Caesar, *Gallic War*, 8,55,2.
14. Cicero, *ad Atticum*, 5,11,2.
15. Appian, *Civil Wars*, 2,98.
16. Cicero, *ad Atticum*, 5,2,3.
17. Cicero, *ad familiares*, 8,1,2.
18. Ibid., 8,1,4.
19. Cassius Dio, *Roman History*, 40,59,3.
20. Cicero, *ad Atticum*, 5,7.
21. Cicero, *ad familiares*, 2,8,2.
22. Ibid., 8,2,2.
23. Suetonius, *Caesar*, 29,1.
24. Cassius Dio, *Roman History*, 40,60,2.
25. Cicero, *ad familiares*, 8,4,4.
26. Ibid., 8,9,2.
27. Ibid., 8,9,5.
28. Ibid., 8,5,2.
29. Ibid., 8,8,5.
30. Contrary to the reintroduction of the veto by the *lex Pompeia*.
31. Cicero, *ad familiares*, 8,8,6.
32. Ibid., 8,8,7.
33. Ibid., 8,8,8.
34. Ibid., 8,8,9.
35. Ibid., 8,10,2.
36. Ibid., 8,10,2.
37. Four-day festivity whose date was fixed from year to year by the consuls who had just taken office.
38. Cicero, *ad familiares*, 8,6,4–5.
39. Ibid., 8,6,5.
40. Ibid., 2,13,3.
41. Cicero, *ad Atticum*, 6,3,4.
42. Appian, *Civil Wars*, 2,101–2.
43. Plutarch, *Caesar*, 29,3.
44. Velleius Paterculus, *Roman History*, 2,48,3–5.
45. Cicero, *ad familiares*, 8,11,3.
46. See Gagliardi, *Cesare*, p. 166.
47. Cicero, *ad familiares*, 8,13,2
48. Gagliardi, *Cesare*, pp. 169–71.
49. Velleius Paterculus, *Roman History*, 2,49,3.
50. Plutarch, *Antony*, 5,3.
51. Cicero, *ad familiares*, 8,14,1.

7 Winds of Civil War

1. Cicero, *ad familiares*, 8,14,2.
2. Meaning senators, *equites* and tribunes of the treasury.
3. Cicero, *ad familiares*, 8,14,3–4.
4. Appian, *Civil Wars*, 2,104–6.

5. Ibid., 2,110–14.
6. Plutarch, *Pompey*, 57,1–9.
7. Cassius Dio, *Roman History*, 40,63,3–64,4.
8. Cicero, *ad Atticum*, 6,8,2.
9. Ibid., 7,1,1.
10. Ibid., 7,1,2.
11. Ibid., 7,1,3.
12. Ibid., 7,1,4.
13. Cicero, *ad familiares*, 14,5,1.
14. Cicero, *ad Atticum*, 6,9,5.
15. Cicero, *ad familiares*, 16,9,3.
16. Appian, *Civil Wars*, 2,118–19.
17. Plutarch, *Caesar*, 30,6; *Pompey*, 59,1.
18. Plutarch, *Pompey*, 58,10.
19. Appian, *Civil Wars*, 2,121–2.
20. Plutarch, *Antony*, 5,4.
21. Cicero, *ad Atticum*, 7,3,4.
22. A conjecture by the sixteenth-century philologist Corradus, though the manuscripts bear the name Gaius.
23. Cicero, *ad Atticum*, 7,3,5.
24. Ibid., 7,4,2.
25. Ibid., 7,5,4.
26. Ibid., 7,6,2. The manuscripts contain the words *opinione valentior*, corrected by Shackleton Bailey to *opinione tamen lenior*.
27. Cicero, *ad Atticum*, 7,7,4.
28. Ibid., 7,7,5.
29. Ibid.
30. Ibid., 7,7,6.
31. Suetonius, *Caesar*, 29,2.
32. Plutarch, *Caesar*, 31,1–2; *Pompey* 59,4–6; Suetonius, *Caesar*, 29,2–4; Appian, *Civil Wars*, 2,126–7.
33. Velleius Paterculus, *Roman History*, 2,49,4.
34. Cicero, *ad Atticum*, 7,8,4.
35. Ibid.
36. Ibid., 7,8,5.
37. Ibid., 7,9,2.
38. Caesar, *Civil War*, 1,1,1–1,2,8.
39. This was supposed, at least by Caesar himself, to be 1 July: see Gagliardi, *Cesare*, p. 37.
40. Cicero, *ad familiares*, 16,11,2.
41. Ibid., 4,7,2.
42. Appian, *Civil Wars*, 2,127–9.
43. One *stádion*, in the Attic, Alexandrian and Roman system of measurement, was approximately 185 metres. In fact, the distance between Rome and Ravenna was some 213 Roman miles as far as Rimini (along the via Flaminia), and another 37 from Rimini to Ravenna (along the via Popilia). Codices of Appian's *Civil Wars* give two improbable figures: 3,300 and 1,300 *stádia*.
44. But his appointment in fact took place after 7 January.
45. Cassius Dio, *Roman History*, 41,1,1–2,2.
46. Caesar, *Civil War*, 1,3,1–5,5.
47. Cicero, *ad familiares*, 16,11,2.
48. Ibid., 6,6,5.
49. Caesar, *Civil War*, 1,5,3–4.
50. Ibid., 1,5,5.
51. Livy, *Periochae*, 109.
52. Appian, *Civil Wars*, 2,129–33.
53. Cassius Dio, *Roman History*, 41,3,1–4.

54. Cicero, *ad familiares*, 8,17,1.
55. Ibid., 16,11,2.
56. Caesar, *Civil War*, 1,6,1–8.
57. Appian, *Civil Wars*, 2,134–5.
58. Cicero, *ad familiares*, 16,11,3.

8 The Rubicon

1. Caesar, *Civil War*, 1,7,1–8,1.
2. Ibid., 1,7,5–6.
3. Cassius Dio, *Roman History*, 41,4,1.
4. Caesar, *Civil War*, 1,5,5.
5. Lucan, *Pharsalia*, 1,183–92.
6. Ibid., 1,192–205.
7. Ibid., 1,213–32.
8. Ibid., 1,254.
9. Ibid., 1,269.
10. Ibid., 1,303–7.
11. Ibid., 1,319–23.
12. Ibid., 1,340–6.
13. Ibid., 1,379–88.
14. Plutarch, *Caesar*, 31,3.
15. Ibid., 32,4.
16. Ibid., 32,5.
17. Ibid., 32,5–9.
18. Suetonius, *Caesar*, 7,2; Cassius Dio, *Roman History*, 37,52,2; 41,24,2.
19. Plutarch, *Pompey*, 60,1–4.
20. Plutarch, *Antony*, 5,10–6,1.
21. Suetonius, *Caesar*, 30,2–5.
22. This was confirmed by Plutarch, *Caesar*, 46, 1–2.
23. Cicero, *On Duties*, 3,82.
24. See p. xvii and Bibliography and Further Notes, p. 303.
25. Suetonius, *Caesar*, 31,1–33,1.
26. Ibid., 81,2.
27. On the prisoner, see Butler and Cary (eds), *Svetoni*, p. 85; on the prisoner and the gold ring, see Canfora, *Cesare*, pp. 163–4
28. Appian, *Civil Wars*, 2,124–41.
29. Ibid., 2,139–41.
30. Velleius Paterculus, *Roman History*, 2,49,4.
31. Cassius Dio, *Roman History*, 41,4,1.
32. Eutropius, *Breviarium* historiae Romanae, 6,19,2.
33. Orosius, *History Against the Pagans*, 6,15,3.
34. A. Veggiani, *Il Rubicone. Studi sull'idrografia e sul territorio dell'antico Urgon-Rubicone*, Il Ponte Vecchio, Cesena, 1995 (a cura di R. Zoffoli).

9 The Escape from Rome

1. This was the speed of Curio's earlier mission, though from Ravenna, some 37 miles further on.
2. Caesar, *Civil War*, 1,11,4.
3. Ibid., 1,8,2–11,3.
4. Cicero, *ad familiares*, 16,12,2.
5. Cicero, *ad Atticum*, 7,21,3. On the second mission, see pp. 186–7

6. Lucan, *Pharsalia*, 1,481–93.
7. Ibid., 1,254–6.
8. Ibid., 2,534–6.
9. Ibid., 5,27–34.
10. Appian, *Civil Wars*, 2,205–8.
11. Plutarch, *Caesar*, 33,1–4.
12. Plutarch, *Pompey*, 60,1–61,3.
13. Appian, *Civil Wars*, 1,141–4.
14. Cassius Dio, *Roman History*, 41,4,2–4.
15. Cicero, *ad Atticum*, 7,11,1.
16. Cassius Dio, *Roman History*, 41,5,1–2.
17. Caesar, *Civil War*, 1,8,2–9,6.
18. Cassius Dio, *Roman History*, 41,5,2–6,1.
19. A probable gap in the text; cf. Dionigi Vottero in Adriano Pennacini (ed.), *Gaio Giulio Cesare. Opera omnia*, Einaudi-Gallimard, Torino 1993, p. 1185.
20. 'Lictors' were magistrates' bodyguards who carried the *fasces*, bundles of rods tied with leather strips, symbol of magisterial power.
21. Caesar, *Civil War*, 1,6,7–8.
22. Lucan, *Pharsalia*, 1,510–22.
23. Cassius Dio, *Roman History*, 41,6,2–4.
24. Plutarch, *Pompey*, 83,6.
25. Cicero, *ad Atticum*, 9,10,2.
26. Cicero, *ad familiares*, 16,12,2.
27. Caesar, *Civil War*, 1,30,5.
28. Plutarch, *Pompey*, 60,6.
29. Caesar, *Civil War*, 1,32,8.
30. Plutarch, *Cato the Younger*, 46,1.
31. Plutarch, *Pompey*, 60,6.
32. Ibid., 57,8–9.
33. Plutarch, *Caesar*, 33,5.
34. Plutarch, *Pompey*, 60,6–61,1; cf. *Moralia*, 204 D.
35. Plutarch, *Cato the Younger*, 52,1–3.
36. Ibid., 53,1.
37. Velleius Paterculus, *Roman History*, 2,49,2.
38. Plutarch, *Caesar*, 33,6; *Pompey*, 61,6.
39. Cicero, *ad Atticum*, 7,11,1–4.
40. Appian, *Civil Wars*, 2,142.
41. Ibid., 2,146–8.
42. Ibid., 2,205–8.
43. Caesar, *Civil War*, 1,14,1–3.
44. Lucan, *Pharsalia*, 1,592–5.
45. Plutarch, *Caesar*, 34,1; *Pompey*, 61,6.
46. Plutarch, *Pompey*, 61,7.
47. Plutarch, *Caesar*, 34,2–4.
48. Plutarch, *Pompey*, 83,7.
49. Appian, *Civil Wars*, 2,148.
50. Cassius Dio, *Roman History*, 41,6,5–6.
51. Caesar, *Civil War*, 1,10,1–11,3.
52. Cassius Dio, *Roman History*, 41,7,1–9,6.
53. For detailed references to each of Cicero's letters discussed here, see *Bibliography and Further Notes*.
54. Cicero, *ad Atticum*, 7,10.
55. Ibid., 7,11,5.
56. Cicero, *ad familiares*, 14,18,1–2.

57. Ibid., 14,14,1.
58. Ibid., 14,14,1–2.
59. Cicero, *ad Atticum*, 7,12,6.
60. Ibid., 7,13a,3 BL.
61. Ibid., 7,14,3.
62. Ibid., 7,16,3.
63. The *lex agraria* of 59.
64. Caesar, *Civil War*, 1,14,4–5.
65. Cassius Dio, *Roman History*, 41,9,7–10,2.
66. Cicero, *ad Atticum*, 7,12,1.
67. Lucan, *Pharsalia*, 2,462.
68. Florus, *Epitome of Roman History*, 2,13,18.
69. Cicero, *ad Atticum*, 7,12,2.
70. Ibid., 7,12,6.
71. Ibid., 7,13a,1 BL.
72. Ibid., 7,13a,2 BL.
73. Ibid., 7,13b,3 BL.
74. Ibid., 7,13b,2 BL.
75. Ibid., 7,14,1.
76. Caesar, *Civil War*, 1,8,2–9,6.
77. Ibid., 1,9,5–6.
78. Ibid., 1,10,1–11,3.
79. A conjecture of Christian Gottfried Schütz (CIↃ); the manuscripts refer to either 500 (IↃ) or 5,000 (IↃↃ).
80. Cicero, *ad Atticum*, 7,14,2.
81. Ibid., 8,11B,2.
82. Ibid., 7,15,3.
83. Ibid., 7,15,2.
84. Ibid., 7,15,3.
85. Cicero, *ad familiares*, 16,12,3.
86. Cicero, *ad Atticum*, 7,17,2.
87. Cicero, *ad familiares*, 16,12,4.
88. Ibid., 16,12,5.
89. See D.R. Shackleton Bailey (ed.), *Cicero: Epistulae ad familiares,* I, Cambridge University Press, Cambridge, 1977, p. 483, with regard to the letter *ad Atticum*, 7,16,2.
90. Cicero, *ad Atticum*, 7,16,2.
91. Ibid., 7,17,1.
92. Ibid., 7,17,4.
93. Ibid., 7,17,5.
94. Ibid., 7,18,2.
95. Ibid., 7,19.
96. Ibid., 7,20,1.
97. Ibid., 7,21,1.
98. Ibid., 7,21,2.
99. Ibid., 7,22,1.
100. Ibid., 7,23,3.
101. Ibid., 7,23,1.

10 Caesar's 'Long March' and Pompey's Flight to Brundisium

1. Caesar, *Civil War*, 1,12,1–16,1.
2. A place that Cicero, on 23–4 January, at Minturnae, still thought to be in Pompeian hands (*ad Atticum*, 7,13b,3 BL).
3. Lucan, *Pharsalia*, 2,462–71.

4. Florus, *Epitome of Roman History*, 2,13,19.
5. Cicero, *ad Atticum*, 7,24,1.
6. Ibid., 7,25.
7. Ibid., 7,26,1.
8. Ibid., 8,11A. On the possibility that it may actually be the first letter received from Pompey, see *Bibliography and Further Notes*.
9. Cicero, *ad Atticum*, 8,11B,2.
10. Ibid., 8,11B,3.
11. Not necessarily *ad Atticum*, 8,11A.
12. Cicero, *ad Atticum*, 8,1,1.
13. Ibid., 8,1,2.
14. It is noted by Jean Bayet in *Cicéron: Correspondance*, V, Les Belles Lettres, Paris, 1964, p. 157, but without setting out any hypothesis.
15. Cicero, *ad Atticum*, 8,1,3.
16. Ibid., 8,2,1.
17. Ibid., 8,2,2.
18. Ibid., 8,2,3.
19. Ibid., 8,2,4.
20. Ibid., 9,10,4.
21. Ibid., 8,3,4.
22. Ibid., 8,3,5.
23. Ibid., 8,3,6.
24. Ibid., 8,3,7.
25. The letter referred to is probably *ad Atticum*, 8,12A.
26. Ibid., 8,6,2.
27. Ibid., 8,7,1.
28. Ibid., 8,4,3.
29. Ibid., 8,8,2.
30. This is *ad Atticum*, 8,12 (Cicero to Atticus – from Formiae, 28 February); the attached correspondence consists of 8,12A (Pompey to the consuls Marcellus and Lentulus – from Luceria, 17–18 February); 8,12B (Pompey to Ahenobarbus – from Luceria, 11–16 February); 8,12C (Pompey to Ahenobarbus – from Luceria, 16 February); 8,12D (Pompey to Ahenobarbus – from Luceria, 17 February).
31. Cicero, *ad Atticum*, 8,11A.
32. Ibid., 8,12B,2.
33. Though Cicero, *ad Atticum*, 8,3,7, refers to a letter.
34. Ibid., 8,12A,3.
35. About whom nothing else is known.
36. Cicero, *ad Atticum*, 8,12C,1–3.
37. Ibid., 8,12C,4.
38. Ibid., 8,12D,1.
39. Ibid., 8,12D,1–2.
40. Ibid., 8,12A,1.
41. Ibid., 8,12A,2.
42. Caesar, *Civil War*, 1,16,2–23,5.
43. All the manuscripts give *XL*, but it is thought this might be *XV* on the basis of Livy, *History of Rome*, 35,40,6, or alternatively it might be *IV*: cf. Vottero, in Pennacini (ed.), *Gaio Giulio Cesare*, p. 1200. A *jugerum* was a measure of land equivalent to just over 2,520 square metres, about a quarter of a hectare (0.623 acres).
44. The thirty or so cohorts were immediately sent to Sicily.
45. Plutarch, *Caesar*, 34,6–9.
46. Seneca, *De Beneficiis*, 3,24.
47. Suetonius, *Nero*, 2,2–3.
48. Caesar, *Civil War*, 2,149–50; cf. 163.
49. Cassius Dio, *Roman History*, 41,11,1–3.

50. Lucan, *Pharsalia*, 2,478–80.
51. Ibid., 2,507–10.
52. Cicero, *ad Atticum*, 8,14,3.
53. Cicero, *ad Atticum*, 8,9b,2 BL.
54. Ibid., 8,11,2–4.
55. The correspondence attached to the letter *ad Atticum*, 8,11 consists of 8,11A and 8,11B, and of the more recent 8,11C and 8,11D.
56. Cicero, *ad Atticum*, 8,11C.
57. Ibid., 8,11D,1.
58. Ibid.
59. Ibid., 8,11D,3.
60. Ibid., 8,11D,4.
61. Ibid., 8,12,6.
62. Ibid., 8,13,1.
63. Ibid., 8,13,2.
64. Ibid., 8,14,1.
65. Ibid., 8,14,3.
66. Ibid., 8,15,3.
67. Ibid., 8,15A,2.
68. Ibid., 8,15A,3.
69. Ibid., 8,16,2.
70. Ibid., 9,1,1.
71. Ibid., 9,1,3.
72. Ibid., 9,2a BL.
73. Ibid., 9,2b,2 BL.
74. Ibid., 9,2b,3 BL.
75. Ibid., 9,3,2.
76. Cicero, *ad familiares*, 8,15,1–2.
77. Cicero, *ad Atticum*, 9,5,2.
78. Ibid., 9,5,3.
79. Vibius Curius was probably a knight and prefect of the cavalry.
80. Cicero, *ad Atticum*, 9,6,1.
81. Ibid., 9,6,2.
82. Ibid., 9,6,3.
83. Ibid., 9,6A.
84. Ibid., 9,7,4.
85. Ibid., 9,7A,2.
86. Ibid., 9,7B,2.
87. Ibid., 9,7C,1.
88. Ibid., 9,7C,2.
89. Ibid., 9,8,2.
90. Ibid., 9,9,2.
91. Ibid., 9,9,3.
92. Ibid., 9,9,4.
93. Hippias sought the help of the Peloponnesians in 500, without success, and indeed led the Persians in 490 against the Athenians at Marathon; according to Herodotus (*Histories*, 6,107,1–2), he too is supposed to have dreamed about making incestuous love with his mother, wrongly interpreting this as an omen that he would return to his own country.
94. Cicero, *ad Atticum*, 9,10,3.
95. Ibid., 9,10,6.
96. Ibid., 9,11,1.
97. This was ibid., 9,6A.
98. Ibid., 9,11,3.
99. Ibid., 9,11,4.

100. Ibid., 9,11A,2.
101. Ibid., 9,12,1.
102. Ibid., 9,13a,1–2 BL.
103. Ibid., 9,13a,4 BL.
104. Ibid., 9,13b BL.
105. Ibid., 9,13A.
106. Ibid., 9,14,1–2.
107. Ibid., 9,14,2.
108. Ibid., 9,14,3.

11 In Caesar's Hands

1. Caesar, *Civil War*, 1,24,1–28,4.
2. The Roman foot was equivalent to just over 29.6 centimetres.
3. Though *ad Atticum*, 9,13A in fact indicates that he had been sent back.
4. Lucan, *Pharsalia*, 2,632–44.
5. Ibid., 2,711–13.
6. Florus, *Epitome of Roman History*, 2,13,18–22.
7. Plutarch, *Caesar*, 35,1–3.
8. Plutarch, *Antony*, 6,4.
9. Plutarch, *Pompey*, 61,2–63,3.
10. Appian, *Civil Wars*, 2,151; 159.
11. Cassius Dio, *Roman History*, 41,10,4–13,4.
12. Caesar, *Civil War*, 1,29,1–31,3.
13. This happened on 23 April: Cicero, *ad Atticum*, 10,16,3.
14. Quintilianus, *Institutio Oratoria*, 11,1,80.
15. Lucan, *Pharsalia*, 3,52–70.
16. Plutarch, *Caesar*; 35,3; *Pompey*, 63,4.
17. Plutarch, *Cato the Younger*, 53,3–5.
18. Appian, *Civil Wars*, 2,160–2.
19. Cassius Dio, *Roman History*, 41,15,1.
20. Cicero, *ad Atticum*, 9,15,1.
21. Ibid., 9,15a BL.
22. Ibid., 9,16,2.
23. Ibid., 9,17,1.
24. Ibid., 9,18,1.
25. Ibid., 9,19,3.
26. Meetings of the Senate were held on that and the next two days. For the date, see in particular Cicero, *ad Atticum*, 9,17,1, and Caesar, *Civil War*, 1,33,3.
27. Caesar, *Civil War*, 1,32,1–33,4.
28. Florus, *Epitome of Roman History*, 2,13,21.
29. An error not infrequent. According to Eutropius, *Breviarium historiae Romanae*, 6,20,1, he had even immediately proclaimed himself dictator.
30. Lucan, *Pharsalia*, 3,71–168.
31. Reference to Pyrrhus's attempts at corruption.
32. Lucan, *Pharsalia*, 3,154–68.
33. Plutarch, *Pompey*, 63,4.
34. Cf. also Plutarch, *Antony*, 6,4.
35. Plutarch, *Caesar*, 35,4–11.
36. Appian, *Civil Wars*, 2,160–7.
37. Cassius Dio, *Roman History*, 41,15,1–18,1.
38. The sum was later given in 46. See Bibliography and Further Notes.
39. Orosius, *Histories Against Pagans*, 6,15,4–6.

40. Pliny, *Natural History*, 19,40; 33,56.
41. Cicero, *ad Atticum*, 10,1,2; cf. *ad familiares*, 4,4,1.
42. Cicero, *ad Atticum*, 10,3.
43. Ibid., 10,3a,1–2.
44. Ibid., 10,4,6.
45. Ibid., 10,4,8.
46. Ibid., 10,4,11–12.
47. Ibid., 10,5,1.
48. Ibid., 10,6,3.
49. Ibid., 10,7,1.
50. Ibid., 10,8,1–4.
51. Ibid., 10,8,4.
52. Ibid., 10,8,6.
53. Ibid., 10,8A,1–2.
54. Ibid., 10,8B,1–2.
55. Ibid., 10,9,1.
56. Ibid., 10,9A,3.
57. Cicero, *ad familiares*, 2,16,1.
58. Cicero, *ad Atticum*, 10,10,2.
59. Ibid., 10,11,4.
60. Ibid., 10,12,2 BL.
61. Ibid., 10,12a,3 BL.
62. Ibid., 10,13,1.
63. Ibid., 10,14,1.
64. Ibid., 10,15,2.
65. Ibid., 10,15,4.
66. Ibid., 10,16,3.
67. Ibid., 10,16,4.
68. Ibid., 10,17,3.
69. Ibid., 10,17,4.
70. Ibid., 10,18,1.
71. Cicero, *ad familiares*, 14,7,2–3.

12 The Battle Fought, the *Res Publica* and the City

1. Cicero to Gaius Cassius Longinus, from Brundisium, August 47.
2. Cicero's correspondence resumes on 5–13 January 48 with a letter he sent to Atticus from Epirus (*ad Atticum*, 11,1). For the whole of 48 we have 14 letters from Cicero to Atticus, of which the first six were sent from Epirus, from Pompey's camp and from Dyrrhachium, purposely omitting matters regarding the military campaign. In addition there are two letters of February and May received by Caelius and Dolabella, sent from Rome and perhaps from Dyrrhachium. For 47, however, we have 36 letters sent by Cicero (including one quoting from a letter sent to Caesar but lost); for 46 we have 101 letters sent and one received; for 45 we have 130 letters sent and 9 received.
3. Cicero, *ad familiares*, 7,3,2–3 (to Marcus Marius, from Rome, April–May 46).
4. Cicero, *ad Atticum*, 11,6,2 (from Brundisium, 27 December 48).
5. Ibid., 13,52,1–2.
6. The principal sources are Caesar's own *Commentaries on the Civil War* (which end with his early exploits in Egypt in November 48 and are continued by three works on the Alexandrine, African and Hispanic wars, written by followers), the descriptions of Appian and Cassius Dio, as well as Suetonius' *Caesar* and five biographies by Plutarch (*Antony*, *Caesar*, *Cato*, *Cicero* and *Pompey*). What remains of Lucan's work ends abruptly with Caesar under siege at Alexandria (10,546); other accounts come from Livy by way of the *Periochae* and from Velleius Paterculus, Florus, Eutropius and Orosius.

7. Caesar, *Civil War*, 1,39,3.
8. Ibid., 1,52,1.
9. Lucan, *Pharsalia*, 3,761–2.
10. Caesar, *Civil War*, 2,18,7.
11. Ibid., 2,21,5.
12. Ibid., 2,32,2–3.
13. Ibid., 3,1,1.
14. Cassius Dio, *Roman History*, 41,43,2.
15. Plutarch, *Cato the Younger*, 53,4; *Pompey*, 65,1.
16. Plutarch, *Cato the Younger*, 53,3.
17. Caesar, *Civil War,* 3,10,8.
18. Appian, *Civil Wars*, 2,236; cf. Lucan, *Pharsalia*, 5,580–93; Cassius Dio, *Roman History*, 41,46,2–4.
19. Caesar, *Civil Wars*, 3,29,3.
20. Appian, *Civil Wars*, 2,252.
21. Ibid., 2,260.
22. Caesar, *Civil War*, 3,73,3–4.
23. Ibid., 3,78,3.
24. Appian, *Civil War*, 2,268.
25. Plutarch, *Pompey*, 66,4.
26. Ibid., 66,6.
27. Plutarch, *Cato the Younger*, 54,11.
28. Appian, *Civil Wars*, 2,270–85.
29. Cassius Dio, *Roman History*, 41,52,1–3.
30. Ibid., 41,55,1–56,1.
31. Plutarch, *Caesar*, 46,1; Suetonius, *Caesar*, 30,4.
32. Plutarch, *Pompey*, 76,2.
33. Cicero, *ad Atticum*, 11,7,3.
34. Ibid., 11,6,5.
35. Ibid., 11,17a BL.
36. Plutarch, *Caesar*, 50,3; Suetonius, *Caesar*, 37,2.
37. Appian, *Civil Wars*, 2,397.
38. Cicero, *ad Atticum*, 12,37a.
39. Appian, *Civil Wars*, 2,440.
40. Cassius Dio, *Roman History*, 41,30,2.
41. Ibid., 41,39,3.
42. Ibid., 42,17,1–21,2.
43. Ibid., 42,22,1–25,3.
44. Cicero, *ad familiares*, 8,17,2.
45. Orosius, *Histories Against Pagans*, 6,14,4–5.
46. Cassius Dio, *Roman History*, 42,23,2.
47. Caesar, *Civil War*, 3,21,3.
48. Cassius Dio, *Roman History*, 42,24,2.
49. Caesar, *Civil War*, 3,22,4.
50. Cicero, *ad Atticum*, 11,7,2.
51. Ibid., 11,10,2.
52. Cassius Dio, *Roman History*, 42,26,1–33,3.
53. Livy, *Periochae*, 113.
54. Cassius Dio, *Roman History*, 42,49,1–55,4.
55. Ibid., 43,14,1–18,6.
56. Plutarch, *Caesar*, 55,1. The Attic *médimnos* was a unit of volume equal to almost 52 litres.
57. Suetonius, *Caesar*, 39,4.
58. Appian, *Civil Wars*, 2,425.
59. Cassius Dio, *Roman History*, 43,21,4; cf. 43,25,2.

60. Cicero, *ad Atticum*, 13,39,1.
61. Cassius Dio, *Roman History*, 43,42,1–3.
62. Caesar, *Civil War*, 1,2,3.
63. Augustus, *Res gestae*, 25,1–3.
64. Florus, *Epitome of Roman History*, 4,8,2.
65. Lucan, *Pharsalia*, 6,420–2.
66. *Précis des Guerres de Jules César, par Napoléon, écrit par M. Marchand a l'Île Sainte-Hélène sous la dictée de l'Empereur*, J.P. Meline, Libraire-éditeur, Bruxelles, 1836, p. 134.
67. Cicero, *ad Atticum*, 8,1,1; Lucan, *Pharsalia*, 1,522
68. Cassius Dio, *Roman History*, 41,9,7.
69. Cicero, *ad Atticum*, 8,11,2.
70. Cassius Dio, *Roman History*, 50,3,4–4,1.

BIBLIOGRAPHY AND FURTHER NOTES

A Note on Sources

It is almost impossible to give even an approximate idea of the quantity and variety of academic studies on the causes and the course of the Civil War of 49–45. In this review we shall look in particular at the main sources and commentaries.

On the correspondence of Cicero, see R. Tyrrell and L. Purser (eds), *The Correspondence of M. Tullius Cicero Arranged According to its Chronological Order*, I–VII, Hodges, Figgis & Co. and Longmans, Green & Co., Dublin and London, 1904–33, 2nd edition; D.R. Shackleton Bailey (ed.), *Cicero's Letters to Atticus*, I–VII, Cambridge University Press, Cambridge, 1965–70; idem (ed.), *Cicero: Epistulae ad familiares*, I–II, Cambridge University Press, Cambridge, 1977; idem (ed.), *Cicero: Epistulae ad Quintum Fratrem et M. Brutum*, Cambridge University Press, Cambridge, 1980. On the various interpretations of Cicero's correspondence, see E. Narducci, 'Boissier, Cicerone, il Cesarismo', now in idem, *Cicerone e i suoi interpreti: Studi sull'Opera e la Fortuna*, ETS, Pisa, 2004, pp. 277–311. On the informative nature of the correspondence, see Cic. *fam.* 2,4,1. For a biography – and bibliography – of Cicero, see E. Narducci, *Cicerone: La parola e la politica*, Laterza, Roma and Bari, 2009; for a chronology, see N. Marinone, *Cronologia ciceroniana*, edited by E. Malaspina, Pàtron, Bologna, 2004, 2nd edition. On his role in the civil war, see P.A. Brunt, 'Cicero's "Officium" in the Civil War', *Journal of Roman Studies* 76, 1986, pp. 12–32. On his correspondence as evidence of the positions of the ruling class, see D.R. Shackleton Bailey, 'The Roman Nobility in the Second Civil War', *The Classical Quarterly* 10, 1960, pp. 253–67. On the figure of Atticus, see E. Narducci, 'Il "personaggio" di Attico: da Cornelio Nepote a Montaigne', in idem, *Cicerone e i suoi interpreti*, pp. 145–89; idem, *Parola*, pp. 218–32.

'Short century' is a definition taken from the expression coined by Eric Hobsbawm for the twentieth century and applied by Emanuele Narducci to the period between the Social War and the reign of Augustus: E. Narducci, 'Cicerone nel "secolo breve"', in idem (ed.), *Cicerone: Prospettiva 2000: Atti del I 'Symposium Ciceronianum Arpinas' (Arpino, 5 maggio 2000)*, Le Monnier, Firenze, 2001, pp. 1–15; on 'Roman revolution' to describe the period from 60 to the reign of Augustus, see R. Syme, *The Roman Revolution*, Oxford University Press, Oxford, 1939; on the 'last generation' of the republic, see E.S. Gruen, *The Last Generation of the Roman Republic*, University of California Press, Berkeley and Los Angeles, 1974.

'Hysterical letters' is an expression coined by J.P.V.D. Balsdon, 'Consular Provinces under the Late Republic, II: Caesar's Gallic Command', *Journal of Roman Studies* 29, 1939, pp. 167–83, 178; 'chronic blindness' is the accusation made by Jérôme Carcopino, in *Les secrets de la correspondance de Cicéron*, I, L'artisan du livre, Paris, 1947, p. 385.

There are 91 surviving letters written by Cicero between 4 January and his departure from Italy on 7 June 49; those received are 12; those sent between other people and attached are 8; those sent by Pompey which have survived through Cicero's correspondence are 2 to Cicero and

301

another 4 to Lucius Domitius Ahenobarbus and to consuls. Cicero's correspondence for the year 52 – a crucial year for the deterioration of the political situation – unfortunately contains only 2 surviving letters, both sent by Cicero. For the year 51, we have 51 sent and 8 received; for the year 50 we have 51 sent and 7 received.

On the works of Caesar, see A. Pennacini (ed.), *Gaio Giulio Cesare: Opera omnia*, Einaudi-Gallimard, Torino, 1993. On Caesar's speed, see M. Rambaud, *L'art de la déformation historique dans les 'Commentaires' de César*, Les Belles Lettres, Paris, 1966, 2nd edition, pp. 251–6. On the writing and reliability of the *Commentaries on the Civil War*, see also D. Vottero, in Pennacini (ed.), *Gaio Giulio Cesare*, pp. 1163–73; for further analysis, see J.H. Collins, 'On the Date and Interpretation of the "Bellum Civile"', *American Journal of Philology* 80, 1959, pp. 113–32; idem, 'Caesar as Political Propagandist', in H. Temporini (ed.), *Aufstieg und Niedergang der römischen Welt*, I, 1, de Gruyter, Berlin and New York, 1972, pp. 922–66; M.T. Boatwright, 'Caesar's Second Consulship and the Completion and Date of the "Bellum Civile"', *The Classical Journal* 84, 1988, pp. 31–40; M. Jehne, 'Caesar und die Krise von 47 v. Chr.', in G. Urso (ed.), *L'Ultimo Cesare: Scritti, riforme, progetti, poteri, congiure (Cividale del Friuli, 16–18 settembre 1999)*, L'Erma di Bretschneider, Roma, 2000, pp. 151–73; K. Raaflaub, 'Bellum Civile', in M. Griffin (ed.), *A Companion to Julius Caesar*, Wiley Blackwell, Chichester, 2009, pp. 175–91; L. Grillo, *The Art of Caesar's 'Bellum Civile': Literature, Ideology, and Community*, Cambridge University Press, Cambridge, 2012.

For a historical commentary to Cornelius Nepos's *Atticus*, see N. Horsfall (ed.), *Cornelius Nepos: A Selection, Including the Lives of Cato and Atticus*, Clarendon Press, Oxford, 1989.

On Trebatius, see W.H. Alexander, 'Cicero on C. Trebatius Testa', *The Classical Bulletin* 38, 1962, pp. 65–9, 74–6.

On Caelius, see P. Cordier, 'M. Caelius Rufus, le préteur récalcitrant', *Mélanges de l'École Française de Rome: Antiquité* 106 (1994), pp. 533–77; Narducci, *Cicerone: La parola*, pp. 257–76.

Apart from Cicero's letters and Caesar's writings, the principal sources for the 49–45 Civil War are, in chronological order: Velleius Paterculus, Lucan, Plutarch, Suetonius, Florus, Appian, Cassius Dio, Eutropius, Orosius.

On the work of Velleius Paterculus and that of Florus, see L. Agnes and J. Giacone Deangeli (eds), *Le storie di G. Velleio Patercolo: Epitome e frammenti di L. Anneo Floro*, UTET, Torino, 1991.

On Lucan's *Pharsalia*, and in particular books I–II, see P. Roche (ed.), *Lucan: De Bello Civili, Book I*, Oxford University Press, Oxford, 2009; E. Fantham (ed.), *Lucan: De Bello Civili, Book II*, Cambridge University Press, Cambridge, 1992. On Lucan and his historical sources, see Roche (ed.), *Lucan*, pp. 42–3; on his ideology, see E. Narducci, *Lucano: Un'epica contro l'impero*, Laterza, Roma and Bari, 2002.

I wish to thank Paolo Esposito for the very helpful exchange of ideas about Lucan.

On Plutarch's *Antony*, see C.B.R. Pelling (ed.), *Plutarch: Life of Antony*, Cambridge University Press, Cambridge, 1988.

On Plutarch's *Cato the Younger*, see C. Bearzot and L. Ghilli (eds), *Plutarco: Vite parallele, Focione e Catone Uticense*, Rizzoli, Milano, 1993.

On Plutarch's *Caesar* see A. Garzetti (ed.), *Plutarchi Vita Caesaris*, La Nuova Italia, Firenze, 1954; C.B.R. Pelling, *Plutarch: Caesar*, Oxford University Press, Oxford, 2011.

On Plutarch's *Cicero*, see A.W. Lintott (ed.), *Plutarch: Demosthenes and Cicero*, Oxford University Press, Oxford, 2013.

On Plutarch's *Pompey*, see E. Luppino Manes and A. Marcone (eds), *Plutarco: Vite parallele, Agesilao e Pompeo*, Rizzoli, Milano, 1989.

On Suetonius' *Caesar*, see H.E. Butler and M. Cary (eds), *C. Svetoni Tranquilli Divus Iulius*, Clarendon Press, Oxford, 1927.

On Appian's *Civil Wars*, see E. Gabba and D. Magnino (eds), *Le 'Guerre civili' di Appiano*, UTET, Torino, 2001; on book II of the *Civil Wars*, see C. Carsana, *Commento storico al libro II delle 'Guerre civili' di Appiano (parte I)*, ETS, Pisa, 2007.

On book XLI of Cassius Dio's *Roman History*, see N. Berti, *La guerra di Cesare contro Pompeo: Commento storico a Cassio Dione libro XLI*, Jaca Book, Milano, 1988; G. Norcio (ed.), *Cassio Dione: Storia romana, I–III*, Rizzoli, Milano, 1995–6.

On Eutropius' *Brevarium*, see F. Bordone and F. Gasti (eds), *Eutropio: Storia di Roma*, Rusconi, Santarcangelo di Romagna, 2014.

On Orosius' *Histories Against the Pagans*, see A. Lippold (ed.), *Orosio: Le storie contro i pagani*, I–II, Fondazione Lorenzo Valla-Mondadori, Milano, 1976.

On the laws, see G. Rotondi, *Leges publicae populi Romani: Elenco cronologico con una introduzione sull'attività legislativa dei comizi romani. Estratto dalla Enciclopedia Giuridica Italiana*, Società editrice libraria, Milano, 1912.

On meetings of the Senate between 68 and 43, see P. Stein, *Die Senatssitzungen der Ciceronischen Zeit (68–43)*, Diss., Münster, 1930.

On the magistratures, see T.R.S. Broughton, *The Magistrates of the Roman Republic*, I–II, American Philological Association, New York, 1951–2; T.R. Shannon, *Supplement to The Magistrates of the Roman Republic*, American Philological Association, New York, 1960.

Prologue

The period of 11–12 January can be determined on the basis of two factors. The first is the time required for Curio and the tribunes, having left Rome on the night between 7 and 8 January, to reach Caesar at Ravenna or, more probably, at Ariminum, calculable as a three-day journey; they would therefore have reached their destination at the earliest on the night between 10 and 11 January, even if news of the Senate decree of 7 January must have preceded them (Suetonius, *Caesar*, 31,1). The second factor is the time it took for news of the capture of Ariminum, but also the later capture of Ancona – but not necessarily the capture of Arretium – to reach Rome by the early part of 17 January. Since Ancona is about 64 Roman miles from Ariminum (1 Roman mile is equivalent to just over 1,480 metres), the legion's footsoldiers would have taken at least another three days to get there; Ancona is about 180 miles from Rome and could take just over two days for a courier travelling at the same speed as Curio, which would suggest that the Rubicon had been crossed no later than 12 January. In terms of the actual date, between the two corresponding possibilities of 11 January 49 in the republican calendar and in the astronomical calendar – 24 November 50 according to Groebe or 16 December 50 for Le Verrier – see J. Carcopino, *Jules César*, Presses Universitaires de France, Paris, 1968, 5th edition, p. 361, n. 2 suggests that the third moon mentioned by Lucan, *Pharsalia*, 1,218–19 is the third full moon of winter, visible from the astronomical date of 17 December 50; Carcopino, in regarding it as confirmation of the system adopted by Le Verrier, favours this as the date for the crossing of the Rubicon (therefore 12 January 49 of the Republican calendar). A useful chronology of the whole period can be found in A.C. Müller, *Untersuchungen zu Caesars italischem Feldzug 49 v. Chr. Chronologie und Quellen*, Diss., München, 1972.

There are a number of misinterpretations linked to Caesar's campaign and phrasing. According to Greek sources, the words Caesar was supposed to have spoken when he was about to cross the Rubicon were in fact 'let the die be thrown': *anerríphtho kúbos* (Plutarch, *Caesar*, 32,8; *Pompey*, 60,1–4; cf. *Moralia*, 206 C: *pâs anerríphtho kúbos*), with the variants *o kúbos anerríphtho* (Appian, *Civil Wars*, 2,140) and *erríphtho kúbos* (Zonaras, *Extracts of History*, 10,7), a proverbial expression documented in Critias (*P. Oxy.* 2078), Aristophanes (fr. 673) and in the form *anerríphtho kúbos*, in Menander (fr. 59). The sixteenth-century vernacular expression 'the die is cast', now in common use, refers to the version *iacta alea est* (Suetonius, *Caesar*, 32), where nevertheless, according to Erasmus (1518), *est* ('is') seems to be a textual corruption of *esto*, the subjunctive form. Curiously, critics don't seem to have given much thought to a crucial element: the translation 'the die is cast' necessarily shifts attention to the irreversibility of Caesar's decision, whereas 'let the die be thrown' seems much more in keeping with the climate of uncertainty – and literally of chance – that accompanies this action, a climate that is self-evident in the main sources, including Suetonius. On the expression in Greek, see J. Taillardat, 'Comica', *Revue des Études Grecques* 64, 1951, pp. 4–20, 4–9; Y. Gomez Gane, '"Il dado è tratto" (Giulio Cesare e Ludovico Domenichi)', *La lingua italiana* 11, 2015, pp. 99–106.

This is Suetonius' version of what happened. As to its reliability, see chapter 8 (the sub-section 'Suetonius' Version and Caesar's Reasons').

On the half-legion, other sources say that Caesar was followed by the whole of Legio XIII, while Livy's lost account mentioned only five cohorts, therefore a total of around 2,500 men.

On the line of the Arno-Rubicon, see U. Laffi, 'La provincia della Gallia Cisalpina', now in idem, *Studi di storia romana e di diritto*, ESI, Roma, 2001, pp. 209–35, 212; M. Sordi, 'Silla e lo "ius pomerii proferendi"', in eadem (ed.), *Il confine nel mondo classico*, Vita e Pensiero, Milano, 1987, pp. 200–11; N. Berti, 'Il Rubicone, confine religioso e politico, e l'inizio della guerra civile tra Cesare e Pompeo', in Sordi (ed.), *Il confine*, pp. 212–33.

I wish to thank Alberto Dalla Rosa for the fruitful exchange of ideas over the value of this 'boundary'.

PART I BACKGROUND

1 The Stage and Its Main Characters

Commentary to Cicero's *De re publica* in J.E.G. Zetzel (ed.), *Cicero, 'De Re Publica': Selections*, Cambridge University Press, Cambridge, 1985.

On the *pomerium* and the Servian Walls, see Livy, *History of Rome* 1,44,3–5; on spatial importance at political and legal level, see P. Catalano, 'Aspetti spaziali del sistema giuridico-religioso romano: "mundus", "templum", "urbs", "ager", "Latium", "Italia"', in W. Haase (ed.), *Aufstieg und Niedergang der römischen Welt*, II, 16,1, de Gruyter, Berlin and New York, 1978, pp. 440–552; on the killing of Remus, see Livy, *History of Rome* 1,7,1–3; on 500,000 inhabitants in the mid-first century, see E. Lo Cascio, 'La popolazione', in idem (ed.), *Roma imperiale: una metropoli antica*, Carocci, Roma, 2000, p. 38; on living conditions, see Z. Yavetz, 'The Living Conditions of the Urban Plebs in Republican Rome', *Latomus* 17, 1958, pp. 500–17.

Commentary to Cicero's *Laws* in A.R. Dyck, *A Commentary on Cicero: De Legibus*, University of Michigan Press, Ann Arbor, 2004.

On the different ideas about *res publica*, see also H.I. Flower, *Roman Republics*, Princeton University Press, Oxford, 2010.

On citizenship, see G. Luraschi, 'Sulle "leges de civitate" ("Iulia", "Calpurnia", "Plautia Papiria")', *Studia et Documenta Historiae et Iuris* 44, 1978, pp. 321–70. On censuses between 114 and 69, see C. Nicolet, *Rendre à César: Économie et société dans la Rome antique*, Gallimard, Paris, 1988, p. 47. On causes and the course of the Social War, see *infra*, chapter 1, 'Pompey: Training and Dominance of a "Teenage Butcher"', pp. 27–32.

On elections and assemblies, see L.R. Taylor, *The Voting Districts of the Roman Republic: The Thirty-five Urban and Rural Tribes*, American Academy, Rome, 1960; eadem, *Roman Voting Assemblies: From the Hannibalic War to the Dictatorship of Caesar*, University of Michigan Press, Ann Arbor, 1966; A. Yakobson, *Elections and Electioneering in Rome: A Study in the Political System of the Late Republic*, Steiner, Stuttgart, 1999.

On knights, see C. Nicolet, *L'ordre équestre à l'époque républicaine*, I–II, De Boccard, Paris, 1966–74.

On the *plebs urbana*, see N. Purcell, 'The City of Rome and the "plebs urbana" in the Late Republic', in *The Cambridge Ancient History*, IX, Cambridge University Press, Cambridge, 1994, 2nd edition, pp. 644–88.

On grain legislation, see C. Virlouvet, 'Les lois frumentaires d'époque républicaine', in *Le ravitaillement en blé de Rome et des centres urbains des débuts de la république jusqu'au haut empire: Actes du colloque international (Naples, 14–16 Février 1991)*, École Française de Rome, Naples and Rome, 1994, pp. 11–29.

On food supply and famine in Rome, see C. Virlouvet, *Famines et émeutes à Rome des origines de la République à la mort de Néron*, École Française de Rome, Rome, 1985; A. Tchernia, 'Le ravitaillement de Rome: les réponses aux contraintes de la géographie', in B. Marin and C. Virlouvet (eds), *Nourrir les cités de Méditerranée: Antiquité–Temps modernes*, Maisonneuve & Larose, Paris, 2003, pp. 45–60; C. Virlouvet, 'L'approvvisionamento de Rome en denrées alimentaires de la République au Haut-Empire', in Marin and Virlouvet (eds), *Nourrir*, pp. 61–82.

On *clientela*, see E. Deniaux, *Clientèles et pouvoir à l'époque de Cicéron*, École Française de Rome, Rome, 1993.

On electoral corruption, see J. Linderski, 'Buying the Vote: Electoral Corruption in the Late Republic', *The Ancient World* 11, 1985, pp. 87–94; E. Deniaux, 'De l'"ambitio" à l'"ambitus": les lieux de la propagande et de la corruption électorale à la fin de la république', in *L'"Urbs": Espace urbain et histoire (Ier siècle av. J.-C.–IIIe siècle ap. J.-C.): Actes du colloque international (Rome, 8–12 mai 1985)*, École Française de Rome, Rome, 1987, pp. 279–304; L. Fascione, L'"ambitus" e la "Pro Plancio"', in B. Santalucia (ed.), *La repressione criminale nella Roma repubblicana tra norma e persuasione*, IUSS Press, Pavia, 2009, pp. 357–82.

Commentary to the *Defence of Murena* in E. Fantham (ed.), *Cicero's 'Pro L. Murena Oratio'*, Oxford University Press, Oxford, 2013.

On the absence of a police corps, see W. Nippel, *Public Order in Ancient Rome*, Cambridge University Press, Cambridge, 1995; on violence, see P.J.J. Vanderbroeck, *Popular Leadership and Collective Behavior in the Late Roman Republic (ca. 80–50 BC)*, Gieben, Amsterdam, 1987; A.W. Lintott, *Violence in Republican Rome*, Oxford University Press, Oxford, 1999, 2nd edition.

Commentary to *Defence of Sestius* in R.A. Kaster, *Cicero: 'Speech on Behalf of Publius Sestius'*, Clarendon Press, Oxford, 2006.

On *contiones* and public opinion, see F. Millar, *The Crowd in Rome in the Late Republic*, University of Michigan Press, Ann Arbor, 1998; H. Mouritsen, *Plebs and Politics in the Late Roman Republic*, Cambridge University Press, Cambridge, 2001; R. Morstein-Marx, *Mass Oratory and Political Power in the Late Roman Republic*, Cambridge University Press, Cambridge, 2004; cf. K.-J. Hölkeskamp, *Reconstructing the Roman Republic: An Ancient Political Culture and Modern Research*, Princeton University Press, Princeton, 2010.

On obstructionist practices, see L. de Libero, *Obstruktion: Politische Praktiken im Senat und in der Volksversammlung der ausgehenden römischen Republik (70–49 v. Chr.)*, Steiner, Stuttgart, 1992; on the relationship between religion and voting, see J. Linderski, *The Augural Law*, in W. Haase (ed.), *Aufstieg und Niedergang der römischen Welt*, II, 16,3, de Gruyter, Berlin and New York, 1986, pp. 2146–312; C. Bergemann, *Politik und Religion im spätrepublikanischen Rom*, Steiner, Stuttgart, 1992.

On the importance of houses on the Palatine Hill, see A. Carandini, '"Domus" e "insulae" sulla pendice settentrionale del Palatino', in idem, *Schiavi in Italia: Gli strumenti pensanti dei Romani fra tarda Repubblica e medio Impero*, NIS, Roma, 1988, pp. 359–87. On urban properties and their value, see S.E. Craver, 'Urban Real Estate in Late Republican Rome', *Memoirs of the American Academy in Rome* 55, 2010, pp. 135–58.

On the terms *nobilitas* and *novitas*, see P.A. Brunt, '"Nobilitas" and "novitas"', *Journal of Roman Studies* 72, 1982, pp. 1–17.

On Roman imperialism, see the classic texts E. Badian, *Roman Imperialism in the Late Republic*, Cornell University Press, New York, 1968; W.V. Harris, *War and Imperialism in Republican Rome, 327–70 BC*, Clarendon Press, Oxford, 1979; and the recent F. Hurlet, '(Re)penser l'Empire romain: Le défi de la comparaison historique', in *La notion d'empire dans les mondes antiques*, Bilan historiographique, Université de Franche-Comté, Besançon, 2011, pp. 107–40.

On *publicani*, see M.R. Cimma, *Ricerche sulle società di publicani*, Giuffrè, Milano, 1981.

On the army, see A. Keaveney, *The Army in the Roman Revolution*, Routledge, London and New York, 2007.

On ideologies, see J.L. Ferrary, 'Le idee politiche a Roma nell'epoca repubblicana', in L. Firpo (ed.), *Storia delle idee politiche economiche e sociali*, I, UTET, Torino, 1982, pp. 723–804; G. Zecchini (ed.), *'Partiti' e fazioni nell'esperienza politica romana*, Vita e Pensiero, Milano, 2009.

On the concept of *libertas*, see C. Wirszubski, *'Libertas' as a Political Idea at Rome During the Late Republic and Early Principate*, Cambridge University Press, Cambridge, 1950; P.A. Brunt, *'Libertas' in the Republic*, in idem, *The Fall of the Roman Republic and Related Essays*, Clarendon Press, Oxford, 1988, pp. 281–350.

On Benjamin Constant, 'ancients' and 'moderns', see most recently L. Fezzi, *Il rimpianto di Roma: 'Res publica', libertà 'neoromane' e Benjamin Constant, agli inizi del terzo millennio*, Le Monnier, Firenze, 2012.

On *provocatio* and justice, see contributions in Santalucia (ed.), *La repressione*, including: F. Coarelli, 'I luoghi del processo' (pp. 3–13), A.W. Lintott, '"Provocatio" e "iudicium populi" dopo Kunkel' (pp. 15–24), M. Jońca, 'The scope of "exilium voluntarium" in the Roman Republic' (pp. 77–91); see also J.-M. David, *Le patronat judiciaire au dernier siècle de la république romaine*, École Française de Rome, Rome, 1992; E. Narducci, *Processi ai politici nella Roma antica*, Laterza, Roma and Bari, 1995; O. Licandro, 'Candidature e accusa criminale: strumenti giuridici e lotta politica nella tarda repubblica', *Index* 25, 1997, pp. 447–71.

On the Senate and its operation, see M. Bonnefond-Coudry, *Le sénat de la république romaine: De la guerre d'Hannibal à Auguste – pratiques délibératives et prise de décision*, École Française de Rome, Rome, 1989; for other problems, see A. Ormanni, *Il regolamento interno del senato romano nel pensiero degli storici moderni sino a Theodor Mommsen: contributo a una storia della storiografia sul diritto pubblico romano*, Giannini, Napoli, 1990.

On the dictatorship and example of Sulla, see A. Keaveney, *Sulla: The Last Republican*, Routledge, London and New York, 2005, 2nd edition; F. Santangelo, *Sulla, the Elites and the Empire*, Brill, Leiden, 2007.

On proscriptions, see F. Hinard, *Les Proscriptions de la Rome républicaine*, École Française de Rome, Rome, 1985; on the dismantling of the 'Sullan constitution', see U. Laffi, 'Il mito di Silla', *Athenaeum* 45, 1967, pp. 177–213, 255–77.

On the *senatus consultum ultimum* and institutional relations with dictatorship, *tumultus* and *iustitium*, see J. Ungern-Sternberg von Pürkel, *Untersuchungen zum spätrepublikanischen Notstandsrecht: 'Senatus consultum ultimum' und 'hostis' – Erklärung*, Beck, München, 1970; cf. A. Guarino, 'Senatus consultum ultimum', in W.G. Becker and L. Schnorr von Carolsfeld (eds), *Sein und Werden im Recht: Festgabe für Ulrich von Lübtow*, Duncker & Humblot, Berlin, 1970, pp. 281–94; T.N. Mitchell, 'Cicero and the "senatus consultum ultimum"', *Historia* 20, 1971, pp. 47–61; C. Masi Doria, '"Salus populi suprema lex esto": Modelli costituzionali e prassi del "Notstandrecht" nella "res publica" romana', in eadem, *Poteri magistratura processi nell'esperienza costituzionale romana*, Jovene, Napoli, 2015, pp. 1–21.

Livy's version of the story about Tarpeia and the subsequent conflict in *History of Rome* 1,11,6–13,5; commentary in R.M. Ogilvie, *A Commentary on Livy: Books 1–5*, Clarendon Press, Oxford, 1965, pp. 74–9.

Romulus defended Rome from the Fidenates who were devastating the fields (Livy, *History of Rome* 1,14,5), Tullus Hostilius defended it from the Albans who set up camp no more than 5 miles away (Livy, *History of Rome* 1,23,3), led first by King Cluilius – who gave his name to the Cluilian Trenches – and then by the dictator Mettius Fufetius, a conflict resolved by the duel between Horatii and Curiatii; Tarquinius Priscus defended it from the Sabines who crossed the River Aniene (Livy, *History of Rome* 1,36,1). Commentary in Ogilvie, *A Commentary*, ad loc.

Livy's version of the banishment of Tarquin in *History of Rome* 1,58,1–60,3; commentary in Ogilvie, *A Commentary*, pp. 223–30; cf. D. Briquel, *Mythe et révolution: La fabrication d'un récit – la naissance de la république à Rome*, Latomus, Bruxelles, 2007.

Livy's version of the story of Porsenna, Horatius Cocles and Mucius Scaevola in *History of Rome* 2,9,1–13,5; commentary in Ogilvie, *A Commentary*, pp. 255–66.

On subsequent events, see in particular Livy, *History of Rome* 2,18,4–5 (501); 2,24,1–8 and 2,26,1–3 (495); 2,43,2 (481); 2,51,1–9 (477); 2,63,2–4 (469); 2,64,3 (468); 3,3,1–6 (465); 3,5,1–4 (464); 3,7,1–3 (463); 3,8,7 (462); 3,15,4–18,11 (460); 3,26,1 (458); 3,30,4 (457); 3,38,1–42,7, 3,51,10 and 3,54,10 (450); 3,66,5–69,10 (446); 4,2,13–14 (445); 4,21,6–10 (435); 4,26,1–12 (431); 5,18,7–12 (396). Commentary in Ogilvie, *A Commentary*, ad loc.

Livy's version of the Sack by the Gauls in 5,35,1–55,5; commentary in Ogilvie, *A Commentary*, pp. 713–52; on the many other sources, see O. Skutsch, 'The Fall of the Capitol', *Journal of Roman Studies* 43, 1953, pp. 77–8; M. Sordi, 'Il Campidoglio e l'invasione gallica del

386 a. C.', in eadem (ed.), *I santuari e la guerra nel mondo classico*, Vita e Pensiero, Milano, 1984, pp. 82–91; U. Roberto, *'Roma capta': Il sacco della città dai Galli ai Lanzichenecchi*, Laterza, Roma and Bari, 2012, pp. 3–23. On what happened, see also D. Briquel, *La prise de Rome par les Gaulois: lecture mythique d'un événement historique*, Presses de l'Université de Paris-Sorbonne, Paris, 2008. On the literary reflection and figure of Camillus, see S.P. Oakley, 'Reading Livy's Book 5', in B. Mineo (ed.), *A Companion to Livy*, Wiley-Blackwell, Chichester, 2015, pp. 230–42. On references to the civil war, see also J.F. Gaertner, 'Livy's Camillus and the Political Discourse of the Late Republic', *Journal of Roman Studies* 98, 2008, pp. 27–52.

On the geese kept at public expense, see also Cicero, *pro Roscio Amerino* 56; Pliny, *Natural History*, 10,51.

On *hic manebimus optime*, see R. Tosi, *Dizionario delle sentenze latine e greche*, Rizzoli, Milano, 1991, p. 371; E. Citernesi and A. Bencini, *'Latinorum': Dizionario del latino contemporaneo*, Le Monnier, Firenze, 1997, p. 114.

On subsequent events, see in particular Livy, *History of Rome* 6,2,7 (389); 6,28,1–4 (380); 6,42,4–8 (367); 7,9,5–6 (361); 7,11,2–9 (360); 7,12,1–4 (359); 7,12,7–11 (358); 7,17,6–9 (355); 7,19,8–10 (353); 7,23,1–4 (350); 7,25,12 (349). Commentary in S.P. Oakley, *A Commentary on Livy: Books VI–X*, I–II, Clarendon Press, Oxford 1997–1998, ad loc.

On Pyrrhus's advance, see Plutarch, *Pyrrhus* 17,9 (300 *stadii* from Rome); Appian, *Samnite War* 10,10 (Anagnia); Florus, *Epitome of Roman History* 1,13,24 (Praeneste); Ampelius, *liber memorialis* 28,3; 45,2 (20 miles); Anonymous, *de viris illustribus*, 35,6 (20 miles); Eutropius, *Breviarium of Roman History* 2,12,1 (Praeneste, 18 miles); cf. P. Corbier, 'Pyrrhus en Italie: réflexion sur les contradictions des sources', *Pallas* 79, 2009, pp. 221–31; A. Kubler, 'Pyrrhus et Hannibal: deux figures de la peur de l'ennemi à Rome', in S. Coin-Longeray and D. Vallat (eds), *Peurs antiques*, Publications de l'Université de Saint-Étienne, Saint-Étienne, 2015, pp. 301–13.

The principal sources on Hannibal's invasion in 211 are Polybius, *Histories* 9,5,8–7,10; Livy, *History of Rome* 26,7,1–11,13; other sources and discussion in E.T. Salmon, 'Hannibal's March on Rome', *Phoenix* 41, 1957, pp. 153–63; cf. Kubler, 'Pyrrhus'.

On Coriolanus, see Livy, *History of Rome* 2,39,2–40,12 (commentary in Ogilvie, *A Commentary*, pp. 331–6); Dionysius of Halicarnassus, *Roman Antiquities* 8,1,1–62,3; other sources and commentary in T.J. Cornell, 'Coriolanus: Myth, History and Performance', in D.C. Braund and C. Gill (eds), *Myth, History and Culture in Republican Rome: Studies in Honour of T.P. Wiseman*, University of Exeter Press, Exeter, 2003, pp. 73–97.

On the events of 342, see Livy, *History of Rome* 7,38,5–41,8 (commentary in S.P. Oakley, *A Commentary on Livy: Books VI–X*, II, pp. 342–87).

I wish to thank Michele Bellomo for his information and our exchange of ideas on this matter.

On the assassination of Tiberius Gracchus, see Plutarcha, *Tiberius Gracchus* 16,1–19,10; Appian, *Civil Wars* 1,64–70; on the death of Gaius Gracchus, see Plutarcha, *Gaius Gracchus*, 15,1–18,1; Appian, *Civil Wars*, 1,114–20; on the *senatus consultum ultimum*, see Cicero, *Philippics*, 8,14.

On the 'marches on Rome' between 88 and 82, see Keaveney, *Sulla*, pp. 45–123; cf. R.A. Bauman, 'The *hostis* Declarations of 88 and 87 BC', *Athenaeum* 51, 1973, pp. 270–93; on the *villa publica* massacre and the conflicting versions, see Keaveney, *Sulla*, pp. 124–6; on proscriptions and consequent difficulties, see also Hinard, *Les Proscriptions*, pp. 17–233.

On Marius and his wars, see R.J. Evans, *Gaius Marius: A Political Biography*, University of South Africa, Pretoria, 1994; on Sertorius, see C.F. Konrad, *Plutarch's 'Sertorius': A Historical Commentary*, University of North Carolina Press, Chapel Hill, 1994.

On Plutarch's *Sulla*, see M.G. Angeli Bertinelli, M. Manfredini, L. Piccirilli and G. Pisani (eds), *Plutarco: 'Le vite di Lisandro e di Silla'*, Fondazione Lorenzo Valla-Mondadori, Milano, 1997.

On the events of 77 and Lepidus, see L. Labruna, *Il console sovversivo: Marco Emilio Lepido e la sua rivolta*, Liguori, Napoli, 1976.

On the march of Octavianus, see L. Canfora, *La prima marcia su Roma*, Laterza, Roma and Bari, 2007.

On Pompey, see in particular E. Meyer, *Caesars Monarchie und das Principat des Pompejus: Innere Geschichte Roms von 66 bis 44 v. Chr.*, Cotta, Stuttgart and Berlin, 1922, 3rd edition; M. Gelzer, *Pompeius*, Bruckmann, München, 1949; J. Van Ooteghem, *Pompée le Grand, bâtisseur d'Empire*, Académie Royale de Belgique, Bruxelles, 1954; J. Leach, *Pompey the Great*, Croom Helm, London, 1978; R. Seager, *Pompey the Great: A Political Biography*, Blackwell, Oxford, 1979 (2002²); K. Christ, *Pompeius: Der Feldherr Roms – Eine Biographie*, Beck, München, 2004; L. Fezzi, *Pompeo*, Salerno editrice, Roma, 2019.

On the Social War, see A. Keaveney, *Rome and the Unification of Italy*, Croom Helm, London and Sydney, 1987, pp. 3–158; S.L. Kendall, *The Struggle for Roman Citizenship: Romans, Allies, and the Wars of 91–77 BCE*, Gorgias Press, Piscataway, 2013; C.J. Dart, *The Social War, 91 to 88 BCE: A History of the Italian Insurgency against the Roman Republic*, Ashgate, Dorchester, 2014.

On citizenship for Transpadanian Gauls, see also E. Gabba, 'Problemi della romanizzazione della Gallia Cisalpina in età triumvirale e augustea', now in idem, *Italia romana*, New Press, Como, 1994, pp. 237–46.

On the death of Pompey's father, see O.D. Watkins, 'The Death of Cn. Pompeius Strabo', *Rheinisches Museum für Philologie* 131, 1988, pp. 143–50.

On the triumph and its value, see T. Itgenshorst, '*Tota illa pompa'. Der Triumph in der römischen Republik*, Göttingen, Vanderhoeck & Ruprecht, Göttingen, 2005.

On the campaign in Sicily and in Africa, see also E. Badian, 'The Date of Pompey's First Triumph', *Hermes* 83, 1955, pp. 107–18.

On the funeral of Sulla, see in particular Vanderbroeck, *Popular*, p. 220; on the position of Pompey during those years, see F.J. Vervaet, 'Pompeius' Career from 79 to 70 BCE: Constitutional, Political and Historical Considerations', *Klio* 91, 2009, pp. 406–34.

On the repression of Lepidus and involvement of Pompey, on his involvement in Spain and on the triumph, see in particular Seager, *Pompey*, pp. 15–21. On economic tensions in Rome, see in particular Vanderbroeck, *Popular*, pp. 220–1.

On the rebellion of Spartacus and its repression, see most recently B. Strauss, *The Spartacus War*, Simon & Schuster, New York, 2009; on the position of Crassus, see F.J. Vervaet, 'Crassus' Command in the War Against Spartacus (73–71 BCE): His Official Position, Forces and Political Spoils', *Klio* 96, 2014, pp. 607–44.

On Crassus, see F.E. Adcock, *Marcus Crassus, Millionaire*, Heffer, Cambridge, 1966; B.A. Marshall, *Crassus: A Political Biography*, Hakkert, Amsterdam, 1976; A.M. Ward, *Marcus Crassus and the Late Roman Republic*, Missouri University Press, Columbia, 1977.

On Plutarch's *Crassus*, see M.G. Angeli Bertinelli, C. Carena, M. Manfredini and L. Piccirilli (eds), *Plutarco, 'Le vite di Nicia e di Crasso'*, Fondazione Lorenzo Valla-Mondadori, Milan, 1993.

On the *contio* and the reconciliation, see in particular Vanderbroeck, *Popular*, pp. 221–2; D. Dzino, '"Annus mirabilis": 70 BC re-examined', *Ancient History* 32, 2002, pp. 99–117.

On Varro, see Gellius, *Attic Nights* 14,7,1–13.

On the figure of Caesar we shall limit ourself to indicating M. Gelzer, *Caesar der Politiker und Staatsmann*, Callwey, München, 1941, 3rd edition; Carcopino, *César*; H. Strasburger, *Caesar im Urteil seiner Zeitgenossen*, Wissenschaftliche Buchgesellschaft, Darmstadt, 1968, 2nd edition; S. Weinstock, *Divus Iulius*, Clarendon Press, Oxford, 1971; Z. Yavetz, *Julius Caesar and his Public Image*, Cornell University Press, Ithaca, 1983; C. Meier, *Giulio Cesare*, Garzanti, Milano, 1993; K. Christ, *Caesar: Annäherung an einem Diktator*, Beck, München, 1994; L. Canfora, *Cesare: Il dittatore democratico*, Laterza, Roma and Bari, 1999; other bibliography in H. Gesche, *Caesar*, Wissenschaftliche Buchgesellschaft, Darmstadt, 1976.

On Gaius Aurelius Cotta, see also J. Malitz, 'C. Aurelius Cotta "cos": 75 und seine Rede in Sallusts Historien', *Hermes* 100, 1972, pp. 359–86.

On the *contio* for the aunt, see also Vanderbroeck, *Popular*, pp. 222–3; on funeral ceremonies, see in particular Polybius, *Histories* 6,53,1–54,3.

On Caesar's premature departure, see also Canfora, *Cesare*, pp. 19–21. Plutarch places the reflection on Alexander during his time as praetor (*Caesar* 11,5–6) and the dream on the night before his crossing of the Rubicon (*Caesar*, 32,9). Suetonius and Cassius Dio (*Roman History*, 37,52,2 and 41,24,2) place the dream during his time as quaestor.

On piracy in general and on Pompey's subsequent campaign, see P. de Souza, *Piracy in the Graeco-Roman World*, Cambridge University Press, Cambridge and New York, 1999.

On Cicero's *On Duties*, see A.R. Dyck, *A Commentary on Cicero: De Officiis*, University of Michigan Press, Ann Arbor, 1996.

On the *lex Gabinia* and the voting, see in particular Vanderbroeck, *Popular*, pp. 223–5; cf. A.M. Ward, 'Cicero's Support of the "lex Gabinia"', *The Classical World* 63, 1969, pp. 8–10; S. Jameson, 'Pompey's "imperium" in 67: Some Constitutional Fictions', *Historia* 19, 1970, pp. 539–60.

On the law of 67 against *ambitus* and on the *rogatio Manilia* on the *liberti*, see in particular Rotondi, *Leges*, pp. 374–5.

On the mutiny of Clodius, see also D. Mulroy, 'The Early Career of P. Clodius Pulcher: A Re-examination of the Charges of Mutiny and Sacrilege', *Transactions and Proceedings of the American Philological Association* 118, 1988, pp. 155–78.

On the voting for the *lex Manilia* on the command of Pompey, see in particular Vanderbroeck, *Popular*, pp. 226–7.

On the emulation of Alexander, see in particular Plutarch, *Pompey*, 2,2; Pliny, *Natural History*, 7,95.

On Pompey's march towards Rome, see in particular Vanderbroeck, *Popular*, p. 234.

2 Plots and Scandals

On the first conspiracy, see F.L. Jones, 'The First Conspiracy of Catiline', *The Classical Journal* 34, 1939, pp. 410–22, favourable to the idea of two conspiracies; H. Frisch, 'The First Catilinarian Conspiracy: A Study in Historical Conjecture', *Classica et Mediaevalia* 9, 1947, pp. 10–36, against the idea that Crassus took part in the first; R. Seager, 'The First Catilinarian Conspiracy', *Historia* 13, 1964, pp. 338–47, against the existence of the first; L. Havas, 'Pompée et la première conjuration de Catilina', *Acta Classica Universitatis Scientiarum Debreceniensis* 3, 1967, pp. 43–53, who suggests that Pompey was sent against Mithridates to favour the first conspiracy; E.S. Gruen, 'Notes on the "First Catilinarian Conspiracy"', *Classical Philology* 64, 1969, pp. 20–4, which thinks about simple demonstrations against Torquatus and Cotta; L. Havas, 'Crassus et la première conjuration de Catilina: Les relations de Cicéron et de Crassus', *Acta Classica Universitatis Scientiarum Debreceniensis* 6, 1970, pp. 35–43, which considers it credible; B.A. Marshall, 'The Vote of a Bodyguard for the Consuls of 65', *Classical Philology* 72, 1977, pp. 318–20, which regards it as false; F.X. Ryan, 'The Consular Candidacy of Catiline in 66', *Museum Helveticum* 52, 1995, pp. 45–8, which regards the candidature of Catiline in 66 as possible.

On the political activity of the censors Crassus and Catulus, see E.G. Hardy, 'The Transpadane Question and the Alien Act of 65 or 64 BC', *Journal of Roman Studies* 6, 1916, pp. 63–82. On the Egyptian question, see *infra*, chapter 4, 'The Pact Falters But Doesn't Collapse', pp. 70–8.

On Caesar's aedileship and the gladiators, see Canfora, *Cesare*, pp. 21–4.

On Marians at the Capitolium, see in particular Vanderbroeck, *Popular*, pp. 229–30.

On the tribunal presided over by Caesar, see M.C. Alexander, *Trials in the Late Roman Republic, 149 BC to 50 BC*, University Press, Toronto, 1990, pp. 108–9. On the crimes of Catiline, see B.A. Marshall, 'Catilina and the Execution of M. Marius Gratidianus', *The Classical Quarterly* 35, 1985, pp. 124–33; cf. also F. Hinard, 'Mais qui donc a tué Gratidianus?', *Kentron* 2, 1986, pp. 118–22.

On Catiline's electoral promises, see in particular Cicero *Catilinarians* 2,18; Sallust *Conspiracy of Catiline*, 21,2; Cassius Dio, *Roman History* 37,30,2; cf. A. Barbieri, 'Le "tabulae novae" ed il "bellum Catilinae"', *Rivista di Cultura Classica e Medioevale* 36, 1994, pp. 307–15.

On the electoral campaign of 64 and the *Commentariolum petitionis*, see D. Nardo, *Il 'Commentariolum petitionis': la propaganda elettorale nella 'Ars' di Quinto Cicerone*, Liviana, Padova, 1970; on the work and the figure of Cicero's brother, see F. Prost, *Quintus Cicéron: Petit manuel de campagne électorale; Marcus Cicéron: Lettres à son frère Quintus*, I, 1 et 2, Les Belles Lettres, Paris, 2017; cf. L. Fezzi, 'Il "Commentariolum petitionis": sguardi dalle democrazie contemporanee', *Historia* 56, 2007, pp. 14–26.

On the dissolution of the *collegia*, see Asconius, *On Cicero's Orations*, pp. 7; 75 C; commentary in B.A. Marshall, *A Historical Commentary on Asconius*, University of Missouri Press, Columbia, 1985, pp. 94–5, 262–3.

On the celestial signs of 63, see Cassius Dio, *Roman History* 37,25,2; Obsequens, *The Prodigies*, 61.

On the agrarian proposal, see J.-L. Ferrary, 'Rogatio Servilia agraria', *Athenaeum* 66, 1988, pp. 141–64; Cicero's speech to the populace in *La legge agraria*, 2,71; commentary in E.J. Jonkers, *Social and Economic Commentary on Cicero's 'De lege agraria orationes tres'*, Brill, Leiden, 1963.

On the number of eligible voters, see Virlouvet, 'Les lois', pp. 20–1.

On the proposals for abolition of debts and the reinstatement of the sons of proscripts, see Cassius Dio, *Roman History*, 37, 25,3–4; on Cicero's opposition to the latter, see also Cicero, *ad Atticum*, 2,1,3; *in Pisonem*, 4; Pliny, *Natural History*, 7,117; Plutarch, *Cicero*, 12,2.

On Cicero's province, see W. Allen Jr, 'Cicero's Provincial Governorship in 63 BC', *Transactions and Proceedings of the American Philological Association* 83, 1952, pp. 233–41.

On the *Catilinarians*, see A.R. Dyck (ed.), *Cicero: Catilinarians*, Cambridge University Press, Cambridge, 2008.

On Catiline's conspiracy as a 'war of information', see L. Fezzi, 'Sulle tracce del "falso": una lettura della congiura di Catilina', *Hormos* 1, 2009, pp. 1–12.

On the trials of Rabirius, see in particular Vanderbroeck, *Popular*, pp. 230–1; Alexander, *Trials*, pp. 110–11; cf. E.J. Phillips, 'The Prosecution of C. Rabirius in 63 BC', *Klio* 56, 1974, pp. 87–101; C. Loutsch, 'Cicéron et l'affaire Rabirius (63 av. J.-C.)', *Museum Helveticum* 39, 1982, pp. 305–15. On Saturninus, see F. Cavaggioni, *L. Apuleio Saturnino 'tribunus plebis seditiosus'*, Istituto Veneto di Scienze, Lettere ed Arti, Venezia, 1998.

On Caesar as *pontifex* and the importance of this, see Canfora, *Cesare*, pp. 25–8.

On the elections of 63, in which Catiline was defeated, see Cicero, *Catilinarians*, 1,11; 1,27; *Defence of Murena*, 51–52; Sallust, *Conspiracy of Catiline*, 26,5; Plutarch, *Cicero*, 14,5–8.

On Cato, see R. Fehrle, *Cato Uticensis*, Wissenschaftliche Buchgesellschaft, Darmstadt, 1983; on his quaestorship, see also L. Fezzi, *Falsificazione di documenti pubblici nella Roma tardorepubblicana (133–31 a.C.)*, Le Monnier, Firenze, 2003, pp. 51–3; on his election for tribunate, see also Vanderbroeck, *Popular*, p. 231.

On Servius Sulpicius Rufus, see *Realencyclopädie der classischen Altertumswissenschaft (RE)*, under the heading *Sulpicius* (n. 95).

On the trial of Murena and on the *lex Tullia de ambitu*, see P. Moreau, 'Cicéron, Clodius et la publication du "pro Murena"', *Revue des Études Latines* 58, 1980, pp. 220–37; G. Poma, 'La "lex Tullia de ambitu" e la difesa ciceroniana di Murena', *Rivista Storica dell'Antichità* 35, 2005, pp. 275–92.

On the letters of Crassus and development of the early stages of reaction, see Fezzi, 'Sulle tracce'.

On the prophecy of the three *Cornelii*, see Cicero, *Catilinarians*, 3,9; Sallust, *Conspiracy of Catiline*, 47,2.

On the Senate decree of 5 December, see in particular A. Drummond, *Law, Politics and Power: Sallust and the Execution of the Catilinarian Conspirators*, Franz Steiner Verlag, Stuttgart, 1995; on Caesar's speech rewritten by Sallust, see Canfora, *Cesare*, pp. 60–8.

On the grain law proposed by Cato, see Virlouvet, 'Les lois', pp. 21–2.

On the crowd that rushed into the Senate for Caesar, on criticisms of Metellus Nepos, on the fight with Cato, on the crowd that surrounds Caesar's house and the involvement of Vettius, see also Vanderbroeck, *Popular*, pp. 233–4.

On *In Defence of Sulla*, see D.H. Berry (ed.), *Cicero: Pro P. Sulla oratio*, Cambridge University Press, Cambridge and New York, 1996.

On the profanation, see P. Moreau, *'Clodiana Religio': Un procès politique en 61 av. J.-C.*, Les Belles Lettres, Paris, 1982; D.F. Epstein, 'Cicero's Testimony at the *Bona Dea* Trial', *Classical Philology* 81, 1986, pp. 229–35; Mulroy, 'The Early Career'; W.J. Tatum, 'Cicero and the *Bona Dea* Scandal', *Classical Philology* 85, 1990, pp. 202–8.

On the attack by the Clodians on the Popular Assembly, see also Vanderbroeck, *Popular*, p. 235.

In a letter of July 65 (*ad Atticum*, 1,2,1) there is reference to an accuser of Catiline, colluding with the defence, with whom Cicero himself must have had dealings; Cicero, *har. resp.*, 42 identifies this person as Publius Claudius Pulcher (later Clodius). On Claudius' help to Cicero during the Catilinarian conspiracy, see Plut. *Cic.* 29,1.

On the attack on the court by supporters of Claudius, see Vanderbroeck, *Popular*, p. 236.

On the blocking of the contract for *publicani*, see Cic. *Att.* 1,17,9; 1,18,7; 2,1,8. On the role of Ahenobarbus in the election of Cicero, see Cic. *Att.* 1,1,3–4.

On decrees against corruption, see Gruen, *Last Generation*, pp. 223–4.

3 The Arrival of the 'First Triumvirate'

On Pompey's march towards Rome and the triumph, see Vanderbroeck, *Popular*, pp. 234, 236.

On Appian's *Mithradatic War*, see P. Gaukowski (ed.), *Appien. Histoire Romaine. La guerre de Mithridate*, Les Belles Lettres, Paris, 2001.

On the dismissal of Pompey's requests and on the role of Cato and Crassus, see Gruen, *Last Generation*, pp. 86–8.

On the *rogatio* of Lucius Flavius, see Seager, *Pompey*, pp. 79–80.

On Crassus' guarantee, see Plutarch, *Caesar*, 11,1; *Crassus*, 7,6; on his work in Spain, see Meier, *Giulio Cesare*, pp. 188–9.

On the impediment on candidature *in absentia*, sources and discussion in C. Ehrhardt, 'Caesar's First Triumph?', *Prudentia* 19, 1987, pp. 50–7; on Caesar's victory, see Cassius Dio, *Roman History*, 37,54,3; on the 'triumvirate', see Canfora, *Cesare*, pp. 69–86.

On the elections for the consulship of 60, see Meier, *Giulio Cesare*, pp. 192–4.

On Caesar's quest for popularity, see Cassius Dio, *Roman History*, 38,7,4–5.

On the legislation and chronology of the consulship, see L.R. Taylor, 'The Dating of Major Legislation and Elections in Caesar's First Consulship', *Historia* 17, 1968, pp. 173–93.

On the *contio* of Pompey and Crassus and on the violence linked to the voting of the agrarian law, see Vanderbroeck, *Popular*, pp. 236–7.

On the opposition of Bibulus, see L. Richardson, 'Cicero, Bibulus, and Caesar's Agrarian Bills of 59 B.C.E.', in G.L. Schmeling and J. D. Mikalson (eds), *'Qui miscuit utile dulci': Festschrift Essays for Paul Lachlan MacKendrick*, Bolchazy and Carducci, Wauconda, 1998, pp. 299–312; on his deterioration after 50, see M.J.G. Gray-Fow, 'The Mental Breakdown of a Roman Senator: M. Calpurnius Bibulus', *Greece and Rome* 37, 1990, pp. 179–90.

On the provision, see C. Carsana, 'Riflessioni sulle "leges Iuliae agrariae" del 59 a.C.: giuramento collettivo e principio di inabrogabilità nel II libro delle "Guerre civili" di Appiano', *Rendiconti dell'Accademia Nazionale dei Lincei* 12, 2001, pp. 259–74.

On the *lex Vatinia de provincia Caesaris*, see M. Gelzer, 'Die "lex Vatinia de imperio Caesaris"', *Hermes* 64, 1928, pp. 113–37; the deadline of 1 March 54 can be obtained from Cicero, *On Consular Provinces*, 36–7.

On the games proclaimed by Gabinius and on the *ludi Apollinares*, see Vanderbroeck, *Popular*, p. 238.

On the Vettius plot, see L.R. Taylor, 'The Date and the Meaning of the Vettius Affair', *Historia* 1, 1950, pp. 45–51; on the *contio*, see also Vanderbroeck, *Popular*, p. 239.

On the inconclusive debates, see Cicero, *In Defence of Sestius*, 40; *Against Vatinium*, 15; *Scholia Ciceroniana Bobiensia*, pp. 130, 146, 151 St.; Suetonius, *Iulius*, 23,1; *Nero*, 2,2.

On Clodius, see W.J. Tatum, *The Patrician Tribune: Publius Clodius Pulcher*, University of North Carolina Press, Chapel Hill and London, 1999; L. Fezzi, *Il tribuno Clodio*, Laterza, Roma and Bari, 2008.

On his adoption and change of name, see also A.M. Riggsby, 'Clodius/Claudius', *Historia* 51, 2002, pp. 117–23.

On his reliance on Cicero, see in particular Cicero, *ad Quintum fratrem*, 1,2,16.

On Clodius' bases of consensus, see Cassius Dio, *Roman History*, 38,12,4; 13,1–3.

On the legislation of Clodius, see also L. Fezzi, 'La legislazione tribunizia di Publio Clodio Pulcro (58 a.C.) e la ricerca del consenso a Roma', *Studi Classici e Orientali* 47, 1999, pp. 245–341.

On Cloelius, see also C. Damon, '"Sex. Cloelius, scriba"', *Harvard Studies in Classical Philology* 94, 1992, pp. 227–50.

On the cost of the grain law, see Cicero, *In Defence of Sestius*, 55; cf. *de domo sua*, 23; *Scholia Ciceroniana Bobiensia*, p. 132 St. Definition of the sum from Plutarch, *Pompey*, 45,4.

On the freeing of slaves and immigration, see in particular Suetonius, *Augustus*, 42,2; Cassius Dio, *Roman History*, 39,24,1.

On the recruitment of gangs, see Vanderbroeck, *Popular*, pp. 240–1; S.M. Cerutti, 'Clodius and the Stairs of the Temple of Castor', *Latomus* 57, 1998, pp. 292–305; cf. J.M. Flambard, 'Clodius, les collèges, la plèbe et les esclaves: Recherches sur la politique populaire au milieu du Ier siècle', *Mélanges d'Archéologie et d'Histoire de l'École Française de Rome* 89, 1977, pp. 115–56; F. Favory, 'Clodius et le péril servile: fonction du thème servile dans le discours polémique cicéronien', *Index* 8, 1978–9, pp. 173–87.

On the laws on Cicero's exile, see also E. Lepore, *Il 'princeps' ciceroniano e gli ideali politici della tarda repubblica*, Istituto Italiano per gli Studi Storici, Napoli, 1954, pp. 123–41; E. Gabba, 'Cicerone e la falsificazione dei senatoconsulti', *Studi Classici e Orientali* 10, 1961, pp. 89–96; P. Moreau, 'La "lex Clodia" sur le bannissement de Cicéron', *Athenaeum* 75, 1987, pp. 465–92; idem, 'La "rogatio" des huit tribuns de 58 av. J.-C. et les clauses de "sanctio" réglementant l'abrogation des lois', *Athenaeum* 77, 1989, pp. 151–78; C. Venturini, 'I "privilegia" da Cicerone ai romanisti', *Studia et Documenta Historiae et Iuris* 56, 1990, pp. 155–96; L. Fezzi, 'La coerenza di Cicerone su "XII tab. 9. 1–2" e il silenzio di Cotta sui "privilegia"', *Revue de Philologie, de Littérature et d'Histoire Anciennes* 88, 2014, pp. 79–105. On Cicero's exile, see most recently A.W. Lintott, *Cicero as Evidence: A Historian's Companion*, Oxford University Press, Oxford, 2008, pp. 175–85.

On the violence connected to the *rogatio de capite civis*, on the *contio* with Caesar and on the violence connected to the *rogatio de exilio*, see also Vanderbroeck, *Popular*, pp. 241–3.

On Cicero's house, see also G.C. Picard, 'L'"aedes Libertatis" de Clodius au Palatin', *Revue des Études Latines* 43, 1965, pp. 229–37; S.M. Cerutti, 'The Location of the Houses of Cicero and Clodius and the Porticus Catuli on the Palatine Hill in Rome', *American Journal of Philology* 118, 1997, pp. 417–26; S. Treggiari, 'The Upper-class House as Symbol and Focus of Emotion in Cicero', *Journal of Roman Archaeology* 12, 1999, pp. 33–56; C. Krause, 'Das Haus Ciceros auf dem Palatin', *Numismatica e Antichità Classiche* 33, 2004, pp. 293–316.

On the violence of Clodius, the inaction of Pompey, the conflict over the first proposed recall from exile, see also Vanderbroeck, *Popular*, pp. 243–4.

On the figure of Milo, see also A.W. Lintott, 'Cicero and Milo', *Journal of Roman Studies* 64, 1974, pp. 62–78.

On Cicero's return, see in particular Moreau, 'La "rogatio"'; Fezzi, 'La coerenza'; on the crowd that flocked from all over Italy and his arrival in Rome, see also Vanderbroeck, *Popular*, pp. 248–9.

On fluctuation in the price of grain and the artificial nature of the famine, see in particular T. Łoposzko, 'La famine à Rome en 57 avant J.-C.', *Quaderni di Storia* 9, 1979, pp. 101–22.

On the attack at the Senate of 9 September, see also Vanderbroeck, *Popular,* cit., pp. 249–51.

On Pompey's task, see in particular Plutarch, *Pompey*, 49,4; on the involvement of Cicero and his brother, see Cicero, *ad Atticum*, 4,1,7; 4,2,6; *ad Quintum fratrem* 2,4,7; 2,5,3; *In Defence of Scaurus*, 39.

For a commentary on Cicero's *de domo sua*, see R.G. Nisbet (ed.), *M. Tulli Ciceronis: De Domo Sua Oratio*, Clarendon Press, Oxford, 1939.

On Cicero's role, especially in 69, see E. Deniaux, 'Le patronage de Cicéron et l'arrivée des blés de Sicile à Rome', in *Le ravitaillement en blé de Rome et des centres urbains des débuts de la république jusqu'au haut empire: Actes du colloque international (Naples, 14–16 Février 1991)*, École Française de Rome, Naples and Rome, 1994, pp. 243–53; on the trial of Verres, see most recently L. Fezzi, *Il corrotto: Un'inchiesta di Marco Tullio Cicerone*, Laterza, Roma and Bari, 2016.

On Clodius' attacks on the house of Cicero, see Vanderbroeck, *Popular*, pp. 251–2.

On *navigare necesse est*, see Tosi, *Dizionario*, p. 555; Citernesi and Bencini, *'Latinorum'*, pp. 184–5.

4 Caesar, Gaul and Rome

On the publication of the *Commentaries on the Gallic War*, see in particular *Gallic War 8 proem.* 4–7; Suetonius, *Iulius*, 56,1; T.P. Wiseman, 'The Publication of De Bello Gallico', in K. Welch and A. Powell (eds), *Julius Caesar as Artful Reporter: The War Commentaries as Political Instruments*, Duckworth, London, 1998, pp. 1–9, which suggests how they may have been composed book by book up to winter 54/53, then books V–VI in winter 53/52 and VII in winter 52/51. Discussion about the attribution of book VIII to Aulus Hirtius – rather than to Caesar himself, except perhaps for the final chapters – in L. Canfora, 'La lettera a Balbo e la formazione della raccolta cesariana', *Annali della Scuola Normale Superiore di Pisa* 23, 1993, pp. 79–103.

On the relationship between conquest and propaganda, see in particular Rambaud, *L'art*; G. Zecchini, *Cassio Dione e la guerra gallica di Cesare*, Vita e Pensiero, Milano, 1978; E.S. Ramage, 'The "Bellum Iustum" in Caesar's "De Bello Gallico"', *Athenaeum* 89, 2001, pp. 145–70; A.M. Riggsby, *Caesar in Gaul and Rome: War in Words*, University of Texas Press, Austin, 2006.

On Caesar's knowledge of Gaul, see J. Harmand, 'Le portrait de la Gaule dans le "De bello Gallico" I–VII', in H. Temporini (ed.), *Aufstieg und Niedergang der römischen Welt*, I, 3, de Gruyter, Berlin and New York, 1973, pp. 523–95.

On the general situation, see in particular T. Rice Holmes, *Caesar's Conquest of Gaul*, Clarendon Press, Oxford, 1911, 2nd edition; J. Harmand, 'La conquête césarienne des Gaules: Le bilan économique et humain', *Rivista Storica dell'Antichità* 12, 1982, pp. 85–130; E. Hermon, *Rome et la Gaule transalpine avant César, 125–59 av. J.-C.*, Jovene, Napoli, 1993; G. Zecchini, *Le guerre galliche di Roma*, Carocci, Roma, 2009.

On the renewed threat of the Helvetii in 60, see Cicero, *ad Atticum*, 1,19,2; 1,20,5.

On the beginnings of the conflict, see G. Walser, *'Bellum Helveticum': Studien zum Beginn der caesarischen Eroberung von Gallien*, Franz Steiner Verlag, Stuttgart, 1998.

On the two new legions recruited in 58, see Caesar, *Gallic War*, 1,10,3 (Legio XI and XII); on the two new legions recruited in 57, see Caesar, *Gallic War*, 2,2,1 (Legio XIII and XIV); on Legio XIII, see in particular J. Rodríguez González, *Historia de las legiones romanas*, Almena, Madrid, 2003, pp. 331–2.

On the fifteen-day *supplicatio*, decreed in autumn 57, see Caesar, *Gallic War*, 2,35,4; cf. Cicero, *On Consular Provinces*, 25–7; *In Defence of Plancius*, 93; *In Defence of Balbus*, 61; *ad familiares*, 1,9,14; Plutarch, *Caesar*, 21,1; Cassius Dio, *Roman History*, 39,5,1; on the money, see Cassius Dio, *Roman History*, 39,25,1.

On the situation in Egypt, see E. Olshausen, *Rom und Ägypten von 116 bis 51 v. Chr.*, Diss., Erlangen, 1963; I. Shatzman, 'The Egyptian Question in Roman Politics (59–54 BC)', *Latomus* 30, 1971, pp. 363–9.

On the scuffle and order of censure, see also Vanderbroeck, *Popular*, pp. 252–3.

On the scandals of the Egyptian affair and the trial of Caelius, see R.G. Austin (ed.), *M. Tulli Ciceronis: Pro M. Caelio Oratio*, Clarendon Press, Oxford, 1963; A.R. Dyck (ed.), *Cicero: Pro Marco Caelio*, Cambridge University Press, Cambridge, 2013; on Clodia, see also M.B. Skinner, *Clodia Metelli: The Tribune's Sister*, Oxford University Press, Oxford and New York, 2011.

On the violence at the *ludi Megalenses*, see also Vanderbroeck, *Popular*, p. 253; T. Köves-Zulauf, 'Ciceros Todfeind Clodius – ein Spielverderber', *Acta Classica Universitatis Scientiarum Debreceniensis* 31, 1995, pp. 141–52.

On the *Response of the Haruspices*, see J.O. Lenaghan, *A Commentary on Cicero's Oration 'De haruspicum responso'*, Mouton, The Hague, 1969.

On the fire, see in particular C. Nicolet, 'Le temple des Nymphes et les distributions frumentaires à Rome à l'époque républicaine d'après des découvertes récentes', *Comptes Rendus des séances de l'Académie des Inscriptions et Belles-Lettres*, 1976, pp. 39–46.

On the *ager Campanus*, see D.L. Stockton, 'Cicero and the "Ager Campanus"', *Transactions and Proceedings of the American Philological Association* 93, 1962, pp. 471–89; G.M. Oliviero, 'La riforma agraria di Cesare e l'"ager Campanus"', in G. Franciosi (ed.), *La romanizzazione della Campania antica*, I, Jovene, Napoli, 2002, pp. 269–86.

On the attacks of Gnaeus Cornelius Lentulus Marcellinus, see Broughton, *Magistrates*, II, p. 207.

On the Luca Conference, see also E.S. Gruen, 'Pompey, the Roman Aristocracy and the Conference of Luca', *Historia* 18, 1969, pp. 295–320; C. Luibheid, 'The Luca Conference', *Classical Philology* 65, 1970, pp. 88–94; A.M. Ward, 'The Conference of Luca: Did It Happen?', *American Journal of Ancient History* 5, 1980, pp. 48–63.

For *On the Consular Provinces*, see H.E. Butler and M. Cary (eds), *M. Tulli Ciceronis, De Provinciis Consularibus Oratio ad Senatum*, Clarendon Press, Oxford, 1924; L. Grillo (ed.), *Cicero's De Provinciis Consularibus Oratio*, Oxford University Press, Oxford, 2015. From §§35–37 it seems that Caesar's appointment ought to end on 1 March 54: Cicero in fact considers it absurd that a province is assigned but not entrusted to a consul of 55 before that date, suggesting that the Gallic provinces remain with Caesar until the end of 54, so that he is replaced, from 1 January 53, by one of the two consuls of 54. On what is obtained by Caesar, see Cicero, *ad familiares*, 1,7,10.

On the return of Cato, the clash with Cicero, the postponement of the consular elections of 56, the violence against Ahenobarbus in early 55, the inauspicious omens adduced by Pompey at the praetorial election of 55, the violent election of Vatinius, the violence during the election of the aediles and the voting at the plebiscite of Trebonius, see also Vanderbroeck, *Popular*, pp. 254–8.

On the *lex Pompeia Licinia*, see L. Gagliardi, *Cesare, Pompeo e la lotta per le magistrature: Anni 52-50 a. C.*, Giuffrè, Milano, 2011, pp. 34–6. This was passed probably some time before 13 November and perhaps before 12 August, but must have had no time limit. It was provided, however, that the Senate could deal with the succession of Caesar only from 1 March 50, as is seen from Cicero, *ad familiares*, 8,9,5 and 8,8,9, and confirmed in Caesar, *Gallic War*, 8,53,1.

On Cato's warning, see Plutarch, *Cato the Younger*, 43,8–10.

On the law on *sodalicia*, see Gruen, *Last Generation*, pp. 229–33; P. Grimal, 'La "lex Licinia de sodaliciis"', in A. Michel-R. Verdière (ed.), *Ciceroniana: Hommages à K. Kumaniecki*, Brill, Leiden, 1975, pp. 107–15; A.M. Milazzo, 'La fattispecie materiale della "lex Licinia de sodaliciis" e le origini del reato associativo', *Studia et Documenta Historiae et Iuris* 79, 2013, pp. 481–99.

On the Theatre of Pompey and other contemporary buildings, see P. MacKendrick, 'Nabobs as Builders: Sulla, Pompey, Caesar', *The Classical Journal* 55, 1960, pp. 241–56.

On the funeral of Julia, see also Vanderbroeck, *Popular*, p. 259.

On the purchase of houses, see also Cicero, *ad Atticum*, 4,16,14; Pliny, *Natural History*, 36,103.

On the electoral scandal, see also Fezzi, *Falsificazione*, pp. 75–8.

On the first rumours regarding Pompey's ambition as absolute leader, see Seager, *Pompey*, p. 133.

On Cato's proposal and the violence, see also Vanderbroeck, *Popular*, p. 258. On the trial *de repetundis* of Scaurus and Cato's involvement in politics, see Alexander, *Trials*, pp. 143–4.

On the overall situation, see K. Morrell, 'Cato and the Courts in 54 B.C.', *Classical Quarterly* 64, 2014, pp. 669–80.

On the trials of Gabinius, see Alexander, *Trials*, pp. 145, 148–9; E. Fantham, 'The Trials of Gabinius in 54 BC', *Historia* 24, 1975, pp. 425–43; R.S. Williams, '"Rei publicae causa ": Gabinius' Defense of His Restoration of Ptolemy Auletes', *The Classical Journal* 81, 1985, pp. 25–38; on the violence, see Vanderbroeck, *Popular*, pp. 260–1. On the flooding of the Tiber and Gabinius, see Cassius Dio, *Roman History*, 39,61,1–63,5.

On the clash between candidates for the consulship, see Vanderbroeck, *Popular*, p. 261.

On the elections postponed in 53, see E.S. Gruen, 'The Consular Elections for 53 BC', in J. Bibauw (ed.), *Hommages à Marcel Renard*, II, Latomus, Bruxelles, 1969, pp. 311–21; Seager, *Pompey*, pp. 134–40.

On the disaster at Carrhae, see G. Traina, *La resa di Roma: 9 giugno 53 a. C., battaglia a Carre*, Laterza, Roma and Bari, 2010; on the curses of 55 and the incitement of the crowd, see also Vanderbroeck, *Popular*, p. 258.

On Pompey's marriage, see Seager, *Pompey*, pp. 140–1.

On Clodius' programme, see T. Łoposzko, 'Gesetzentwürfe betreffs der Sklaven im Jahre 53 v.u.Z.', *Index* 8, 1978–9, pp. 154–66.

On Cicero's *pro Milone*, see A.C. Clark (ed.), *M. Tulli Ciceronis pro T. Annio Milone ad Iudices Oratio*, Clarendon Press, Oxford, 1895.

On the fights on the *via Sacra* and between Clodius and Milo, see Vanderbroeck, *Popular*, p. 262.

On Mark Antony's attempt to kill Clodius, see G. Traina, *Marco Antonio*, Laterza, Roma and Bari, 2003, pp. 18–20.

On the failure of the consuls of 53 in the elections of consuls and praetors, see Seager, *Pompey*, p. 142.

On Milo's electoral expenses and on the lack of an *interrex*, see Ascon. p. 31 C; cf. Marshall, *Historical Commentary*, pp. 162–3.

On Britannia, see C.F.C. Hawkes, *Britain and Julius Caesar*, Oxford University Press, Oxford, 1978.

On the twenty-day *supplicatio*, passed in autumn 55, see Caesar, *Gallic War*, 4,38,5; Cassius Dio, *Roman History*, 39,53,2.

On the position of Cato, see Fehrle, *Cato*, pp. 174–7.

On Clodius in Transalpine Gaul, see Cicero, *On the Response of the Haruspices*, 42.

PART II ROME IN CHAOS

5 From the Death of Clodius to a Sole Consul

Commentaries on Asconius in Clark (ed.), *Milone*, pp. 94–118; Marshall, *Historical Commentary*; R.G. Lewis (ed.), *Asconius: Commentaries on Speeches by Cicero*, Oxford University Press, Oxford and New York, 2006; on the use of the records of the Senate, see in particular G.V. Sumner, 'Asconius and the "Acta"', *Hermes* 93, 1965, pp. 134–6.

On the events of 52, we follow J.S. Ruebel, 'The Trial of Milo in 52 BC: A Chronological Study', *Transactions and Proceedings of the American Philological Association* 109, 1979, pp. 231–49.

On Fulvia, see also C.L. Babcock, 'The Early Career of Fulvia', *American Journal of Philology* 86, 1965, pp. 1–32.

On the purchase of the house, see Pliny, *Natural History*, 36,103.

Regarding the arrival of the corpse, only Appian, *Civil Wars*, 2,77 states that the people spent the night in the Forum.

On the funeral, see also Vanderbroeck, *Popular*, pp. 263–4; G.S. Sumi, 'Power and Ritual: The Crowd at Clodius' Funeral', *Historia* 46, 1997, pp. 80–102.

On the fasces, see Clark (ed.), *Milone*, p. 98.

On Pompey's gardens, see Marshall, *Historical Commentary*, p. 170.

On the *contio* of Caelius Rufus, see Vanderbroeck, *Popular*, p. 264; the presence of Cicero at the *contio* of 27 January is supported by just one manuscript of Asconius (cf. Marshall, *Historical Commentary*, p. 171).

On the *senatus consultum ultimum*, passed between 3 and 10 February, see Ruebel, 'The Trial', p. 238; cf. H. Appel, 'Pompeius Magnus: His Third Consulate and the "senatus consultum ultimum"', *Biuletyn Polskiej Misji Historycznej* 7, 2012, pp. 341–60; Cassius Dio places the decision on the Palatine Hill, on the afternoon of Clodius' funeral, at the same time as the election of the *interrex*, and claims that the mandate to defend the state would have gone not just to the tribunes and to Pompey (without mention of the *interrex*), but also to Milo, who for that very reason would return into action (Cassius Dio, *Roman History*, 40,49,5); the historian suggests, however, that the decision to give Pompey responsibility for the levy happened later, due to the continuance of fighting and along with the changing of robes (40,50,1); immediately after, on the arrival of Pompey, in a meeting at the Theatre of Pompey, under military protection, he suggests the decision was made to dig up the bones of Clodius and rebuild the Curia (40,50,2).

On observations to Cicero's *De Legibus*, see Dyck, *A Commentary*, pp. 400–1, and in particular C. Martino, *Mentioning the Unmentionable: The Troublesome After-life of P. Clodius Pulcher* (awaiting publication). My thanks to the author for our discussion.

On the creation of the sole consul, see Gruen, *Last Generation*, pp. 153–5; J.T. Ramsey, 'How and Why Was Pompey Made Sole Consul in 52 BC?', *Historia* 65, 2016, pp. 298–324.

On permission to choose a colleague, see Plutarch, *Pompey*, 54,8; on the co-opting of his father-in-law, exculpated thanks to Pompey, see Appian, *Civil Wars*, 2,95; Cassius Dio, *Roman History*, 40,51,2–3; on the receptiveness to Caesar, see Suetonius, *Caesar*, 26,1.

On the two new laws, see Marshall, *Historical Commentary*, pp. 178–80. So far as the new trial was concerned, only three days were provided – at least so far as the *vis* was concerned – to collect the depositions of the witnesses (who were therefore limited to those who were more compelling), which were then sealed by the jury. On the fourth day, the parties would be called to attend, producing an equal number of names of judges. On the fifth day, eighty-one names would be drawn, and, immediately after, the prosecution would speak for two hours and the defence for three. Before the verdict, prosecution and defence would both reject five names from each of the orders, until the final number of fifty-one jurors was reached.

With regard to the trial *de ambitu*, since there were many accusers, a *divinatio*, 'divination' or 'presentiment', was held in front of Torquatus, the quaestor of that court. The purpose was to identify which of the petitioners was most suitable. The choice fell on the older Appius Claudius, the same man who had pursued the prosecution *de vi*, whereas Publius Valerius Leo and Gnaeus Domitius, perhaps a son of Gnaeus Domitius Calvinus (consul in 53), acted as signatories. Appius Claudius asked that Milo produce fifty-four slaves, giving their names; Milo replied that they were no longer in his *potestas*. Claudius was then allowed to choose as many as he wished of Milo's slaves, in order to submit them to interrogation. Schola said that Clodius had intended to remain at his Alban estate but was told of the death of his architect Cyrus, to whom both he and Cicero were testamentary heirs, a version confirmed by Gaius Clodius. Cicero, *In Defence of Milo*, 46 observes however that the previous day Clodius had left the architect while he was on the point of dying, and it was hardly credible that he had indeed returned on receiving the news. Cicero, *In Defence of Milo*, 46 goes on to state that Quintus Arrius and Gaius Clodius were also witnesses.

On the course of the trial, see also Vanderbroeck, *Popular*, p. 265.

Earlier speech of Brutus in Asconius, *On Cicero's Orations*, p. 41 C; Quintilianus, *Institutio Oratoria*, 3,6,93; 10,1,23; 10,5,20; *Scholia Ciceroniana Bobiensia*, p. 112 St.

On the structure of *pro Milone*, of fundamental importance is Clark (ed.), *Milone*, pp. L–LVII:

– *Exordium* (1–5), with praise of the judges and of Pompey, whose soldiers were regarded as protection;
– *Praeiudicia* (7–22), aimed at showing, through other historical or legendary cases, that murder could sometimes be justified, that the Senate was pleased about the death of Clodius and had not considered it *contra rem publicam*, and desired an investigation but not new proceedings, as did Pompey too;
– *Narratio* (24–9), on the intentions and character of Clodius. He had brought uncivilized slaves from the Apennines, with whom he had devastated the public woods and sacked Etruria; he had then said, both before the Senate and before the people, that Milo could not be deprived of his office of consul, but of his life yes; when Favonius asked him what hope he had in speaking such madness while Milo was still alive, he had answered that Milo would be dead in the space of three or four days; Favonius had immediately reported the words 'to Marcus Cato, here present' (26). Clodius' premeditation was clear. Having heard about Milo's annual visit to Lanuvium, he had left Rome the day before to ambush him in front of his own farm; he had left in such haste as to abandon a turbulent *contio*. Milo, on the other hand, having remained in the Senate until the assembly had been dismissed, had returned home and left with his wife and at such an hour that Clodius could already have been on his return journey, had he so wished. When he met him, Clodius was on horseback, without encumbrances, carriages, baggage, without his usual companions of Greek origin, or his wife who was almost always present. Milo was travelling in a carriage, with his wife, a cloak wrapped around him, encumbered by a large retinue of maidservants and boys. He came across Clodius in front of Clodius' farm, towards the eleventh hour (around 5 pm), and not the ninth (3 pm), as Asconius reports. Immediately, from higher ground, many of Clodius' men had attacked him with missiles, and those in front had killed the driver of the carriage. Milo, having thrown his cloak back over his shoulders, had jumped down, strenuously defending himself, while those who were with Clodius had drawn their swords. Some hurried to strike Milo from behind while others, thinking him dead, began to attack the slaves at the end of the line. Some of these died, but others, seeing the battle around the carriage and having heard from Clodius himself that Milo had been killed, without their master having ordered it, 'did what every man would have wished of his men in a similar situation' (29);
– *Tractatio* (32–71), on the interest that Clodius had in the death of Milo and on the violence to which he had always resorted:
  1. *ex causa* (32–4): the ambush was useful only to Clodius: he would have become praetor with two consuls who would have left him to act, all the more because he had some 'incendiary' (33) laws ready, in the hands of Sextus Clodius;
  2. *ex vita* (36–41): Milo would have become consul, preventing Clodius from pursuing acts of violence. If he had wanted to kill him, in the past, he would have had plenty of legitimate opportunities. And then, why stain his hands during an election campaign?
– *Argumentum* (44): the words of Favonius are recalled once again;
– This leads to considerations on *tempus* (45–52). Clodius had hurried away from a *contio*; he could have known Milo's movements, but Milo couldn't have known his. Schola had given evidence about the victim's return before the death of his architect Cyrus, a version confirmed by Gaius Clodius: 'I believe indeed that the messenger, who is said to have brought news of Cyrus's death, did not inform him of that, but told him that Milo was approaching. After all, what did he have to say about Cyrus, whom Clodius, on his departure from Rome, had left more dead than alive? I had been with him, had sealed Cyrus's testament together with Clodius, because he had publicly made his will and had appointed him and me as heirs. The

day before, at the third hour, Clodius had left him at the very point of death: the day after, at the tenth hour, was news sent to him that he was dead? . . . for what reason, then, did he hasten to return to Rome, why had he ventured along the road in the depth of night? . . . And just as Clodius, rather than attempting that journey, ought to have avoided arriving in the city by night, so Milo, supposing he wanted to set an ambush, if he knew that Clodius was about to arrive in the city at night, he could have positioned himself there and waited. He would have killed him at night. Everyone would have believed him if he had denied it. He would have killed him in some place that was dangerous and full of brigands. Everyone would have believed him if he had denied it: everyone wants to save him, even now that he confesses it. The brunt of the blame would have fallen on the place itself, a den of outcasts.' (48–50);

– Next are considerations on *locus* (53–4). Clodius, on his return from Aricia, stopped at his Alban villa, and it was exactly there that the ambush occurred, in a place where 'thanks to underground passageways built with the criterion of a madman, there was comfortable space for 1,000 men ready for everything' (53). Clodius suddenly, at a late hour, had left the villa and gone towards that of Pompey, whom he well knew then to be at Alsium. All of this to waste time and wait for Milo;

– Next are considerations on *facultas* (55–6). Milo was hampered by the number and nature of his companions, and by the presence of his wife; he was saved by the courage of his slaves;

– Then a *locus communis contra quaestiones* (57–60) on slaves. Milo had freed them because they had saved him, even if someone would be suspicious that he hadn't lavished them with gifts; he had freed them to prevent them being subjected to torture. That system is criticized: 'Come on, then, what kind of examination could it have been? Let's give an example: "Hey, you, Rufio! Be careful not to lie. Was it Clodius who laid an ambush for Milo?" – "Yes": then he'll certainly get crucified. – "No": and his long-awaited freedom is his. What is there more serious than such an examination? They, those due to give evidence, are separated in a flash from their companions, thrown into a cell so that no one can talk to them. After spending a hundred days at the disposal of the prosecutor, they are presented by him as his witnesses in court. Is any examination more impartial and more honest than that?' (60);

– There is then a *consecutio* and *locus communis contra rumores* (61–6): Milo's return to Rome and placing his trust in Pompey, who yet had certain suspicions, was a sign of innocence, as was his indifference to the charges of sedition and conspiracy to kill, above all in relation to Pompey;

– There is then the *pars adsumptiva*, or *extra causam* (72–91). The murder of Clodius was something positive; it is followed by a devastating picture of the man, praise for Milo's energy, a description of the condition of Rome if Clodius had been praetor: 'in his house he was already drawing up laws that would have made us slaves of our servants' (87); 'a new law, found in his house together with other Clodian laws, would have made our slaves his *liberti* (89). He also recalled the violence towards the tribune of the plebs Marcus Caelius Rufus, the celebrations decreed in Etruria, the widespread joy wherever news of the death of Clodius was heard;

– The *epilogus* and *commiseratio* follow (92).

Fragments of the real speech but doubts about its existence in J.N. Settle, 'The Trial of Milo and the Other Pro Milone', *Transactions and Proceedings of the American Philological Association* 94, 1963, pp. 268–80.

On later trials of Milo, see Asconius, *On Cicero's Orations*, p. 54 C (cf. pp. 36, 38–9 C). The following day marked the beginning of the trial *de ambitu* at the court of Torquatus, which led to a conviction in his absence. The prosecutor, Appius Claudius again, had declared he would forego the prescribed recompense; it was undersigned by Publius Valerius Leo and Gnaeus Domitius. A few days later – probably once again in his absence – at the court of Marcus Favonius, Milo was convicted *de sodaliciis*, prosecuted by Publius Fulvius Neratus, who received the reward provided by law. He was once again convicted *de vi*, perhaps according to the *lex*

Plautia, before the court of Lucius Fabius, prosecuted by Lucius Cornificius and Quintus Patulcius.

On Milo's goods to Philotimus, see also A. Haury, 'Philotime et la vente des biens de Milon', *Revue des Études Latines* 34, 1956, pp. 179–90.

On the trials of Saufeius and Cloelius, see Ascon., pp. 54–6 C. After Milo, the first to be tried under the *lex Pompeia de vi* was Marcus Saufeius, who had led the attack on the inn at Bovillae and the killing of Clodius. His accusers were Lucius Cassius (Longinus?), Lucius Fulcinius and Gaius Valerius. He was defended by Cicero and Caelius and acquitted by a single vote. The orders, this time, were divided: the majority of the tribunes of the treasury voted to acquit (10 against 6), while senators and knights, by a slim majority were in favour of conviction (respectively 10 to 8 and 9 to 8). Asconius observed that it was hatred of the victim that saved Saufeius, since, having led the attack, his situation was even weaker than that of Milo. A few days later, Saufeius was also tried by the court of Gaius Considius, under the *lex Plautia de vi*, with the additional charge of having occupied places *edita* and having with him a *telum*. His accusers were Gaius Fidius, Gnaeus Aponius, Marcus Seius and at least one other person. He was defended by Cicero and Marcus Terentius Varro Gibba. This time he was acquitted by a wider majority (32 to 19), though a majority of the tribunes of the treasury voted to convict. Sextus Cloelius, who had incited the crowd to carry the body of Clodius into the Curia, was then prosecuted – probably under the *lex Pompeia* – by Gaius Caesennius Filo and Marcus Alfidius, and defended by Titus Flacconius. He was convicted by a large majority (46 votes), whereas only two senators and three knights voted for acquittal.

On the speech in support of Scipio, see Plutarch, *Pompey*, 55,7; Appian, *Civil Wars*, 2,93–94; on the choice of Scipio as colleague, see Plutarch, *Pompey*, 55,4; Appian, *Civil Wars*, 2,95.

On the trial of Scaurus, see Vanderbroeck, *Popular*, p. 265; Alexander, *Trials*, pp. 156–7.

On the timescales for a candidature, see Gagliardi, *Cesare*, pp. 23–61. Technically, Caesar could again become consul only from 1 January 48, since Sulla's law of 82 provided a compulsory interval of ten years. Furthermore, it seems that according to the *lex Licinia Pompeia* of 55, no successor could be appointed before 1 March 50. Caesar probably considered that his proconsulate should last until 31 December 49, but some have suggested earlier dates. It is a much debated question, and Cicero himself described it as unclear (*Marc.* 30).

On the proposal of the ten tribunes and the later request to make an exception, see Gagliardi, *Cesare*, pp. 63–87.

On Caesar at Ravenna and the role of Cicero, see Cicero, *ad Atticum*, 7,1,4 (from Athens, 16 October 50).

On the law on the government of provinces, see in particular Gagliardi, *Cesare*, pp. 89–104; C.E.W. Steel, 'The "Lex Pompeia de prouinciis" of 52 BC: A Reconsideration', *Historia* 61, 2012, pp. 83–93; on the influence of Cato, see K. Morrell, *Pompey, Cato, and the Governance of the Roman Empire*, Oxford University Press, Oxford, 2017.

On the earlier Senate decree, see Cassius Dio, *Roman History*, 40,46,2; 40,56,1.

On the end of Pompey's *cura annonae*, the only information is a letter from Cicero (*ad familiares*, 13,75), written at the end of 52 or early 51.

On the strange subsequent event and the correction of the law, see in particular Gagliardi, *Cesare*, pp. 105–49.

On the games of the aediles, see Plutarch, *Cato the Younger*, 46,2–3.

On the defeat of Cato, see Plutarch, *Cato the Younger*, 49,3–4; on the possible role for Caesar, cf. Caesar, *Civil War*, 1,4,1.

On the *supplicatio* granted to Caesar, see Caesar, *Gallic War*, 7,90,8; cf. Cassius Dio, *Roman History*, 40,50,4, who refers instead to sixty days.

6 Winner in a Tight Corner

On recruitment in Cisalpine Gaul, see Caesar, *Gallic War*, 7,1,1; reserves were formed to what remained as ten legions (cf. 7,7,5; 7,57,1).

On druids, see Caesar, *Gallic War*, 6,13,3–14,6; cf. G. Zecchini, *I Druidi e l'opposizione dei Celti a Roma*, Jaca Book, Milano, 1984.

On Vercingetorix, see in particular Y. Le Bohec, 'Vercingétorix', *Rivista Storica dell'Antichità* 28, 1998, pp. 85–120; G. Zecchini, *Vercingetorige*, Laterza, Roma and Bari, 2002.

On the relationship between Caesar and Labienus, see M.-W. Schulz, *Caesar und Labienus: Geschichte einer tödlichen Kameradschaft: Caesars Karriere als Feldherr im Spiegel der Kommentarien sowie bei Cassius Dio, Appianus und Lucanus*, G. Olms, Hildesheim, 2010.

On the loan of Pompey's Legio I and the Senate's decision of 50, in the light of the whole matter of the restitution of the legions, see Carsana, *Commento*, pp. 120–1, 123.

On the position of Sulpicius cf. Cicero, *ad familiares*, 4,1–6; on that of Marcellus, then defended in 46, cf. Cicero, *ad familiares*, 4,7–11; *In Defense of Marcellus* (passim); see also *Realencyclopädie der classischen Altertumswissenschaft* (RE), under the heading *Claudius* (n. 216).

On the route taken by Cicero and his stay in Cilicia in 51, see Marinone, *Cronologia*, pp. 146–8; on the whole question and on the correspondence of the period, see *infra* chapter 7, 'A Proposal from Caesar'.

The letter on the punishment of the citizen of Novum Comum is Cicero, *ad Atticum*, 5,11,2 (Athens, 6 July 51). Plutarch, *Caesar*, 29,2 records that the consuls 'took citizenship away from the inhabitants of Novum Comum, a *colonia* recently established by Caesar in Gaul, and the consul Marcellus had one of the senators of Novum Comum who had come to Rome beaten with rods, adding that he was inflicting these bruises as a sign of his not being Roman: that he should go to Caesar to show them'; Suetonius, *Caesar*, 28,4 notes that Marcellus 'also proposed that the colonists sent to Comum by virtue of the bill of Vatinius be deprived of their citizenship on the ground that it had been granted for electoral reasons and through abuse of power'. Cf. G. Luraschi, 'La "lex Vatinia de colonia Comum deducenda" ed i connessi problemi di storia costituzionale romana', in *Proceedings of the conference to mark the centenary of the Rivista archeologica Comense*, Noseda, Como, 1974, pp. 363–400.

On the reconstruction and date of the proposal of Marcellus, see Gagliardi, *Cesare*, pp. 108–15, 151. Cf. *Gallic War*, 8,53,1; Plutarch, *Caesar*, 29,1; Suetonius, *Caesar*, 28,2–29,1; Appian, *Civil Wars*, 2,97; 99; Cassius Dio, *Roman History*, 40,59,1. On the definition of the relative decree as *auctoritas*, see Cicero, *ad Atticum*, 5,2,3 (10 May 51).

On Cicero's meeting with Pompey between 19 and 21 May 51, see Cicero, *ad Atticum*, 5,2,2 (Venusia, 15 May 51); 5,6 (Tarentum, 18–19 May 51); 5,7 (Tarentum, 20 May 51); *ad familiares*, 2,8,2 (Athens, 6 July 51); 8,1,3 (Rome, after 24 May 51).

On rumours about Pompey's journey to Spain, see Cicero, *ad Atticum*, 5,11,3; *ad familiares*, 3,8,10.

About the failure to reach a decision on 1 June and on the role of Pompey, cf. Appian, *Civil Wars*, 2,99.

On the trial of Marcellus, see Alexander, *Trials*, p. 162.

On the bribe to Paullus, see Appian, *Civil Wars*, 2,101; on the corruption of Paullus and also among the ruling class, see Plutarch, *Caesar*, 29,3; Plutarch, *Pompey*, 58,2; on the basilica, sources in Carsana, *Commento*, p. 112.

On the Senate meeting after March, see Appian, *Civil Wars*, 2,103.

On the question and political position of Curio, see W.K. Lacey, 'The Tribunate of Curio', *Historia* 10, 1961, pp. 318–29, who does not think there was corruption; on Caesar's practice of paying politicians, see N.A. Coffee, 'Caesar chrematopoios', *The Classical Journal* 106, 2011, pp. 397–421.

Explanations in Plutarch, *Caesar*, 29,3; Suetonius, *Caesar*, 29,1; Appian, *Civil Wars*, 2,101–2; Cassius Dio, *Roman History*, 40,60,2–62,4.

On the proposal of 13 November, see Gagliardi, *Cesare*, pp. 53–6, 164–7.

On the Senate's acceptance of candidature *in absentia*, see Gagliardi, *Cesare*, pp. 167–71.

On attempts at corruption in relation to Lentulus Crus, see also L. Hayne, 'Caesar and Lentulus Crus', *Acta Classica* 39, 1996, pp. 72–6.

On violence in the election of Antony, see Vanderbroeck, *Popular*, p. 266.

7 Winds of Civil War

In general, on Caesar's peace proposals and their sincerity, up to Pharsalus, see F.A. Sirianni, 'Caesar's Peace Overtures to Pompey', *L'Antiquité Classique* 62, 1993, pp. 219–37.

Date and discussion of Caesar's proposal in Gagliardi, *Cesare*, pp. 161–4, 172–3; Carsana, *Commento*, p. 115.

On celebrations in honour of Curio, see Vanderbroeck, *Popular*, pp. 266–7.

On Pompey at a school of rhetoric, see Suetonius, *Rhetors*, 25, 3.

On Atticus' visit to Pompey, see Cicero, *ad Atticum*, 7,2,5–6 (from Brundisium, 24 November 50).

On Cicero's campaign, see D. Caiazza, 'Il proconsolato di Cicerone in Cilicia', *Ciceroniana* 1, 1959, pp. 140–56; M. Wistrand, *'Cicero imperator': Studies in Cicero's Correspondence 51–47 BC*, Acta Universitatis Gothoburgensis, Göteborg, 1979.

On the problem of paying Pompey's troops between summer 51 and summer 50, see Cicero, *ad familiares*, 8,4,4; 8,14,4.

On the payment of Caesar's legions, see Carsana, *Commento*, p. 123. On Appius Claudius Pulcher and the disaffection of troops in relation to Caesar, see Plutarch, *Caesar*, 29,5; *Pompey*, 57,7; Appian, *Civil Wars*, 2,116–17.

On the censure of Appius Claudius Pulcher, see also Cicero, *ad familiares*, 8,14,4.

On the possibility that Caesar, *Civil War*, 1,7,8–8,1 and *Gallic War*, 8,54,4–5 are misleading on the positioning beyond the Alps of the legions prior to the Rubicon, and in particular Legio XII, which joined Caesar at the beginning of February (1,15,3), and of Legio VIII, which joined him in the early days of the siege of Corfinium (1,18,5), as well as that of the horsemen of Noricum, see Ottmer, *Die Rubikon-Legende*.

On the Senate meeting of 1 December, in Plutarch there is a certain confusion regarding a speech to the people delivered by the new tribune Mark Antony on 21 December (for the actual speech and dating, see in particular Cicero, *ad Atticum*, 7,8,4–5), and regarding the Senate meeting of 1 January 49 and that of 7 January 49, while Cassius Dio makes no mention of the matter. In Plutarch, *Antony*, 5,5–9 the account of the division of the Senate over the prospects relating to Caesar and Pompey is preceded by that of the public reading of messages that Antony is said to have received from Caesar, and followed by his being driven out of the Senate, which had occurred after speeches by Cato and Lentulus Crus, and lastly the escape; Antony is also confused with Curio, who was tribune the previous year.

In Plutarch, *Caesar*, 30,2–31,3 Curio went proposing to the people that both Caesar and Pompey should leave their command, finding approval among the crowd; Antony read out a letter to the people in spite of opposition from the consuls; Scipio proposed then in the Senate to declare Caesar a public enemy unless he laid down his arms by a certain day; when the consuls asked if it seemed appropriate that Pompey discharged his army and repeated the question with regard to Caesar, in the first case, very few were in favour, in the second almost everyone, but when Antony proposed that both should leave their commands, all unanimously approved; Scipio however violently objected and the consul Lentulus Crus ended the meeting and all changed their robes in sign of mourning; mildly worded letters then arrived from Caesar, and Cicero also set about mediating, but in the end Lentulus did not agree to the pact: he drove Antony and Curio from the Senate and they fled from Rome.

In Plutarch, *Pompey*, 58,4–59,6 Curio put forward the request, supported by Antony and by Lucius Calpurnius Piso Caesoninus; it was proposed at first that only Caesar should leave his command, obtaining the majority, but then, when asked that both should leave their command, only twenty-two senators were on Pompey's side; he went out, was applauded by the people; Marcellus objected, the Senate voted to change their dress and all went to Pompey; immediately after, Antony read a letter from Caesar to the people, which asked that both should leave their posts; Lentulus however did not summon the Senate; nor did Cicero succeed with the compromise proposal due to the opposition of Lentulus and Cato.

Appian's account of the Senate meeting of 1 December 50 is in 2,118–19; cf. *Civil War*, 8,52,3–5 (mention of Curio's action).

Description of Curio's escape in Appian, *Civil Wars*, 2,123–4; other sources in Carsana, *Commento*, pp. 123–4.

Cicero's letters on the way towards Rome: Cicero, *ad Atticum*, 7,3; 7,4; 7,5; 7,6; 7,7; 7,8; 7,9.

On Lucius Cornelius Balbus, see Cicero, *In Defence of Balbus* (passim) and J. Lamberty, '"Amicus Caesaris": der Aufstieg des L. Cornelius Balbus aus Gades', in A. Coşkun (ed.), *Roms auswärtige Freunde in der späten Republik und im frühen Prinzipat*, Duehrkohp und Radicke, Göttingen, 2005, pp. 155–73.

On Cicero's appointment and on other sources, see R. Tyrrell and L. Purser, 'Cicero's "Command in Campania"', in eidem (edd.), *Correspondence*, IV, pp. 558– 61; D.R. Shackleton Bailey, 'Cicero's Command in 49', in idem (ed.), *Cicero's Letters to Atticus*, IV, pp. 438–40.

On Curio's suggestions to Caesar, see Appian, *Civil Wars*, 2,125 (2,124 refers to an army of 5,000 foot soldiers and 300 horsemen arrived from the ocean, returning from Britannia and then crossing the Alps).

Later proposal in Velleius Paterculus, *Roman History*, 2,49,4; Plutarch, *Caesar*, 31,1–2; *Pompey*, 59,4–6; Suetonius, *Caesar*, 29,2–4; Appian, *Civil Wars*, 2,126–7. On this complex moment, cf. in particular Carsana, *Commento*, pp. 124–7.

On Cicero's debt, see M. Ioannatou, *Affaires d'argent dans la 'Correspondance' de Cicéron: L'aristocratie sénatoriale face à ses dettes*, De Boccard, Paris, 2006, pp. 288–90.

Plutarch, *Pompey*, 59,3–4 refers to a letter read by Antony to the crowd, but it is probably the one brought by Curio; difficulties in recruitment Plutarch, *Pompey*, 59,2.

On the letter and its contents, cf. Caesar, *Civil War*, 1,5,5; 1,9,3; Cicero, *ad familiares*, 16,11,2; Suetonius, *Caesar*, 29,2; Plutarch, *Antony*, 5,5; *Caesar*, 30,1–3; 31,1; *Pompey*, 59,3–4; Appian, *Civil Wars*, 2,126–28; Cassius Dio, *Roman History*, 41,1,1–3. Antony's interpretation in Plutarch, *Antony*, 5,5; *Caesar*, 30,3; *Pompey*, 59,3.

On the debate of 1 January, see Berti, *La guerra*, pp. 29–31; Carsana, *Commento*, pp. 126–7. Cf. G. Hinojo Andrés, *'Misso ad uesperum senatu omnes qui sunt eius ordinis a Pompeio euocantur', Caes., 'civ.' I,3*, in *Emerita*, 46, 1978, pp. 113–15

On the meetings of the 2, 5 and 6 January, cf. Caesar, *Civil War*, 1,5,4 (two-day assembly); A. Kirsopp Michels, *The Calendar of the Roman Republic*, Princeton University Press, Princeton, 1967, charts 1 and 2. Cassius Dio, *Roman History*, 41,2,2–3,1, reconstructed as follows: Antony and Quintus Cassius block the decisions with the veto on 1 January and the following day, then the Senate votes to change its dress, decision once again obstructed by the tribunes, but officially recorded and applied.

Plutarch reports the proposal of a compromise by which "Caesar would leave Gaul and discharge his army, except for two legions with which he would wait in Illyricum for his second consulship" (*Pompey*, 59,5); according to another version it would have supported Caesar's proposal "that they gave him Cisalpine Gaul and Illyricum with two cohorts" (*Caesar*, 31,1), but establishing a negotiation, seeking to "persuade Caesar's friends to be content with the aforesaid provinces and only 6,000 soldiers" (31,2); but Lentulus Crus would not agree to the deal.

On Plutarch and the events of 7 January, cf. *Antony*, 5,9–10; *Caesar*, 31,2; *Pompey*, 59,1.

On the order to assemble 130,000 Italic soldiers, see Appian, *Civil Wars*, 2,134 and Carsana, *Commento*, pp. 130–1.

Cassius Dio, as we have seen, also refers to the treasury being entrusted to Pompey, but he later gives more information (*Roman History*, 41,6,3–6).

Reference to meetings before 17 January is probably also in Caesar, *Civil War*, 1,30,5, where it is recorded how Cato, before withdrawing from Sicily, had reproached Pompey for having guaranteed, during a Senate meeting, that he was ready for war. A Senate decree that would have given authority to take sums from the provinces is mentioned afterwards, where there is reference to sums levied from Asia (3,32,6).

On the sending of ambassadors to Massilia, see Caesar, *Civil War*, 1,34,3; on the fortification of the strongholds in Latium, see Lucan, *Pharsalia*, 2,447–52; Florus, *Epitome of Roman History*, 2,13,18 refers to castles of Italy equipped with small garrisons.

PART III FROM THE RUBICON TO
THE SURRENDER OF ROME

8 The Rubicon

Among the studies of the differences between the versions, see R.A Tucker, 'What Actually Happened at the Rubicon?', *Historia* 37, 1988, pp. 245–8; P. Bicknell and D. Nielsen, 'Five Cohorts against the World', in C. Deroux (ed.), *Studies in Latin Literature and Roman History*, Latomus, Bruxelles, 1998, pp. 138–66; A. Rondholz, 'Crossing the Rubicon: A Historiographical Study', *Mnemosyne* 62, 2009, pp. 432–50; J. Beneker, 'The Crossing of the Rubicon and the Outbreak of Civil War in Cicero, Lucan, Plutarch, and Suetonius', *Phoenix* 65, 2011, pp. 74–99.

On Caesar's fabrications in timescale, see Rambaud, *L'art*, pp. 134–40; Canfora, *Cesare*, pp. 158–65.

On Lucan's version, see also Roche (ed.), *Lucan*, pp. 203–22. On the use of cavalry, see Caesar, *Gallic War*, 7,56,4; *civ.* 1,64,5; it is interesting to note that, for the crossing of the Sicoris, Lucan offers only the picture of men crossing the river using their arms (*Pharsalia*, 4,149–52).

On the figure of Asinius Pollio, see G. Zecchini, 'Asinio Pollione: dall'attività politica alla riflessione storiografica', in W. Haase (ed.), *Aufstieg und Niedergang der römischen Welt*, II, 30,2, de Gruyter, Berlin and New York, 1982, pp. 1265–96.

Against the idea of being fearful of a trial, see Shackleton Bailey, *Cicero's Letters to Atticus*, I, pp. 38–40; Gruen, *Last Generation*, pp. 494–5; C.T.H.R. Ehrhardt, 'Crossing the Rubicon', *Antichthon* 29, 1995, pp. 30–41; R. Morstein-Marx, 'Caesar's Alleged Fear of Prosecution and His *ratio absentis* in the Approach to the Civil War', *Historia* 56, 2007, pp. 159–78. On the dynamics that led to the conflict, see the now classic K. Raaflaub, *Dignitatis contentio: Studien zur Motivation und politischen Taktik im Bürgerkrieg zwischen Caesar und Pompeius*, Beck, München, 1974.

Suggestions about the influence of Labienus on the remaining five cohorts in Bicknell and Nielsen, 'Five Cohorts', pp. 156–7.

On the controversy, see P. Aebischer, 'Considérations sur le cours du Rubicon', *Museum Helveticum* 1, 1944, pp. 258–69; C. Ravara Montebelli, 'Il passaggio del Rubicone', in eadem (ed.), *'Alea iacta est': Mostra tenuta presso l'Archivio di Stato di Rimini dal 25 settembre al 25 novembre 2010*, Il ponte vecchio, Cesena, 2010, pp. 15–46.

Sul *decretum Rubiconis*, see I. Di Stefano Manzella, 'L'interazione fra testo e manufatto / monumento in epigrafia', in *Acta XII Congressus internationalis epigraphiae graecae et latinae (Barcelona, 3–8 Septembris 2002)*, I, Institut d'Estudis Catalans, Barcelona, 2007, pp. 393–418, 416–17.

9 The Escape from Rome

On the situation of the cities in Italy, see F. Santangelo, *Performing Passions, Negotiating Survival: Italian Cities in the Late Republican Civil Wars*, in H. Börm, M. Mattheis and J. Wienand (eds), *Civil War in Ancient Greece and Rome: Contexts of Disintegration and Reintegration*, Franz Steiner Verlag, Stuttgart, 2016, pp. 127–48.

On the embassy of Lucius and Roscius, see R. Tyrrell and L. Purser, 'The Negotiations of Lucius Caesar', in eidem (edd.), *Correspondence*, IV pp. 561–4; K. von Fritz, 'The Mission of L. Caesar and L. Roscius in January 49 BC', *Transactions and Proceedings of the American Philological Association* 72, 1941, pp. 125–56; D.R. Shackleton Bailey, 'The Credentials of L. Caesar and L. Roscius', in idem (ed.), *Cicero's Letters to Atticus*, IV, pp. 441–7. On the version of Cassius Dio, see Berti, *La guerra*, pp. 36–40.

On the meeting of 17 January, there is most probably a reference, though veiled, in Caesar, *Civil War*, 1,6,7–8 (order to abandon Rome), then repeated in 1,33,2 (threats to those who remained). The date of the 17th emerges from Cicero, *ad Atticum*, 9,10,2.

On the possibility of meetings during the days immediately before, see Meyer, *Caesars Monarchie*, starting from Plutarch, *Pompey*, 60,1.

On the role of Cicero or Volcatius Tullus in Appian, see Carsana, *Commento*, p. 136.

References to Pompey's command the following year in Caesar, *Civil War*, 3,3; 3,16; 3,79; Lucan, *Pharsalia*, 5,44–49; Plutarch, *Cato the Younger*, 53,4; *Pompey*, 64,3; 65,1; 66,1; Cassius Dio, *Roman History*, 41,43,2. The only reference by Cicero to the *tumultus* was the military levies (cf. Cicero, *ad familiares*, 16,12,3); on the *tumultus*, see Masi Doria, 'Salus populi'; on the whole question, see F.J. Vervaet, 'The Official Position of Cn. Pompeius in 49 and 48 BCE', *Latomus* 65, 2006, pp. 928–53.

On the declaration, see also P. Jal, '"Hostis" ("publicus") dans la littérature latine de la fin de la république', *Revue des Études Anciennes* 65, 1963, pp. 53–79.

The only study on the description of the panic at this moment is F. Barrière, '"Sic quisque pavendo / dat vires famae" (Lucain, "Bellum ciuile", 1,484–5): étude de la peur dans Rome à l'arrivée de César en 49 av. J.-C.', in Coin-Longeray and Vallat (eds), *Peurs*, pp. 325–38.

On the value of Cicero's correspondence in understanding the alignment of the *nobiles* and for historical investigation, see Shackleton Bailey, 'The Roman Nobility'.

Pompey's followers – with numerical references, where possible, to the related headings in the *Realencyclopädie der classischen Altertumswissenschaft (RE)* – were: Lucius Aelius Tubero 150 (praetor), Sextus Atilius Serranus, Marcus (Aurelius) Cotta 109 (praetor), Lucius Caecilius Metellus 75 (tribune in 49), Quintus Caecilius Metellus Pius Scipio Nasica 99 (consul in 62 and pontifex), Marcus Calpurnius Bibulus 28 (consul in 59), Gnaeus Calpurnius Piso (Frugi) 95 (proquaestor in 49), Gaius Cassius Longinus 59 (tribune in 59), Gaius Claudius Marcellus 217 (consul in 49), Marcus Claudius Marcellus 229 (consul in 51), Appius Claudius Pulcher 297 (censor in 50 and augur), Lucius Cornelius Lentulus Crus 218 (consul in 49), Publius Cornelius Lentulus Spinther 238 (consul in 57 and pontifex), Publius Cornelius Lentulus Spinther 239 (augur), Faustus Cornelius Sulla 377 (quaestor in 54 and augur), Lucius Domitius Ahenobarbus 27 (consul in 54 and pontifex), Gaius Fannius 9 (praetor and pontifex), Lucius Julius Caesar 144, Marcus Junius Brutus 53 (quaestor in 53, legate in 49 and pontifex), Licinius (Crassus) Damasippus 65 (senator), Publius Licinius Crassus Dives Junianus 75 (tribune in 53), Lucius Livius Ocella 25 (praetor), Aulus Manlius Torquatus 70 (praetor), Lucius Manlius Torquatus 80 (praetor in 49), Minucius Rufus 50, Quintus Minucius Thermus 67 (praetor), Marcus Ottavius 33 (curule aedile in 50), Marcus Opimius 9, Otacilius Crassus 9, Aulus Plautius (Silvanus?) 8 (praetor in 51), Pompey Rufus 43, Marcus Porcius Cato 20 (praetor in 54), Marcus Publicius 12 (senator), Marcus Pupius Piso 10–12 (senator), Sextus Quinctilius Varus (quaestor in 49), Publius Rutilius Lupus 27 (praetor in 49), Servius Sulpicius 21 (senator), Servius Sulpicius Rufus 95 (consul in 51), Marcus Terentius Varro 84 (praetor), Gaius Valerius Flaccus 169 (legate in 53–51).

Caesar's followers were: Marcus Acilius Glabrio (cf. 15, 16, 39), Lucius Aemilius Buca 37, Marcus Aemilius Lepidus 73 (praetor in 49 and pontifex), Gaius Antistius Reginus 39 (legate in 53–49?), Gaius Antistius Vetus 47 (tribune in 56), Gaius Antonius (Hybrida) 19 (consul in 63), Gaius Antonius 20 (quaestor in 51?), Lucius Antonius 23 (quaestor in 50), Mark Antony 30 (tribune in 49 and augur), Marcus Appuleius 2, 3, 14?, (Aurelius) Cotta (tribune in 49), Lucius Calpurnius Bestia 24–25 (aedile), Quintus Cassius 21 (senator?), Lucius Cassius Longinus 65, Quintus Cassius Longinus 70 (tribune of the plebs in 49 and augur), Marcus Claudius Marcellus Aeserninus 232, Tiberius Claudius Nero 254, Gaius Claudius Pulcher 303 (praetor in 56), Lucius Cornelius Cinna 107, Publius Cornelius Dolabella 141 (senator and XVvir), Publius Cornelius Lentulus Marcellinus 232, Gnaeus (Cornelius) Lentulus Vatia 241, Publius Cornelius Sulla 386 (consul designate in 65), Gaius Didius 2, Gnaeus Domitius 11, Gnaeus Domitius Calvinus 43 (consul in 53), Quintus Fabius Maximus Sanga 108, 143 (praetor), Marcus Furius Bibaculus 37, Furius Crassipides 54, Quintus Hortensius 8 (senator), Sextus Julius Caesar 152–153 (flamen of Jove), Decimus Junius Brutus Albinus 55a (quaestor in 50?), Marcus Junus Silanus 171–172 (legate in 53), L. (Juventius) Laterensis 15, Marcus Licinius

Crassus 56 (quaestor in 54, pontifex), Lucius Marcius Censorinus 48, Lucius (Marcius) Figulus 64, Lucius Marcius Philippus 77 (tribune in 49 and augur), Quintus (Marcius) Filippus 83 (senator), Quintus Mucius Scaevola 23 (tribune in 54 and augur), Gaius Norbanus Flaccus 9a, Gaius Papirius Carbo 35 (praetor in 62), Lucius Pinarius Scarpus 24, Publius Plautius Hypsaeus 23 (praetor), Gaius Scribonius Curio 11 (tribune in 50, pontifex), Lucius Sempronius Atratinus 26, Gaius Servilius Casca Longus 53, Publius Servilius Isauricus 67 (praetor in 54, augur?), Servius Sulpicius Galba 61 (praetor in 54, augur), Publius Sulpicius Rufus 93 (legate in 55–49), Servius Sulpicius Rufus 96, Marco Terentius Varro Gibba 89, Marcus Valerius Messalla Rufus 268 (consul in 53 and augur), Lucius Volcatius Tullus.

Notable among the 'neutrals' were: Manius Aemilius Lepidus 62 (consul in 66), Lucius Aemilius (Lepidus) Paullus 81 (consul in 50), Lucius Aurelius Cotta 102 (censor in 64), Lucius Calpurnius Piso Cesoninus 90 (censor in 50), Gaius Claudius Marcellus 214 (praetor in 80 and augur), Gaius Claudius Marcellus 216 (consul in 50), Lucius Julius Caesar 143 (consul in 64), Lucius Marcius Philippus 76 (consul in 56), Marcus Perperna 5 (censor in 86), Publius Servilius Vatia Isauricus 93 (censor in 55), Aulus Terentius Varro Murena 91.

Cicero's correspondence (between 17 January and 10 February): *ad Atticum*, 7,10 (Cicero to Atticus – from Rome, 17–18 January); 7,11 (Cicero to Atticus – from Rome or from Campania, 17–22 January); 7,12 (Cicero to Atticus – from Formiae, 21–22 January); *ad familiares*, 14,18 (Cicero with his son to Terentia and Tullia – from Formiae, 22 January); 14,14 (Cicero to Terentia and Tullia – from Minturnae, 23 January); *ad Atticum*, 7,13a BL TP (= 7,13 T OCT CP L; Cicero to Atticus – from Minturnae, 22–23 January); 7,13b BL TP (= 7,13a T OCT CP L; Cicero to Atticus – from Minturnae, 23–24 January); 7,14 (Cicero to Atticus – from Cales, 25 January); 7,15 (Cicero to Atticus – from Capua, 26 January); *ad familiares*, 16,12 (Cicero to Tiro – from Capua, 27 January); *ad Atticum*, 7,16 (Cicero to Atticus – from Cales, 28 January); 7,17 (Cicero to Atticus – from Formiae, 2 February); 7,18 (Cicero to Atticus – from Formiae, 3 February); 7,19 (Cicero to Atticus – from Formiae, 3 February); 7,20 (Cicero to Atticus – from Capua, 4–5 February); 7,21 (Cicero to Atticus – from Cales, 8 February); 7,22 (Cicero to Atticus – from Formiae, 8–9 February); 7,23 (Cicero to Atticus – from Formiae, 9–10 February).

Quoted also is *ad Atticum*, 8,11B (Cicero to Pompey – from Formiae, 15–16 February).

10 Caesar's 'Long March' and Pompey's Flight to Brundisium

On Pompey's patronage of Auximum, see *Inscriptiones Latinae Selectae* 877.

On Caesar's advance we can suppose this approximate dating, between the crossing of the Rubicon and arrival at Corfinium (15 February): occupation of Pisaurum, Fanum, Ancona (prior to 15 January); occupation of Arretium (17 January); council of war at Teanum Sidicinum and rejection of Caesar's proposal (23 February); arrival at Ariminum or Ancona of the ambassadors and consequent occupation of Auximum and Iguvium (1–4 February), and continuation of the march south, while Pompey ordered troops to converge on Luceria; Caesar joined by Legio XII (5 February); retreat to Corfinium by Lentulus Spinther (from Asculum), by Thermus (from Iguvium) and by Vibullius, with the cohorts recruited in Picenum (towards 7–8 February). Cf. also Pennacini, *Gaio Giulio Cesare*, p. 1199.

Cicero's correspondence (between 10 and 24 February): *ad Atticum*, 7,24 (Cicero to Atticus – from Formiae, 10–11 February); 7,25 (Cicero to Atticus – from Formiae, 10–12 February); 7,26 (Cicero to Atticus – from Formiae, 12–15 February); 8,11A (Pompey to Cicero – from Luceria, 10 February); 8,11B (Cicero to Pompey – from Formiae, 15–16 February); 8,1 (Cicero to Atticus – from Formiae, 15–16 February); 8,2 (Cicero to Atticus – from Formiae, 17 February); 8,3 (Cicero to Atticus – from Cales, 18–19 February); 8,6 (Cicero to Atticus – from Formiae, 20–21 February); 8,7 (Cicero to Atticus – from Formiae, 21–23 February); 8,4 (Cicero to Atticus – from Formiae, 22 February); 8,8 (Cicero to Atticus – from Formiae, 23–24 February).

On the identification of Cicero, *ad Atticum*, 8,11A, see Shackleton Bailey, *Cicero's Letters to Atticus*, IV, pp. 341–2.

On the capture of Corfinium, see R. Tyrrell and L. Purser, 'The Forces at Corfinium and its Neighbourhood', in eidem, *Correspondence*, IV, pp. 564–5; G. Veith, 'Corfinium, eine kriegsgeschichtliche Studie', *Klio* 13, 1913, pp. 1–26; D.R. Shackleton Bailey, 'Exspectatio Corfiniensis', in idem (ed.), *Cicero's Letters to Atticus*, IV, pp. 448–59. In defence of the conduct of Ahenobarbus, in addition to Shackleton Bailey, see K. von Fritz, 'Pompey's Policy Before and After the Outbreak of the Civil War of 49 BC', *Transactions and Proceedings of the American Philological Association* 73, 1942, pp. 145–80; A. Burns, 'Pompey's Strategy and Domitius' Stand at Corfinium', *Historia* 15, 1966, pp. 74–95.

On the number of Ahenobarbus' cohorts: Caesar, *Civil War*, 1,15,5–7 says that Vibullius and Hirrus had thirteen cohorts, Domitius around twenty. The figures given by Pompey vary between thirty-one (Cicero, *ad Atticum*, 8,12A,1; 3) and thirty cohorts (Cicero, *ad Atticum*, 8,11A).

Cicero's correspondence (between 25 February and 25 March): *ad Atticum*, 8,9b BL (= 8,9,3–4 TP = 8,9a T OCT CP = 8,9 L; Cicero to Atticus – from Formiae, 25 February); 8,11 (Cicero to Atticus – from Formiae, 27 February); 8,11C (Pompey to Cicero – from Canusium, 20 February); 8,11D (Cicero to Pompey – from Formiae, 27 February); 8,12 (Cicero to Atticus – from Formiae, 28 February); 8,13 (Cicero to Atticus – from Formiae, 1 March); 8,14 (Cicero to Atticus – from Formiae, 2 March); 8,15 (Cicero to Atticus – from Formiae, 3 March); 8,15A (Balbus to Cicero – from Rome, around end of February – 1 March); 8,16 (Cicero to Atticus – from Formiae, 4 March); 9,1 (Cicero to Atticus – from Formiae, 6 March); 9,2a BL (= 9,2 TP T OCT CP L, Cicero to Atticus – from Formiae, 7 March); 9,2b BL (= 9,2a TP T OCT CP L, Cicero to Atticus – from Formiae, 8 March); 9,3 (Cicero to Atticus – from Formiae, 9 March); *ad familiares*, 8,15 (Caelius to Cicero – from Albintimilium, c.9 March); *ad Atticum*, 9,5 (Cicero to Atticus – from Formiae, 10–11 March); 9,6 (Cicero to Atticus – from Formiae, 11–12 March); 9,6A (Caesar to Cicero – on the march to Brundisium, c.5 March); 9,7 (Cicero to Atticus – from Formiae, 13 March); 9,7A (Balbus and Oppius to Cicero – from Rome, 7–10 March); 9,7B (Balbus to Cicero – from Rome, 9–12 March); 9,7C (Caesar to Oppius and Balbus – on the march, 3–5 March); 9,8 (Cicero to Atticus – from Formiae, 14 March); 9,9 (Cicero to Atticus – from Formiae, 17 March); 9,10 (Cicero to Atticus – from Formiae, 18 March); 9,11A (Cicero to Caesar – from Formiae, 18–20 March); 9,11 (Cicero to Atticus – from Formiae, 20 March); 9,12 (Cicero to Atticus – from Formiae, 20–21 March); 9,13a BL (= 9,13,1–7 TP CP = 9,13 T OCT; Cicero to Atticus – from Formiae, 22–23 March); 9,13b BL (= 9,13,8 TP = 9,13a T OCT CP = 9,13 L; Cicero to Atticus – from Formiae, 24 March); 9,13A (Balbus to Cicero – from Rome, c.22–23 March, with copy of a letter sent by Caesar to Oppius and Balbus on 9–10 March); 9,14 (Cicero to Atticus – from Formiae, 24–25 March, with part-copy of a letter sent by Caesar to Pedius on 14 March).

On the fact that Oppius and Balbus handled Caesar's political affairs, see Wiseman, 'The Publication', n. 18.

On the relationship between Pompey and Theophanes, see B.K. Gold, 'Pompey and Theophanes of Mytilene', *American Journal of Philology* 103, 1985, pp. 312–27.

Cicero, *ad Atticum*, 9,10,4 refers to a *volumen* of Atticus' letters (cf. L. Canfora, *Totalità e selezione nella storiografia classica*, Laterza, Bari, 1972, p. 125), probably 13.

On the *nékyia*, see Cicero, *ad Atticum*, 9,10,7; 9,11,2; 9,18,2; cf. Hinard, *Les Proscriptions*, pp. 213–17.

11 In Caesar's Hands

Cicero's correspondence (between 25 March and 2 April): *ad Atticum*, 9,15 (Cicero to Atticus – from Formiae, 25 March); 9,15a BL T OCT CP (= 9,15,6 TP; Cicero to Atticus – from Formiae, 25–26 March, with the copy of a letter sent to Cicero from Matius and Trebatius on their way from Capua, 23–24 March); 9,16 (Cicero to Atticus – from Formiae, 26 March, with the copy of a letter sent by Caesar to Cicero c.20 March); 9,17 (Cicero to Atticus – from Formiae, 27 March); 9,18 (Cicero to Atticus – from Formiae, 28–29 March); 9,19 (Cicero to Atticus – from Arpinum, 31 March–2 April).

On the garrison at Hydruntum referred to in Appian, see Carsana, *Commento*, p. 143.

On Caesar's naval transport, see M. B. Charles, *Caesar and Maritime Troop Transport in the Civil War (49–45 BC)*, in C. Deroux (ed.), *Studies in Latin Literature and Roman History*, XV, Latomus, Brussels, 2010, pp. 130–152.

On Cato's flight from Sicily, see also D.C. Yates, *The Role of Cato the Younger in Caesar's Bellum Civile*, *The Classical World* 104, 2011, pp. 161–174.

On the role of Asinius Pollio cited by Plutarch and Appian, see Carsana, *Commento*, pp. 143–4.

Velleius Paterculus mentions only an explanation by Caesar 'in the Senate and to the assembly of the people of his motives, and of the tragic state of need for which he had been compelled by the arms of others to take up arms' (*Roman History*, 2,50,2) and Suetonius speaks of an investigation in the Senate of the 'political situation' (*Caesar*, 34,2).

Cicero's correspondence (between 3 April and 11 June): *ad Atticum*, 10,1 (Cicero to Atticus – from Laterium, 3 April); 10,3 (Cicero to Atticus – from Arcanum, 7 April); 10,3a (Cicero to Atticus – from Arcanum, 7 April); 10,4 (Cicero to Atticus – from Cumae, 14 April); 10,5 (Cicero to Atticus – from Cumae, 16 April); 10,6 (Cicero to Atticus – from Cumae, c.17–21 April); *ad familiares*, 4,1 (Cicero to Sulpicius Rufus – from Cumae, c.21–22 April); *ad Atticum*, 10,7 (Cicero to Atticus – from Cumae, 21–22 April); *ad familiares*, 4,2 (Cicero to Sulpicius Rufus – from Cumae, 28–29 April); 5,19 (Cicero to Mescinius Rufus – from Cumae, c.28 April); *ad Atticum*, 10,8 (Cicero to Atticus – from Cumae, 2 May); 10,8A (Antony to Cicero – from Campania, c.1 May); 10,8B (Caesar to Cicero – on his way to Massilia, 16 April); 10,9 (Cicero to Atticus – from Cumae, 3 May); 10,9A (= *ad familiares*, 8,16; Caelius to Cicero – from Liguria, 16 April); *ad familiares*, 2,16 (Cicero to Caelius – from Cumae, 2–4 May); *ad Atticum*, 10,10 (Cicero to Atticus – from Cumae, 3 May, with the copy of a letter of Antony sent to Cicero on 2–3 May, perhaps from Misenum); 10,11 (Cicero to Atticus – from Cumae, 4 May); 10,12 BL T OCT CP L (= 10,12,1–3 TP; Cicero to Atticus – from Cumae, 5 May); 10,12a BL T OCT CP L (= 10,12,4–7 TP; Cicero to Atticus – from Cumae, 6 May); 10,13 (Cicero to Atticus – from Cumae, 7 May); 10,14 (Cicero to Atticus – from Cumae, 8 May); 10,15 (Cicero to Atticus – from Cumae, 10–12 May); 10,16 (Cicero to Atticus – from Cumae, 14 May); 10,17 (Cicero to Atticus – from Cumae, 16 May); 10,18 (Cicero to Atticus – from Cumae, 19–20 May); *ad familiares*, 14,7 (Cicero to Terentia – from Caieta, 7–11 June).

On Caelius' plan, see D.R. Shackleton Bailey, '*Caelianum illud*', in idem (ed.), *Cicero's Letters to Atticus*, IV, pp. 461–9.

12 The Battle Fought, the *Res Publica* and the City

On the events of the civil war from 49 to 45 we shall limit ourself to indicating, for the completeness of its sources, the still highly authoritative T. Rice Holmes, *The Roman Republic and the Founder of the Empire*, vol. III, Clarendon Press, Oxford, 1923. So far as attention to the 'maritime' aspect of Pompey's strategy is concerned, see M.J.G. Gray-Fow, '"Qui mare teneat" (Cic. "Att." 10, 8): Caesar, Pompey, and the Waves', *Classica et Mediaevalia* 44, 1993, pp. 141–79, with a very useful list of naval battles between 49 and 45.

Lucan, with poetic creativity, depicts Cicero at Pharsalus, talking with Pompey about war: 'their weapons quiver in their hands, each impatient for the signal that is late: hurry, or the trumpets will sound before you' (*Pharsalia*, 7,82–3).

On Caesar's hostility to Cato, see Canfora, *Cesare*, pp. 285–9.

On the defence of Marcellus, Ligarius and Deiotarus, see Narducci, *Cicerone: La parola*, pp. 383–8.

On the army rebellion at Placentia, see Suetonius, *Caesar*, 69; Appian, *Civil Wars*, 2,191–5; Cassius Dio, *Roman History*, 41,26,1–35,5.

On Caesar's fiscal policy in 49, see M.W. Frederiksen, 'Caesar, Cicero and the Problem of Debt', *Journal of Roman Studies* 56, 1966, pp. 128–41, who suggests the following sequence: (1) temporary measures in 49 and 48 to create valuations; (2) a law in 49, later continued in 46 or

45, *de modo credendi et possidendi*, which limited the possession of currency and required investment in Italy; (3) a law on the *cessio bonorum*, in 46 or in 45. Cf. P. Simelon, 'Aspects de la situation socio-économique en Italie entre 49 et 45 av. J.-C.', *Acta Classica Universitatis Scientiarum Debreceniensis* 21, 1985, pp. 73–100.

On Caesar's distributions, see Appian, *Civil Wars*, 2,198. P.D.A. Garnsey, *Famine and Food Supply in the Graeco-Roman World: Responses to Risk and Crisis*, Cambridge University Press, Cambridge, 1988, p. 202 also ascribes Cassius Dio, *Roman History*, 41,16,1 to the same occasion.

About Caelius and Milo and then Dolabella, see P. Simelon, 'À propos des émeutes de M. Caelius Rufus et de P. Cornelius Dolabella (48–47 av. J.-C.)', *Les Études Classiques* 53, 1985, pp. 387–405; Cordier, 'Caelius'.

On the earthquake and its destruction, see Cassius Dio, *Roman History*, 41,14,2; on living conditions in general, see Yavetz, 'The Living Conditions', pp. 516–17.

On the example of Curio, see K.E. Welch, 'Antony, Fulvia, and the Ghost of Clodius in 47 BC', *Greece and Rome* 42, 1995, pp. 182–201. If we accept Purser's conjecture as correct at Cicero, *ad Atticum*, 11,23,3 (*de statua*), Dolabella actually proposed erecting a statue to Clodius.

Appian's version (*Civil Wars*, 2,385–6) is different (Caesar travelled across Asia to deal out justice for the extortions of the *publicani*), but confirms that he moved when he came to hear that Antony and his troops were holding the Forum.

On the mutiny of soldiers in Campania, between January and September 47, see Plutarch, *Caesar*, 51,2–4; Suetonius, *Caesar*, 70; Appian, *Civil Wars*, 2,386–96; Cassius Dio, *Roman History*, 42,52,1–55,3; cf. Frontinus, *Stratagems*, 1,9,4.

On the dissolution of the *collegia*, fiscal measures, reduction of the number of those having rights to grain, distribution of land, public works, donations and triumphs and their consequences, see the classic Z. Yavetz, *'Plebs' and 'Princeps'*, Clarendon Press, Oxford, 1969, pp. 45–57.

As observed by Carcopino, *César*, p. 469 n. 2, there is no reason to reject the suggestion of Cassius Dio, for the reason that the news about Munda would have had to take at least thirty-three days to reach Rome. The publication of Caesar's dispatch could have been delayed, in view of the coincidence with 21 April.

We have limited ourself to quoting, in order, T. Mommsen, *The History of Rome*, vol. 2, Cambridge, Cambridge University Press, 2010; Meyer, *Caesars Monarchie*, pp. 312–18; von Fritz, 'Pompey's Policy'; Burns, 'Pompey's Strategy'; L.G. Pocock, 'What Made Pompeius Fight in 49 BC?', *Greece and Rome* 6, 1959, pp. 68–81; A. Powell, '"An Island amid the Flame": The Strategy and Imagery of Sextus Pompeius, 43–36 BC', in A. Powell and K.E. Welch (eds), *Sextus Pompeius*, Duckworth, London, 2002, pp. 103–33; K.E. Welch, *'Magnus Pius': Sextus Pompeius and the Transformation of the Roman Republic*, Classical Press of Wales, Swansea, 2012.

On the work of Sextus Pompey, the sources provide much information.

In 41 famine afflicted Rome, for traffic by sea had been cut off by Pompey and the lands of Italy were no longer cultivated owing to the war; whatever was produced served for the troops. The people committed robberies in the city at night and actions even worse than theft, and they committed them with impunity: the general opinion attributed them to the soldiers. The people shut their shops and drove out the magistrates, for they no longer felt a need for magistrates or for crafts in a city reduced to hunger and infested with brigands (Appian, *Civil Wars*, 5,72–73).

In December 40, 'since grain was reserved for the army, the people openly cursed the war and the victory, and running from house to house in search of grain, they plundered all they could find' (*Civil Wars*, 5,138). Even afterwards, 'the merchants of the East couldn't put to sea for fear of Pompey and Sicily, those of the West due to Sardinia and Corsica held by Pompey's troops, those of the opposite shore of Africa due to the same that controlled the sea from both sides' (*Civil Wars*, 5,280). Everything rose in price and the masses pressed for a settlement with Pompey; for which there was a revolt by the people, tired of funding the civil war, in which Octavian came close to being lynched. When he tried to reach a peace, concluded in summer 39, the admiral 'Menodorus wrote to Pompey from Sardinia that he should either pursue the war or procrastinate, since the famine was fighting for them and, if he waited, the peace conditions would be more favourable' (*Civil Wars*, 5,293). But in 38 the pact was broken, and Rome returned to famine, as Appian once again records (*Civil Wars*, 5,325–9). After several naval defeats, Octavian found himself pressed 'by hunger and by the people who were once again urging him for an agreement and scorned war because it was contrary to the pacts' (*Civil Wars*, 5,384), which led to other agreements. Once again in 36, there were popular insurrections in remembrance of Pompey the Great, to which Octavian had to send Maecenas, on two occasions, to calm the city (*Civil Wars*, 5,414; 5,470).

Regarding the difficulties about using Cicero's writings as evidence, the matters already raised should be taken into account. The letter of May 51 doesn't imply that Pompey had spoken about a naval blockade (*ad familiares*, 2,8,2). The first hint of deserting Rome appears in December 50, in a letter which – with the spirit of a *suasoria* – sketched out all the possibilities: 'when hostilities have begun will it be better to defend the city or abandon it so as to prevent him having any supplies and other reinforcements?' (*ad Atticum*, 7,9,2).

That the problem of supplying the city was being experienced, appears for the first time in a letter to Atticus with the explanation of one letter to Pompey (though not explicit):'keep a firm hold on the coast if he wants to be sure of grain supplies from the provinces' (*ad Atticum*, 8,1,2). Pompey's plan takes form, however, in three very 'anxious' letters of March 49, where we read that Pompey had, as his 'first plan, to throttle Rome and Italy with hunger; then devastate the countryside, to set fire to everything, not to keep their hands off the possessions of the rich' (*ad Atticum*, 9,7,4), and 'to kill with hunger the most ancient and most sacred mother, our country!', thanks to the fleet assembled 'from Alexandria, from Colchis, from Tyros, from Sidon, from Aradus, from Cyprus, from Pamphylia, from Lycia, from Rhodes, from Chios, from Byzantium, from Lesbos, from Smyrna, from Miletus, from Coos', put together to 'intercept supplies to Italy and to occupy the provinces that give us grain' (*ad Atticum*, 9,9,2). Lastly, rereading his correspondence to Atticus, Cicero states that 'our Gnaeus has been pondering this disgrace for two years, so much so that he is minded to ape Sulla, so that all he has thought about for so long is proscriptions' (*ad Atticum*, 9,10,6). But this, of course, was an effective instrument for reproaching Atticus.

ACKNOWLEDGEMENTS

The idea for this work was conceived after I took part in the research group *Palingenesie der römischen Senatsbeschlüsse* (509 v.Chr.–284 n.Chr.), at the Institut für Rechtsgeschichte of the Westfälische Wilhelms-Universität Münster, operating under the auspices of the Alexander von Humboldt Foundation, and directed by Pierangelo Buongiorno. Several underlying propositions were usefully considered during the course of a 'lectura' organized at the University of Padua, at the Centro Interdipartimentale di Ricerca Studi Liviani, promoted by Gianluigi Baldo and presently directed by Maria Veronese.

Grateful thanks to Lia Di Trapani, incomparable editor, and to Flavio Raviola, incomparable reader.

Respectful and heartfelt thanks to two ever-present figures who have once again generously offered me their advice and encouragement: Umberto Laffi, who previously guided my studies with passion and enthusiasm, and Arnaldo Marcone, who has contributed so much in steering and nourishing my interests.

I dedicate this book with particular thanks to my father, Mario Fezzi, lawyer, pianist and lover of history, who died on 5 July 2016. Many of my passions I owe to him.

INDEX